AMERICAN SACRED SPACE

RELIGION IN NORTH AMERICA

Catherine L. Albanese and Stephen J. Stein, *editors*

William L. Andrews, editor. *Sisters of the Spirit: Three Black Women's Autobiographies of the Nineteenth Century.*

Mary Farrell Bednarowski. *New Religions and the Theological Imagination in America.*

David Chidester. *Salvation and Suicide: An Interpretation of Jim Jones, the Peoples Temple, and Jonestown.*

Thomas D. Hamm. *God's Government Begun: The Society for Universal Inquiry and Reform, 1842–1846.*

Thomas D. Hamm. *The Transformation of American Quakerism: Orthodox Friends, 1800–1907.*

Jean M. Humez, editor. *Mother's First-Born Daughters: Early Shaker Writings on Women and Religion.*

Carl T. Jackson. *Vedanta for the West: The Ramakrishna Movement in the United States.*

David Kuebrich. *Minor Prophecy: Walt Whitman's New American Religion.*

John D. Loftin. *Religion and Hopi Life in the Twentieth Century.*

Colleen McDannell. *The Christian Home in Victorian America, 1840–1900.*

Ronald L. Numbers and Jonathan M. Butler, editors. *The Disappointed: Millerism and Millernarianism in the Nineteenth Century.*

Richard W. Pointer. *Protestant Pluralism and the New York Experience: A Study of Eighteenth-Century Religious Diversity.*

Sally M. Promey. *Spiritual Spectacles: Vision and Image in Mid-Nineteenth-Century Shakerism.*

Russell E. Richey. *Early American Methodism.*

A. Gregory Schneider. *The Way of the Cross Leads Home: The Domestication of American Methodism.*

Richard Hughes Seager. *The World's Parliament of Religions: The East/West Encounter, Chicago, 1893.*

Ann Taves, editor. *Religion and Domestic Violence in Early New England: The Memoirs of Abigail Abbot Bailey.*

Thomas A. Tweed. *The American Encounter with Buddhism, 1844–1912: Victorian Culture and the Limits of Dissent.*

Valarie H. Ziegler. *The Advocates of Peace in Antebellum America.*

AMERICAN SACRED SPACE

David Chidester and
Edward T. Linenthal, editors

Indiana University Press

Bloomington and Indianapolis

The paper used in this publication meets the minimum requirements of American National Standard for Information Sciences—Permanence of Paper for Printed Library Materials, ANSI Z39.48-1984.

Manufactured in the United States of America

Library of Congress Cataloging-in-Publication Data

American sacred space / David Chidester and Edward T. Linenthal, editors.
p.   cm. — (Religion in North America)
Includes bibliographical references and index.
ISBN 0-253-32915-9 (alk. paper) — ISBN 0-253-21006-2 (pbk. : alk. paper)
1. Sacred space—United States. 2. United States—Religion.
I. Chidester, David. II. Linenthal, Edward Tabor, date.
III. Series.
BL581.U6A48   1995
291.3'5'0973—dc20
95-3986

I 2 3 4 5 00 99 98 97 96 95

for Walter H. Capps

CONTENTS

Jennifer Hope

Adriene Cole

Contents

FOREWORD

Over fifty years ago Sidney E. Mead first published his ground-breaking essay "The American People: Their Space, Time, and Religion." In it he argued that it was "not too much to say that in America space has played the part that time has played in the older cultures of the world." "Americans during their formative years were a people in movement through space," Mead wrote. They were "a people exploring the obvious highways and the many unexplored and devious byways of practically unlimited geographical and social space. The quality of their minds and hearts and spirits was formed in that great crucible—and in a very short time."[*]

If Mead was right, his insight did not inspire a bevy of American religion scholars to turn their efforts to the study of American sacred space. In fact, until now, there has been remarkably little direct consideration of space and place in American religion. There has been some study of churches and other religious buildings and of public commemorative sites as they function in what has been called civil religion. And there has been some notice of natural landscapes and how they have worked to support a sense of the sacred. But the notion of American sacred space has neither been consistently theorized nor explored across a range of manifestations. Its study has not been integrated in a sustained way into the general comparative study of space in the history of religions. And even more troubling for those who study American religious history, the historical narratives that chronicle American religious experience have not attended well to issues of space and place.

From the perspective of this relative historiographical silence, the present volume is a pioneering effort. Editors and authors join forces here to theorize the concept of American sacred space and to examine the production and presence of sacred space in a series of important American case studies. What they find banishes easy pieties about sacred space as peaceful center and cosmic point of harmonial orientation. In fact, as the editors show, such easy pieties were early questioned in the theoretical literature

[*] See Sidney E. Mead, *The Lively Experiment: The Shaping of Christianity in America* (New York: Harper & Row, 1963), 6–7. The essay was originally published in the *Journal of Religion* 34 (1954): 244–55.

about sacred space, and the work of Mircea Eliade went hand in hand with a more conflictual understanding of sacred space that came from Gerardus van der Leeuw. But the strength of this new collection of essays comes from more than its conformance to one model for the study of sacred space. Rather, these essays challenge, divert, and direct the received theoretical model by their introduction of a body of evidence that pushes it even further toward the conflictual pole. These essays begin to tell how American religious history can be narrated in terms of the contested zones and spaces it has inhabited.

Arising in the midst of the contact of peoples in a nation of, mostly, immigrants—and their competition over goods that seemed in short supply and goals that seemed to clash—American sacred space intensified conflict modalities and never allowed them to rest. Indeed, in this context American exceptionalism cannot be banished from the scholar's horizon, as political correctness seems to demand. It returns, instead, as the exceptionalism of the heavily conflictual, as the persistent testimony to the stresses and strains of pluralism. Thus, the production and presence of sacred space in America invite a reconsideration of general theory in comparative religions and a filling out of the contested side of its understanding. At the same time, American sacred space demands a serious scholarly consideration in its own right, for it promises to help us write American religious culture in clearly revisionist terms.

Practically speaking, the cases presented in this volume only begin to explore the many ways in which conflict and sacred space in America go hand in hand. Studies of nature and the land by these authors, for example, gravitate toward Native American themes when, in fact, numerous other cases might be cited without any reference to Indian peoples. Examinations of domestic space spotlight educational concerns, when other expressions of domestic sacred spheres might be included. No formal treatment of the inner space promoted by a host of American metaphysical religions is presented. And the way that America itself functions as mythic cipher in other people's consciousness is unraveled mostly from the perspective of just one nation, as author David Chidester looks at America with borrowed South African eyes.

What all of this adds up to is a conscious *beginning*. Editors Chidester and Linenthal underline that fact in the synthetic outreach of their theoretical exposition and in the comprehensive bibliography they include. The other authors, with remarkable symmetry, point again and again to the conflictual nature of American sacred space, even as they contribute distinct and original perspectives toward their material. In sum, this is a volume that opens doors to new academic worlds and that invites us to enter them with the intent of staying and discovering. Still more, this volume is also a primer to accompany the student of American religion who steps across the portals. It is both an explorer's manual for a new way of studying American religiosity and an introductory key to its decipherment.

Catherine L. Albanese
Stephen J. Stein, Series Editors

PREFACE

THIS BOOK ENGAGES American sacred space. It uncovers and recovers the sacred character of American land and environments, mountains and monuments, homes and museums, and foreign and domestic perceptions of America through carefully detailed case studies. Each case study, however, awakens new possibilities for further exploration by charting the undiscovered territory of American sacred space. Unfamiliar as this inquiry might be, however, the contours and dynamics of American sacred space that are recollected here will also register for most American readers as hauntingly familiar. After all, Americans live in this space. We offer this book in anticipation of future explorations of the strange and familiar dimensions of American sacred space.

After our introduction, which sets out a theoretical framework for the investigation of sacred space, the discovery of American sacred space begins with Robert Michaelsen's examination of the legal conflicts that have arisen between Native American veneration and Euroamerican commodification of land. Bron Taylor modifies and extends this theme through a close examination of the efforts of environmental activists to defend land and wilderness areas from the encroachments of commodification and exploitation. By focusing upon the establishment of the Mount Rushmore monument in the Black Hills of North Dakota and Wyoming, Matthew Glass further develops the tensions between Native American claims on sacred land and Euroamerican economic and political interests. As these chapters show, American sacred space has been produced from the beginning out of multicultural relations and intercultural conflict. Clearly, these conflictual relations persist in the present.

From conflicts over sacred land, the chapters in this book proceed to specific issues of domestic and foreign sacred space in America. Although the home might seem to be a safe place, a haven in a heartless world, Colleen McDannell analyzes the contested efforts by conservative Protestants to establish the home as a sacred enclave in a hostile environment. Moving from the local to the national, Edward T. Linenthal documents the controversies surrounding the creation of the Holocaust Memorial Museum in Washington, D.C. While that museum has raised controversial questions about commemorating a "foreign" event at the national sacred center, foreign perceptions of America, as David Chidester suggests in a chapter on America as sacred space in South Africa, have in their turn also defined the sacral place of America in the world. Returning home by entering the ambiguous and often ironic space of a postmodern America, Rowland Sherrill concludes the case studies of this volume by moving through the contemporary dislocations and disorientations of an American imagination of space.

This book on American sacred space is the product of genuine collaboration. All of the authors are friends, even close friends, besides being colleagues and co-conspirators in a common project, the ongoing revitalization of the study of American religion. As editors, we have relied upon the intangible bonds of friendship during the long process of bringing this book to publication. We thank the Board of Directors for support. At Indiana University Press, we have benefited from the encouragement and criticism of the editors of the Religion in North America Series, Stephen Stein and Catherine Albanese. Both have helped refine this project. However, by testing this book out on her students while it was still in manuscript, Catherine Albanese has shown us that it definitely has the potential to stimulate thought. We could ask for nothing better.

The process of editing this book has required a transcendence of spatial limits. One of us lives in the midwestern heartland of America; the other lives about as far away as you can go from America without falling off the edge of the earth. The chapters in this book reflect this creative tension between closeness and distance. Each chapter is intimately American in character, but also profoundly global in scope. We find it difficult to be impartial about this book that we have had the privilege of editing on American sacred space. All we can say is that this is exactly the kind of book that we would like to read.

AMERICAN SACRED SPACE

I

INTRODUCTION

David Chidester and Edward T. Linenthal

Over the past few years, we have both somehow convinced our respective universities that we had to go to the Hawaiian Islands to conduct research on American sacred space. Obviously, the fiftieth state of the Union is rich in sacred sites. From the ancient *heiaus*, burial grounds, places of refuge, and sacred valleys, waterfalls, and volcanoes of traditional Hawaiian religion, through the Buddhist temples, Shinto shrines, and multitude of Christian churches, to the national monument of the USS *Arizona* at Pearl Harbor, certain places have been marked out of Hawaiian space for a special kind of attention. At first glance, the traditional Hawaiian sacred site and the national shrine at Pearl Harbor—the most ancient, the most modern—appear to have little in common. They seem to speak to alien worlds. However, the *heiau* and the battlefield continue to be reproduced as sacred sites through similar spatial practices. For purposes of analysis, we will identify those practices here as ritualization, reinterpretation, and the contest over legitimate ownership of the sacred. *→ Practices of sacred sites*

While one of us explored ancient, primordial sites, the other examined the local emplacement of an American patriotic orthodoxy in Hawaii. In search of the sacred, we immediately had to recognize that these places were intimately entangled in such "profane" enterprises as tourism, economic exchange and development, and the intense conflict of contending nationalisms. As tourist attractions, Hawaiian sacred sites promised access to an ultimate or transcendent reality, a promise usually captured in advertising brochures in the phrase, "experience of a lifetime!" Tourist propaganda raised significant questions about the relation between representation and reality. On the island of Maui, for example, visitors were urged to visit the "Seven Sacred Pools." Truth in advertising, however, would have required the admission that the pools were neither seven, since there were actually twenty-four, nor sacred, because they had been used by warriors, not for ritual, but for the more mundane purpose of bathing. As a sacred tourist site, therefore, the "Seven Sacred Pools" was emblematic of the kind of postmodern simulation that has come to characterize international tourism. Nevertheless, ancient sacred sites had been marked out as national parks and tourist destinations in ways that recalled practices of religious ritualization. For example, at *Pu'uhonua o Hōnaunau*, the sacred place of refuge on the Big Island, ritual rules and observances, *kapu* laws, had traditionally placed strict proscriptions on conduct. Under the supervision of the National Parks Service, however, the ritual rules had been revised. On entering the sacred precincts, visitors were advised of the new *kapu* laws by a sign that read, "No picnicking, sunbathing, or smoking."

As in ancient times, this ritualized consecration of a site identified the precise conditions under which that sacred place could be desecrated. In general, desecration can take two forms, defilement or dispossession. In the first case, desecration registers as a violation of the ritual order through which the purity of a sacred place is maintained. While most tourists observed the ritual regulations established by the National Parks Service at *Pu'uhonua o Hōnaunau*, the journalist and social critic Hunter S. Thompson selected its most sacred enclosure for his own manic refuge from the world, constantly smoking, occasionally sunbathing, and picnicking, periodically calling out to the Park Ranger to bring more ice for his whiskey. Although a serious offense, defilement is a form of desecration that can be easily addressed through rites of purification or rites of exclusion, such as excommunication, banishment, or execution, which effectively eliminate a polluting influence from the pure space of the sacred. In Hunter S. Thompson's case, the Park Ranger apparently dealt with his defiling presence by denial. "You are *not here*," the ranger reportedly told him. "The heiau is kapu. *Nobody* can be here."[1] However, the second type of desecration, the dispossession of a sacred site, is much more difficult to redress. Under conditions of dispossession, ritual acts of consecration can only be performed in exile, alienated from their sacred ground. At *Pu'uhonua o Hōnaunau*, as well as at other dispossessed sacred sites on the Islands, Hawaiian traditionalists gained access by night, after the tourists had gone, to reconsecrate the precincts and remember the contours of a lost sacred place. In an important sense, ritual thereby became an act of reclamation.

Accordingly, recent reinterpretations of traditional Hawaiian sites have been advanced in reaction to their perceived desecration. At *Pu'uhonua o Hōnaunau*, which had traditionally established different places for the king and the priests, the physical separation of royal from priestly spheres had provided a lens through which Hawaiians could think about relations between religious and political forces in the larger society. In this respect, the sacred site had been a tangible medium through which people could reflect upon the harmonies and tensions of the Hawaiian social order. Consecration, therefore, had depended, not only upon maintaining ritual purity, but also upon the interpretive potential of the site, its efficacy in giving location to certain ways of thinking about human relations in Hawaii.[2] Under conquest and colonization, however, everything changed, including ways of thinking. Anticipating the approach of January 17, 1993, which would mark the centenary of the overthrow of the Hawaiian nation, various sovereignty groups mobilized funds and popular support. They sponsored twice-monthly programs of Sovereignty Education. They advanced campaigns for self-governance. They claimed a right of national self-determination that demanded recognition by the Hawaiian State, the U.S. federal government, and the community of nations under international law. In that context, *Pu'uhonua o Hōnaunau* and other sacred sites were reinterpreted as highly charged places to focus attention upon the oppression and liberation of the Hawaiian nation. As their meaning was dramatically recast, ancient sacred places became potent counter-sites of political resistance.   → MICHAELSON ARTICLE & LARGER THEME

In the early 1990s the conflict of interpretation over the meaning of sacred sites was embedded in political struggles and legal battles over their legitimate ownership. Contests over sacred space entered the court system. On Oahu a highway was being built over two ancient *heiaus*. A golf course was being planned on an ancient burial ground on Maui. The geothermal drilling project on the Big Island of Hawaii was boring deep into the volcano of the goddess, Pele. Legal actions sought to protect these sacred sites from defilement. But they also tried to establish new terms for the legitimate use and ownership of these sacred places. In that context, ritualization and reinterpretation were both exercised as strategic maneuvers on a battlefield. Ancient sacred places became modern sites of struggle over nationality, economic empowerment, and basic civil and human rights to freedom of religion and self-determination. In the 1990s the struggle continued.

If sacred places could be battlefields, battlefields could also be sacred places. December 7, 1991, marked the fiftieth anniversary of the Japanese bombing of Pearl Harbor, recalling a "day of infamy," but also an event that has been sanctified and commemorated at the national monument of the USS Arizona Memorial. Like other American battlefields, this memorial site has been ritualized by its demarcation from profane space, by its ceremonial displays, and by the pilgrimages to its sacred precincts of tourists, veterans, survivors, and other devotees of an American patriotic faith.[3] Tourist pilgrims come to pay their respects, but also to buy such relics as T-shirts, books, slides, videotapes, maps, and photographs, illustrating a "venerative consumption" that enables visitors to take some part of the sacred shrine back home. As both shrine and tomb, however, the USS Arizona Memorial has a unique place among the battlefields that punctuate the American patriotic landscape. The memorial commemorates the sacrifice, but also houses the remains, of American sanctified dead. Accordingly, the USS Arizona Memorial is a particularly charged sacred site at which Americans can enact the ongoing ritual relations between the living and the dead that form such an important part of a national patriotic faith.

The fiftieth anniversary celebration was an occasion for special ritual observances at Pearl Harbor. Commemoration, however, was also an opportunity for reinterpretation, as different readings of America were asserted by speakers at the site. Some participants remembered World War II as the last "good war," drawing familiar patriotic lessons about American heroism, divine mission, and the redemptive power of martial sacrifice, while others called for an end to all wars that could only happen in a new era of international friendship and cooperation. These different readings highlighted the fact that Pearl Harbor has been the site of a particularly intense conflict of interpretation. Chief Historian of the National Park Service Edwin C. Bearss noted that his office received "more questions and complaints about the historical interpretation and management of this site than about all the other historical areas of the National Park System put together."[4] This conflict of interpretation was intensified by a popular perception that the National Park Service was sponsoring a reinterpretation of Pearl Harbor that not only included, but even glorified, Japanese perspectives on the event. Conflicting interpretations, therefore, could be situated in contests over the legitimate, authentic ownership of the site, a question of ownership intensified by American insecurities about economic competition with Japan.

As an indication of popular involvement in this contest, people from all over America wrote to their congressmen, to the President, and to the staff of the Memorial to complain about the National Park Service's management of the sacred site. The most serious criticism asserted that the Park Service was not an appropriate guardian of the sacred memory of those

Americans who died in the attack on Pearl Harbor. Some proposed that the site should be transferred into the care and supervision of the U.S. Navy. Many, however, like syndicated columnist Thomas Sowell, just demanded that the sacred site should be taken away from the National Park Service, insisting that "people who are squeamish about telling the truth and apologetic about being Americans are the last people to be left in charge of a national shrine like that at Pearl Harbor."[5] Obviously, the controversy surrounding the fiftieth anniversary celebrations at Pearl Harbor involved conflicting interpretations, and competing appropriations, not only of an historical event, but also of the meaning and power of America. Like the ancient *heiau*, the "national shrine" at Pearl Harbor had become a site of struggle over the legitimate use and ownership of sacred space. Many Americans perceived Pearl Harbor as a sacred place that had been made more intensely sacred because it seemed in danger of being defiled or dis-possessed. New ritualizations, competing reinterpretations, and contest-able reappropriations of its symbolic power all appeared to place the site at risk. Like any production of sacred space, however, these practices also re-vitalized the site as a place at which important religious concerns and in-terests could be adjudicated precisely because they were at stake. In simi-lar ways, sacred space has been ritualized, reinterpreted, and contested all over America.

KEY TERMS

I. Sacred Space

PURPOSE of BOOK

This book is an opportunity to rethink what anthropologist Rodney Needham once called "that contested category of the sacred" by exploring the meaning and power of sacred space in America. What is the sacred? In the study of religion, two broad lines of definition have been advanced, one substantial, the other situational. In the first instance, some definitions of the sacred presume to have penetrated and reported its essential character. Familiar substantial definitions—Rudolph Otto's "holy," Gerardus van der Leeuw's "power," or Mircea Eliade's "real"—might be regarded as at-tempts to replicate an insider's evocation of certain experiential qualities that can be associated with the sacred. From this perspective, the sacred has been identified as an uncanny, awesome, or powerful manifestation of reality, full of ultimate significance.[6] By contrast, however, a situational analysis, which can be traced back to the work of Emile Durkheim, has located the sacred at the nexus of human practices and social projects. Fol-lowing Arnold van Gennep's insight into the "pivoting of the sacred," si-

[handwritten marginalia:] RELIGION — 1. SUBSTANTIAL — Penetration of essential sacred character / "holy," "power," "real" / Uncanny, awesome, powerful manifestation of reality — 2. SITUATIONAL: DURKHEIM — nexus of practices & social projects

tuational approaches have recognized that nothing is inherently sacred. Not full of meaning, the sacred, from this perspective, is an empty signifier. As Claude Lévi-Strauss proposed, the sacred is "a value of indeterminate signification, in itself empty of meaning and therefore susceptible to the reception of any meaning whatsoever."[7] In this respect, the term is better regarded as an adjectival or verbal form, a sign of difference that can be assigned to virtually anything through the human labor of consecration. As a situational term, therefore, the sacred is nothing more nor less than a notional supplement to the ongoing cultural work of sacralizing space, time, persons, and social relations. Situational, relational, and frequently, if not inherently, contested, the sacred is a by-product of this work of sacralization.

The divergence between a substantial and situational definition of the sacred is perhaps most evident in the analysis of sacred space. Mircea Eliade held that the sacred irrupted, manifested, or appeared in certain places, causing them to become powerful centers of meaningful worlds. On the contrary, Jonathan Z. Smith has shown how place is sacralized as the result of the cultural labor of ritual, in specific historical situations, involving the hard work of attention, memory, design, construction, and control of place. Not merely an opposition between "insider" and "outsider" perspectives, this clash between substantial and situational approaches to definition and analysis represents a contrast between what might be called the poetics and the politics of sacred space.[8]

While the poetics of sacred space has been most prominent in the study of religion, the politics of its construction and contestation has always been a subtext, even in attempts to work out a substantial, essentialist definition of the sacred. In his landmark text in the phenomenology of religion, *Religion in Essence and Manifestation*, Gerardus van der Leeuw imaginatively explored the implications of his substantial definition of the sacred, "power," in spatial terms. In a chapter on sacred space, Van der Leeuw celebrated a poetics of sacred space, a romantic imagination most evident in his enthusiasm for natural sacred sites, the forests and caverns, rocks and mountains, waterfalls and springs, in which the sacred has often been located. However, Van der Leeuw's implicit distinction between natural and built environments was in tension with his recognition elsewhere that the very category of "nature" was a nineteenth-century invention, and, therefore, could not stand as a stable, independent term in his analysis of sacred space. In the poetics of the sacred, "natural" and "arti-

ficial" sacred sites were equivalent as positions in which power was localized.[9]

In concentrating primarily upon built environments, Van der Leeuw
outlined an inventory of typical sacred places that have appeared in the
history of religions. Van der Leeuw's inventory was a basic series of homologies through which he asserted the metaphoric equivalence of home,
temple, settlement, pilgrimage site, and human body. According to Van
der Leeuw, a home was a temple, a temple a home. The city of Jerusalem,
which he identified as sacred space in its most "typical form," was a temple in the beginning and would be a temple in the end. The pilgrimage site,
as a home, temple, or sacred settlement away from home, could ultimately
be found at the center of the body in the human heart. Sacred places, therefore, formed a recursive series of metaphoric equivalences. The only reason
we can speak of these places as sacred is because they can be discerned as
transferable metaphors for the same kind of powerful space. In addition,
however, and concurrently, Van der Leeuw tracked a second series of homologies, consisting of synecdoches for the items in the first series, that
linked the hearth (of the home), the altar (of the temple), the sanctuary (of
the settlement), the shrine (of the pilgrimage site), and the heart (of the
human body). At the heart of each sacred place, therefore, was another
heart, a center of power located at the core of each sacred center. Although
these homologies were not explicitly schematized or theorized by Van der
Leeuw, remaining implicit in his analysis, the two series of equivalences
established a basic vocabulary for the analysis of sacred places. As they
recurred in his analysis, they provided the key terms for a poetics of sacred
space. → key THEORETICAL IDEAS → could this apply to music?

At the same time, even if unintended, Van der Leeuw laced his analysis
with hints of a politics of sacred space. First, we can identify a politics of
position. In some moments, like Eliade, Van der Leeuw attributed sole,
transcendent, and ultimate agency to sacred power, even holding that sacred power actually positioned itself in the world. Geographer David
Harvey has referred to such a mystification as the "aestheticization of politics," an exercise of poetic imagination "in which appeal to the mythology
of place and person has a strong role to play."[10] However, this mystifying
of power, a kind of "mystical intuitionism" of sacred space, was tempered
by Van der Leeuw's recognition, however it might have been submerged in
his text, that the positioning of a sacred place was a political act, whether
that positioning involved, in his own terms, selection, orientation, limita-

KEY
TERM

David Chidester and Edward T. Linenthal

tion, or conquest. Ultimately, Van der Leeuw recognized that every establishment of a sacred place was a conquest of space.

Second, we can observe that Van der Leeuw consistently linked sacred space with a politics of property. A sacred place was not merely a meaningful place; it was a powerful place because it was appropriated, possessed, and owned. In several important passages of his text, Van der Leeuw referred to the sacred power of property, even suggesting, perhaps somewhat enigmatically, that property was the "realization of possibilities."[11] However, since "possibility" was a technical term in his analytical vocabulary, Van der Leeuw linked power, possibility, and property as forces in the production of sacred space. Recently, cultural analysts have shown a growing interest in the importance of symbolic objects as sacred property. In particular, analysts have documented the ways in which exclusive claims on the ownership of sacred objects can serve political interests. As Norbert Peabody has noted, "For many years now it has been a commonplace observation in history and anthropology that the monopolistic possession of sacred objects, heirlooms, talismans, or regalia helps perpetuate political rule." Likewise, the ownership of the "intellectual property" of religious symbols, myths, or rituals can be shown to operate in economic contexts and to serve specific social or political interests.[12] In a similar way, symbolic space can also be appropriated. The sacred character of a place can be asserted and maintained through claims and counter-claims on its ownership. The sacrality of place, therefore, can be directly related to a politics of property.

Third, we can recognize another relational, situational aspect of sacred space by paying attention to the politics of exclusion. Van der Leeuw proposed that a sacred place, such as a home, was a space in which relations among persons could be negotiated and worked out. Some persons, however, were left out, kept out, or forced out. In fact, the sanctity of the inside was certified by maintaining and reinforcing boundaries that kept certain persons outside the sacred place. By recognizing this process of excluding persons, even if in passing, Van der Leeuw raised the possibility that a politics of exclusion might be an integral part of the making of sacred space.

Fourth, and finally, Van der Leeuw ultimately positioned sacred space, and his analysis of sacred space, in the context of a politics of exile. Insistently, he highlighted a modern loss of the sacred, or alienation from the sacred, or nostalgia for the sacred, in his use and interpretation of basic data of religion. Repeatedly, Van der Leeuw noted that primitives had it;

some peasant folk had retained it; but moderns had entirely lost it. This historical and essentially political situation of exile from the sacred entailed two theoretical implications for Van der Leeuw's phenomenology of sacred space: the most sacred places were remote, and the most authentic religious experience in relation to sacred space was homesickness. "The house is an organic unity," Van der Leeuw noted, recalling his foundational poetic figure for a sacred place, "whose essence is some definite power, just as much as is the temple or church." The modern house, however, was not sacred. Its unity had been dispersed, its position displaced, its boundaries dissolved, its sovereign ownership alienated. As a result of modernization, Van der Leeuw lamented, "it is difficult for us, semi-americanized as we already are . . . to form any idea of its unitary power."[13] In the politics of exile, the sacred was positioned in relation to human beings who found themselves to be out of position. The historical "pivoting of the sacred" in the modern world had made all "semi-americanized" human beings political exiles from the sacred.

what about mental spaces such as meditation? Could these intangible spaces be considered?

? but key term

2. The Production of Sacred Space

RITUALIZATION, REINTERPRETATION, INTERPRETATION

Attention to the politics of position and property, exclusion and exile, in the "pivoting of the sacred" promises new ways of understanding how specific sites and environments, geographical relations and symbolic orientations, can be produced and reproduced as sacred space in America. As a preliminary orientation, some defining features of the production of sacred space, which we have already observed in Hawaii as ritualization, reinterpretation, and contests over legitimate ownership, can be briefly thematized here.

First, we can identify sacred space as ritual space, a location for formalized, repeatable symbolic performances. As sacred space, a ritual site is set apart from or carved out of an "ordinary" environment to provide an arena for the performance of controlled, "extraordinary" patterns of action. Although ritual might enact a myth, signal a transition, reinforce political authority, or express emotion, ritualization is perhaps best understood as a particular type of embodied, spatial practice. Performed in a set-apart, extraordinary symbolic space, rituals can act out and embody perfectly the way things "ought to be." That ritualized, controlled pattern of action, however, can be performed in conscious tension with the way things are normally perceived to be in the ordinary world.[14] In this tension between an extraordinary ritualized place and ordinary space, there is an observable dialectic in the role of ritual in the production of sacred space. Ritual acts of worship, sacrifice, prayer, meditation, pilgrimage, and ceremonial consecrate sacred space. Conversely, however, the demarcation of a set-apart, special place gives ritual acts their very character as a type of highly charged symbolic performance. Since ritual is a defining feature of sacralization, explorations of sacred space and places in America will require particular attention to ritual practices and performances. *[→ KEY THEME, RITUAL]*

The human body plays a crucial role in the ritual production of sacred space. Ritual action manipulates basic spatial distinctions between up and down, right and left, inside and outside, and so on, that necessarily revolve around the axis of the living body. Spatial practices—the "techniques of the body," the formalized "gestures of approach," and the location and direction of embodied movement—all contribute towards producing the distinctive quality and character of sacred space.[15] As Pierre Bourdieu has proposed, embodied practice produces a *habitus*, a localized fusion of thought and action in and through which human beings negotiate the social relations and practical knowledge of their worlds. Rather than the temple, settlement, or pilgrimage site, Bourdieu's primary example of a ritualized *habitus*, agreeing with Van der Leeuw on the point, was the home. "Through the intermediary of the divisions and hierarchies it sets up between things, persons, and practices," Bourdieu has observed, "this tangible classifying system continuously inculcates and reinforces the taxonomic principles underlying all the arbitrary provisions of this culture."[16] Through embodied practices, the ritualized *habitus* of the home, like the *habitus* of other sacred sites, is produced and reproduced as a dynamic spatial ordering of knowledge and power.

Ritualized disciplines of the body, which regulate its gestures and rhythms, its speaking, eating, and excreting, situate embodied practices in place. In the domestic space of the home, for example, American rituals of dining emerged during the nineteenth century to define the table as the focus for a particular kind of cultural *habitus*. As a "tangible classifying system," the dining table, with its prescribed embodied practices, became a ritualized space for distinguishing among different classes of persons, reinforcing a cultural knowledge which held that brutes feed, barbarians eat, but only "cultured man" dines.[17]

If embodied practices can consecrate, they can also desecrate a sacred place. Throughout the history of religions, the production of sacred space has depended upon control over purity.[18] Often purity has been associated with the ritualized control of bodily excretions. Rabbinic Judaism, for ex-

Embodied practice can consecrate space ....

ample, adapted biblical proscriptions for maintaining the sanctity of a camp or settlement to the ritual demands for creating a pure space for prayer. When sanctifying such a place, the Mishna asked, "how far should one distance oneself from excrement?" The answer, according to one account, was "Four cubits."[19] In that exact measurement, which suggested a meticulous management and control of the embodied practices that produce ritual space, the rabbis specified the precise condition for the consecration, but also for the potential desecration, of a sacred place of worship. By contrast, Chinese practitioners of the meditation traditions of Ch'an Buddhism encountered a different problem in managing and controlling the excretions of the body in relation to sacred space. If the Buddha essence, the *Dharmakaya*, was everywhere, then, in principle, sacred space was coextensive with the universe. "Since the Dharmakaya fills all space," one Ch'an master complained, "where in the entire universe can I find a place to shit?"[20] These two approaches to sacred space suggest contrasting relations between the body and ritual purity. In a defiling world, ritual purity can be achieved by control of the body. In a pure world, however, the body poses a different kind of problem. If sacred space is everywhere, where does the profane body fit? Can the body itself be holy, a source of pure actions, extensions, or excretions that cannot defile sacred space?

In America these two dispositions towards the body have defined different "gestures of approach" to the production of sacred space. At one extreme, rigorous discipline of the body has been required for the production and maintenance of sacred space. Accordingly, some American strategies have demanded a meticulous ritual control over embodied space in the interests of purity. As American theologian Jonathan Edwards declared, "This world is all over dirty. Everywhere it is covered with that which tends to defile the feet of the traveller." Body and soul had to be defended from defilement. From Edwards's perspective, however, the body itself was a microcosm of the defiling world. "The inside of the body of man," Edwards held, "is full of filthiness, contains his bowels that are full of dung, which represents the corruption and filthiness that the heart of man is naturally full of."[21] In a world so thoroughly defiled, almost nothing can be done to establish purity. It cannot be constructed through ritual, but must depend upon an unmerited grace. Nevertheless, American heirs of Jonathan Edwards have persisted in observing various ritualized practices for exercising control over the body in the interest of establishing purity in a defiling world.

During the 1950s, the American poet Allen Ginsberg proposed a symbolic strategy for dealing with the dilemma, similar to the Ch'an Buddhist case, of living in a world in which sacred space extended everywhere. Ginsberg declared: "The world is holy! The soul is holy! The skin is holy! The nose is holy! The tongue and cock and hand and asshole holy!"[22] In a world so completely pure, almost anything can be done, since even the body, in all its extensions and apertures, is a pure space. Although Ginsberg's symbolism of the body must be regarded as a minority report, it nevertheless highlights, by stark contrast, the dominant, conventional symbolism of the body in America, a disposition more consistent with the concerns of Jonathan Edwards, as Americans have drawn upon the human body in the ritual production and maintenance of sacred space. In all its gestures and motions, its rhythms and workings, the body is necessarily an integral part of the ritual production of sacred space.

Second, sacred space is significant space, a site, orientation, or set of relations subject to interpretation because it focuses crucial questions about what it means to be a human being in a meaningful world. The geographer Neil Smith has observed that "the production of space also implies the production of meaning, concepts and consciousness of space which are inseparably linked to its physical production."[23] In its material production and practical reproduction, sacred space anchors a worldview in the world. As the anthropologist Robert Redfield suggested, a worldview is comprised of at least two dimensions: classification of persons, and orientation in space and time.[24] Sacred space is a means for grounding classifications and orientations in reality, giving particular force to the meaningful focus gained through these aspects of a worldview. As significant space, sacred places focus a classification of persons, carving out a place for a human identity that can be distinguished from superhuman persons, perhaps to be worshiped, and those classified as subhuman who can be excluded, manipulated, dominated, degraded, or sacrificed. Furthermore, sacred places focus more general orientations in space and time that distinguish center from periphery, inside from outside, up from down, and a recollected past from a meaningful present or an anticipated future. "Symbolic orderings of space and time," as the geographer David Harvey has noted, "provide a framework for experience through which we learn who or what we are in society."[25] Therefore, to understand the symbolic orderings of American sacred space, considerable attention will have to be paid to the interpretive labors that have gone into making space significant. As a heuristic device, we can distinguish among three domains— natural environments, built environments, and mythic orientations—that

3 DOMAINS

represent overlapping and interweaving arenas in which differing interpretations of space as sacred have been advanced.

Natural environments have been subject to interpretation and reinterpretation throughout American history. From the religious practices of American Indians to the spiritual politics of modern environmentalists, the religious interpretation of land and landscape, which Catherine Albanese has recently identified as "nature religion," has defined an open set of interpretive strategies for investing the natural environment with sacred significance.[26] All this interpretive industry, however, suggests that nature, in its human meaning and significance, is a cultural product. During the nineteenth century, for example, a romantic naturalism transferred a sacred web of sentiment from God to nature. As Leo Marx has observed, "The movements of the heavenly bodies, space (an awesome, unimaginable infinity of space) and the landscape itself all were to become repositories of emotions formerly reserved for a majestic God."[27] Some analysts have argued, however, that this nineteenth-century religious valorization of nature disguised the political, social, and economic forces at work in the production of American space. On the one hand, romantic nature religion obscured the military conquest of American Indian societies that made natural environments available for appropriation by "Nature's Nation," the United States. Such a religious interpretation of nature operated to naturalize conquest, thereby serving, in the words of Barbara Novak, as "the rhetorical screen under which the aggressive conquest of the country could be accomplished."[28] On the other hand, romantic religious sentiments about nature have blurred a recognition of the economic production, packaging, and presentation of natural environments in America. As Neil Smith has observed, wilderness and wildlife areas, such as Yellowstone or Yosemite, are "produced environments in every conceivable sense." They are "neatly packaged cultural experiences of environment on which substantial profits are recorded each year."[29] Therefore, nature in America is not a "natural" but a thoroughly cultural production of space.

Built environments are more obviously constructed as cultural locations of religious meaning and significance.[30] Clearly, places of worship, such as churches, synagogues, mosques, and temples, have been marked off, ritualized, and interpreted as specific sites of sacred space in America.[31] Often these sites operate as "nodal points" in a network of sacred places that defines some larger religious landscape. For example, an Aztec temple, the spatial arrangements of Puritan New England, the churches of colonial Virginia, the settings of early nineteenth-century evangelical camp meetings, the architecture of communitarian socialism, the transformations of American synagogues, and the sites of Mormon sacred geography have all comprised different spatial networks of "nodal points" in the production of alternative religious orientations in American space.[32]

Extending the interpretation of specific sites, many other built environments have been identified and analyzed as sacred space in America. A preliminary inventory would have to include the following sites: cities;[33] homes;[34] schools;[35] cemeteries;[36] hospitals, asylums, and prisons;[37] tourist attractions;[38] museums;[39] and even shopping malls.[40] At one time or another, each of these sites has been interpreted as a sacred place in America. As we have noted, the "pivoting of the sacred" that occurs through the work of ritualization and interpretation allows virtually any place to become sacred. What kind of interpretive labor, however, would endow a place like a post office with sacred significance? As Jacques Derrida once confessed, "When I enter the post office of a great city I tremble as if in a sacred place."[41] Seeming to pivot wildly in this case, sacred meaning and significance, holy awe and desire, can coalesce in any place that becomes, even if only temporarily, a site for intensive interpretation.

In America these constructed religious environments are inevitably positioned in relation to a patriotic landscape. Centered in the ritual core of Washington, D.C., this national sacred geography is punctuated by shrines, memorials, monuments, and battlefields at which patriotic orthodoxy has been ritualized and reinterpreted. As Wilbur Zelinsky has argued, American nationalism, particularly as it moved towards celebrating increasingly statist or centralist symbols of national identity and power, became locally embedded all over the country in a patriotic network of sacred places. However, as we have seen, a national shrine such as Pearl Harbor has localized, not only the interpretive framework of an orthodox patriotic faith, but also the conflict of interpretations that advance competing visions of America's place in the world.[42]

While grounded in specific sites, environments, or geographical relations, religious worldviews embody broader spatial orientations that locate human beings in a meaningful, powerful world. Interpretations of sacred space entail strategies of symbolic or mythic orientation. In the study of religion, an earlier concern with the importance of symbolic centers for spatial orientation has been more recently modified to recognize that every center has a periphery, every symbolic centering also decenters those persons and places that stand on or beyond a center's periphery.[43] Therefore, attention to geographical relations between center and periph-

ery locates specific sacred sites or environments within a larger network
of political, social, economic, and symbolic relations of power.

As another example of an advance in the analysis of spatial orientation
in the study of religion, Jonathan Z. Smith has offered the useful distinction between two general spatial orientations, locative and utopian. Locative space is a fixed, bounded, sacred cosmos, reinforced by the imperative
of maintaining one's place, and the place of others, in a larger scheme of
things. By contrast, utopian space is unbounded, unfixed to any particular
location, a place that can only be reached by breaking out of, or being liberated from, the bonds of a prevailing social order.[44]

At the same time, however, general symbolic or mythic orientations toward sacred space—symbolizing center and periphery, inside and outside,
up and down, fixed and free—might be entangled with symbols of class
location, racial classification, or ethnic identification. They also might be
embedded in systems of economic exchange. In the modern economy of
sacred space, the symbolic medium of money, which has been described as
"the 'space' of the capitalist world," produces an empty, infinite extension
through which, in principle, all commodities can pass and freely circulate.
By altering perceptions of space, money has become the primary symbol
of mobility, access, and ownership in the production of modern American
sacred space.[45] Sacred space is often, if not inevitably, entangled in politics.
Since the nineteenth century, the most potent mythic orientations have
linked sacred space with nationalism, celebrating the "sacred nation" as
the most encompassing spatial symbol of inclusion (and exclusion) in the
world. In this respect, the spatial orientation of American nationalism,
like many other nationalisms, has been particularly ambivalent. American
nationalism has been locative in defending its boundaries and borders, but
utopian in its appeals to a manifest destiny of territorial expansion and its
aspiration to transcend all geographical limits in assuming a position of
world power.[46]

Third, and finally, sacred space is inevitably contested space, a site of
negotiated contests over the legitimate ownership of sacred symbols. As
Michel Foucault insisted, "space is fundamental in any exercise of
power."[47] Conversely, power is asserted and resisted in any production of
space, and especially in the production of sacred space. Since no sacred
space is merely "given" in the world, its ownership will always be at stake.
In this respect, a sacred space is not merely discovered, or founded, or constructed; it is claimed, owned, and operated by people advancing specific
interests. As Jonathan Z. Smith once observed, "Where we have good eth-

nography, it's always clear that myth and ritual are owned by certain subsets within the collective."[48] The same is clear for sacred space. Sacred places are arenas in which power relations can be reinforced, in which relations between insiders and outsiders, rulers and subjects, elders and juniors, males and females, and so on, can be adjudicated. But those power relations are always resisted. Sacred places are always highly charged sites for contested negotiations over the ownership of the symbolic capital (or symbolic real estate) that signifies power relations. Although spearheaded by specific cultural entrepreneurs, cultural brokers, or cultural workers, struggles over the ownership of sacred space inevitably draw upon the commitment of larger constituencies that hold an investment in the contest. The analysis of sacred space in America, therefore, will require not only attention to how space has been ritualized and interpreted but also to how it has been appropriated, contested, and "stolen" back and forth in struggles over power in America.[49]

3. Contested Sacred Space

This insistence on the contested character of sacred space must seem strange for readers who are only familiar with the vantage point adopted and promoted by Mircea Eliade. In popular works of interpretation, such as *Patterns of Comparative Religion, The Sacred and the Profane* and *The Myth of the Eternal Return*, Eliade developed three basic axioms for the analysis of sacred space in the history of religions. First, sacred space is set apart on a horizontal dimension from ordinary, homogeneous space. Second, sacred space—as center, *omphalos*, or *axis mundi*—allows for passage between different levels of reality. Third, sacred space is a revelation, an irruption or manifestation of the real, a hierophany. While these axioms, and their application, have been criticized within the history of religions, they have occasionally been accepted uncritically by humanistic geographers as if they were the sole contribution of the study of religion on the topic of sacred space. For example, the geographer Robert David Sack has invoked the authority of Eliade to observe that mountains, rivers, and other "features of the landscape, which to the outsider may have no significance, have emotional import and anchor the emotions to places. Such places become a part of the mythology of a culture. They become holy places, places which are believed to have been created and molded by gods and spirits."[50] In keeping with an Eliadian approach to sacred space, the geographer's observation is framed entirely in the passive voice. Human

Key Theme/Thought

agency, including all the ritual, interpretive, social, economic, and political labor that goes into consecrating space, is erased by attributing all the action to "holy places" and "gods and spirits." *They* become sacred; *they* anchor emotions; *they* create and mold a mythological environment. Instead of contributing to an analysis, these assumptions merely announce a mystical theology of sacred space. Attention to the contested character of sacred space might provide a necessary corrective to this analytical naivete, whether it takes the form of theological dogmatism or mystical intuitionism, that holds out for a view of sacred space as simply "given" or "revealed."

This book reopens the investigation of sacred space by creatively subverting Eliade's axioms. Sacred space may be set apart, but not in the absolute, heterogeneous sense that Eliade insisted upon. Against all the efforts of religious actors, sacred space is inevitably entangled with the entrepreneurial, the social, the political, and other "profane" forces. In fact, as the case studies in this book demonstrate, a space or place is often experienced as most sacred by those who perceive it at risk of being desecrated by the very forces—economic, social, and political—that made its consecration possible in the first place. In one way or another, the chapters of this book set to rest the Eliadian notion that the sacred is necessarily the opposite of the profane or absolutely separate from the profane. *Key!*

Sacred space may involve "levels of reality." Often, however, the most significant levels of reality in the formation of sacred space are not "mythological" categories, such as heaven, earth, and hell, but hierarchical power relations of domination and subordination, inclusion and exclusion, appropriation and dispossession. A certain theological dogmatism might hold, for example, that the city of Jerusalem is "really" sacred. But, as one geographer has observed, "Jerusalem could symbolize both a religious center of the Judeo-Christian world and a contested, occupied city."[51] This ambivalence is not peculiar to Jerusalem; it is part of the reality of sacred space. Therefore, sacred space anchors more than merely myth or emotion. It anchors relations of meaning and power that are at stake in the formation of a larger social reality.

Finally, the assertion that the sacred irrupts or manifests is a mystification that obscures the symbolic labor that goes into making space sacred. It erases all the hard work that goes into choosing, setting aside, consecrating, venerating, protecting, defending, and redefining sacred places. This mystification is even more seriously misleading, however, when it covers up the symbolic violence of domination or exclusion that is frequently involved in the making of sacred space. Sacred places have been exploited by dominant political and economic interests, and they have been reclaimed and even desecrated by those who have been dominated or excluded, all in the context of often violent contests over power and purity. As the case studies in this book show, power and purity are not inherent in sacred space. Power is always at stake in the symbolic, yet also material, struggles over appropriation and dispossession. Purity is always at stake in struggles over inclusion and exclusion. Advancing analysis, rather than a mystical theology, the authors of this volume have had to enter a more complex, contested world of sacred space.

Why should sacred space be inherently contested? Although the chapters of this book examine specific cases of conflict over sacred space, two general reasons might be suggested. First, sacred space is contested for the simple reason that it is spatial. The academic discipline of human geography has advanced several attempts to account for the inevitable conflict that occurs over space and place in human relations. Adopting a geometrical mode of analysis, geographer John Urry has suggested that the spatial dynamics of conflict can be explained by the fact that no two objects can occupy the same point in space. "Hence," Urry has concluded, "space is necessarily limited and there has to be competition and conflict over its organization and control."[52] Whether explained as competition over scarce resources in a human ecology, or as relations of domination and resistance in class struggle, conflict has been analyzed by geographers as a necessary feature of spatiality. Therefore, we should not be surprised that sacred space is entangled in competition over scarce spatial resources, including conflicts over the hypothetical resource of spatiality itself.

However, sacred space is inevitably contested for a second, and perhaps, at first glance, contradictory reason. When space or place becomes sacred, spatially scarce resources are transformed into a surplus of signification. As an arena of signs and symbols, a sacred place is not a fixed point in space, but a point of departure for an endless multiplication of meaning. Since a sacred place could signify almost anything, its meaningful contours can become almost infinitely extended through the work of interpretation. In this respect, a sacred place is not defined by spatial limits; it is open to unlimited claims and counter-claims on its significance. As a result, conflict in the production of sacred space is not only over scarce resources but also over symbolic surpluses that are abundantly available for appropriation. Although "the sacred" might be regarded as an empty signifier, a sign that by virtue of its emptiness could mean anything or nothing, its emptiness is filled with meaningful content as a result of specific strategies of symbolic engagement. Not merely interpretive, these symbolic strategies are powerful, practical maneuvers in the field of sacred symbols. Arguably, as already suggested, these symbolic maneuvers are what make something sacred. Characteristic modes of symbolic engagement in the production of sacred space include strategies of appropriation, exclusion, inversion, and hybridization.

Appropriation and exclusion are two strategies most often employed in attempts to dominate sacred space by advancing special interests of power or purity. In strategies of appropriation, power is asserted in claims to legitimate, authentic ownership. Strategies of exclusion often reinforce those claims in the name of purity. Significantly, the dynamics of both of these strategies for dominating sacred space are most clearly suggested by their oppositions—a space is sacred if it is at risk of being stolen, sacred if it can be defiled. Due to the inherent surplus of signification in "the sacred," no appropriation can ever be final, no exclusion can be total, and, therefore, conflict over ownership and control of the symbolic surplus remains endemic in sacred space. In this respect, a space or place is perhaps revealed at its most sacred when people are willing to fight, kill, or die over its ownership and control.

The other two strategies, inversion and hybridization, are particularly suited for resistance to domination. They lend themselves to projects of reversal, or innovation, or even to the kinds of "desecration" that symbolize alternative relationships to sacred space. Strategies of inversion reverse a prevailing spatial orientation—the high becomes low, the inside becomes outside, the peripheral becomes central—but they may subtly retain its basic oppositional structure. Spatial inversions are often found in millenarian movements that promise an imminent reversal of the prevailing social order. By contrast, the strategy of hybridization, found in practices of mixing, fusing, or transgressing conventional spatial relations, presents "the possibility of shifting *the very terms of the system itself.*"[53] Appearing most dramatically in carnival, festival, or street theater, but also in any spatial practice that mixes up conventional distinctions, the strategy of hybridization, as Homi Bhabha has noted, "terrorizes authority with the *ruse* of recognition, its mimicry, its mockery."[54]

Such reversals and mixtures of dominant spatial relations produce new places, or reclaim old places, as a type of space that Foucault called a heterotopia, "a kind of effectively acted utopia in which the real sites, all the other real sites that can be found within the culture, are simultaneously represented, contested, and inverted."[55] A utopia might have no real place in the world. But a heterotopia, in Foucault's sense, can be located as a real site for altering spatial relations. At *Pu'uhonua o Hōnaunau*, for example, Hunter S. Thompson produced a hybrid sacred site by mixing up the spatial distinctions of Hawaiian tradition and the National Park Service, producing a surrealistic heterotopia for gonzo journalism. At Pearl Harbor, some commentators argued that the inclusion of Japanese perspectives, which blurred the spatial distinction between allies and enemies, threatened to turn that sacred site into a hybrid space. Frequently, the counter-strategies of inversion or hybridization are resisted by dominant cultural interests. The specific contours of dominant spatial orientations might even be defined or reinforced by repressing illicit inversions or mixtures. However, it might be argued that all sacred sites are produced through mixing and manipulating cultural and material relations. After all, Pearl Harbor itself is a hybrid of national park, patriotic monument, and military cemetery. In spite of the efforts of religious actors to sanctify space, there are no pure places in the world. Through appropriation and exclusion, inversion and hybridization, sacred space is produced and reproduced. Relational, situational, and contested, sacred places are necessarily located within these conflictual strategies of symbolic engagement.

[handwritten: Ethnography can be an effective tool to understand the level of purity] *[handwritten: 1-3 - ENVIRONMENT]*

4. American Sacred Space *[handwritten: 4-5 - BUILT]*

American sacred sites, environments, and spatial orientations have been intensely contested. The essays collected in this volume reopen the exploration of contested American sacred space. They begin with the land. The first three essays explore conflicts over land that have been pursued not only by military, legal, or economic force but also in and through highly charged sacred symbols. The specific conflicts examined here—over land and property rights, over the preservation of wilderness areas, and over the significance of the Black Hills—are richly suggestive of the ways in which sacred space in America has appeared at the nexus of clashing, contradictory symbolic projects.

The contests over sacred space, place, and power waged throughout American history between Euroamericans and American Indians have especially revealed the contested contours of American sacred space. While American Indian approaches to sacred space might be regarded as environmental, European conquerors and colonizers enacted military, legal, and architectural rituals that transformed the American environment in conformity to alien ideals of sacred space. In and through those ritual enactments of power, position, and possession, the sanctity of property rights represented a fundamental, nonnegotiable religious commitment for dominant Euroamerican interests. A re-examination of the history of land as property clarifies the prevailing religious interests, the "fetishism of commodities," that set the terms and conditions for negotiating power and place in the American environment.

If sacred space is recognized as contested space, then the acts of radical environmentalists in the 1980s and 1990s take on new significance. Although often branded in the media as "terrorists," radical environmentalists, such as in the movement known as Earth First!, have resorted to dramatic rituals of resistance, from civil disobedience to industrial sabotage, in defense of what they have perceived as a sacred natural order. In addition to practicing these rituals of resistance, radical environmentalists have mobilized other symbolic instruments of power, including innovative myths, rituals, and forms of communal organization, that have supported a resacralization of the environment. In particular, wilderness areas have assumed a crucial significance, revered for their inviolable sanctity and defended when that sanctity is violated. The struggles of radical environmentalists are especially suggestive of the inherently contested character of sacred space. Among other things, they show how sacred space is perceived as sacred precisely because it is always in danger of desecration. In the midst of this tension between the desire for consecration and the danger of desecration, radical environmentalists have engaged in a kind of ritualized guerrilla warfare over sacred space in America. Although apparently a marginal, fringe movement in modern America, the activists of radical environmentalism have mobilized forces in the ongoing contest over sacred space that has been central to the religious and political life of America as a whole.

As one front on which the symbolic warfare over American environments has been waged, the Black Hills of South Dakota and Wyoming has focused an ongoing conflict of interpretation over the meaning and power of American sacred space. Competing religious interpretations of the Black Hills were provided in the nineteenth century by Lakota prophets and U.S. Army generals. In the twentieth century, conflicting religious interpretations of the region have continued to be advanced by Native Americans, environmentalists, mining and logging industries, government agents, and others, each claiming to have penetrated, in mutually exclusive ways, the central meaning and significance of the Black Hills. At the center of this conflict, the patriotic edifice of Mount Rushmore has substantially altered the terms of engagement in this struggle. Part patriotic monument, part entrepreneurial initiative, and part intrusion on the landscape, Mount Rushmore has focused attempts to define the meaning of this natural environment. This conflict of interpretation, however, has underwritten and perhaps disguised a more fundamental struggle over legitimate access to and ownership of the area. The conflict over the meaning of the Black Hills, therefore, illustrates a more basic conflict over place and power in an American sacred environment that reveals the contested character of sacred space throughout America.

The next two essays explore the symbolic and material construction of two built environments, the Christian home and the Holocaust Memorial Museum. Both the home and the museum have been produced as specific sacred sites. At first glance, the home might seem the locus of the ordinary, the everyday, or the mundane in American symbolic life. However, domestic space in America has also been set apart as a special, sacred site of religious significance. What has been called a "cult of domesticity" emerged in nineteenth-century America to ritualize human relations between males and females, elders and juniors, family and strangers, and so on. These symbolic relations were all centered and reinforced in the domestic architecture, discourses, and practices of the home. Giving the "cult of domesticity" an explicitly religious content, conservative Christians in the late twentieth century have worked hard to construct a domestic sacred place set apart from the larger space of America. An examination of this particular type of domestic space in the worlds of conservative Christians reveals how the home has operated as a specific sacred site, not only idealized and promoted, but also constructed, negotiated, and even sometimes resisted in practice as a nexus of religious meaning and power.

The Holocaust Memorial Museum raises the question of how an ostensibly "foreign" event should be commemorated at the heart of the American patriotic landscape. As an examination of the construction of this museum demonstrates, sacred places are places of memory. The significance of memory for sacred space in America is nowhere better revealed than in shrines, monuments, battlefields, and other specific sites of ritualized commemoration that anchor collective recollections of an American past in the present. As a case study in the production of a sacred site for memory, this examination of the Holocaust Memorial Museum, located at the ceremonial center of the American patriotic landscape adjacent to the Washington Mall, reveals both persistent and changing aspects of American sacred space at the end of the twentieth century. The negotiations over space and memory in the construction of that memorial site have focused crucial and intensely contested issues concerning America's place in the world. Not only a ritualized recollection of the past, however, the Holocaust Memorial Museum, in the ways that it commemorates the past and gives shape to a public memory, suggests that specific sacred sites may symbolically open or foreclose possible futures for America. In this respect, memory of the past might produce the space of the future.

The last two essays investigate symbolic or mythic orientations towards the meaning and power of America as a whole. That sacred totality, however, is revealed, ironically, in a range of alienated, dislocated, or foreign visions of America. A significant dimension of American sacred space appears in the ways in which America has registered and has been represented as a "foreign" space in other parts of the world. As a symbolic totality, the meaning and power of America in the world might best be revealed outside of the geographical boundaries of the United States. At the very least, certain aspects of America as sacred space can only be discerned outside of America. Adopting the distinction between utopian and locative space, it is possible to explore the ways in which America has operated as a potently ambivalent sacred space in the world. In South Africa, for example, America has been a symbol of sudden, apocalyptic liberation, most evident in the "American" movement that mobilized a large following during the 1920s with its promise of the imminent advent of black American liberators. More recently, however, America has symbolized the center of a locative, dominant, and often oppressive world order. Through a case study of America as sacred space in South Africa, some general conclusions can be drawn about the ways in which America's ambivalent sacred significance has been external to America yet at the same time central to the meaning and power of America in the world.

In a radically decentered America, modern spatial orientations often seem more like disorientation. America fails to appear as a single, uniform, coherent space, as a meaningful totality "from sea to shining sea," as it might appear in the patriotic orthodoxy. Rather, America appears as an ironic space in which the differences between location and dislocation have become obscured in disorienting, dangerous, but nevertheless revealing and sometimes revelatory ways. In the immediacy of a modern subjectivity, as mediated, however, through distinctive narrative strategies, or, more often, as fragmented and multiplied under the effects of modernity, American sacred space has been rediscovered as mobile and pluriform, harrowing, yet still perhaps hallowed, suggesting a mythic orientation that is not securely anchored in a stable sacred landscape but is at risk in a modern world of media and mobility. These considerations raise significant questions about the future of sacred space in America. A spatial "disalienation," particularly in the midst of the endlessly signifying, but essentially meaningless, "hyperreality" of a postmodern world, as the critic Fredric Jameson has observed, will require more than merely a new recognition of the significance of place. It depends upon more than merely developing new techniques for "cognitive mapping." A recovery of place, in Jameson's terms, depends upon a cultural politics dedicated to "a practical reconquest of a sense of place."[56] Not the home, therefore, but the battlefield, provides the governing metaphor in such a poetics and politics of space. In the explorations of sacred space advanced in this book, we find ourselves over and over again on the battlefield. Ritualized and reinterpreted, American sacred space remains contested space.

Obviously, American sacred space is a rich, complex field for investigation. Each chapter in this book combines historical depth with a detailed, sensitive analysis of current conflicts over the ritualization, reinterpretation, and authentic ownership of the sacred in America. It should be clear, however, that this book merely charts some of the possibilities. Our exploration of American sacred space in this volume marks only a beginning. Much work remains to be done. Crucial issues have been raised in these chapters by documenting symbolic and material conflicts over property and land, environment and ecology, patriotism and resistance, purity and defilement, inclusion and exclusion, and foreign and domestic perceptions of America. In the end, however, we are left with a lingering question that is implicitly raised by the chapters of this book: Are we exploring distinctively American sacred space or sacred space that only happens—by accident of geography, by coincidence of history—to be located within America? This is a problem. On the one hand, the authors in this volume adopt a broadly comparative perspective, drawing upon theoretical initiatives that have been advanced in the general history of religions. In this respect, there is nothing unique about American sacred space. Its production has followed the same strategies of ritualization, interpretation, and contestation that can be observed in the creation of sacred space and sacred places everywhere else in the world.

On the other hand, however, each chapter of this book is deeply immersed in some specific localization of American sacred space. In meticulous detail, each chapter grounds larger issues of the production and construction of sacred space within American historical experience. By focusing upon the land and the environment, the religious home and the commemorative museum, the foreign imagination and the domestic alienation, these essays directly engage the question, "What is American about American sacred space?" The answer to this question, we suggest, resides in the details, in the specific character and contours of American struggles to produce, construct, and negotiate the sacred. As the case studies in this book suggest, these struggles have inevitably been conducted in and through human relations, through relations that have been negotiated between Native Americans and Euroamericans, between capitalist entrepreneurs and pagan environmentalists, between Christian fundamentalists and secular society, between Jews and a patriotic establishment, between African-Americans and official American foreign policy towards Africa, between the people and a popular culture. What is American about American sacred space can be found precisely in these networks of overlapping, conflicting human relations that have made America and have forged its historical experience.

American historical experience has shaped the production of sacred space in America in distinctive ways that need to be acknowledged. The production of sacred space also involves time; it depends, not only upon a symbolic conquest or construction of place, but also upon the temporal processes of ritual and practice, memory and narrative, and the ongoing engagement with historical factors and change. Each chapter of this book, in different ways, locates the production of sacred space in a dramatic history of social change. Since each account is necessarily grounded in a specific locale within the American cultural landscape, no single "master narrative" based on these case studies can hope to encompass the diversity of historical change in the whole of America. At the risk of drawing very broad generalizations, we can only hint at some of the basic features of American historical experience that have influenced the symbolic and material production of American sacred space.

First, without necessarily reviving Frederick Turner's classic frontier thesis we can recognize the ways in which American historical experience has been shaped by frontier situations. As recent comparative research has proposed, a frontier is not a line, border, or boundary; it is a zone of intercultural contact and interchange. Opening with the encounter of two or more previously separated cultures, a frontier zone closes when one has established hegemony. In American history, the encounter between Euroamerican and Native American cultures opened frontier zones that closed—unevenly, but inexorably—across North America during the nineteenth century. Hegemony was established, not only over a diversity of American Indian societies, but also over African-Americans who were incorporated as forced labor. However, as the chapters by Michaelsen, Taylor, and Glass show in this volume, the hegemony established on those closed frontiers has remained unstable and contested. Of course, throughout American history, there are many examples of frontiers as zones of encounter and conflict. For example, as immigrants streamed into northern urban centers by the millions in the late nineteenth and early twentieth century, they often lived in ethnic enclaves that provided reassuring orientation in an unfamiliar place. Traditional music, foods, and language helped transform new world space into a community in which to live and work. The old world was, in part, recreated in the midst of the new world. Such ethnic space was not immune from various incursions: from other immigrant groups competing for jobs and living space, from the seemingly corrosive effects of public education—carried out in "secular" space where the pull of tradition was weakened—and from the lure of the evocative myth that had drawn so many to the New World to begin with, America as a land of promise and redemption, a land where immigrants could begin again. Disorientation, dislocation, and alienation, were imbedded in the immigrants' consciousness, try though they might to use their former identities as a buffer to soften the impact of their new condition.

Various peoples met, clashed, and were changed in urban zones of conflict. Traditional social structures broke apart, as Catholic married Protestant, and Protestant married Jew; new music was created, as fluid rhythms of jazz floated oblivious to ethnic boundaries. New religions—the Nation of Islam, for example—were formed in response to the bitterly resented omnipresence of white ownership of urban economic space. Race and class shaped the boundaries of urban frontiers, every bit as much as had fences on the western frontier, as exclusionary policies were encoded in zoning regulations, redlining, and the ominous metaphor of the city as a modern jungle, inhabited by human predators, those "others" of urban modernity. But no frontier has ever been so closed that it has not allowed scope, however limited, for counter-maneuvers of resistance and recovery. As part of the arsenal of the "weapons of the weak," the symbolic resources of narrative and ritual have been drawn into struggles to keep frontier zones open for the recovery of sacred space.

Second, the historical development of the American legal system has lent a distinctive character to the production of American sacred space.

America has been imagined by many as a free space, as a land of liberty, largely by virtue of the constitutional rights enshrined in the laws and upheld by the courts of the United States. At its inception, the American constitutional guarantee of civil rights was limited in scope, because it excluded children, women, African-Americans, Native Americans, and Euroamericans without property from the right to vote. However, as the scope of civil inclusion was gradually, haltingly extended, the courtroom increasingly became a crucial location for adjudicating conflicts over American sacred space. It is significant that so many of the chapters in this book find themselves in the courtroom. Clearly, as Michaelsen recounts, the courts have been sites of struggle for contesting American Indian sacred places. Taylor documents the civil lawsuit against the U.S. Forest Service over Mt. Graham; Glass alludes to the American Indian Movement taking its struggle over the Black Hills to the U.S. Supreme Court. Although most appeals have been unsuccessful, they have nevertheless shown that the courtroom has developed into the principal arena for conducting the politics of American sacred space. Certainly, the influence of the American legal system has extended into other areas of American religious and symbolic life. For example, behind the initiatives in home schooling recounted by Colleen McDannell stand crucial Supreme Court decisions during the 1960s that interpreted the First Amendment constitutional limits on establishing religion, through prayer, devotional Bible reading, or religious instruction, in the public schools. In the most litigious nation on earth, American courts have focused, but also, to a certain extent, have defused and ameliorated religious conflict over sacred space in America.

Third, a distinctive managerial ethos has emerged out of American historical experience to influence the production and preservation of sacred space. Drawing upon a Christian religious ethics of stewardship or custodianship, this management style has especially characterized the sanctification of natural environments and wilderness areas. By placing them under the bureaucratic management of federal agencies—the U.S. Forest Service, the National Park Service—their enduring sanctity has been secured. This managerial ethos has also been crucial in creating and maintaining national sites of a patriotic orthodoxy in America. Under federal regulation and bureaucratic supervision, this managerial ethos has operated on the basis of an implied consensus. In most cases, the grounds for consensus have remained invisible because they have been delegated to committees. However, as Linenthal shows in this volume, the production of sacred space by committee can be an intensely contested process, especially when upholders of the managerial ethos have to negotiate every detail with stakeholders making competing claims on that space.

Fourth, the commodification of space, which Michaelsen documents in his analysis of the Euroamerican ideology of property rights, has pervaded every aspect of the production of sacred space in America. Certainly, as we argue, the issue of "ownership" has been a consistent feature of sacred space everywhere in the world. Since they are not simply "given," sacred places must inevitably be appropriated. However, the commodification of space—in the right of discovery, in the right of entitlement, in the right to development, in the right to access and use—has entailed distinctive spatial consequences in American historical experience. Quite literally, sacred space can be bought and sold. The history of the American preservation movement clearly illustrates the deeply felt need to identify, shelter, and preserve places deemed historic through purchase, if necessary. As most chapters in this book note, efforts to secure sacred space in America have often been directed towards removing them from the marketplace or protecting them from any contaminating contact with economic exchange, entrepreneurial enterprise, or motives of financial gain. However, to put the issue bluntly, the very production of sacred space depends upon money. Perhaps echoing a Protestant aversion to the buying and selling of sacred relics, benefices, or indulgences, many Americans have assumed that sacred space must be outside of the cycle of economic exchange. However, if all space is commodified, not only real estate, but also air space, air waves, intellectual property, and all the works of the human imagination, then sacred space cannot escape the economic forces of ownership and alienation.

Fifth, America has witnessed a series of dramatic and extensive information revolutions that has substantially affected the historical production of sacred space in America. If the production of sacred space depends upon intensive interpretation, then that hermeneutics of place must be grounded in shared information. The face-to-face encounters of oral tradition and folklore, conversation and confession, argument and debate, characterized the dominate verbal mode of transmitting information among all segments of the American population—Native American, African-American, and Euroamerican—until well into the nineteenth century. While the kingdom of print certainly expanded in the nineteenth and twentieth centuries, it never completely conquered these oral forms of information exchange. Perhaps in hindsight, we will view print as a brief interlude in the history of communication. As the twentieth century draws to a close, with print already submerged under radio, television, and computer networks, we face the prospect of an emergent "cyberspace" in which information explodes in every direction. As hinted by Chidester and developed by Sherrill in this volume, this rapidly changing information technology already shows signs of altering the contours and experiential dynamics of American sacred space.

Sixth, American historical experience has produced a national orientation, supported by specific national sites, that has been saturated with a distinctive kind of patriotic sacrality. All sacred sites in America, linked together in complex and often conflicting ways, encourage the cumulative perception that America, in all its manifest diversity, is a national unity. "This land is your land, this land is my land," because we share the same historical geography of sacred sites "from sea to shining sea." However, as the chapters in this book show, Americans do not in fact share the same historical geography. They do not all live in the same America. While John Winthrop and his ideological descendants could view America as the new Israel, the chosen land, African-Americans held in bondage spoke of America as the oppressive Egypt, alien space transformed only briefly during the Civil War into the promised land of the north. Members of new religions of the nineteenth century—Shakers and Mormons, for example—expressed the optimism that the Kingdom of God was indeed at hand by constructing clearly defined sacred space in which their sanctified life could be led. Some Pentecostalists draw rigid lines between the space of their church—where the baptism of the Holy Spirit transforms their lives—and the "world," a threatening and evil place to be resisted. In many ways, the boundaries they draw between sacred space and everyday space are more pronounced than cloistered monks, who, while seemingly cut off from the "world," seek to sanctify all space through their identification with the natural—and sacred—rhythms of everyday life. As the chapters by Linenthal and Chidester in particular suggest, the question of what "belongs" in American sacred space remains intensely contested. At the ceremonial core of American sacred space, does a ritualized commemoration of a "foreign" event belong? At the distant periphery, do foreigners have any claim on defining the sacred space of America? In these questions, America's past is recast, its future foretold. While the national question in America has always been an intercultural conflict of interpretations, the future of

America will inevitably and increasingly be global. In the process, any distinction between national sacred space, growing out of American historical experience, and international sacred space will be blurred.

Seventh, and finally, American historical experience has fashioned a national, public, or civil religion that has depended heavily upon the production of sacred space. Independent of any organized religious institution, whether church, temple, synagogue, or mosque, this civil religiosity is as firmly implanted on American soil as it is in the American calendar or in American creeds. It encompasses elements of the patriotic landscape that celebrate the nation, as well as places that mourn abandoned ideals, the National Park Service site of the Manzanar concentration camp for Americans of Japanese ancestry during World War II, for example. However, as Sherrill observes in this book, American civil religion is currently undergoing yet another time of trial. Following Robert Bellah's initial formulation of the notion of American civil religion, we might regard the first period of trial during the American Revolution as the challenge of national independence, the Civil War of the 1860s as the challenge of national unity, and the Vietnam era of the 1960s as the challenge of national integrity. Entering the twenty-first century, America confronts new challenges, although still undefined, that seem to be emerging as distinctively spatial. As the chapters in this book suggest, the challenge to American civil society and civil religion will be decidedly spatial, especially when they involve the profound conflicts over space and place that arise under conditions of alienation, dislocation, and disorientation.

As the chapters of this book demonstrate, the question of the meaning of America is constantly being raised in specific sacred places. Made sacred through the work of ritualization, the labor of intensive interpretation, and the struggles of contestation, these sites enact a politics of the sacred that remains crucial for the life of the nation. In most cases, this politics is a micro-politics: Contests over sacred meaning and power are anchored in specific locations—a courtroom in Arizona, a forest in California, a mountain in North Dakota, a home in Texas, a memorial museum in Washington, D.C., a baseball stadium in New York—but these local instances of sacred politics resonate with larger questions of national memory of the past and aspirations for the future. At these sites, local sacred space is negotiated and renegotiated in ways that shape the religious contours and character of the entire nation.

Historians of religions have not been the only ones to notice the importance of sacred space in the formation of modern nationalisms. In 1977 the

French Marxist Regis Debray insisted on the sacred character of any nationalism. As Debray proposed:

> We should not become obsessed by the determinate historical form of the nation-state but try to see what that form is made out of. It is created from a natural organization proper to *homo sapiens*, one *through which life itself is rendered untouchable or sacred. This sacred character constitutes the real national question.*

In specifying the sacred substance of the national question, Debray pointed explicitly to two "anti-death processes," the production of sacred time and sacred space. In the first case, the national question depends upon "a delimitation of time, or the assignation of origins." Like Eliade, who documented the "myth of the eternal return" in the history of religions, Debray observed that the mythic temporal origin, the "zero point or starting point is what allows ritual repetition, the ritualization of memory," with ritual reenactment "signifying defeat of the irreversibility of time." In the second instance, the national question depends upon the "delimitation of an enclosed space." Within the highly charged confines of that delimited sacred space, whether a sacred site, environment, or territory, national interests intersect with "an encounter with the sacred." The national question, according to Debray, raises over and over again the problem of the precise location of "a sacred space within which divination could be undertaken." In the production of sacred space and places, meaning and power coalesce; the national question is answered in the ritualization of memory and the divination of a shared future.[57]

With careful attention to local detail, the chapters of this book show how America has been produced out of sacred material. Clearly, America has been constructed and contested at the intersection of many sacred spaces. In an important sense, the authors of the essays collected in this book have rediscovered America. Not content with the guidebooks, formulas, and comforts of academic tourism, the authors have risked the uncharted dangers of exploration to see America new. At the very least, that work of rediscovery reveals that America has not been a single space, but an arena of multiple centers, changing environments, shifting geographical relations, and ambivalent symbolic orientations, all contested and at stake in the dynamics of sacred space in America. The essays collected in this volume are intended to be suggestive, and perhaps even challenging and provocative, in charting new territories for further discovery. In that spirit, we propose this itinerary through some of the sites, environments, and spatial orientations in which America has appeared as sacred space. America may not appear the same again.

Notes

1. Hunter S. Thompson and Ralph Steadman, *The Curse of Lono* (New York: Bantam Books, 1983), 158.

2. See Valerio Valeri, *Kingship and Sacrifice: Ritual and Society in Ancient Hawaii* (Chicago: University of Chicago Press, 1985).

3. See Edward Tabor Linenthal, *Sacred Ground: Americans and Their Battlefields*, 2nd ed. (Urbana: University of Illinois Press, 1993).

4. Memo, "Pearl Harbor Anniversary Commemoration: History Division Report," from chief historian to Associate Director, Cultural Resources, April 6, 1992, US-SAMA.

5. Thomas Sowell, "Park Service turns its back on patriotism," *Honolulu Star-Bulletin*, December 11, 1991.

6. Rudolf Otto, *The Idea of the Holy*, trans. John W. Harley (London: Oxford University Press, 1950). For a discussion of sacred space that draws upon the work of Otto, Van der Leeuw, and Eliade, see Larry E. Shiner, "Sacred Space, Profane Space, Human Space," *Journal of the American Academy of Religion*, 40 (1972): 425–36. On the "uncanny" and the sacred, see Sigmund Freud, "The Uncanny," in James Strachey (ed.), *Complete Psychological Works* (London: Hogarth, 1953–74): 17:220, and Lorne Dawson, "Otto and Freud on the Uncanny and Beyond," *Journal of the American Academy of Religion*, 57 (1989): 288–311. For a classic exploration of the poetic imagination of space, see Gaston Bachelard, *The Poetics of Space*, trans. Maria Jolas (New York: Orion Press, 1964). Attention to the experiential, imaginative, and poetic dynamics of sacred space has characterized the work of geographer Yi-Fu Tuan in, for example, "Geopiety: A Theme in Man's Attachment to Nature and to Place" in David Lowenthal and Martyn J. Boyden (eds.), *Geographies of the Mind* (New York: Oxford University Press, 1976), 11–40; Tuan, *Space and Place: The Perspective of Experience* (Minneapolis: University of Minnesota Press, 1977); and Tuan, "Sacred Space: Explorations of an Idea," in Karl W. Butzer (ed.), *Dimensions of Human Geography* (Chicago: University of Chicago, Department of Geography Research Paper No. 186, 1978). A sensitive development of this experiential approach has recently been undertaken in Belden C. Lane, *Landscapes of the Sacred: Geography and Narrative in American Spirituality* (New York: Paulist Press, 1988). Assuming a similar substantial, essential, or experiential definition of sacred space, a popular guidebook to American sacred sites, or what the editor calls sacred "vortexes," celebrates the mystical causation and character of places that are "concentrated points of psychic or soul energy put there by cosmic and natural forces of earth and sky; or caused by the interaction of human awareness and the eternal vitalities of nature which still resonate at the site, long after the person has departed." Frank Joseph (ed.), *Sacred Sites: A Guidebook to Sacred Centers and Mysterious Places in the United States* (St. Paul, Minn.: Llewellyn Publications, 1992), xii.

7. Claude Lévi-Strauss, "Introduction à l'oeuvre de Marcel Mauss," in Marcel

Mauss, *Sociologie et anthropologie: précédé d'une introduction à l'oeuvre de Marcel Mauss* (Paris: Presses universitaires de France, 1950), xlix; cited in Jonathan Z. Smith, *To Take Place: Toward Theory in Ritual* (Chicago: University of Chicago Press, 1978), 107. See also Jacques Derrida, "Structure, Sign, and Play in the Discourse of the Human Sciences," in *Writing and Difference*, trans. Alan Bass (Chicago: University of Chicago Press, 1978), 289-91. David Parkin has identified three responses to Durkheim's distinction between sacred and profane in the analysis of space: (1) Eliade's proposal that sacred space is centered, differentiated, and heterogeneous in relation to a profane that is homogeneous and undifferentiated; (2) Lévi-Strauss's structural analysis of the ways in which the "mythogeographical" and the social interpenetrate in all symbolic and spatial relations; and (3) the more recent emphasis on the role of embodied practices in the production of sacred space that is associated with the work of Pierre Bourdieu. See David Parkin, *Sacred Void: Spatial Images of Work and Ritual among the Giriama of Kenya* (Cambridge: Cambridge University Press, 1991), 3-6. On the "pivoting of the sacred," see Arnold van Gennep, *The Rites of Passage*, trans. Monika B. Vizedom and Gabrielle L. Caffee (Chicago: University of Chicago Press, 1960), 12-13.

8. Mircea Eliade, *Patterns in Comparative Religion*, trans. Rosemary Sheed (New York: Harper and Row, 1958), 367-85; Eliade, *Sacred and Profane*, trans. Willard R. Trask (New York: Harcourt, Brace, 1961), 20-65; Jonathan Z. Smith, "The Wobbling Pivot," in *Map is Not Territory: Studies in the History of Religions* (Leiden: E. J. Brill, 1978), 88-103; and Smith, *To Take Place*, passim. On spatial poetics and politics, see Peter Stallybrass and Allon White, *The Politics and Poetics of Transgression* (London: Methuen, 1986).

9. Gerardus van der Leeuw, *Religion in Essence and Manifestation*, trans. J. E. Turner, foreword by Ninian Smart (Princeton: Princeton University Press, 1986; orig. German ed. 1933; orig. English trans. 1938), 52-53.

10. David Harvey, *The Condition of Postmodernity: An Enquiry into the Origins of Cultural Change* (Oxford: Blackwell, 1989), 209.

11. Van der Leeuw, *Religion in Essence and Manifestation*, 210.

12. Norbert Peabody, "In Whose Turban Does the Lord Reside? The Objectification of Charisma and the Fetishism of Objects in the Hindu Kingdom of Kota," *Comparative Studies in Society and History*, 33 (1991): 727; Simon Harrison, "Ritual as Intellectual Property," *Man* (N.S.), 27 (1992): 225-44.

13. Van der Leeuw, *Religion in Essence and Manifestation*, 395-96.

14. Jonathan Z. Smith, *Imagining Religion: From Babylon to Jonestown* (Chicago: University of Chicago Press, 1982), 63. For a useful discussion of theoretical problems in the analysis of ritual, with special attention to ritualization as embodied social practice, see Catherine Bell, *Ritual Theory, Ritual Practice* (New York and Oxford: Oxford University Press, 1992).

15. The analysis of ritualized "techniques of the body" was initiated by Marcel Mauss, "Techniques of the Body," trans. Ben Brewster, *Economic Sociology*, 2 (1973): 70-88. The phrase, "gestures of approach," appears in Eliade, *Patterns in Comparative Religion*, 370-71. For a creative analysis of location and direction, or embodied *deictic* relations, in the production of sacred space, see James W. Fernandez, "Location and Direction in African Religious Movements: Some Deictic Contours of Religious Conversion," *History of Religions*, 25 (1986): 353-67. For an overview of the analysis of the body in the study of religion, see Lawrence Sullivan, "Body Works: Knowledge of the Body in the Study of Religion," *History of Religions*, 30 (1990): 86-99.

16. Pierre Bourdieu, *Outline of a Theory of Practice*, trans. Richard Nice (Cambridge: Cambridge University Press, 1977), 89. Bourdieu has defined the *habitus* as embodied practices of classification and orientation. "The schemes of the habitus, the primary forms of classification, owe their specific efficacy to the fact that they function below the level of consciousness and language, beyond the reach of introspective scrutiny or control by the will. Orienting practices practically, they embed what some would mistakenly call values in the most automatic gestures or the apparently most insignificant techniques of the body . . . and engage the most fundamental principles of construction and evaluation of the social world." *Distinction: A Social Critique of the Judgement of Taste* (Cambridge: Harvard University Press, 1984), 466. On the embodied practical strategies and tactics of ordinary life, see Michael de Certeau, *The Practice of Everyday Life*, trans. Steven Rendell (Berkeley: University of California Press, 1984). The importance of embodied spatial practices in the social production of social space is developed in Henri Lefebvre, *The Production of Space*, trans. Donald Nicholson-Smith (Oxford: Blackwell, 1991).

17. John F. Kasson, "Rituals of Dining: Table Manners in Victorian America," in Kathryn Grover (ed.), *Dining in America 1850-1900* (Amherst: University of Massachusetts Press, 1987), 114. See also Theodore C. Humphrey and Lin T. Humphrey (eds.), *"We Gather Together": Food and Festival in American Life* (Ann Arbor: UMI Research Press, 1988). On the European history of body disciplines, including table manners, see Norbert Elias, *The Civilizing Process: The Development of Manners, Changes in the Code of Conduct and Feeling in Early Modern Times* (New York: Urizen Books, 1978).

18. See the classic work of Mary Douglas, *Purity and Danger* (London: Routledge, 1966).

19. Baruch M. Bokser, "Approaching Sacred Space," *Harvard Theological Review*, 78 (1985): 279-99.

20. Bernard Faure, "Space and Place in Chinese Religious Traditions," *History of Religions*, 26 (1987): 337-56.

21. Jonathan Edwards, *Images and Shadows of Divine Things*, (ed.) Perry Miller (Westport, Conn.: Greenwood Press, 1977), 44.

22. Allen Ginsberg, *Collected Poems, 1947-1980* (New York: Harper and Row, 1984), 134.

23. Neil Smith, *Uneven Development: Nature, Capital, and the Production of Space* (Oxford: Blackwell, 1984), 77.

24. Robert Redfield, *The Papers of Robert Redfield*. vol. 1, *Human Nature and the Study of Society*; vol. 2, *The Social Uses of Social Science* (Chicago: University of Chicago Press, 1963). This definition of worldview has been developed in David Chidester, *Salvation and Suicide: An Interpretation of Jim Jones, the Peoples Temple, and Jonestown* (Bloomington: Indiana University Press, 1988).

25. Harvey, *Condition of Postmodernity*, 214.

26. Catherine L. Albanese, *Nature Religion in America: From the Algonkian Indians to the New Age* (Chicago: University of Chicago Press, 1990). For an introduction to American sacred land, see Robert S. Michaelsen, "Sacred Land in America: What Is it, How Can it Be Protected?" *Religion*, 16 (1986): 249-68. Obviously, the history of American Indian land has been a chronicle of dispossession and desecration. See Wilcomb E. Washburn, "The Moral and Legal Justification for Dispossessing the Indians," in James Smith (ed.), *Seventeenth-Century America: Essays in Colonial History* (Chapel Hill: University of North Carolina Press, 1959), 15-32; and Steve Talbot, "Desecration and

American Indian Religious Freedom," *Journal of Ethnic Studies*, 12,4 (1985): 1–18. For the controversial thesis that the land became increasingly sacred during the nineteenth century precisely because it was being dispossessed and thereby desecrated, see Sam Gill, *Mother Earth: An American Story* (Chicago: University of Chicago Press, 1987). In the literature contrasting American Indian and Euroamerican interpretations of land, the crucial difference is often identified as the Euroamerican commodification of land. See, for example, William Cronon, *Changes in the Land: Indians, Colonists, and the Ecology of New England* (New York: Hill and Wang, 1983). For deep background on the transfer of land from human relations to commodity, see Robert C. Palmer, "The Origins of Property in England," *Law and History Review*, 3 (1985): 1–50; and Palmer, "The Economic and Cultural Impact of the Origin of Property, 1180–1220," *Law and History Review*, 3 (1985): 375–96. For a useful discussion of different orientations toward land as a cultural space, resource, commodity, or trust, see Joseph G. Jorgensen, "Land Is Cultural, So Is a Commodity: The Locus of Difference among Indians, Cowboys, Sod-Busters, and Environmentalists," *Journal of Ethnic Studies*, 12,3 (1984): 1–21. However, an alternative Euroamerican interpretation of the natural environment, taking nature's side against "Lord Man," and, in the process, "rediscovering America," was pioneered by the prophet of wilderness, John Muir. See Michael P. Cohen, *The Pathless Way: John Muir and the American Wilderness* (Madison: University of Wisconsin Press, 1984); and Frederick Turner, *Rediscovering America: John Muir in His Time and Ours* (New York: Viking, 1985). Artists, photographers, and writers played an important role in representing wilderness areas as "sacred places," even influencing the U.S. Congress to set aside the first national wilderness parks in the world. See the chapter by William H. Goetzmann in Stanley H. Palmer and Dennis Reinhartz (eds.), *Essays on the History of North American Discovery and Exploration* (College Station: A & M Press, 1988). In this American wilderness ideology, specific natural sites, such as Yosemite, the Grand Canyon, Yellowstone, the Grand Tetons, and the Indiana Dunes on the shores of Lake Michigan, had to be preserved as undeveloped areas. Among recent studies of the preservation and defense of wilderness environments, see Richard A. Bartlett, *Yellowstone: A Wilderness Besieged* (Tucson: University of Arizona Press, 1985); Robert W. Righter, *Crucible for Conservation: The Creation of Grand Teton National Park* (Boulder: Colorado Associated University Press, 1982); and, on conflicts over the Indiana Dunes, see J. Ronald Engel, *Sacred Sands: The Struggle for Community in the Indiana Dunes* (Middletown, Conn.: Wesleyan University Press, 1983); and Kay Schaeffer and Franklin Schaeffer, *Duel for the Dunes: Land Use Conflict on the Shores of Lake Michigan* (Urbana: University of Illinois Press, 1983). For a review of controversies over the conservation of wilderness and other public lands in the 1980s, see C. Brant Short, *Ronald Reagan and the Public Lands: America's Conservation Debate, 1979–1984* (College Station: Texas A & M University Press, 1989). Modern environmentalism, which has operated in many respects like a religious movement, has been subject to a variety of interpretations. For different analyses of the environmentalist movement, see Mary Douglas and Aaron Wildavsky, *Risk and Culture: An Essay on the Selection of Technical and Environmental Dangers* (Berkeley: University of California Press, 1982); Samuel P. Hays, *Beauty, Health, and Permanence: Environmental Politics in the United States, 1955–1985* (Cambridge: Cambridge University Press, 1987); and Roderick Frazier Nash, *The Rights of Nature: A History of Environmental Ethics* (Madison: University of Wisconsin Press, 1989). On the political spirituality or spiritual politics of ecology, see James Lovelock, *Gaia: A New Look at Life on Earth* (New York: Oxford University Press, 1979);

and Jonathon Porritt, *Seeing Green: The Politics of Ecology Explained* (New York: Blackwell, 1985). In the interpretation of natural environments, gendered differences might be observed. Based on an analysis of literary texts, Annette Kolodny has argued that the "rape" of the environment, and the violence of the frontier, in which people, land, and landscape were violated, has shaped basic male perceptions of nature. By contrast, female visions of nature have been more human, humane, and ecologically responsible. See Annette Kolodny, *The Lay of the Land* (Chapel Hill: University of North Carolina Press, 1975); and Kolodny, *The Land before Her: Fantasy and Experience of the American Frontiers, 1630–1860* (Chapel Hill: University of North Carolina Press, 1984). For the argument that the frontier, and the frontier myth of redemption through violence, were crucial to the formation of American perceptions, or perhaps, following Kolodny on this point, American male perceptions of the environment, see Richard Slotkin, *Regeneration through Violence: The Mythology of the American Frontier, 1600–1860* (Middletown, Conn.: Wesleyan University Press, 1973); Slotkin, *The Fatal Environment: The Myth of the Frontier in the Age of Industrialization, 1800–1890* (New York: Atheneum, 1985); and Slotkin, *Gunfighter Nation: The Myth of the Frontier in Twentieth-Century America* (New York: Atheneum, 1992).

27. Leo Marx, *The Machine in the Garden: Technology and the Past Oral Ideal of America* (New York: Oxford University Press, 1964), 96.

28. Barbara Novak, *Nature and Culture: American Landscape and Painting 1825–1875* (New York: Oxford University Press, 1980), 38. See Perry Miller, *Nature's Nation* (Cambridge, Mass.: Harvard University Press, 1967).

29. N. Smith, *Uneven Development*, 57.

30. For a review of literature on the spatial analysis of built environments, see Denise L. Lawrence and Setha M. Low, "The Built Environment and Spatial Form," *Annual Review of Anthropology*, 19 (1990): 453–505. A useful survey of literature on the material culture of religion in America, with significant implications for the study of sacred space, is provided in Colleen McDannell, "Interpreting Things: Material Culture Studies and American Religion," *Religion*, 21 (1991): 371–87.

31. A blend of phenomenological and theological reflection on places of worship can be found in Harold W. Turner, *From Temple to Meeting House: The Phenomenology and Theology of Places of Worship* (The Hague: Mouton, 1979). For an excellent analysis of the social and economic forces at work in the production of the sacred space of one place of worship, see Pamela C. Graves, "Social Space in the English Medieval Parish Church," *Economy and Society*, 18 (1989): 297–322. For an American case study, see David J. Goa, "Three Urban Parishes: A Study of Sacred Space," *Material History Bulletin*, 29 (Spring 1989): 13–23.

32. The analysis of "nodal points" has been advanced in Edward W. Soja, *Postmodern Geographies: The Reassertion of Space in Critical Social Theory* (London: Verso, 1989), 149, 151. On the Aztec temple, see David L. Carrasco, "Templo Mayor: The Aztec Vision of Place," *Religion*, 11 (1981): 275–97; and Johanna Broda, David Carrasco, and Eduardo Matos Moctezuma, *The Great Temple of Tenochtitlan: Center and Periphery in the Aztec World* (Berkeley: University of California Press, 1987). On Puritan churches as sacred space, see James P. Walsh, "Holy Time and Sacred Space in Puritan New England," *American Quarterly*, 32 (1980): 79–95. On spatial relations in colonial Virginia, see Rhys Isaac, *The Transformation of Virginia, 1740–1790* (Chapel Hill: University of North Carolina Press, 1982); and Dell Upton, *Holy Things and Profane: Parish Churches in Colonial Virginia* (Cambridge, Mass.: MIT Press, 1986). On camp meeting

sites, see Ellen Weiss, *City in the Woods: The Life and Design of an American Camp Meeting on Martha's Vineyard* (New York: Oxford University Press, 1987). On utopian architecture, see Dolores Hayden, *Seven American Utopias: The Architecture of Communitarian Socialism, 1790–1975* (Cambridge, Mass.: MIT Press, 1979). On synagogues in America, see Jack Wertheimer (ed.), *The American Synagogue: A Sanctuary Transformed* (New York: Cambridge University Press, 1988). On Mormon sacred geography, see Richard Francaviglia, *The Mormon Landscape* (New York: AMS Press, 1978).

33. A classic overview of the city is provided in Lewis Mumford, *The City in History: Its Origins, Its Transformations, and Its Prospects* (New York: Harcourt Brace and World, 1961). "Virtually everywhere," as Anthony Giddons has observed, "the generation of power in the city has been expressed in religious terms." *A Contemporary Critique of Historical Materialism*. Volume 1, *Power, Property, and the State* (London: Macmillan, 1981), 145. In the study of religion, cities have received special attention as sacred sites. In addition to the now-classic works of Paul Wheatley, *The Pivot of the Four Quarters* (Chicago: Aldine, 1971); and Stanley J. Tambiah, "The Galactic Polity in Southeast Asia," in *Culture, Thought, and Social Action* (Cambridge: Harvard University Press, 1985), 252–86; see also David L. Carrasco, "City as Symbol in Aztec Thought: The Clues from the *Codex Mendoza*," *History of Religions*, 20 (1981): 199–223; Diana Eck, "The City as a Sacred Center," *Journal of Developing Societies*, 2 (1986): 149–281; Bardwell Smith and Holly Baker Reynolds (eds.), *The City as a Sacred Center: Essays on Six Asian Contexts* (Leiden: E. J. Brill, 1987); Jeffrey F. Meyer, *The Dragons of Tiananmen: Beijing as a Sacred City* (Columbia: University of South Carolina Press, 1991); and the remarkable analysis of Protestant and Catholic conflicts over sacred space in the city of Lyon in Natalie Z. Davis, "The Sacred and the Body Social in Sixteenth-Century Lyon," *Past and Present*, 90 (1981): 40–70. Beyond paying some attention to the ceremonial center of Washington, D.C., the analysis of urban sacred space has been underdeveloped in American studies. On America's sacred urban center, see Kenneth R. Bowling, *The Creation of Washington, D.C.: The Idea and Location of the American Capital* (Washington, D.C.: George Mason University, 1991). On the interpretation of the symbolic and material "texts" of American cities, see Grady Clay, *Close-up: How to Read the American City* (Chicago: University of Chicago Press, 1980). For a discussion of symbolic tensions and transpositions between urban and rural space in American cities, see James L. Machor, *Pastoral Cities: Urban Ideals and the Symbolic Landscape of America* (Madison: University of Wisconsin Press, 1987).

34. As noted, theories of the production of sacred places and the relevant dispositions towards sacred space have often been anchored in the home. In addition to Van der Leeuw and Bourdieu, see David E. Sopher, "The Landscape of Home: Myth, Experience, Social Meaning," in D. W. Meinig (ed.), *The Interpretation of Ordinary Landscapes: Geographical Essays* (Oxford: Oxford University Press, 1979), 129–49; but also see the cautionary observation that "home" might resist any easy crosscultural translation in J. Z. Smith, *To Take Place*, 30. For an insightful analysis that situates the sacralization of the home in relation to both local and larger social environments, see Juan Eduardo Campo, "Shrines and Talismans: Domestic Islam in the Pilgrimage Paintings of Egypt," *Journal of the American Academy of Religion*, 55 (1987): 285–305; and Campo, *The Otherness Paradise: An Inquiry into the Religious Meanings of Domestic Space in Islam* (Columbia: University of South Carolina Press, 1991). The history of domestic housing in America has been recounted in Gwendolyn Wright, *Building the Dream: A Social History of Housing in America* (New York: Pantheon, 1981). For a discussion of

the American home as refuge, sacred enclosure, or recreational vehicle, see Joel Schwartz, "Home as Haven, Cloister, and Winnebago," *American Quarterly*, 39 (1987): 467–73. Nineteenth-century Protestant and Catholic homes in America have been reconstructed in Colleen McDannell, *The Christian Home in Victorian America 1840–1900* (Bloomington: Indiana University Press, 1986); the Catholic home in Ann Taves, *The Household of Faith: Roman Catholic Devotions in Mid-Nineteenth-Century America* (Notre Dame: University of Notre Dame Press, 1986). During the nineteenth century, it has been argued, the American "cult of domesticity" enclosed women in a sacralized home that was a space of both subordination and empowerment. See Mary Ryan, *The Empire of the Mother: American Writing about Domesticity, 1830–1860* (New York: Institute for Research in History and Haworth Press, 1982). Between the 1870s and 1930s, that domestic space also localized the "sacralization" of children, transforming them from objects of utility to objects of sentiment. See Viviana A. Zelizer, *Pricing the Priceless Child: The Changing Social Value of Children* (New York: Basic Books, 1985). With reference to Mary Douglas's work on purity and symbolic order, the ritualized purification of the American home has been analyzed in Phyllis Palmer, *Domesticity and Dirt: Housewives and Domestic Servants in the United States, 1920–1945* (Philadelphia: Temple University Press, 1989). For an analysis of the dynamic, ritualized relations between home and neighborhood in an Italian Catholic community, see Robert Anthony Orsi, *The Madonna of 115th Street: Faith and Community in Italian Harlem, 1880–1950* (New Haven: Yale University Press, 1985).

35. As Robert Michaelsen once observed, the American public school has operated as if it were the established church of a common, public, or civil religion. "Is the Public School Religious or Secular?," in Elwyn A. Smith (ed.), *The Religion of the Republic* (Philadelphia: Fortress Press, 1971), 22–44. A recent account of the ritualization of the school that occurred when flag ritual was introduced at the end of the nineteenth century is found in Scot M. Guenter, "Flag Ritual Comes to the Public Schools: Development and Dissemination of the Pledge of Allegiance," *The American Flag, 1777–1924: Cultural Shifts from Creation to Codification* (Rutherford: Fairleigh Dickinson University Press, 1990), 114–53. Differences in identifying the specifically Christian religious interests at work in public schooling seem to depend largely upon whether the analyst emphasizes the role of Protestant liberals or evangelicals in the nineteenth-century formation of the American common school. For this contrast, compare Charles Leslie Glenn Jr., *The Myth of the Common School* (Amherst: University of Massachusetts Press, 1988); and David B. Tyack and Elisabeth Hansot, *Managers of Virtue: Public School Leadership in America, 1820–1980* (New York: Basic Books, 1982). From a revisionist perspective, the school has appeared as a space for ritualizing and reinforcing American ideals of personal discipline and social order. See David Nasaw, *Schooled to Order: A Social History of Public Schooling in the United States* (New York: Oxford University Press, 1979).

36. The comparative study of cemeteries as sacred space owes much to the foundational work, originally published in 1907, of Robert Hertz, "A Contribution to the Study of the Collective Representation of Death," in Rodney Needham (ed.), *Death and the Right Hand* (London: Cohen and West, 1960), 27–86. See Richard Huntington and Peter Metcalf, *Celebrations of Death: The Anthropology of Mortuary Ritual* (Cambridge: Cambridge University Press, 1979). The classic analysis of the cemetery as a sacred place in America was advanced by W. Lloyd Warner, *The Living and the Dead: A Study of the Symbolic Life of Americans* (New Haven: Yale University Press, 1959). For general

surveys of American cemeteries, see David E. Stannard (ed.), *Death in America* (Philadelphia: University of Pennsylvania Press, 1974); Wilbur Zelinsky, "Unearthly Delights: Cemetery Names and the Map of the Changing American Afterworld," in Lowenthal and Boyden (eds.), *Geographies of the Mind*, 171–95; and David Charles Sloane, *The Last Great Necessity: Cemeteries in American History* (Baltimore: Johns Hopkins University Press, 1991). Specific case studies of cemeteries have recently appeared: For example, a recent study of Mount Auburn Cemetery in Boston has identified the tensions inherent in the cemetery's divergent symbolic roles as a private sanctuary for meditation, a recreational garden for pleasure, and a place of public and patriotic commemoration for the nation's honored dead. See Blanche Linden-Ward, *Silent City on a Hill: Landscapes of Memory and Boston's Mount Auburn Cemetery* (Columbus: Ohio State University Press, 1989). A detailed comparison of three cemeteries in Texas has identified the different sacred geographies of death in a "southern folk cemetery," a Mexican cemetery, and a German cemetery. See Terry G. Jordan, *Texas Graveyards: A Cultural Legacy* (Austin: University of Texas Press, 1982). On conflicts over the desecration of American Indian burial sites, see Robert Bieder, *A Brief Historical Survey of the Expropriation of American Indian Remains* (Boulder: Native American Rights Fund, 1990); and the articles by Jane Hubert, Randall H. McGuire, Jan Hammil and Robert Cruz, Stephen Moore, and Larry J. Zimmerman collected in Robert Layton (ed.), *Conflict in the Archaeology of Living Traditions* (London: Unwin Hyman, 1989), 131–216. For an excellent analysis of conflicts over a sacred burial site at the nexus of urban zoning regulations, environmental protection legislation, property development, and internal struggles within a Native American community, see Johnny P. Flynn and Gary Laderman, "Purgatory and the Powerful Dead: A Case Study of Native American Reparation," *Religion and American Culture*, 4 (1994): 51–75.

37. The recognition that hospitals, asylums, and prisons operate as ritualized "institutions of exclusion" has depended upon the work of Michel Foucault, *The Birth of the Clinic: An Archaeology of Medical Perception*, trans. A. M. Sheridan Smith (New York: Random House, 1973); Foucault, *Madness and Civilization: A History of Insanity in the Age of Reason*, trans. Richard Howard (New York: Random House, 1965); and Foucault, *Discipline and Punish: The Birth of the Prison*, trans. Alan Sheridan (New York: Vintage Books, 1975). On the emergence of the hospital as a powerful site in America, see Paul Starr, *The Social Transformation of American Medicine* (New York: Basic Books, 1982). On the asylum as ritualized space, see Erving Goffman, *Asylums: Essays on the Social Situation of Mental Patients* (New York: Penguin, 1961). On the history of the asylum in America, see David J. Rothman, *The Discovery of the Asylum: Social Order and Disorder in the New Republic* (Boston: Little, Brown, 1971); and Rothman, *Conscience and Convenience: The Asylum and its Alternatives in Progressive America* (Boston: Little, Brown, 1980). The prison has been analyzed as an important ritual site in American culture, particularly as a site for the "rites of execution" that enact supreme power and reinforce a symbolism of order in America, in Louis P. Masur, *Rites of Execution: Capital Punishment and the Transformation of American Culture* (New York: Oxford University Press, 1989). The space of the prison, with its rituals of discipline, punishment, confinement, and execution, has even been identified as a crucial factor in the social formation of the United States. See Thomas L. Dumm, *Democracy and Punishment: Disciplinary Origins of the United States* (Madison: University of Wisconsin Press, 1987).

38. Theoretical analysis of pilgrimage and pilgrim sites has benefited from the work

of Victor Turner, "Pilgrimages as Social Processes," *Dramas, Fields, and Metaphors Symbolic Action in Human Society* (Ithaca: Cornell University Press, 1974), 166–230; and Victor Turner and Edith Turner, *Image and Pilgrimage in Christian Culture* (New York: Columbia University Press, 1976). For a crosscultural collection of essays, see Robert Ousterhout (ed.), *The Blessings of Pilgrimage* (Urbana: University of Illinois Press, 1990). An exemplary analysis of sacred space in Japan, with particular attention to pilgrimage in its historical context, can be found in Allan G. Grapard, "Flying Mountains and Walkers of Emptiness: Toward a Definition of Sacred Space in Japanese Religions," *History of Religions*, 20 (1982): 195–221. The study of pilgrimage in America, however, remains undeveloped. Pilgrimage to American sacred sites registers as a type of tourism, as illustrated by a popular guidebook such as Paul Lambourne Higgins, *Pilgrimages USA: A Guide to the Holy Places of the United States for Today's Traveller* (Englewood Cliffs, N.J.: Prentice-Hall, 1985). The interpretation of tourism itself as pilgrimage, and tourist attractions as modern pilgrim sites, was pioneered in Dean Mac-Cannell, *The Tourist: A New Theory of the Leisure Class* (New York: Schocken Books, 1976). See Valene L. Smith (ed.), *Hosts and Guests: The Anthropology of Tourism*, 2nd ed. (Philadelphia: University of Pennsylvania Press, 1989); and Eric Lead, *The Mind of the Traveler: From Giligamesh to Global Tourism* (New York: Basic Books, 1991). On tourist attractions as pilgrim sites in America, see John Sears, *Sacred Places: American Tourist Attractions in the Nineteenth Century* (New York and Oxford: Oxford University Press, 1989). For a discussion of pilgrimage linked with a poetic imagination, see Lawrence Buell, "The Thoreuvian Pilgrimage: The Structure of an American Cult," *American Literature*, 61 (1989): 175–99. For an important recovery of aimless, utopian pilgrimage, animated by a different kind of literary imagination, see Stephen Prothero, "On the Holy Road: The Beat Movement as Spiritual Protest," *Harvard Theological Review*, 84 (1991): 205–22.

39. As a site of powerful cultural representations and symbolic constructions, the museum has been recently analyzed in James Clifford, "On Collecting Art and Culture," *The Predicament of Culture: Twentieth-Century Ethnography, Literature, and Art* (Cambridge, Mass.: Harvard University Press, 1988): 215–51. On the museum as a sacred site—a modern "temple," a place for enacting a "ritual of citizenship," a locus for "ritual criticism"—see Duncan F. Cameron, "The Museum: A Temple or the Forum," *Cahiers d'Histoire Mondiale*, 14 (1972): 189–202; Carol Duncan, "Art Museums and the Ritual of Citizenship," in Ivan Karp and Steven D. Lavine (eds.), *Exhibiting Cultures: The Poetics and Politics of Museum Display* (Washington, D.C.: Smithsonian Institution Press, 1991), 88–103; and Ronald L. Grimes, "Ritual Criticism of Field Excavations and Museum Displays," *Ritual Criticism: Case Studies in Its Practice, Essays on Its Theory* (Columbia: University of South Carolina Press, 1990), 63–88. Museums are ritualized sites of memory, places that preserve, commemorate, and recreate the past, that "foreign country," in the present. See Michael Wallace, "Visiting the Past: History Museums in the United States," *Radical History Review*, 25 (1981): 63–96; and the last two chapters of David Lowenthal, *The Past is a Foreign Country* (Cambridge: Cambridge University Press, 1985). On the production of collective memory more generally, see Paul Connerton, *How Societies Remember* (Cambridge: Cambridge University Press, 1989). Museums are also sites for intensive interpretation. For a detailed, insightful analysis of the particular order of the world represented at the American Museum of Natural History in New York, see Mieke Bal, "Telling, Showing, Showing Off," *Critical Quarterly*, 18 (1992): 556–94. As a particular kind of representational site, international

expositions have operated, like museums, as symbolic edifices for interpreting the place of America and Americans in the world. See Robert Rydell, *All the World's a Fair: Visions of Empire at American International Expositions, 1876-1916* (Chicago: University of Chicago Press, 1984); and Paul A. Tenkotte, "Kaleidoscopes of the World: International Exhibitions and the Concept of Culture-place, 1851-1915," *American Studies*, 28 (1987): 5-29. Increasingly, American museums have been contested sites. On conflicts over the ownership of cultural artifacts, including sacred or ritual objects, see Phyllis Mauch Messenger (ed.), *The Ethics of Collecting Cultural Property: Whose Culture? Whose Property?* (Albuquerque: University of New Mexico Press, 1989); and Michael M. Ames, *Museums, the Public, and Anthropology: A Study in the Anthropology of Anthropology* (Vancouver: University of British Columbia Press, 1986).

40. Ira G. Zepp, *The New Religious Image of Urban America: The Shopping Mall as Ceremonial Center* (Westminster, Md.: Christian Classics, 1986). See also Mark Gottdiener, "Recapturing the Centre: A Semiotic Analysis of the Shopping Mall," in Gottdiener and Alexandros P. Lagopoulos (eds.), *The City and the Sign* (New York: Columbia University Press, 1986), 288-302.

41. Jacques Derrida, *The Post Card: From Socrates to Freud and Beyond*, trans. Alan Bates (Chicago: University of Chicago Press, 1987), 69. Like Derrida, however, Catholic devotees of the national shrine of Saint Jude might have had reason to imagine the post office as a sacred place, since, as Robert Orsi has shown, they could, in effect, make a pilgrimage to the sacred site in Chicago by staying home and sending their petitions through the mail. Robert Orsi, "The Center Out There, in Here, and Everywhere Else: The Nature of Pilgrimage to the Shrine of Saint Jude, 1929-1965," *Journal of Social History*, 25 (1991): 213-32.

42. Wilbur Zelinsky, *Nation into State: The Shifting Symbolic Foundations of American Nationalism* (Chapel Hill: University of North Carolina Press, 1989).

43. In addition to the previously cited works by Eliade and J. Z. Smith (n.8), and by Wheatley, Tambiah, and Carrasco (n.33), see Edward Shils, "Center and Periphery," in *Selected Essays of Edward Shils* (Chicago: University of Chicago Press, 1970), 1-14; Charles H. Long, *Significations: Signs, Symbols, and Images in the Interpretation of Religion* (Philadelphia: Fortress Press, 1986); and Arjun Appadurai, "Theory in Anthropology: Center and Periphery," *Comparative Studies in Society and History*, 28 (1986): 356-61. Advances in the analysis of spatial, symbolic, and material relations between sacred centers and peripheries has received special attention in the introduction to David Carrasco (ed.) *To Change Place: Aztec Ceremonial Landscapes* (Boulder: University Press of Chicago, 1991), xvii-xix. For geographical analysis, see Jean Gottman (ed.) *Centre and Periphery: Spatial Variation in Politics* (Beverly Hills and London: Sage Publications, 1980).

44. J. Z. Smith, *Map is Not Territory*, 67-102, and Jonathan Z. Smith, *Drudgery Divine: On the Comparison of Early Christianities and the Religions of Late Antiquity* (Chicago: University of Chicago Press, 1990), 121-42.

45. Harvie Ferguson, *The Science of Pleasure: Cosmos and Psyche in the Bourgeois World View* (London: Routledge, 1990), 161.

46. On nationalism as a religious orientation, see Carlton Hayes, *Nationalism: A Religion* (New York: Macmillan, 1960); and Ninian Smart, "Religion, Myth, and Nationalism," in Peter H. Merkl and Smart (eds.), *Religion and Politics in the Modern World* (New York: New York University Press, 1983), 15-28.

47. Michel Foucault, "Space, Knowledge, and Power," in Paul Rabinow (ed.), *The*

Foucault Reader (New York: Pantheon, 1984), 252. See Foucault, "Questions of Geography," in Colin Gordon (ed.), *Power/Knowledge: Selected Interviews and Other Writings 1972–1977* (New York: Pantheon, 1980), 63–77.

48. Robert G. Hamerton-Kelly (ed.), *Violent Origins': Walter Burkert, Rene Girard, and Jonathan Z. Smith on Ritual Killing and Cultural Formation* (Stanford: Stanford University Press, 1987), 188.

49. David Chidester, "Stealing the Sacred Symbols: Biblical Interpretation in the Peoples Temple and the Unification Church," *Religion*, 18 (1988): 137–62. On power relations in ritual, see Maurice Bloch, *From Blessing to Violence: History and Ideology in the Circumcision Ritual of the Merina of Madagascar* (Cambridge: Cambridge University Press, 1986); and Bell, *Ritual Theory, Ritual Practice*, 169–223. Contested symbolic politics has become a prominent theme of cultural analysis, even appearing in the titles of such recent works as Richard Edwards, *Contested Terrain: The Transformation of the Workplace in the Twentieth Century* (New York: Basic Books, 1979); John H. Mollenkopf, *The Contested City* (Princeton: Princeton University Press, 1983); Leslie Fowler, *Shared Symbols, Contested Meanings: Gros Ventre Culture and History, 1778–1984* (Ithaca: Cornell University Press, 1987); John Emmeus Davis, *Contested Ground: Collective Action and the Urban Neighborhood* (Ithaca: Cornell University Press, 1991); Jane M. Gaines, *Contested Culture: The Image, the Voice, and the Law* (Chapel Hill: University of North Carolina Press, 1991); John Eade and Michael J. Sallnow (eds.), *Contesting the Sacred: The Anthropology of Christian Pilgrimage* (London: Routledge, 1991); and Robert J. Mason, *Contested Lands: Conflict and Compromise in New Jersey's Pine Barrens* (Philadelphia: Temple University Press, 1992).

50. Robert David Sack, *Conceptions of Space in Social Thought: A Geographic Perspective* (London: Macmillan, 1980), 30, with reference to Mircea Eliade, *Australian Religion* (Ithaca: Cornell University Press, 1973), 42.

51. Rob Shields, *Places on the Margin: Alternative Geographies of Modernity* (London: Routledge, 1991), 23. See Roger Friedland and Richard D. Hecht, "The Politics of Sacred Place: Jerusalem's Temple Mount/al-haram al-sharif," in Jamie Scott and Paul Simpson-Housely (eds.), *Sacred Places and Profane Spaces: Essays in the Geographics of Judaism, Christianity, and Islam* (Westport, Conn.: Greenwood Press, 1991), 21–61.

52. John Urry, "Social Relations, Space and Time," in Derek Gregory and John Urry (eds.), *Social Relations and Spatial Structures* (New York: St. Martin's Press, 1985), 30.

53. Stallybrass and White, *The Politics and Poetics of Transgression*, 58.

54. Homi Bhabha, "Signs Taken as Wonders: Questions of Ambivalence and Authority under a Tree Outside Delhi, May 1817," in Henry Louis Gates Jr. (ed.), *"Race," Writing, and Difference* (Chicago: University of Chicago Press, 1986), 176. On carnival and street theater as a strategy of ritual resistance to domination, see Susan G. Davis, *Parades and Power: Street Theatre in Nineteenth-Century Philadelphia* (Philadelphia: Temple University Press, 1986).

55. Michel Foucault, "Of Other Spaces," *Diacritics*, 16 (1986): 24.

56. Fredric Jameson, "Postmodernism, or the Cultural Logic of Late Capitalism," *New Left Review*, 146 (July/August 1984): 89.

57. Regis Debray, "Marxism and the National Question," *New Left Review*, 105 (1977): 26–27.

2

DIRT IN THE COURT ROOM
Indian Land Claims
and American Property Rights
Robert S. Michaelsen

The land they settled on was ours. We knew not but the Great
Spirit had sent them to us for some good purpose, and therefore
we thought they must be a good people. We were mistaken.
—Lenape (Delaware) Indian[1]

I fear . . . that God Land will be . . . as great a God with us English
as God Gold was with the Spaniards.   —Roger Williams[2]

The earth, and all that is therein, is given to men for the support
and comfort of their being.   —John Locke[3]

Land is, more than anything else, the immediate reason for conflict
between Indians and non-Indians.   —Milner Ball[4]

① Case study
② Navajo medicine men/women & development of land around SF

I. Introduction

"WHAT IS A medicine man?" the U.S. District Court judge asked in response to the efforts of the Navajo Medicine Men's Association to stop the *what*
expansion of a ski resort on National Forest Service land on the slopes of
the San Francisco Peaks. The attorney for the Navajo, in supporting documents and in his direct response, pointed out that soil and other items
from these peaks, and from the three other sacred mountains of the Navajo
people, are carried in the medicine man's pouch. Thus he moved adroitly
from the microcosmic to the macrocosmic, from the bit of dirt in the
pouch to the massive landform. In a word, he made a mountain out of a
molehill.[5]

In the Navajo cast of characters medicine men and women are healers,

subject

43

persons of power, because they possess the formulas and symbols for restoring balance in their patients by putting them back into harmony with the world. They do this by "singing" a chant or "way" and by using all of the powers at their command. Those powers are embodied and symbolized in their medicine pouches.

Here is the image, then: dirt—real dirt—introduced as evidence in a court of law. The overriding argument between Indians and European Americans involves dirt—soil, land. Whose is it? Who controls it? What does it signify?

The dirt in the medicine pouch is analogous to the white man's deed or title. It is symbolic of and even embodies the claimant's right to the land. Likewise, the medicine pouch, which gives its owner special power in the community, is analogous to the white man's bundle of rights which protects his property and gives him standing in a court of law. While no American court is likely to grant such analogous status to the medicine pouch or the dirt in it, the appurtenances of a court of law suggest the utmost seriousness, and legal concepts relative to property often assume a sacred character. It was Sir William Blackstone, the influential English jurist, who defined a "deed" by which title to land is conveyed from one to another as "the most solemn and authentic act a man can possibly perform."[6]

While the attorney for the Navajo Medicine Men's Association may not have had analogy in mind, he and his clients were strongly interested in claiming and securing certain rights relative to the San Francisco Peaks. They rested their case primarily on the free exercise clause of the First Amendment to the Constitution—the right freely to practice their religion. That practice involves, they claimed, a time-honored relationship with the mountains as they are. Hence any man-imposed physical changes and additions constitute a threat to the free exercise of their religion. By extension, then, the Navajo Medicine Men's Association was claiming a time-honored *right* to the mountains as they are. Such an implied claim need not be understood as involving ownership in the white man's sense but possibly something more akin to a conservation easement. In any case, a claim is implied.

More obviously, the Navajo were arguing religion as commonly understood among white people—relationships with ultimate power or powers, that which is sacred, holy. That, the court could handle. Indeed, it might even accept the argument that for the Navajo that dirt has some sort of ultimate significance but not of a sort that embraces a status similar to that of a title.

2. Sacred Geography

> It is said that that area is not even a part of this world that we live in here. That that place up there, the high country, belongs to the spirit and it exists in another world apart from us. —Karuk Indian[7]

> This high country is our religion . . . [T]his mountain is sacred to my people. —Yakima Indian[8]

But, put in the language of the major culture, religion and land *are* intimately related in traditional Native American cultures. While land may be regarded as sacred in some generalized sense, specific areas are more significant in that they are sources and locales of power and identity. They may tie the people to each other and to their past. These locales may also be places in which shamans and other types of religious leaders or people of power are empowered. Such specific places are critically significant, then, to individual and communal identity and well-being.

The Navajo religion is closely tied to the earth.[9] The supreme object of the Navajo way is to live in harmony with the earth, the land. Building ski lifts and other facilities on the sacred mountain destroys the harmony of the area, according to the Navajo argument. That threatens Navajo well-being.

Landforms are of great importance to the Navajo. A mountain like the San Francisco Peaks is not only the residence of deities, it is itself a deity. Hence "to gouge [the land] or to erect structures on it violates the [land form] in much the same way the actions would offend a human body . . . [C]utting, digging or other man-made disturbances of the natural state . . . causes the sacred deity to lose its healing power and inhibits the effectiveness of the religious ceremonies and thus interferes with the healing of the Navajo people and the restoration of harmony, balance and natural order to their lives."[10]

Sacred geography was also at stake in another recent court case—*Lyng*—in which three Indian tribes of northwest California sought to stop the National Forest Service from developing a road through an area regarded by the tribes (Karuk, Yurok, and Tolowa) as especially sacred and called "the high country." These tribes, like the Navajo, claimed that the preservation of this land in its pristine condition was essential to the free exercise of their religion. Like the Navajo, their case implied a claim, a right, to the land as it is.

This high country, the contested area, is located in a relatively remote area in the Siskyou Mountains that includes three prominent peaks, the highest points in the area and hence among the chief centers of power. In the Indians' view, the roots of the area's power lie in the life and continuing presence of certain immortals who inhabited America before humans came upon the earth and who withdrew when the Indians came into the country. In the withdrawal process they were transformed into animals, rocks, trees, immortal spirits, etc., and they continue to exercise a powerful influence in those forms. This power in the high country is enhanced by the presence of the souls or spirits of deceased people of power.

The three tribes involved in the court case which focused on the high country, while springing from different ethnic roots and speaking different and mutually unintelligible native languages, came, by virtue of geographic proximity and intermarriage, to share many cultural and religious beliefs and practices. The Karuk are of Hokan stock and are thought to be among the earliest inhabitants of the region. The Yurok, the most studied of the three groups, are of Algic stock (as is also the Algonquian family). The Tolowa are of Athapascan stock. Although external pressures from the late nineteenth century to the present have had a devastating impact on these groups, a relatively large and vital indigenous population still lives in the area and a substantial number still follows or seeks to follow the traditional religious patterns.[11]

Mountains and high places played and play a central role in the religious life of all three peoples. A Tolowa informant told anthropologist Cora Du-Bois more than sixty years ago that among her people a girl or woman who felt the inclination to become a "doctor" or shaman was taken to a "lucky mountain" where she danced "facing the east." Falling into a trance state she dreamed about the mountains as sources of power. Dreams about the ocean were regarded, on the other hand, as "bad omens."[12]

"Among the Yurok . . . ," anthropologist Alfred L. Kroeber reported, "the person whom the spirits have visited in dreams, ascends high peaks where he spends one or more nights until he has acquired powers."[13] Kroeber's "Yurok collaborator," Robert Spott, reported on one woman shaman that "For several summers she danced . . . at a peak [which] looks out over the ocean. Then at last while she was sleeping," a woman came to her in a dream and gave her her power in the form of an object called a "pain." Even after gaining control over this object, it was still necessary for her to go up to the peak where there was a "tsektsel" or "prayer seat" on which she would "sit down and think."[14] Among the Karuk also, according to anthropologist John P. Harrington, "doctors acquired and kept their status by performing the ceremony of mountain pilgrimages."[15]

Mountains also played a significant role in the world renewal ceremonies among the Yurok and Karuk. The routine of the master of ceremonies or priest in these ceremonies was a rigorous one which typically involved ritual treks to special places, including, in some instances, mountain peaks. He (and all priests seem to have been men) would also ritually "feed the mountains."[16] The ceremonies, the objectives of which were the prevention of disease, famine and calamity (or the assurance of health, food, and stability) for another year and the reestablishment and firming of the earth, required precision of action in a specific spot.[17]

The role of mountains is especially significant in certain Karuk versions of the world renewal ceremony, as reported by E. W. Gifford. Stone piling with an opening to "the sacred mountain" is a preliminary activity to the ceremony at one locale. On the third day the priest goes to this mountain. At another locale the focal center of the ceremony is "a sacred mountain" which is several miles away and which remains the orientation point throughout the ceremony. The priest "keeps his eye on it as he follows prescribed journeys,"[18] and after he has built a fire at each of the prescribed locales that he must visit, he leaves two fire sticks or tongs pointed toward the mountain. On the final, climactic night, two of the priest's assistants, called "priestesses" by Gifford, "make a miniature figure of the sacred mountain's two peaks with damp sand." When they have finished making the sand model they take fir trimmings from their hair rolls and insert the little fir needles into the model. As they put needles into the model they pray that all kinds of trees will grow well. The priest then stands beside (or on) this sacred sand pile while a certain dance is performed. He must stand all night and gaze in the direction of the mountain.[19]

Hence, since the religious and cultural life of the Northwest Indians is rooted in the existence and activities of prehuman creatures, and since these creatures are still in some sense present in specific sites, these sites assume enormous importance to that life. The religious life of these people is rooted thereby in the soil, in the rocks, in the trees, in the mountains in their area. Typically these physical features were named; "every feature of their landscape of any importance whatsoever had its precise name . . . and . . . a precise significance. . . . " In a very real sense, then, the "indigenous peoples of the region were geographers *par excellence*."[20]

Hence the evidence they presented in making their case included whatever they could muster in court to show the location and the contours of their "high country."

a. Conflicting Worlds

> Even if we assume that [building a road through the "high country"] will "virtually destroy . . . the Indians' ability to practice their religion," the Constitution simply does not provide a principle that could justify upholding [the Indians'] claims. —The U.S. Supreme Court[21]

> Because of the immense cultural and religious significance of land in Indian life, the power to destroy Indian land rights carries with it the power to destroy Indian identity. —Coulter and Tulberg[22]

Unfortunately for the Indian claimants, and perhaps for others as well, the courts were not persuaded by the dirt in the Navajo medicine pouches or by the high country representations and arguments of the Northwest California Indians. Both lost their cases, as did several other tribes and individuals who launched similar complaints involving sacred sites.[23] The final blow to the religion-based Native American land claims came in 1988 when the Supreme Court spoke decisively on the subject in *Lyng v Northwest Indian Cemetery Protective Association*. The Court held that if the Indian complainants were successful in their efforts to assure protected access to sacred sites on public lands that would constitute the imposition of "religious servitude" on the contested areas. Going to the heart of the Indians' implied property right claim, the Court exclaimed that, if successful in that claim, they would gain "*de facto* beneficial ownership of some rather spacious tracts of public property." This could lead to a "far from trivial . . . diminution of the Government's property rights . . . Whatever rights the Indians may have to use of [such areas]," the Court concluded, "those rights do not divest the Government of the right to use what is, after all, *its* land."[24]

While the Court was willing to acknowledge that the contested area might be significant to the religious practice of the Indians, it concluded that the Indians' free exercise of religion claim clearly did not override the Government's property rights. Further, the Court gave no weight whatsoever to such constructs of the white man's law as aboriginal title or Indian title, constructs which, in theory, seem to be in the same league as concepts of governmental ownership, but which, in practice, carried no weight in this and similar Indian land claims cases.

A little dirt in a medicine pouch over against all of the power embodied

KEY ISSUE / QUESTION / DEBATE & ARTICLE

in the symbols and institutions of governmental ownership; high country protection against all of the pressures of a governmentally sanctioned policy of "multiple use" of national forests. Beneath these conflicts is a fundamental clash of worlds epitomized in sharply different views of dirt, soil, land and of property rights thereto; on the one side, the possibility of nearly absolute and unrestricted individual or corporate ownership, which involves the right to use the land and to "alienate" it as one wishes (within some limits); on the other side, an understanding of a relationship to the land which is more communitarian than individual and which may entail both the right of use and the responsibility of care, but which does not entail the right to alienate the land.[25] Attitudes of white men have ranged from eager—even greedy—desire for iron-clad ownership, the prevalent view, to an almost mystical sense of the beauties of the land. While Indian views have generally been much more communally based, individual vision seekers have experienced close relationships to specific places, relationships symbolized, as in the Navajo singers' case, through dirt and other items in the medicine pouch.[26]

Another way to put the contrast between white and Indian views is to ask: Does the land belong to me or do I belong to the land? Mae Wilson Tso, a fifty-year-old Navajo medicine woman, stated one pole well in another court case involving her resistance and that of several other Navajo to forced removal from land on Black Mesa on which they had lived all their lives.[27] "We have an obligation and a responsibility to the land to remain here and care for it," protested Tso. We are "instructed to be caretakers of the land."[28] This medicine woman, mother of nine, dramatically illustrated that each Navajo is tied to the land from birth. When a child is born, his or her afterbirth is offered back to the earth. As the child grows, he or she is bound to the land in many other ways. Contrast this with the prevailing understanding of land in America: land is a resource to be developed, exploited. It is a commodity, to be used or used up, to be bought and sold for a profit. I own the land, it does not own me. *KEY TERM*

Further, in the prevailing Western view this ownership is reinforced, or undergirded or guaranteed, by a system of law in which property is not just the thing in itself or the resources themselves but the "bundles" of legal relations and rights through which human behavior is controlled in regard to them. Land as property can refer to "either the thing owned which is the object of the bundle of relations which constitute ownership, or it can refer to the bundle of relations themselves." Ownership of property is understood, then, in terms of sets of rights which include the right of use, enjoy-

Description of western concept of man's relationship to land

ment and alienation of the property, and exclude impingement by others on it; and which are spelled out in and transferred through legal documents (titles, deeds, abstracts) and can be defended in courts of law. These rights may be possessed and exercised by individuals as well as legally defined communities such as corporations and civil or governmental entities.[29]

In contrast, traditional Indian understanding of land as property involves the land itself. It is rooted in the soil and in experience on the land. Hence it is closer to the material reality than the prevailing Western abstractions in laws, titles, etc. Insofar as it is represented in abstractions it is likely to be so as a living reality—or possibly in a drawing or a medicine bundle. The Indian understanding may also be based on long uninterrupted possession and use. Communal ownership is often understood to include the dead and the yet to be born as well as the living. Here, then, is an organic view rather than a structural one, a view in which there are no sharply marked distinctions between past, present, and future, between nature and supernature, and in which boundaries were determined by use, which varied over time, and consisted of landmarks, watercourses, etc., which were characterized by a certain fluidity.

These differences between white and Indian views are deeply rooted in once completely separate histories. Over five hundred years, however, the paths of these disparate peoples have crossed and recrossed until they have become like the characters in Sartre's *No Exit*—like it or not, they are bound to live together in apparently everlasting tension. Nowhere is this tension more evident than in their approaches to and uses of land. And the focal point of the tension, that point where it becomes most evident, is the courtroom where the enormous body of law which has evolved out of Indian-white relations is brought into full display.

In power terms, stronger has been pitted against weaker, as Europeans and Euro-Americans have overwhelmed the indigenous peoples and taken possession of most of their land. Nonetheless, that overriding power has been and continues to be moderated by forces of law and conscience and by the remarkable capacity of the weaker party to survive by adapting traditional ways, while selectively adopting the ways of the major culture.

3. The Paraphernalia and Presumptions of Power over Land

The language of power over land is evident in the Supreme Court's use in *Lyng v Northwest Indian Cemetery Protective Association* of words

like "ownership" and "property rights." The American glossary of power
concepts and signs includes, in addition to these words: "discovery," "settlement," "possession," "use" (and "multiple use"), "vacant," "waste,"
"occupancy," "alienation," "extinguishment," "title," "deed," "fee simple," "survey," "cadastral survey," "plat," "preemption," "homestead,"
"fence," "improvement," "cultivation," "plant," "develop," "allotment,"
and "allotment in severalty." These concepts and signs, rooted in European history, ideology and practice, have added up to a complete mapping
of the land and a totality of claim over it.

a. "Discovery" and Its Progeny → descended from offspring

> There are moments in history to which one can point and say, "At this
> hour, on this day, the history of the world was changed forever." Such
> a moment occurred at two o'clock on the morning of October 12, 1492,
> when a cannon, fired from the Spanish caravel *Pinta*, announced the
> sighting of land . . . It was the new world. —N. Scott Momaday[30]

"Discovery" of what came to be called "America" confronted the Europeans with a whole new set of geographical, political, legal, theological,
moral and religious questions. What was this land? Part of the Indies? A
separate continent? The site of the Garden of Eden? Who or what were
these creatures that inhabited this strange world? Human beings? Barbarians? An inferior people? Prospective converts to Christianity? Prospective
slaves? How should they be treated? What claims did they have on the
land? What claims did the European "discoverers," conquerors, and settlers have? Quite naturally, the Europeans turned to or relied on their own
long-established world views to answer these questions. By the fifteenth
century they had had extensive contacts with foreigners, "barbarians,"
"infidels." The crusades had been supported and justified by appeal to the
supremacy of Christianity and of the Pope and the consequent obligation
to Christianize and civilize the non-believers. Quite logically, then, when
Spanish authorities appealed to the Pope for support of their "discovery"
of, and consequent right to, the new world, he obliged by dividing the
newly "discovered" world between the Spanish and the Portuguese. Papal
supremacy was also the foundation of Spanish justification of conquest of
the natives. This is illustrated most strikingly in the *Requerimiento*
which Spanish conquistadores were expected to read to natives before taking up arms against them. That document embodies in brief compass the
whole Christian cosmology and chain of command: from the one supreme
creator and sovereign God to His Son, Jesus Christ, to the Vicar of Christ,

SACRED = POWER

the Pope, to the King and Queen of Spain, to their representatives. As God, the creator, is ruler of all the world, so His living representative on earth functions in His stead. Acknowledgement of this superior and supreme authority would bring peace; failure to acknowledge would bring war and enslavement to that authority.

While Protestant monarchs, such as those of the Netherlands and of England, did not accept the supremacy of the Pope, they did assume the supremacy of Christianity and of their own claims to land as Christian monarchs. Hence Queen Elizabeth authorized Sir Humphrey Gilbert in 1578 "to discover and take possession of such remote, heathen, and barbarous lands, as were not actually possessed by any Christian prince or people." Sir Walter Raleigh was later authorized "to discover, search, fynde out, and view such remote heathen and barbarous landes, Countries and territories not actually possessed of any Christian prynce, nor inhabited by Christian People . . . " As further enticement to Raleigh the Queen's letters patent granted him and his heirs "for ever all soyle of all such landes countreys and territories . . . discovered or possessed," "full power" to take possession, and "full power to dispose thereof and of every parte in fee simple or otherwise according to the order of the lawes of England . . . "[31]

Protestant colonizers, such as the Puritans of New England, did not rely so much on the authority of the Christian monarch as on that of the Scriptures. But the immediate result was much the same. Thus John Cotton, using 2 Sam. 7:10 as his text[32] in his sermon on the theme "God's Promise to His Plantation," delivered to the departing Puritans in Southampton in 1630, proclaimed that God had prepared the way for their settlement in the new world. God makes room for his people in three ways: (1) by lawful war; (2) by purchase or other friendly means; and (3) by making a country

> though not altogether void of inhabitants, yet void in that place where they reside. Where there is a vacant place there is liberty for the sons of Adam or Noah to come and inhabit, though they neither buy it nor ask their leave. Abraham and Isaac, when they sojourned amongst the Philistines, they did not buy land to feede their cattle, because they said There is roome enough.

Cotton then allied Scripture with nature:

> It is a principle of nature that in vacant soil, he that takes possession of it, and bestows culture and husbandry upon it, his right it is. And the ground of this is from the Grand Charter given to Adam and his posterity, Genesis 1:28, "Multiply, and replenish the earth, and subdue it."[33]

John Winthrop, Cotton's fellow Puritan, declared in 1629 that most of the land in America came under the legal rubric of vacuum domicillium; the logic of this concept is that if one builds upon or cultivates the land it is his. Winthrop assumed that the natives, being a "savage people," who neither built permanent structures nor cultivated the land, had no more claim to the land than one of occupancy. Actual use of the land created, on the other hand, a civil and superior title to it.[34]

The Puritans were consistent in their use of this view of vacant or "waste" land. When they settled in the Connecticut River Valley, they claimed the land as "The Lord's waste," to which they had "a common right . . . with the rest of the sons of Noah." They also used the argument of vacancy against each other.[35]

John Cotton's parting spiritual advice to the Puritans assembled in Southampton in 1630 was "Offend not the poor natives, but as you partake in their land, so make them partakers of your precious faith, as you reap their temporals, so feed them your spirituals."[36] A fair bargain? Fair enough for the Puritan settlers, at least. This sense of the fairness of the deal was bolstered in an early seal of New England which features an almost naked Indian, holding a bow in one hand and an arrow in the other and saying: "Come over and help us." Spirituals for temporals.

Hence, the Puritan ideologues and movers went even farther than their Catholic counterparts in providing justification for taking over the land. In their reliance on natural law theory, they stressed the centrality of use in laying claims to possession, and to natural law theory they added biblical proof texts even more liberally and literally than the Catholic moral theologians did. This usage is illustrated in a grand way by the scriptural verses inscribed by Daniel Gookin on the title page of his Historical Collection of the Indians in New England, which include Psalm 2, verse 8: "Ask of me, and I shall give thee, the heathens for thine inheritance, and the uttermost parts of the earth for thy possession."[37] References to such biblical texts were also incorporated into the laws of Massachusetts Bay.[38]

The views of Catholic and Puritan ideologues regarding land rights and possession in America were substantially reinforced by the natural law views of John Locke. In the beginning, Locke wrote in a much quoted phrase, "all the world was America."[39] Locke was not merely stating some abstraction; he apparently meant that this "virgin" land was exactly the way all land was at the beginning of human history.[40] Like the mind, the natural world was in the beginning a tabula rasa to be written upon, a wild and unused resource to be tamed and exploited by human labor. Insofar as this land was "property," it was held by divine intention in common. But since God meant that land should be used for human benefit, i.e., to support the "greatest conveniences of life" that human beings "were capable of drawing from it, it cannot be supposed," Locke argued, that God "meant it should always remain common and uncultivated." In actuality, God "gave it to the use of the industrious and rational," who through their labor on the land gained property rights to it.[41] "As much land as a man tills, plants, improves, cultivates, and can use the product of, so much is his Property. He by his labour does, as it were, inclose it from the common." This enclosure, far from being disadvantageous to others, actually enhances and increases "the common stock of mankind: for the provisions serving to the support of human life, produced by one acre of enclosed and cultivated land, are . . . ten times more than those which are yielded by an acre of land of an equal richness lying waste in common."[42]

To illustrate his point Locke asks his readers "whether in the wild woods and uncultivated waste of America, left to nature, without any improvement, tillage, or husbandry, a thousand acres yield the needy and wretched inhabitants as many conveniences of life as ten acres of equally fertile land do in Devonshire, where they are well cultivated?"[43] To Locke, the answer was obvious. The Native Americans had wasted the land by not developing it. Hence they had no lasting property rights in it; it was only "common sense" that the European discoverers do what the natives had not done.

The European conquerors and colonizers of the new world assumed, then, that by virtue of both God-derived authority and natural law, discovery gave them exclusive right to possess the land either by conquest or purchase. This is not to suggest that the rights of Indians were entirely ignored. While failing to recognize that the Indians had "discovered" America long before the white man, European theorists did acknowledge that they had a continued right of occupancy in their soil—called variously "aboriginal title," "original Indian," or simply "Indian title."[44] Nonetheless, the closer the Indians' approaches to and uses of land were to those of the Europeans, the more the latter acknowledged Indian rights. For example, in New England Indian rights to "improved" land—land which they had systematically cultivated and on which they had built more or less permanent structures—were more substantially acknowledged than were Indian claims to "vacant" or "waste" land. Furthermore, "praying Indians," that is, those converted to Christianity, were generally granted land on which to develop their separate communities. It is noteworthy, however, that the the final arbiter in land allocations and disputes was the General Court (or General Assembly in Rhode Island)—i.e., the entity in which ultimate sovereignty was vested. In this respect these agencies were successors to the Crown, whether acknowledged by the Crown or not. They were the beneficiaries and the repositories of the rights of discovery.[45]

b. Symbolic Acts and Signs of Discovery   *similar to Indian traditions*

[When the European explorers and colonizers could not settle immediately or fully on the land they claimed, they established their right to that land by ceremonial acts and proclamations. Thus, on October 12, 1492, Columbus consummated his discovery of America by planting the royal banner on the shore of San Salvador and taking possession of the land in the name of Ferdinand and Isabella. And everywhere he went he raised crosses and made claims for his sovereigns—Jesus Christ and Christ's vice-regents.

In performing these symbolic acts and making these claims, Columbus was following established practice among European monarchs and their representatives, a practice which, as astronaut Neil Armstrong's act of planting the American flag on the surface of the moon indicates, continues in some form even to the present day. On his first voyage Vasco da Gama carried *padroes* or stone pillars to set up as marks of discovery and overlordship. When Sir Francis Drake put ashore on the coast of California (just where is still disputed) he left "a plate of brass, fast nailed to a great and firm poste" to claim New Albion for Queen Elizabeth. These sorts of practices continued among the Americans. For example, Captain James Biddle of the United States Navy, in response to orders to take formal possession of the lands at the mouth of the Columbia River following the War of 1812, took three boats and more than fifty well armed officers and men ashore at Cape Disappointment to perform the necessary ceremonies—or as much as he could remember of them. Here, "in the presence of several natives," according to his own account, "displaying the flag of the United States, turning up a sod of soil, and giving three cheers, I nailed up against a tree a leaden plate in which were cut the following words: 'Taken possession of in the name and on the behalf the United States, by Captain James Biddle, Commanding the United States Ship Ontario. Columbia River, August 1818.'" After another salute was fired the landing party took on water and wood and then departed, leaving behind, as Vernon Carstensen puts it, "some puzzled natives."[46] Some natives were more than puzzled by this sort of ritual behavior, however. In the mid-eighteenth century the

Shawnees tore down and "trampled under foot with contempt" the symbols of French ownership which had been hung on trees along the Allegheny and Ohio rivers.[47] To be on the safe side in preserving the emblems of their claims to sovereignty, the French took to burying lead plates safely out of view. Whatever the means—monuments set upon the land or plates buried beneath it, "words pronounced upon the air, written on a piece of paper, or set down in a book of public record"—all established and registered title and perpetuated a right to a given piece of land, so far as the Europeans and their successors were concerned.[48] Such symbolic acts encapsulated the power resident in that right.

c. The Doctrine of Discovery Developed

Today, more than five hundred years after Columbus put ashore in the "Indies," debate swirls around his "discovery" and its impact. This much is clear, however: Whether Columbus discovered America or someone else did, his act of discovery and the associated symbols of possession were supported by a world view which took on legal significance in the doctrine or right of discovery; that doctrine rests at the base of European and subsequent American claims to the land. Hence some form of European discovery is crucial to American property law. → interesting concept

Indeed, the doctrine of discovery, as propounded by European monarchs, formed the foundation of the approaches to land that prevailed in the American colonies, and subsequently, in the American states, under the Articles of Confederation, and still prevails in American constitutional law. Under this doctrine, sovereignty over land, as understood among European monarchs and in prevailing interpretations of natural law, rested with the European monarchs and their successors among the American political jurisdictions. It did not rest with the American Indians, whose right to the land was understood solely as a right of occupancy, and not one of ultimate ownership and control. Under this doctrine Indians could "alienate" or sell or cede their land only to the sovereign authority, and not directly to private individuals or groups.

The proponents of the doctrine of discovery often conveniently forgot or downplayed the Indians, relative to the land. The most available device was to assume that the land was vacant—hence, free to be taken by the first claimants. As early in the life of the new republic as 1810, Chief Justice John Marshall, the chief architect of American constitutional theory relative to land, described Indian-occupied territories as "vacant lands within the United States."[49] While that view was often supported by the notion that the Indians were wanderers, hunters who ranged wide over the land but never settled permanently in any one place, and hence had no sustainable claim to particular areas; still, there were people on the land, people who had to be dealt with in some way—both in reality and in theory. As indicated, the most common ways of dealing with whatever hold or claim they might have on their lands were purchase or conquest. When it came to theory, the view that prevailed in the long run was that the land rights of the Indians were no more than rights of occupancy. -7 KEY TERM

The attorney for Peck, the winner in *Fletcher v Peck*, 1810, put the prevailing view well in his statement before the Supreme Court:

> What is Indian title? It's a mere occupancy for the purpose of hunting. It is not like our tenures; they have no idea of a title to the soil itself. It is overrun by them, rather than inhabited. It is not a true and legal possession . . . It is a right not to be *transferred* but *extinguished*. It is a right regulated by treaties, not by deeds of conveyance. It depends upon the law of nations, not upon municipal right.
>
> The Europeans found the territory in possession of a rude and uncivilized people . . . They had no idea of property in the soil but a right of occupation. A right not individual but national. This is the right gained by conquest. The Europeans always claimed and exercised the right of conquest over the soil.
>
> The rights of [conquering] governments are allodial [free from the tenurial rights of a feudal overlord]. The crown of Great Britain granted lands to individuals, even while the Indian claim existed, and there has never been a question respecting the validity of such grants. When that claim was extinguished, the grantee was always admitted to have acquired a complete title. The Indian title is a mere privilege which does not affect the allodial rights.[50]

This argument is worth quoting at length, not only because so much of the generally prevailing view is captured in it, but also because it is the view which the Court itself accepted.

The doctrine of discovery and its progeny finally took on the full clothing of American constitutional law thirteen years after *Fletcher v Peck* in *Johnson and Graham's Lease v McIntosh*. This case involved much more directly than *Fletcher* the issue of Indian land rights. It pitted two claimants to an area of land against each other. One had secured the land by purchase directly from the Indians, the other through the federal government. The Court found for the latter.

Discovery, Chief Justice Marshall wrote for the Court, "gave title to the government by whose subjects, or by whose authority, it was made, against all other European governments, which title might be consummated by possession."[51] Discovery, in the case under review, was traced back to the issuance by James I of letters patent on May 23, 1609, to the colony of Virginia.[52] In something of an understatement Marshall observed that the rights of the original inhabitants were "to a considerable extent, impaired."

> They were admitted to be the rightful occupants of the soil, with a legal as well as just claim to retain possession of it, and to use it according to their own discretion; but their rights to complete sovereignty, as independent nations, were necessarily diminished, and their power to dispose of the soil at their own will, to whomsoever they pleased, was denied by the original fundamental principle, that discovery gave exclusive title to those who made it.[53]

The doctrine of discovery, then, "gave an exclusive right to [the United States] to extinguish the Indian title of occupancy, either by purchase or by conquest." This doctrine then led to the vesting of "absolute title" in the federal government,[54] a title which subsequently could be transferred to individuals or groups or corporations by purchase or outright grant.

d. From Discovery to Possession and Ownership

> That the lands of this country were taken from [the Indians] by conquest, is not so general a truth as is supposed. I find in our historians and records, repeated proofs of purchase, which cover a considerable part of the lower country; and many more would doubtless be found on further search. The upper country we know has been acquired altogether by purchases made in the most unexceptionable form.
> —Thomas Jefferson[55]

> The conduct of the Americans of the United States toward the aborigines is characterized, . . . by a singular attachment to the formalities of law. Provided that the Indians retain their barbarous condition, the Americans take no part in their affairs; they treat them as independent nations and do not possess themselves of their hunting grounds without a treaty of purchase; and if an Indian nation happens to be so encroached upon as to be unable to subsist upon their territory, they kindly take them by the hand and transport them to a grave far from the land of their fathers. —Alexis de Tocqueville[56]

From discovery followed possession and from possession, ownership. Gradually the Indian "occupants" of the continent were displaced through conquest and removal from their land or through purchase of it. In the infancy of the new republic, twelve tribes in the Northwest Territory were forced to cede large tracts of their lands in the eastern part of the territory in the Treaty of Greenville, 1795. With the Louisiana Purchase in 1803, some 828,000 square miles, most of it tribal homelands, became available for future non-Indian expansion and as a "dumping ground" for Indians removed from east of the Mississippi. Between the American Revolution and the end of the nineteenth century, the United States took possession of more than two billion acres of land claimed by indigenous tribes and nations. About half of this area was purchased by treaty or agreement at an average price of seventy-five cents an acre; much of the remainder was claimed or confiscated by the United States without compensation.[57] And so the story continued as Indian lands shrank to a minute fraction of their original size.[58]

e. Rectangles and Circles: Dividing the Land

> You have noticed that everything that an Indian does is in a circle, and that is because the Power of the World always works in circles, and everything tries to be round . . . But the Wasichus [whites] have put us in these square boxes. —Black Elk[59]

> The land has been made into arithmetic. —Fictional Montana Homesteader[60]

Rivers and streams afforded the most obvious access for Europeans to this new world. And the most obvious boundaries within it. Yet, in their claims following discovery Europeans relied more on straight lines than on meandering water courses to describe boundaries and support possession. Looking at a map of the land claims of the thirteen states upon the winning of independence, one is impressed with the prevalence of these horizontal and vertical lines. This grid pattern is interrupted only by such obvious bodies of water as the Great Lakes and the Ohio and Mississippi rivers.[61]

Seven of the original thirteen states laid claim to land west of the mountains: Massachusetts, Connecticut, New York, Virginia, North Carolina, South Carolina, and Georgia. All of these except New York claimed sea-to-sea grants under the terms of their original charters from the English Crown. For example, in 1732 George II granted a charter to the founders of the colony of Georgia to "all the lands and territories" from the northern reaches of the Savannah River on the north and the southern reaches of the Altamaha River on the south westward "in direct lines to the South Sea."[62]

This straight-line pattern continued to prevail in the survey, and division into rectangles, of the public domain following the land cessions to the federal government by these seven states. Thomas Jefferson proposed in 1784 that these lands, when gained from the Indian occupants, be divided into "Hundreds of ten geographical miles square, each mile containing 6,086 feet and four tenths of a foot, by lines to run and marked due North and South, and others crossing these at right angles . . . " These hundreds, he further proposed "shall be subdivided into lots of one mile square each, or 850 acres and four tenths of an acre by marked lines running in like manner due North and South, and others crossing these at right angles." This proposal was forwarded to the Continental Congress with the approval of a committee which was chaired by Jefferson.[63]

While Jefferson's proposal was not followed in precise form, the system that came to prevail clearly reflected the same straight-line, right-angle approach to land. The land ordinances of 1785 and 1787 specified that the basic square was to be six miles in size, constituting a township, and that the township was to be divided into lots of 640 acres each.

[Americans became firmly attached to this rectangular system of dividing the land. They insisted upon its use even in areas—such as the arid west—where it made even less sense then it did in the more humid east.] In his monumental report to the Congress on the arid region of the United States in 1878, John Wesley Powell maintained that settlers of that region "should not be hampered with the present arbitrary system of dividing lands into rectangular tracts."[64] He urged instead that the land be surveyed in such a way as to correspond with topography and especially with sources of water. But his report was ignored by the Congress, as were his recommendations to the constitutional conventions of several western states that they lay out their political boundaries along watersheds so as to avoid some of the inevitable conflicts over water usage.[65]

The first public land surveys under the rectangular system in the new nation were done in eastern Ohio in 1786. These and subsequent surveys included the placement of monuments or markers at the four corners of each section and a record of the survey which included a description of the monuments, how marked, and a plat, which is a graphic representation of the survey. The record and the plat served subsequently as the legal basis for all transactions involving public lands. By the middle of the twentieth century more than ninety percent of the total public area in the continental United States had been surveyed in this fashion.[66] Thus a monumental cadastral net was cast over most of the land west of the Appalachians, and the survey details of each segment or square of this net were carefully recorded and described in the public records. The land, while remaining a physical reality, also became a legal abstraction which could be owned and *another example of ... sacred ... turned into ... concept* → KEY CONCEPTUAL IDEA

sold or otherwise transferred from one person or entity to another. Land became property and property meant rights not things. It is as though some artist had reduced the physical reality to a colossal canvas and had also proceeded to document each detail on the canvas.[67]

While the recording system used in the United States was an American innovation,[68] the practice of marking land with boundary markers is deeply rooted in Western history. Its significance is suggested in a legend or myth involving the Roman god Terminus, the god of boundaries. Numa Pompilius, legendary second king of Rome, had *termini* or boundary stones, made to mark dividing lines between neighbors. Property rights were further sanctified by Numa through the erection of a temple to Terminus. The temple had no roof, symbolizing that the god of boundaries could not himself be bound, or in more earthly terms, that property rights extend without limits into the space above the lines. Further evidence of the power of Terminus is suggested in the story of the building of the Capitoline Temple. To accomplish this feat it was necessary that altars and temples to several gods which were on the summit of the Capitol be removed. Augurs were charged to seek the assent of the gods to this temporary dislocation. Terminus refused to be moved. Boundaries are sacrosanct.

f. Titles and Deeds

extremely sacred

> Most of them [the Mashpees] just kept on using the land in the same old communal way we Indians always did before the white man came over here with his walls and fences and bits of paper. —Mabel Avant, Mashpee Wapanoag historian[69]

> The title of the Cherokee to their lands is the most ancient, pure and absolute known to man; its date is beyond the reach of human record; its validity confirmed by possession and enjoyment antecedent to all pretense of claim by any portion of the human race. —Cherokee Memorial to Congress[70]

The primary purpose of the massive survey of public lands in the new nation was to provide a basis for the disposal of the land by grant or sale. That process was consummated by the granting of "title" through the instrument of a "deed." In law a title to land means legal right to the possession of that property and the evidence of such right. Evidence is typically provided in the form of a "deed," which, to allude to Blackstone again, "is a writing sealed and delivered by the parties" and is called a deed because of the solemnity with which it is executed and the authenticity it implies.[71] "Clear" title may be demonstrated by an abstract which rehearses the history of the legal possession of the land or real property involved and which in the case of land in America is rooted in "discovery" of the land by some European monarch or designee. Hence the survey provides a foundation for conversion to a legal document, a written instrument symbolizing and signifying possession of the land surveyed.

Rectangles and right angles, solemn "deeds" and written "titles" symbolized the white man's approach to land. It is an approach which stands in sharp contrast to that of a people who lived intimately on the land, who knew it in all of its contours, undulations, ups and downs, who were keenly aware of its watercourses, and who assumed the rights of use by tradition embedded in their minds.

g. "Improving the Land"

Under the Preemption Act of 1841, which one scholar has described as "the most important agrarian measure ever passed by Congress,"[72] up to 160 acres of surveyed public domain land "to which the Indian title has been . . . extinguished" became available to qualified individuals who could pay $1.25 per acre and "who shall inhabit and *improve* the same . . . " Qualified people included heads of families, widows, and single men over 21 who were citizens or had filed intentions to become one.[73] "Improvement" and the right of preemption of public domain land had been tied together in congressional land acts since early in the nineteenth century.[74] Later, under the Homestead Act of 1862, public lands became available without a per acre cost to essentially the same class of people described in the Act of 1841. "[A]bsolute title" would be theirs following "actual settlement and cultivation" of the land for five years and the payment of a recording fee.[75]

The association of improvement with the rights of ownership of land was a common one in the colonies. It also involved a concept of ownership which differed sharply from that of the Native Americans. The impact of this concept on both the Indians and the land was devastating.[76] Indians were deprived of control over large areas which they had previously regarded as theirs. The Massachusetts Court acknowledged Indian ownership of only those lands which they had improved or "subdued."[77] The implication was that Indians did not own any other kind of land or land used for any purpose other than agricultural development. Native American approaches to land use or ownership tended, however, to be communal or tribal rather than individual, and rights of use or access among them were fluid, changing from season to season as they themselves moved from place to place following the hunt, the spawning of the fish, the maturation of plants and the ripening of fruit. Hence "ownership" was not tied in a narrow way to permanent settlement and improvement or cultivation. (This is not to imply that Indian nations did not acquire and defend territory.)

With improvement, cultivation, came fences—not only to mark boundaries but also to keep out roving animals, both wild and domesticated. Bounded land and the fence were, as Milner Ball points out, the "primary characteristic" of the property law which the settlers brought with them.[78]

h. Land as "Real Property"

> I am a lady now. I married a Lord! —Scottish immigrant girl who married an Iowa homesteader[79]

> Nothing can be sold, but such things as can be carried away.
> —Black Hawk[80]

Possession, survey, marking and recording, and improvement brought the evolution of land law or the law of real property, the core of the common law. A major thrust of that evolution may be described in shorthand form as involving a transition from the law governing the lord of the manor in medieval England to that involving the lord of the homestead in nineteenth-century America. Freehold tenure replaced feudal tenure.

As ownership and dominion went hand in hand in the case of the lord of the manor, so the homesteader was, in the ideology at least, free to do with his land whatever he chose to do. The law of real property developed in such a manner as to disencumber the processes of possession, use, exclusion and sale. The instruments of this law continued to be the symbolic representations of the power over the land—the title, for example. "The title of our lands," asserted Jesse Root in 1798, "is free, clear, and absolute, and every proprietor of land is a prince in his own domains, and lord paramount of the fee."[81] The primary form of title employed was the "fee simple" title. Fee simple ownership entails the most extensive and exclusive rights of use, exclusion and disposition. It was often described as "absolute ownership." The only limits to which it is subject are those involved in society's right to tax, to condemn and to police. Fee simple title was closely allied in development with "allodial" title which means free of rent or services demanded by some lord or other claimant, leaving the exclusive right to land in the hands of the owner, subject only to the societally imposed limitations indicated.

Possession of real property was a consuming goal among Americans. "Free or cheap land," Everett Dick points out, "was the lodestone that pulled multitudes of Europeans to America [and] the motive that irresistibly drew the Easterner" to the West.[82] Possession of land and all the rights and privileges attached thereto equaled power. "There is nothing which so generally strikes the imagination and engages the affections of mankind, as the right of property," declared Blackstone. To the aspirant that right meant "sole and despotic dominion . . . over the external things of the world, to the total exclusion of the right of any other individual in the universe."[83]

As the nation developed, however, power in the possession of land, of a particular place, was enhanced, seemingly, as that land became a commodity, a good that could be exchanged for a greater good. Blackstone's absolute dominion over the land, which entitled the owner to "undisturbed enjoyment" of his property, gave way to a more "dynamic, instrumental, and . . . abstract view . . . that emphasized . . . productive use and development."[84] Even in the eighteenth century Lord Dunsmore, the Royal Governor of Virginia, complained to King George that the settlers of Virginia "acquire no attachment to Place: But wandering about Seems engrafted in their Nature . . . They . . . even imagine the Lands further off, are still better than those upon which they are settled."[85] And in the nineteenth century, land development and land trading reached frenzied proportions. Land law was modified in such a way as to favor enterprise, and industrial and urban development, over pastoral settlement. Land became a way of enhancing wealth, understood in monetary terms.[86] Power became as portable as the paper which symbolized it.

G. van der Leeuw defines "property" as "the name given to the realization of possibilities . . . " "Possessions" are "sacred" and "inalienable"; they embody and enhance power. Freehold tenure brings power in the possession of land; the ability to alienate that land, to turn it into a negotiable commodity, multiplies the power and extends the scope of the owner. Hence, land, rather than being a static entity, assumes a dynamic quality like a gift, which goes the rounds and returns to the giver in enhanced form.[87]

Whatever the form of land law, however, the Indians were losers. European and subsequent American claims based on "discovery" and possession tended to ignore the natives or to regard them as temporary impediments to land possession. And if the natives were puzzled by such acts as those of Captain Biddle at Cape Disappointment in 1818, they certainly must have been puzzled and even angered by claims based on actual occupation or efforts of the would-be possessors to buy or trade for land.[88] But, as Carstensen correctly observes, "The land system spread upon the United States owes much to the values expounded by Blackstone; it owes little more than place names to the Indians."[89]

One might think the development and use of public lands in the late nineteenth and the twentieth centuries represents an exception to Carstensen's generalization about the prevalence of Blackstonian and the absence of Indian values. But even that development has been dominated by an understanding or ideology of land as commodity. Even land which remained public, Milner Ball points out, "was generally rendered into commodities through extraction and marketing of the underlying minerals, timber sales, and leases of grazing ranges."[90] Hence the National Forest Service policy of "multiple use."

i. Land as an Instrument to "Civilize" the Natives

> You ask me to plow the ground! Shall I take a knife and tear my mother's bosom? You ask me to cut grass and make hay and sell it to be rich like white men! But how dare I cut my mother's hair?
> —Smohalla, Shahaptian, 1860s[91]

> The head chief [of the Cherokees] told us that there was not a family in that whole nation that had not a home of its own. There was not a pauper in that nation, and the nation did not owe a dollar. It built its own capitol, . . . schools and . . . hospitals. Yet the defect of the system was apparent. They have got as far as they can go, because they own their land in common. [Under this] system there is no enterprise to make your home any better than that of your neighbors. There is no selfishness, which is at the bottom of civilization. Till this people will consent to give up their lands, and divide them . . . so that each can own the land he cultivates, they will not make much more progress.
> —Senator Henry L. Dawes[92]

In the course of their "civilizing" and "Americanizing" efforts among Indians, white Americans, and especially those who regarded themselves as "friends of the Indians," attempted to convert Indians into private landholders and to instill the Blackstonian values in them. Under the terms of the General Allotment Act of 1887, tribal (communal) lands were to be broken up into individual parcels—alloted in severalty—on which individual Indians, through patience and hard work, could eventually gain their own share of the American dream. Under the terms of the Act actual possession, receipt of that magical title and the power it symbolized, could not occur until after twenty-five years in proving the claim and oneself. The "success" of the Act is indicated in the fact that of the 138 million acres of tribal land holdings in 1887, only 48 million remained in Indian hands in 1934 when the allotment policy was discontinued. Of the land distributed under the Allotment Act to individuals by the Dawes Commission "only 5 percent is in Indian hands today, and more than 50 percent of all reservation land in the United States is owned by non-Indians."[93] Hence reservations are like checkerboards and the effectiveness of tribal or reservation control is considerably diminished.

Perhaps as important as the loss of land itself is the undermining of the symbolic world in which land played such a central role. The magnitude and significance of this loss is suggested in the fact that Indian religious ideology was fundamental and religious leaders played significant roles in most land disputes. Separation from familiar land and landmarks threatened tribal identity and well-being.[94]

4. "The Return of the Native"

When the committee from Plymouth had purchased the territory of Eastham of the Indians, "it was demanded, who laid claim to Billingsgate?" which was understood to be all that part of the Cape north of what they had purchased. The answer was, there was not any who owned it. "Then," said the committee, "that land is ours." The Indians answered that it was. This was a remarkable assertion and admission. The Pilgrims appear to have regarded themselves as Not Any's representatives. Perhaps this was the first instance of that quiet way of "speaking for" a place not yet occupied, or at least not improved as much as it may be, which their descendants have practiced, and still are practicing so extensively. Not Any seems to have been the sole proprietor of all America before the Yankees. But history says, that when the Pilgrims had held the lands of Billingsgate many years, at length "appeared an Indian who styled himself as Lieutenant Anthony," who laid claim to them, and of him they bought them. Who knows but a Lieutenant Anthony may be knocking at the door of the White House some day? At any rate, I know that if you hold a thing unjustly, there will surely be the devil to pay at last. —Henry David Thoreau[95]

The analysis to this point suggests a story of unrelieved loss for the Indians. That is not far from the truth. However, in recent times Native Americans have realized some redress for inequities involved in what Felix *operating under white [?] majority*

Cohen called "the largest real estate transaction,"[96] and others have dubbed the most extensive land grab, in history. In addition, a few Indian tribes have even won some significant land claims.

In the treaty-making period, up to 1871, some 370 treaties were negotiated by the United States government with American Indian tribes and nations. The great majority of these involved land cessions. But, as one observer has remarked, "it would be difficult, indeed, to find a land cession made by the Indians entirely of their own volition."[97] Through these treaties and some additional agreements the United States purchased or otherwise gained possession of some 95 percent of its public domain for an estimated $800 million.[98]

Nonetheless, the making of treaties involved a recognition of some degree of tribal autonomy—a *de jure* acknowledgment of sovereignty, however limited. When Congress unilaterally and arbitrarily discontinued treaty making with Indian nations or tribes in 1871, their status in dealing with the United States became more clouded and their means of appeal for redress of grievances, including alleged violation of treaty agreements, became even less obvious. This is very evident in federal courts.

a. Indian Resort to Federal Courts

The Cherokee Nation, perhaps the most advanced in appropriating the ways of the white world, was the first to turn to the federal courts for redress of grievances involving control of land. In a move to stave off efforts of the state of Georgia to emasculate and to destroy the Cherokee Nation, in violation of treaty guarantees given to the Cherokee by the United States, and in the face of the refusal of President Andrew Jackson to stand behind those guarantees, the Cherokee Nation turned to the Supreme Court.[99] However, the Court majority rejected the Cherokee plea on a jurisdictional ruling: it declared that Nation to be neither a foreign nation nor a state under Art. III, Sec. 2 of the Constitution and hence without standing to sue. The Cherokee are more correctly "denominated domestic dependent nations," opined Chief Justice Marshall in an oxymoron which was to assume near-classic proportions in American Indian law. "They occupy a territory to which we [the United States] assert[s] a title independent of their will, which must take effect in point of possession when their right of possession ceases."[100] The progeny of the "law" of discovery live on in this decisively important decision. Hence, the Court failed the Cherokee in this case.

Indian access to federal courts was further limited in 1863 when the

Court of Claims was restricted in its jurisdiction from handling claims based on treaty articles.[101] This meant that an Indian tribe seeking redress had to rely on a special Congressional act giving the Court of Claims jurisdiction. Obtaining such an act often consumed years, followed by additional years of litigation in the Court of Claims. By 1946, when the Indian Claims Commission was established, almost two hundred claims had been filed with the Court of Claims but only twenty-nine awards had been granted. Hence, following the end of treaty making, and especially in the late nineteenth and early twentieth centuries, Indian autonomy was severely undercut. The Marshall Court recognized Indian tribes as domestic dependent *nations* in *Cherokee Nation*, but increasingly, federal courts regarded them as disappearing peoples.

b. The Indian Claims Commission

> Things last longer on paper than they do in your head. —Commissioner Edward P. Smith to a delegation of Otoe Chiefs, 1863.[102]

In still another effort once and for all to "redress" American wrongs in appropriating or misappropriating Indian lands, and finally to settle "the Indian problem," the United States Congress enacted the Indian Claims Commission Act in 1946.[103] Under the provisions of that act the Commission was empowered to "hear and determine" a variety of "claims against the United States on behalf of any Indian tribe, band, or other identifiable group of American Indians residing within the territorial limits of the United States," including claims based on treaties "revised on the ground of fraud, duress, unconscionable consideration, [or] mutual or unilateral mistake" and "claims arising from the taking by the United States, whether as the result of a treaty of cession or otherwise, of lands owned or occupied by a claimant without the payment for such lands of compensation agreed to by the claimant . . . ."[104] The original act specified a five-year time limit for the filing of such claims.

This Congressional response to past injustices, seemingly laudatory in a historical context characterized by neglect and inaction, was still a grudging one since the jurisdiction of the Indian Claims Commission and the Court of Claims was limited under the act to monetary damages in claims successfully brought against the United States. The Commission did not have the authority to award or recommend the return of land.

Despite the fact that filing claims with the Commission was an involved and costly process, almost all of the 176 identifiable tribes and

not a genuine offering

bands filed one or more claims during the five year period, 1946–1951. Altogether a total of some 375 claims was filed, of which only 26 had been adjudicated by the end of the five-year period. The great majority of these claims involved grievances over tribal land acquisition by the U.S., including charges of inadequate compensation, fraud, failure to live up to treaty agreements, or outright unjustifiable confiscation. The determination of tribes and the depth of resentment over past grievances is suggested not only by the number of claims filed, but also by the fact that to succeed in such claims, the tribes had to prove *exclusive* use or occupation of the land from "time immemorial" (later modified to "a long time"), no small task for a people without written histories and court records. —] people where work to anthropologists could one in handy

The life of the Indian Claims Commission was extended several times up to 1978, when it was required to close shop. In the thirty-plus years of the Commission's existence some 225 money awards were made involving a total of $818 million. The size of these awards ranged from a few hundred dollars to over $17.5 million.[105] Awards were made in response to approximately 35 percent of the claims filed. Approximately 30 percent were denied, approximately 15 percent were referred to the Court of Claims, and the remainder were disposed of in other ways.[106]

Tribal efforts to regain land continued to be dependent on suit which, until 1966, could be launched only with Congressional approval. In that year Congress passed a statute which authorized Indian tribes with governing bodies recognized by the Secretary of the Interior to file suit in federal courts.[107] Since that time the number of suits has burgeoned. The story of one of these is especially revealing in that it involved enormous amounts of land and also dramatically illustrates the role of land recovery in tribal rebirth.

c. Restitution of Land

In February of 1964 five women of the Passamaquoddy tribe were arrested by Maine troopers and booked for trespassing on land the tribe claimed belonged to them by virtue of a 1795 treaty. They and other Passamaquoddies had sought to block the construction of a road through the property, which a white developer claimed belonged to him. The tribe hired an attorney who reached an agreement with the prosecuting attorney in the trespass case that neither side would set foot on the contested property until the question of ownership had been settled. The prosecutor then set aside the charge of trespass against the five women.

Little did these five Passamaquoddy women realize that their sit-in on a

—] Passamaquoddy tribe

sand pile would set in motion one of the most complex and significant land claims cases in American history. Before the case was settled out of court several years later, the Passamaquoddy tribe and their neighbors, the Penobscot Nation, would lay claim to over twelve and a half million acres of their aboriginal territory, an area involving nearly two-thirds of the state of Maine, and would seek millions in monetary damages for trespassing.

Ironically enough, the doctrine of "discovery" operated in the Indians' favor in this case. The key to their success in achieving a negotiated settlement which involved the state of Maine, the United States government, and several lumber companies with large timber holdings in Maine, was a federal district court ruling[108] that the treaty of 1795 had been negotiated by the state (Massachusetts, the forerunner to Maine in this territory) in violation of the Indian Trade and Intercourse Act of 1790, an act which required that all Indian land transactions be negotiated through the federal government.[109] This decision, then, cast a legal shadow over all of the state's subsequent dealings involving land presumably acquired from the Passamaquoddy and Penobscot through the treaty of 1795.

After complex legal and other negotiations, maneuvers, thrusts, and counter-thrusts over more than a decade, the tribes were finally awarded $81.5 million by the federal government in 1980, which they were able to use in purchasing at market value up to 300,000 acres of publicly and privately held land. They also secured a number of additional concessions from both the state and the federal governments, including formal recognition by the federal government—an action which brought them a number of additional benefits. Thus was achieved what one member of the Penobscot Nation referred to as "the rebirth" of an Indian tribe and an Indian nation in the state of Maine.[110]

The suit of the Passamaquoddies and the Penobscots both stimulated and drew upon other eastern Indian land lawsuits based on the Indian Trade and Intercourse Acts of the early years of the federal republic. The bases on which all of these cases rested included decisively significant decisions that a) the Indian Trade and Intercourse Acts applied in such cases, since this meant that b) inasmuch as the federal government had not been involved in the initial land negotiations about which the Indians were pleading, it had to be involved in some way in their plea,[111] and c) the cases were not subject to such common shut-off valves as statutes of limitations or the legal doctrine of laches (under which a case may be thrown out of court because of undue delay in bringing it). Altogether some dozen land claims were brought by eastern Indian tribes under these conditions in a twenty-year period, most of them in the 1970s. Some of these claims resulted in land settlements similar to but much smaller than those negotiated by the Passamaquoddy and Penobscot.[112]

d. Land and the Free Exercise of Religion

> Tall remembered what the Cree leaders told him, that survival was
> their religion. —fictional character[113]

The most striking Indian victory in a land claim in which the free exercise of religion played a central role occurred in the ultimate success of the Taos Indians in securing, through an act of Congress, not the courts, sole control of 44,000 acres in the Blue Lake watershed in 1970 after being at the mercy of National Forest Service policy for 64 years. The significance of this act in the larger picture is suggested by the statement of anthropologist John Bodine that "this was the first time in the history of United States-Indian relations that a claim for land, based on the practice of aboriginal religion, successfully ended in the restoration of that land to an Indian reservation."[114]

This encouraging note is somewhat soured, however, by the realization that victory for the Taos Indians in their efforts to secure the return of the Blue Lake watershed to their control was achieved after long and arduous work in the political arena. It was also a victory without parallel in its magnitude.[115] The strong—even adamant—support of governmental property rights by the Supreme Court in the *Lyng* case eighteen years after the Taos success is, however, more representative of and authoritative for what can be expected in free exercise of religion-based land claims. In other words, appeal to the freedom of religion is not likely to add weight to such claims in American courts.

There is, however, a happy ending of sorts in the story of efforts of the Northwest California Indians to stop the building of an all-weather road through their most sacred area. The land area under litigation in *Lyng* was declared by Congress to be a part of the Siskiyou Wilderness and hence preserved from the kind of development which the Indians were resisting. Their loss in the Court was reversed by a victory in the political arena.

e. Other Rights

By virtue of their status as "domestic, dependent nations," Indian tribes and their members can also lay claim to various other rights related to and different from land rights. Tribes have the power to levy and collect taxes and are exempt generally from state taxation and, by virtue of some treaties and federal statutes, from some forms of federal taxes. Aboriginal rights, treaties, statutes, and executive orders guarantee—or are appealed to in support of—certain rights to hunt, fish and gather. And, as a result of court interpretation, tribes generally have maintained significant water rights: The "Winters Doctrine"[116] holds that the establishment of Indian reservations entailed the right to sufficient water to carry out the purposes of the reservations. In not specifying just what amount of water might be involved, this "doctrine" leaves much room for litigation. Indeed, litigation proceeds apace and public controversy continues at a slow boil over Indian water, hunting, fishing and gathering rights, powers of taxation and control (over gambling, for instance), as well as land rights. But, by and large, the stakes are highest, both economically and culturally, when land is the central issue.

5. Continuing Conquest

The white man never sleeps. —Russel Jim, Yakima[117]

The history of human affairs convinces us that it is always a misfortune to hold the position of a weaker party. —Cherokee response to the Dawes Commission[118]

While Indian lands have become part of the United States, Indian communities have neither been allowed to remain isolated as independent political entities nor have they been granted full status within the American political system. Consequently, American Indians have been forced to live within a political/legal no-man's-land from which there seems to be no possibility of extrication. —Vine Deloria[119]

American law is designed to protect property rights. How do tribal Indians fare under that law? How has the white man's law protected their property rights? The fact is that Indian tribes or nations have not done well under the property law, which is so important to and in the majority culture. Further, even property rights unique or nearly unique to Indian tribes as "domestic dependent nations" or "quasi-sovereign" entities have eroded substantially. Hence, since land has traditionally been of major significance in Indian identity and well-being, it appears that the government of the United States, by persistently reducing tribal land holdings and control over land, has continued, directly or indirectly, a policy of conquest.

At the foundation of tribal-governmental relations is Congressional supremacy—absolutism might be more appropriate, although the Supreme

strong statement

Court has distinguished between *plenary* and *absolute* power. Citing a variety of opinions, the editors and authors of *Cohen's Handbook of Federal Indian Law*, 1982 edition, state that "Perhaps the most basic principle of all Indian law . . . is that those powers which are lawfully vested in an Indian tribe are not, in general, delegated powers granted by express acts of Congress, but rather 'inherent powers of a limited sovereignty which has never been extinguished.' "[120] Nevertheless, Congress, as beneficiary of the doctrine of discovery, has the authority and the power to extinguish tribal title almost at will. The Supreme Court has seldom intervened. In addition, the effect of that Court's decisions in several recent cases has been further to limit tribal sovereignty.

Ultimate Congressional control of Indian land was first affirmed in the twentieth century in a case in which Indian claimants argued that a Congressional statute involving their land did not accord with the original treaty made between them and the United States. In this decision the Court, while affirming that "the Indian right of occupancy of tribal lands" has been understood to be "sacred, or . . . as sacred as the fee of the United States in the same lands," also affirmed Indian dependence on the federal government—the ward-guardian relationship first stated by Chief Justice Marshall in *Cherokee Nation*. Then the Court, absolving itself of any responsibility to monitor that trustee relationship in a land dispute of the sort before it, stated that "plenary authority over the tribal relations of the Indians has been exercised by Congress from the beginning, and the power has been deemed a political one, not subject to be controlled by the judicial department of the government."[121] In effect, then, the only recourse open to the Indian claimants was appeal to Congress itself.

Seen in a perspective which fuses history with constitutional doctrine—the only perspective which makes sense in dealing with American Indian law—the notion of plenary federal power over Indian affairs is, as Robert N. Clinton points out, a "legal myth."[122] Initially, in the early federal republic, Indian tribes were regarded as independent sovereign states or entities. Indians are mentioned three times in the Constitution: (1) "Indians not taxed" are excluded from the count apportioning taxes and representatives to Congress;[123] (2) language also used in the Fourteenth Amendment, paragraph 2; and (3) Congress is authorized to "regulate Commerce with foreign Nations, among the several States, and with Indian Tribes."[124] These references clearly imply that Indians are outside the boundaries of the Federal polity. However, over time and directly or indirectly, Indian tribes have been subsumed under a variety of Federal powers including the Treaty Clause,[125] the Property Clause,[126] and the war powers of Congress.[127] The treaty power was used extensively in dealing with Indian tribes for over eighty years. Treaties, while often coerced and seldom satisfactory to the Indian tribes, did constitute an acknowledgment by the United States of some degree of independence for Indian tribes. They also had (and, to some degree, still have) the force of law. However, the practice of treaty making was arbitrarily and unilaterally discontinued by the Congress in 1871. That action, along with a series of other acts—congressional, executive and judicial—in the late nineteenth century, signaled an increasing effort to undermine and even destroy Indian tribes and tribal authority. ➤ rhetoric is growing stronger here

Two Supreme Court cases illustrate this point and one of them set the stage for the full exploitation of the notion of federal plenary power over Indian affairs. In the early 1880s one Crow Dog, a Brule Sioux, murdered Spotted Tail, a well-known tribal leader. Crow Dog was punished according to tribal law. But he was also arrested and imprisoned by federal authorities and faced trial in a federal court. He sought a writ of habeas corpus on the ground that the United States did not have jurisdiction over an act committed by one tribesman over another within tribal boundaries. The Supreme Court found in *Ex Parte Crow Dog*, that the federal court was, indeed, without jurisdiction and that Crow Dog's imprisonment was illegal. A writ was issued and Crow Dog was released. A great outcry followed, Congress passed a law giving the United States authority over "major" crimes committed in Indian country,[128] and shortly thereafter Kagama, a Hoopa Indian who murdered "Ike," a fellow tribesman, and who also argued absence of federal jurisdiction, was not as lucky as Crow Dog. In *Kagama* the Supreme Court ruled that, following the Major Crimes Act, the federal Circuit Court of California did have jurisdiction and hence, that Kagama and his accomplice should be tried for their crime. The Court held, then, that the Congress had the authority to extend federal power into the internal affairs of Indian tribes; hence, tribal sovereignty was further weakened.

As ultimate sovereign, then, Congress has both the responsibility of trustee and the power of eminent domain. In effect, it wears two hats, or rather it owns two hats; it can hardly wear both of them at the same time.[129] By and large, in the past century the Supreme Court has been more impressed with the latter than the former hat—with Congressional power more than with Congressional responsibility. In a curious twist of logic, however, the trust responsibility can become a source of, rather than a check on, "plenary" power. Lurking in the background is the fundamental question of whether in Indian affairs the Congress is subject to the Constitution. This question has been most sharply focussed in cases involving clashes between the Congressional power of eminent domain and the "taking clause" of the Fifth Amendment,[130] cases in which the trust responsibility has often functioned so as to shield the federal government from liability under that clause.

Does Congress have the authority and the power to take without compensation land occupied by Indians since "time immemorial?" The Court responded in the affirmative in 1955 in another landmark decision, *Tee-Hit-Ton*. Appealing to the "taking clause," the Tlingit Indians of Alaska claimed that they had been deprived of land by the United States without adequate compensation. They also argued that at the time of European contact they were at a relatively advanced stage of land use and that their claim to aboriginal title to the land was thereby enhanced. The Supreme Court did not agree. In statements which embody the prevailing view of Congressional absolutism relative to Indian land claims the Court concluded that Indian "occupancy" of land within the United States is "permissive"—at the discretion of the sovereign nation—and that such occupancy, when "not specifically recognized as ownership by action authorized by any Congress . . . may be extinguished by Congress in its own discretion without compensation."[131] Aboriginal title proved, then, to be a thin reed.[132] The Court concluded further that the Tlingit had been, at the time of European contact, hunters and gatherers and hence, had no greater claim to aboriginal title than continental Indian tribes.

Twenty-five years later the Court reached a different conclusion. In *Sioux Nation* the Court recognized that the Congress, in unilaterally taking from the Sioux 7.3 million acres of resource-rich Black Hills land in violation of the 1868 Treaty of Fort Laramie and without just compensation, had acted not as a guardian, but as a conqueror. Still, a close look at that decision and its aftereffects reveals some sobering realities: (1) The amount of the award was based on a calculation that the land was worth $17.5 million in 1877—an amount which is probably considerably short of its actual value at that time. (2) The award by the Supreme Court of a total of $106 million (including interest figured at 5 percent per year) brought a culmination of sorts to well over 50 years of complex and frustrating legal and political actions initiated by the Sioux, actions which required, among other things, that a not inconsiderable fraction of the final award—ten percent—be paid to attorneys for the Indians. (3) The actual award of the funds depends upon the unanimous agreement among the various tribes of the Sioux Nation to accept it and upon the approval of Congress, as guardian, of the manner in which the money would finally be allocated. To date, that has not happened.[133] In the meantime, the account has grown to over $300 million.[134] (4) Most significantly, the award was a monetary one in lieu of land. The issue, as the Court understood it, and as it was brought before the Court by the Indian plaintiffs, was adequate compensation, not governmental confiscation of land. In effect, the Court held that when the government took the land without tribal consent, it did so as a guardian "transmut[ing] land into money" rather than as a sovereign exercising eminent domain.[135]

After the Court's decision was handed down in *Sioux Nation*, the more vocal Sioux maintained that what was obligatory upon the United States was the return of the land, not a monetary award. Consequently, each of the tribes that had joined together in filing the action in *Sioux Nation* rejected the monetary award.[136] The Oglala Sioux Tribe promptly brought suit against the United States to regain their lost land.[137] This suit was unsuccessful.[138] Despite all of this, the Court's decision in *Sioux Nation* does suggest that the power of Congress in Indian affairs is not totally beyond constitutional checks.

More recently the Court has held that the General Allotment Act of 1887 considerably diminished the treaty rights of the Yakima Nation to "exclusive use and benefit" of their land and to control of residence on that land.[139] The central issue in *Brendale* was the extent of Yakima authority to zone land within the reservation. Eighty percent of the reservation land is trust land, held in trust by the United States for the tribe or its individual members. The remaining twenty percent is fee land—owned in fee by both Indians and non-Indians. Tribal zoning laws applied to all fee land as well as trust land. Yakima County zoning laws did not apply to trust land within the Yakima reservation but did apply to fee land. A conflict existed between these zoning restrictions. Two non-Indian fee owners were granted building permits by the county but denied such permits by the tribe. Concluding that to apply tribal zoning ordinances to non-members is to impose "a sort of equitable servitude" on them, the Court supported the superior claim of the county ordinances. The Court thereby concluded that "the Yakima Nation no longer retains the 'exclusive use and benefit' of all the land within the reservation boundaries established by the Treaty," thereby diminishing tribal control over land within tribal boundaries.[140]

Hence, tribal holding and control of land continue to be eroded. The extent of the erosion is suggested in cases such as those cited here. It is also dramatically evident in the fact that, even since the passage of the Indian Reorganization Act in 1934, an act which reversed the policy of the General Allotment Act under which Indians lost control over approximately two-thirds of the land they had controlled in 1887, Indians have lost almost two million acres of their land by condemnation proceedings alone.[141]

The truth is that the Supreme Court has ultimately left the fate of Native Americans in the hands of the Congress or the legislative branch. As the history of Indian-governmental relations clearly demonstrates, that indeed amounts to a very uncertain fate. Since the end of the treaty making period—an end brought about by Congressional fiat—official policy toward Indian tribes has undergone more than one complete reversal: the policy of assimilation which extended for over fifty years until the enactment of the Indian Reorganization Act in 1934, which accorded some degree of tribal autonomy and extended through the Roosevelt administration. Autonomy was replaced by termination during the Eisenhower administration. Termination was reversed under the Kennedy administration. The policy of self-determination was instituted under President Nixon in 1970 and has more or less continued to the present time. These directions and redirections of federal policy suggests that the wind can change at most any time.

6. Continuing Contest: The Issue of Tribal Sovereignty

This land is my land; this land is your land.—Woody Guthrie

Whereas, the lands and waters, forests, fish, game, wild rice, fruits and berries of mother earth are the most valuable and revered cultural and economic asset of Indian people; and Whereas, these assets must be preserved for the use and benefit of ourselves, our children, our children's children and their children after them . . . —Conservation Code, Lac Courte Oreilles Chippewa Indians[142]

Without the land, tribes could not survive as spiritual, cultural, political, and economic entities. —Sharon O'Brien[143]

Oka was unheard of in the United States until the summer of 1990. Then news came of armed conflict there between Mohawk "warriors" and Canadian soldiers. This conflict erupted in a controversy over expansion of a municipal golf course on land the Mohawks claimed as their own. Failing to resolve the conflict in the courts or through discussions with public officials, some Mohawks blockaded the bridge which is the main artery to Montreal from the south. There followed a standoff between the Mohawks and local police officials, a decision by the Canadian government to deploy up to 3,700 soldiers to Oka and other areas inhabited by Mohawks, and the death of one of those soldiers. This series of conflicts exacerbated tensions, not only between Mohawks and the larger white community, but also within the Mohawk community itself. It also led, as such events do, to various studies and reports by official groups. The conclusions of one of these reports is worth citing because it highlights underlying concepts and conflicts about land and sovereignty which also characterize the scene in the United States:

> Across the country [Canada] the land rights of indigenous people have become intertwined with questions regarding residual sovereignty that may or may not be recognized or entrenched under the Constitution. Indigenous people cannot see how they can exercise any real collective land rights without jurisdiction over their own communities. The position taken by the Longhouse people [one of the traditional groups within the Mohawk community] suggests, on the other hand, an unqualified assertion of sovereignty, making constitutional reform irrelevant from this perspective. . . . The holistic worldview of many indigenous cultures means that concepts such as land and self-government or sovereignty are often inseparable.

The report goes on to stress the Mohawk insistence, in this instance, on the linkage of land with sovereignty issues.[144] This issue of tribal sovereignty also hovers in the background, and sometimes in the foreground, in much of the conflict over land in the United States.

On balance, Indian resort to the courts to protect or regain control of land has been less than a success story; it has not put a stop to the erosion of tribal land holdings and control that has gone on ever since Europeans first settled on them. Even the seemingly happy story of the Passamaquoddies and the Penobscots, recounted above,[145] has produced ambiguous results for the tribes. They have improved their economic status and thereby gained more voice in the larger political arena. But they have also experienced divisions and continuing erosion of their cultural identity and coherence and their sovereignty. Their status is more akin to that of a municipality than an independent or even "quasi-sovereign" nation. If the "Maine tribes had a political and social culture to preserve through the exercise of self-government," one informed observer notes, "then the settlement must be considered a defeat."[146]

Nonetheless, possession, recovery and control of land have become increasingly more important to tribal Indians in their renewed struggle for political power and sovereignty in the late twentieth century. "It is the demand for land," Stephen Cornell points out, "that leaves Native Americans on reservations and thereby contributes to their survival as nations. . . ." Such a land base helps preserve tribal identity and, in a world in which their power is very limited, "ultimately gives bargaining power to . . . tribes."[147]

7. Conclusion

Seen within the larger arena of the American polity, the Indian struggle to maintain or to regain land and to strengthen tribal sovereignty may seem as insignificant as the bit of dirt in a medicine pouch held up as evidence before the majestic bar of a federal court. It is, nonetheless, impressive in its persistence and prophetic in its implications for that polity. Indian resort to the courts in land claims cases has been fraught with frustration. Yet efforts continue. Control of land is seen as essential to control of culture—to nationhood.

It should not be difficult for other Americans to identify with peoples for whom specific land areas (soil, dirt) are integrally significant—so much so that their very identity and existence as unique peoples is threatened, or, at a minimum, greatly altered, by loss of control over those areas. Edward T. Linenthal has graphically spelled out the importance to American identity and national pride of certain "sacred ground." No case illustrates this better than an instance in which the Congress used its power of eminent domain to appropriate private property on the site of the Gettysburg Battlefield, an act which was upheld by the Supreme Court. This conversion of private property into public land was justified in the name of national honor, memory, unity and survival. Hence, there "can be no well founded doubt" that the proposed use of this private property "is a public one," the Supreme Court unanimously declared. This ground, the Court elaborated, is "so closely connected with the welfare of the Republic itself as to be within the powers granted Congress by the Constitution for the purpose of protecting and preserving the whole country." This action, then, "touches the heart and comes home to the imagination of every citizen, and greatly tends to enhance his love and respect" for the country.[148]

While the courts and Americans generally might have difficulty in seeing dirt in a medicine pouch as similar to the embodiment of property rights in a title, they might possibly grasp that it symbolizes for the Indians involved the very ground of communal being and hence well-being. What would remain, then, would be a balancing of conflicting claims and interests. Such a balancing might well be guided by the spirit of the Northwest Ordinance of 1787: "The utmost good faith shall always be observed towards the Indians, their lands and property shall never be taken from them without their consent."[149]

Seen in historical perspective, which includes 500 years of conquest, exploitation, suppression, and attempted eradication, one might well conclude that the remarkable fact is that not only do Native Americans continue to survive in this country, but that they can also vigorously pursue their rights—due in part to the fact that the country has recognized those rights, however grudgingly. Terms—even euphemisms—such as "discovery," "allotment," "relocation," and "termination"—capture events that are embarrassing to a nation which frequently pledges liberty and justice for all. Still, while bent on "reduction" or even destruction of the native peoples that very nation also, through treaties and treaty substitutes, made many promises to those peoples. The most significant of those promises, "the essential promise," is the guarantee of what Professor Charles F. Wilkinson calls "a measured separatism on their reservation homelands."[150] And many tribes and reservations have survived destruction or disintegration and persist in claiming what was promised to them. Such claims pose more of a moral threat to settled American myths than an economic threat to American property interests. Will the nation abide by its promises? While the answer appears to be more no than yes, claims continue to be filed and the courts continue to deal with them. In fact, very few other modern nations have afforded their indigenous peoples such an ongoing forum for pressing such claims. Indeed, perhaps the most amazing thing about Indian-governmental relations in this country is the fact they are characterized by an unparalleled volume of litigation involving land claims, sovereignty issues, and related matters. These claims span more than 150 years.[151] Hence, while the story of Indian land claims is replete with dark chapters only occasionally relieved by light episodes, it is there for the telling and it is far from a closed book.[152]

This is not to downplay the fact that many, if not most, such claims have not received fair and even-handed treatment. Nor is it to forget that property rights are extensions of power. Power is channeled and to some degree controlled as these rights are spelled out in laws and policies. While

Indian claims relative to land may be enhanced through patient pursuit of rights embodied in such laws and policies, a shift in power relationships can also enhance such claims. Such a shift is sought in the stress on the sovereignty of Indian tribes[153] and through related appeals to international, over and above national, tribunals.[154]

Nonetheless, perhaps one should not entirely dismiss the importance even to power relations of what might be called the moral factor in Indian-white relations in this country. The words of the Northwest Ordinance, as pious, platitudinous, and hypocritical as they may sound today, do resonate for some Americans, Americans who can and sometimes do make a difference in enhancing the power of a relatively powerless people. In an even more ultimate sense such a shift of power may occur through an expanding awareness among all Americans of the value of land, of dirt, as a spiritual resource. A fundamental shift in perspective may come with a seemingly simple awareness that a deed is not the dirt, a title is not the land, property is rights not the soil, and "a map is never the country itself."[155]

While the courts have not been in the business of acknowledging the value of land as a spiritual resource, an increasing number of Americans do acknowledge and appreciate it. True, the number is still a distinct minority of the American people, but it is a growing minority. And, as Chief Seattle reminded Americans more than a century ago, even the majority does not walk alone on the land.

Table of Court Cases

Attakai v United States, 746 F. Supp. 1395 (D. Ariz. 1990). Navajo claim that removal from home land in connection with governmental enforcement of the Navajo-Hopi Land Settlement Act violated their free exercise of religion denied. Affadavit of Mae Tso. (See *Manybeads*.) *Lyng* precedential.

Badoni v Higginson, 638 F. 2d 172 (10th Cir. 1980); *cert. denied*. Navajo claims that inundation of Lake Powell and flooding of Rainbow Bridge area violated their free exercise of religious rights denied. (See Carl W. Luckert, *Navajo Mountain and Rainbow Bridge Religion*, Flagstaff: Museum of Northern Arizona, 1977).

Brendale v Confederated Tribes and Bands of the Yakima Nation, 492 U.S. 408 (1989). The Yakima Nation does not have the authority to restrict the use of fee land on the reservation which is owned by nonmembers of the tribe.

The Cherokee Nation v The State of Georgia, 30 U.S. 1 (1831). Inasmuch as the Cherokee Nation is not a foreign state (but a "domestic dependent nation") the Court does not have jurisdiction, under Art. III, Sec. 2 of the Constitution, to decide a dispute over land between the State of Georgia and the Cherokee Nation.

County of Yakima v Confederated Tribes and Bands of the Yakima Indian Nation, 112 S. Ct. 683 (1992). Allows states to impose an ad valorem tax on fee-patented lands owned by Indians and permits foreclosure of such parcels.

Duro v Reina, 110 S. Ct. 2053 (1990). Within their territorial jurisdiction, tribal courts do not have jurisdiction over Indians committing crimes who do not belong to the tribe.

Ex Parte Crow Dog, 109 U.S. 556 (1883). Federal Court does not have jurisdiction over crime of murder committed by one tribesman against another in tribal territory. Reversed in *Kagama* after passage of the Major Crimes Act.

Fletcher v Peck, 10 U.S. 87 (1810). Title of the State of Georgia superior to Indian title by virtue of the doctrine of discovery.

Frank Fools Crow v Gullet, 541 F. Supp. 785 (D. S.D. 1982); 706 F. 2d 856 (8th Cir. 1983), *cert. denied*. Cheyenne and Sioux blocked in their efforts to stop the further development of a state park on sacred Bear Butte in South Dakota.

United States v Gettysburg Electric Railway Company, Supreme Court of the U.S., Nos. 599 and 629, October Term, 1895. Congress within its authority to use right of eminent domain to possess private land for public purpose on site of Gettysburg battle.

Johnson and Graham's Lease v McIntosh, 21 U.S. 543 (1823). Case in which the doctrine of discovery was spelled out in some detail by the Court.

Lone Wolf v Hitchcock, 187 U.S. 553 (1903). Congress has plenary authority over tribal Indians, which authority is not subject to control by the courts.

Lyng v Northwest Indian Cemetery Protective Association, 485 U.S. 439 (1988). Northwest California Indians' attempt to stop the completion of a Forest Service road through their most sacred area denied.

Millirrpum v Nabalco Pty. Ltd. and the Commonwealth of Australia, 17 *Federal Law Review*, 141 (1971). Aboriginal land claims upheld.

Montana v United States, 450 U.S. 544 (1981). Indian tribal assertion of civil jurisdiction over nonmembers on non-Indian land within the reservation is inconsistent with their dependent status as wards.

Narragansett Tribe of Indians v Southern R.I. Land Dev. Corp., 418 F. Supp. 798 (D. R.I. 1976). Limited gains in land and money for the Narragansett Tribe.

Navajo Medicine Men's Association v Block, D. D.C., 1981, district court opinion published in *Indian Law Reporter*, 8: 3073–79. See *Wilson*.

Northwest Indian Cemetery Protective Ass'n v Peterson, 565 F. Supp. 586 (N. D. Calif. 1983). See *Lyng*.

Oglala Sioux Tribe v United States, 650 F. 2d 140 (1981), cert. denied, 1985. Following Supreme Court decision in *Sioux Nation* awarding money in lieu of land, the Oglala Sioux tribe brought suit to quiet their title to seven million acres in the Black Hills; Court dismissed suit because Congress, by enacting the Indian Claims Commission Act, established the exclusive remedy for tribe's claim under Fifth Amendment of an unconstitutional taking of land by the United States.

Oliphant v Suquamish Indian Tribe, 435 U.S. 191 (1978). Absent a specific congressional act, the jurisdiction of tribal courts does not extend to non-Indians against whom criminal charges have been filed.

Passamaquoddy Tribe v Morton, 388 F. Supp. 649 (1975), affm'd, 528 F. 2nd 370, 1st Cir. (1975). State violated the Indian Trade and Intercourse Act of 1790; hence, Indian tribe has standing under that Act to make claims on the State of Maine.

Sequoyah v Tennessee Valley Authority, 480 F. Supp. 608 (E. D. Tenn. 1979); 620 F. 2d 1159 (6th Circ. 1980), cert. denied. Attempt by Eastern Cherokee to stop the impoundment of the Little Tennessee River, and hence the flooding of sacred sites, behind the Tellico Dam, denied.

Tee-Hit-Ton v United States, 348 U.S. 272 (1955). Tee-Hit-Ton Indians not entitled to compensation under the Fifth Amendment for the taking by the United States of certain timber lands allegedly belonging to them.

United States v Kagama, 118 U.S. 375 (1886). Congress, as guardian, has authority over the internal affairs of Indian tribes in the Major Crimes Act. Kagama, accused of murdering a fellow tribesman in tribal territory, subject to jurisdiction of federal court. (*Ex Parte Crow Dog* reversed.)

United States v Mazurie, 419 U.S. 544 (1975). Tribe has authority to regulate commerce within tribal boundaries if the Congress has delegated such authority.

United States v Means, 585 F. 2d 404 (8th Cir. 1988). Absent Forest

Service act of direct prohibition of religious rites or denial of access to a site in the Black Hills for temporary use, Indian claimants did not demonstrate a burden on their free exercise of religion rights; district court reversed.

United States v Sioux Nation, 448 U.S. 371 (1980). The 1877 Act which divested the Sioux Nation of the Black Hills effected a taking of property, and that taking implied an obligation on the part of the government to make just compensation to the Sioux Nation, including an award of interest.

Wilson v Block, 708 F. 2d 735 (D. C. Cir. 1983), *cert. denied*. Three suits were combined in *Wilson: Hopi Indian Tribe v. Block, Navajo Medicine Men's Association v. Block*, and *Wilson*. The Hopi and Navajo free exercise of religion claims were denied in this case, which involved the issue of the expansion of a ski resort on National Forest land in an area regarded by them as sacred.

Winters v United States, 207 U.S. 564 (1908). The establishment of Indian reservations entailed the right to sufficient water to carry out the purposes of the reservation.

Notes

1. As reported by Moravian missionary John Heckewelder in "An account of the History, Manners, and Customs of the Indian Nations Who Once Inhabited Pennsylvania and the Neighboring States" (Philadelphia: A. Small, 1819). Reprinted in *Memoirs of the Historical Society of Pennsylvania* (Philadelphia: J. B. Lippincott & Co., 1876), vol. 12, p. 79.

2. Letter "To my honored kind friend Mr. Winthrop, Governor, at Hartford," May 28, 1664. Reprinted in *The Complete Writings of Roger Williams* (New York: Russell & Russell, 1963), vol. 6, p. 319. For an insightful discussion of Williams's understanding of the land issue see Conor Cruise O'Brien, *God Land: Reflections on Religion and Nationalism* (Cambridge: Harvard University Press, 1988), pp. 30-33.

3. "Of Property," in the second *Treatise of Government*, ch. V, § 26. See "Two Treatises of Government," in *The Works of John Locke*, (1823 reprint, Aalen: Scientia Verlag, 1963), 5: 353.

4. "Constitution, Court, Indian Tribes," *American Bar Foundation Research Journal*, 1987, p. 14.

5. *Navajo Medicine Men's Association v. Block*, D. D. C., 1981, district court opinion published in *Indian Law Reporter*, 8: 3073-79, background material in "Official Transcript of Hearing in the United States District Court for the District of Columbia," May 29, 1981, p. 26, unpublished; also, among the other unpublished materials gener-

ated in connection with this case, see various affidavits, including especially, that of Norris Nez, February 20, 1981 ("Each medicineman carries a pouch of mountain dirt. Dirt from each of the four sacred mountains is placed there."), and the "Memorandum of Points and Authorities in Support of Plaintiffs' Motion for Summary Judgment," n. d., n. pp. The "Memorandum" points out that as early as 1868, in treaty negotiations between the Navajo and the United States, the Navajo laid claim to the sanctity of their four mountains. "When the Navajo were first created," their spokesman said, "four mountains were pointed out to us . . . inside of which we should live [and] that was to be our country . . . " (Citing "Proceedings of Council with the Navajo Indians," May 28, 1868, National Archives.) The "Memorandum" also adds that the modern–day Great Seal and flag of the Navajo Tribe depict the four sacred mountains surrounding Navajo land. (Court cases cited in this essay are listed below. I have also used unpublished materials such as those cited here.)

6. As quoted under the fourth definition of "deed" in *The Compact Edition of the Oxford English Dictionary* (New York: Oxford University Press, 1971), vol. 1, p. 667. Lawrence M. Friedman points out that "Some of the greatest American trials, in terms of cost, time, and acrimony, have been trials over title to land" (*A History of American Law*, 2d ed. [New York: Simon & Schuster, 1985], p. 243).

7. "Transcript of Trial," unpublished, p. 74; court decision published as *Northwest Indian Cemetery Protective Association v. Peterson*, 565 F. Supp. 586 (N. D. Calif. 1983).

8. Robert Jim, former chairman, Yakima Nation, referring to Mt. Adams, quoted in Sharon O'Brien, *American Indian Tribal Governments* (Norman: University of Oklahoma Press, 1989), p. 217.

9. "Navaho," writes Gladys A. Reichard, "have an extraordinary interest in geography" (*Navaho Religion: A Study of Symbolism*, Bollingen Series [Princeton: Princeton University Press, 1963], p. 19).

10. From affidavits of Navajo medicine men and women in connection with *Navajo Medicine Men's Association v. Block*, 1981, district court opinion published in *Indian Law Reporter*, 8: 3073–79.

11. See Dorothea J. Theodoratus, Joseph L. Chartkoff, and Kerry K. Chartkoff, "Cultural Resources of the Chimney Rock Section, Gasquet-Orleans Road, Six Rivers National Forest," United States Department of Agriculture—Forest Service, Six Rivers National Forest, Contract No. 53-9158-8-6045, 1979.

12. "Tolowa Notes," *American Anthropologist*, 34 (1932): 256.

13. "The Religion of the Indians of California," *University of California Publications in American Archaeology and Ethnology*, 4, no. 6 (1907): 328. While Kroeber used the typical "he," he also pointed out that the majority of the shamans among Northwest California Indians were women, p. 329.

14. Robert Spott and Alfred L. Kroeber, "Yurok Narratives," *University of California Publications in American Archaeology and Ethnology*, 35, no. 9 (1935): 160.

15. "Tobacco among the Karuk Indians of California," United States Bureau of Ethnology *Bulletin*, no. 94 (1932): 8.

16. Ibid., 233, 247.

17. See Alfred L. Kroeber and E. W. Gifford, "World Renewal: A Cult System of Native California," *University of California Anthropological Records*, 13, no. 1 (1949): 3.

18. Ibid., 22.

19. Ibid., 28.

20. Thomas Buckley, "The 'High Country': A Summary of New Data relating to the Significance of Certain Properties in the Belief Systems of Northwestern California Indians," Prepared for the United States Dept. of Agriculture—Forest Service, Six Rivers National Forest, Eureka, Ca. 1976, p. 3.

21. The Supreme Court majority in *Lyng v Northwest Indian Cemetery Protective Association*, 485 U.S. 439 (1988): 451–52.

22. Robert T. Coulter and Steven M. Tulberg, "Indian Land Rights," in *The Aggressions of Civilization: Federal Indian Policy since the 1880's*, eds. Sandra L. Caldwalader and Vine Deloria Jr. (Philadelphia: Temple University Press, 1984), p. 186.

23. The Hopi Indian Tribe in a case linked with the Navajo case in *Wilson v Block*, 708 F. 2d 735 (D. C. Cir. 1983), *cert. denied*; other Navajo in an earlier case involving the rainbow bridge and Lake Powell (*Badoni v. Higginson*, 638 F. 2d 172 [10th Circ. 1980], *cert. denied*); Cherokee in their attempt to stop the flooding of the Little Tennessee River above the Tellico Dam (*Sequoyah v Tennessee Valley Authority*, 480 F. Supp. 608 [E. D. Tenn. 1979], 620 F. 2d 1159 [6th Cir. 1980], *cert. denied*; and Cheyenne and Sioux in their efforts to stop the further development of a state park on the slopes of the sacred Bear Butte (*Frank Fools Crow v Gullet*, 541 F. Supp. 785 [D. S. D. 1982], 706 F. 2d 856 [8th Cir. 1983], *cert. denied*. All of these cases involved appeal to the free exercise clause of the First Amendment in an effort to protect sacred sites from destruction or desecration.

24. 485 U.S. 439 (1988): 452–53.

25. Among the Navajo, Amos Rapaport notes, "[s]ome things are communally owned: no individual can own timber, water or saltbush. Farm and range 'belong' to the family through 'inherited use ownership' " ("The Pueblo and the Hogan: A Cross-cultural Comparison of Two Responses to an Environment," in *Shelter and Society*, ed. Paul Oliver [New York: Praeger, 1969], p. 76). Joseph G. Jorgensen points out that "powerful and tenacious legacies about land from pre-Contact society are Indian versions of concepts that are similar to the English law concepts of *stewardship* and *usufruct*." However, he adds, "No American Indian society recognized forms of land ownership in which owners could alienate the land" ("Land is Cultural, So Is a Commodity: The Locus of Differences among Indians, Cowboys, Sod-busters, and Environmentalists," *Journal of Ethnic Studies*, 12, no. 3 [1985]: 15).

26. The white man, observed a Seneca Indian, may be interested in owning the land or in contemplating its beauty but the Indian first of all asks, "where are my medicines?" Ake Hultkrantz states in this connection that "the Indian veneration of nature is specific, not general" ("Feelings for Nature among North American Indians," in *Belief and Worship in Native North America*, ed. Christopher Vecsey [Syracuse: Syracuse University Press, 1981], p. 122). See also Christopher Vecsey's statement that the Indians love "particular locations, particular aspects of their environment" ("American Indian Environmental Religions," in *American Indian Environments: Ecological Issues in Native American History*, eds. Christopher Vecsey and Robert W. Venables [Syracuse: Syracuse University Press, 1980], p. 25).

27. Once designated by the Government as Navajo-Hopi joint use land it had become, by Congressional act in 1974, Hopi land (*Statutes at Large of the United States of America*, 88: 93rd Cong., 2d sess., P. L. 93–351, Dec. 22, 1974, p. 1712).

28. From an unpublished affidavit, dated June 15, 1988, taken in connection with *Attakai v. United States*, 746 F. Supp. 1395 (D. Ariz. 1990). Tso's understanding of the relationship between humans and the land is reminiscent of that of the Australian Abo-

rigines. After hearing testimony and examining evidence concerning the Aborigines' view of the land, an Australian judge concluded in a well-known land claims case that "it seems easier to say that the clan belongs to the land than that the land belongs to the clan" (*Milirrpum v Nabalco Pty. Ltd. and the Commonwealth of Australia*, 17 *Federal Law Review*, 141 [1971]: 270-71).

29. See J. C. Smith, "The Concept of Native Title," *University of Toronto Law Journal*, 24 (1974): 6.

30. "The Becoming of the Native: Man in America before Columbus," in *America in 1492: The World of the Indian Peoples before the Arrival of Columbus*, ed. Alvin M. Josephy Jr. (New York: Alfred A. Knopf, 1992), p. 14.

31. David Beer Quinn, ed., *The Roanoke Voyages, 1584-1590: Documents to Illustrate the English Voyages to North America under the Patent Granted to Walter Raleigh in 1584* (London: For the Hakluyt Society, 1955), 1: 82, for Raleigh. The Gilbert quote is taken from *Johnson and Graham's Lease v McIntosh*, 21 U.S. 543 (1823), p. 577.

32. "Moreover I will appoint a place for my People Israel, and I will plant them, that they may dwell in a place of their OWN, and MOVE NO MORE" (translation quoted by Cotton).

33. John Cotton, "God's Promise to His Plantations" (London, 1634; reprinted in Boston, 1686), pp. 4-5.

34. John Winthrop, "General Considerations for the Plantation in New England, with an Answer to Several Objections" (London, 1629), reprinted in *Winthrop Papers* (Boston: The Massachusetts Historical Society, 1931), 2: 117-21.

35. See Ruth Barnes Moynihan, "The Patent and the Indians," *American Indian Culture and Research Journal*, 2, no. 1 (1977): n. 23.

36. Cotton, "God's Promise to His Plantations," p. 19. Cf. the instructions given by the Council of the London Virginia Company to the "first adventurers" in 1606: "In all your passages you must have great care not to offend the naturals, if you can eschew it." Trade with them first, before "they perceive you mean to plant among them." (Quoted in Charles C. Royce, *Indian Land Cessions in the United States*, Eighteenth Annual Report of the Bureau of American Ethnology, 1896-97 [Washington, D.C., 1899], Part 2, p. 563.)

37. Daniel Gookin (London, 1674). See *Historical Collections of the Indians in New England* with notes by Jeffrey H. Fiske (Towtaid: n. p., 1970), p. 141.

38. See Francis Jennings, *The Invasion of America: Indians, Colonization and the Cant of Conquest* (Chapel Hill: University of North Carolina Press, 1975), p. 83.

39. Locke, "Of Property," ch. V, § 49, p. 366.

40. See Robert A. Williams Jr., "Documents of Barbarism: The Contemporary Legacy of European Racism and Colonialism in the Narrative Traditions of Federal Indian Law," *Arizona Law Review*, 31, no. 2 (1989): 237-78 and his *The American Indian in Western Legal Thought: Discourses of Conquest* (New York: Oxford University Press 1990).

41. "Of Property," ch. V, § 34, p. 357.

42. Ibid., ch. V, § 31, p. 356.

43. ch. V, § 37, pp. 359-60.

44. See Robert N. Clinton, "The Proclamation of 1763: Colonial Prelude to Two Centuries of Federal-State Conflict over the Management of Indian Affairs," *Boston University Law Review*, 69 (1989): 331, including n. 5.

45. James Warren Springer correctly points out that scholars have tended to base

their generalizations about English attitudes toward Indian land rights on Puritan statements rather than on actual court records. The latter show that Puritan acknowledgment of Indian land rights is evident in the fact that Indians had access to courts, could sue and be awarded compensation for trespass, and were in some cases even granted fee simple title to land. See Springer, "American Indians and the Law of Real Property in Colonial New England," *American Journal of Legal History*, 30 (1986): 25–58. Scholars have also tended to ignore or underplay the importance of the Royal Proclamation of 1763, in which George III acknowledged Indian sovereignty over large areas—chiefly west of the Appalachians—and sought to centralize authority for dealing with Indians, including land transactions, in the Crown. The Proclamation, while only of slight influence in American law, has been of considerable importance in Canadian law. Furthermore, in recognizing Indian sovereignty and insisting upon centralized authority, it set a precedent for the federal government in the United States. (For a detailed treatment of the Proclamation, see Clinton, "The Proclamation of 1763.")

46. The words of Drake are from his "The World Encompassed," as quoted in Herbert E. Bolton, "The Plate of Brass," in *Drake's Plate of Brass: Evidence of the Visit of Francis Drake to California in the Year 1579* (Berkeley: California Historical Society, 1953), p. 9. The Biddle account is reproduced in Vernon E. Carstensen, ed., *The Public Lands: Studies in the History of the Public Domain* (Madison: University of Wisconsin Press, 1963), p. xiv.

47. Gregory Evans Dowd, *A Spirited Resistance: The North American Indian Struggle for Unity, 1745–1815* (Baltimore: Johns Hopkins Press, 1992), p. 23, quoting from a letter from Captain Raymond to La Jonquiere, Fort Miami, Jan. 5, 1750.

48. Carstensen, *The Public Lands*, p. xv.

49. *Fletcher v Peck* 10 U.S. 87 (1810), pp. 142–43. Emphasis added. See Williams, *The American Indian in Western Legal Thought*, pp. 308–09.

50. *Fletcher*, 122–24. This case is described by Petra T. Shattuck and Jill Norgren as being "best known in law as the case first used by the Court to extol the sanctity of vested rights in property . . . " (*Partial Justice: Federal Indian Law in a Liberal Constitutional System* [Oxford: Berg, 1991], p. 30).

51. *Johnson and Graham's Lease v McIntosh*, 21 U.S. 543 (1823), p. 573.

52. The land in dispute was part of the land Virginia claimed until the state ceded it to the federal government in 1784. Subsequently, following the decisive victory of General Anthony Wayne at the Battle of Fallen Timbers in 1794, the Indians who occupied the land were forced to cede it to the federal government.

53. *Johnson*, p. 574.

54. Ibid., 587–88. In *Johnson*, some say, Marshall was bent upon developing an "Americanized law of real property." (See Shattuck and Norgren, *Partial Justice*, p. 34 and p. 64, n. 79.)

55. *Notes on the State of Virginia*, 1787, ed. William Paden (Chapel Hill: University of North Carolina Press, 1955), p. 96.

56. *Democracy in America*, 1835, edited by Henry Reeve, as revised by Francis Bowen (New York: Vintage Books, 1954), vol. 1, ch. 8, p. 369.

57. See Lawrence Russel Barsh, "Indian Land Claims Policy in the United States," *North Dakota Law Review*, 58 (1982): 7.

58. For details see Royce, *Indian Land Cessions*. On the significance of the doctrine of discovery see the Introduction to Royce by Cyrus Thomas.

59. As quoted in John G. Neihardt, *Black Elk Speaks: Being the Life Story of a Holy Man of the Oglala Sioux* (Lincoln: University of Nebraska Press, 1961), pp. 198-200. Cf. Raymond J. De Mallie, *The Sixth Grandfather: Black Elk's Teachings Given to John G. Neihardt* (Lincoln: University of Nebraska Press, 1984), pp. 290-91.

60. In Ivan Doig, *Dancing at the Rascal Fair* (New York: Harper & Row, 1987; Harper Perennial, 1988), p. 89.

61. See Roy M. Robbins, *Our Landed Heritage: The Public Domain, 1776-1936* (Princeton: Princeton University Press, 1942), p. 6.

62. Royce, *Indian Land Cessions*, p. 634.

63. *Journals of the Continental Congress*, 5 (1784): 324; draft dated April 27, 1784 in *The Writings of Thomas Jefferson*, ed. John Leicester Ford, 3 (1894): 475-83.

64. John Wesley Powell, *Report on the Lands of the Arid Region of the United States, with a More Detailed Account of the Lands of Utah*. 45th Cong., 2d sess., H. R. Exec. Doc. no. 73 (1878), p. 39. "Arid" was understood by Powell to involve that area west of the isohytel line of twenty inches where the mean annual rainfall is less than the twenty inches normally necessary for unirrigated crops.

65. See Wallace Stegner, *The American West as Living Space* (Ann Arbor: University of Michigan Press, 1987), pp. 11-12.

66. There are 6,000 volumes of cadastral survey notes and 100,000 survey plats in the official records. These records contain the original title evidence to approximately one billion acres of public domain now in private hands and 400 million acres of land still in the public domain. (See Earl G. Harrington, "Cadastral Surveys for the Public Lands of the United States," in Carstensen, ed., *The Public Lands*, pp. 35-41.)

67. The practice of surveying the land by points of the compass and recording the results did not originate with the founders of the new nation. As William Cronon notes, "Whereas the earliest deeds in New England tended to describe land in terms of its topography and use . . . later deeds described land in terms of lots held by adjacent owners and marked territories using the surveyors abstractions of points of the compass and metes and bounds" (*Changes in the Land: Indians, Colonists, and the Ecology of New England* [New York: Hill & Wang, 1983], p. 74).

68. Ibid.

69. Quoted in Paul Brodeur, *Restitution: The Land Claims of the Mashpee, Passamaquoddy, and Penobscot Indians of New England* (Boston: Northeastern University Press, 1985), p. 22.

70. In O'Brien, *Tribal Governments*, p. 57.

71. As quoted in *Oxford English Dictionary*, compact edition, vol. 1, p. 667, "deed, 4."

72. Robbins, *Our Landed Heritage*, p. 91.

73. *Statutes at Large of the United States of America*, 5, 27th Cong, 1st sess. (1841), ch. 16, pp. 453-58, quotation on p. 458. Emphasis added.

74. Ibid. 26th Cong, 1st sess. (1840), ch. 32, p. 382, and vol. 4, 18th Cong., 1st sess. (1824), ch. 154, p. 39, e. g.

75. Ibid., 37th Cong., 2d sess. (1862), ch. 75, p. 393.

76. See Cronon, *Changes in the Land*, e. g.

77. Ibid., p. 63, n. 14, and p. 185; Nathaniel B. Shurtleff, ed., *Records of the Governor and Company of Massachusetts Bay* (Boston: M. White, 1853), pp. 3, 281.

78. *Lying Down Together: Law, Metaphor, and Theology* (Madison: University of Wisconsin Press, 1985), p. 96.

79. Quoted in Everett Dick, *The Lure of the Land: A Social History of the Public Lands from the Articles of Confederation to the New Deal* (Lincoln: University of Nebraska Press, 1970), p. 2.

80. Black Hawk in 1833, in *Black Hawk: An Autobiography,* ed. Donald Jackson, (Urbana: University of Illinois Press, 1955), p. 114.

81. As quoted in Lawrence M. Friedman, *A History of American Law,* 2d ed. (New York: Simon & Schuster, 1985), p. 234.

82. Dick, *The Lure of the Land,* p. 1.

83. As quoted in Morton J. Horwitz, *The Transformation of American Law, 1780–1860* (Cambridge: Harvard University Press, 1977), p. 174, n. 1.

84. Ibid., p. 31.

85. As quoted in Dick, *The Lure of the Land,* p. 5.

86. See Friedman, *A History of American Law,* p. 413, and Paul M. Kurtz, "Nineteenth Century Anti-Entrepreneurial Nuisance Injunctions—Avoiding The Chancellor," *William and Mary Law Review,* 17 (1976): 621–70.

87. *Religion in Essence and Manifestation,* trans. J. E. Turner (New York: Harper & Row, 1963), p. 210 and pp. 355–56 on sacrifice of property; cf. David Chidester on "negotiated claims on the ownership of symbols as claims to their power" in "Saving the Children by Killing Them: Redemptive Sacrifice in the Ideologies of Jim Jones and Ronald Reagan," *Religion and American Culture: A Journal of Interpretation,* 1, no. 2 (1991): 177–201, and, on the gift, Lewis Hyde, *The Gift: Imagination and the Erotic Life of Property* (New York: Random House Vintage Books, 1979).

88. The great chief Tecumseh is reported to have exploded at the notion when confronted with it: "Sell the land! Why not sell the air, the clouds, the great sea as well as the land?" (as quoted in Randolph C. Downes, "Land, Indian Concept of Ownership of," *Dictionary of American History,* rev. ed. [New York: Scribners, 1976] vol. 4, p. 90). He and his brother—Tenskwatawa, "The Prophet,"—staunchly resisted land cessions to the whites and opposed those Indian leaders who made them (see Dowd, *A Spirited Resistance,* pp. 138–41). Encounter with Anglo-Americans and their views of land tenure may have led Tecumseh, however, to embrace aspects of their notion of ownership. Land could not be owned in the traditional view. Yet, in conflict with his white adversaries, Tecumseh asserted a kind of Indian ownership of the land they sought (see R. David Edmunds, *Tecumseh and the Quest for Indian Leadership* [Boston: Little, Brown & Co., 1984], pp. 97–98, 109). Many Seneca objected to the sale of their land to the State of New York, and Handsome Lake, the Seneca "prophet," was among the foremost objectors (see Anthony F. C. Wallace, *The Death and Rebirth of the Seneca* [New York: Vintage, 1972], p. 259). The Cayuse Chief Pee-o-pee-o-max-a-max, when he was offered trinkets, blankets and other objects for land at the Walla Walla Treaty Council of 1855, responded incredulously: "Goods and Earth are not equal: goods are for using on the Earth. I do not know where they have given land for goods" (as quoted in Carstensen, *The Public Lands,* p. xiii). These leaders understood and embraced the fluid power of negotiable goods, but land was not in the same category. While one might claim powers in and through landforms and might negotiate those, one could not turn the land itself into a negotiable item. Still, perhaps the white man lived in a world of greater fantasy and magic than the Indian did when he assumed that a title could embody absolute ownership of land and a deed transfer that ownership.

89. Ibid., p. xiv.

90. *Lying Down Together,* pp. 96–97.

91. Quoted in O'Brien, *Tribal Governments*, p. 212.

92. Author of the General Allotment Act, as quoted in Angie Debo, *And Still the Waters Run* (New York: Gordian Press, 1966), pp. 21–22.

93. O'Brien, *Tribal Governments*, p. 216. Land allotted to individual Indians often ended up, through sale, fraud, mortgage foreclosures and tax sales, in the hands of non-Indians. In addition, tribal land considered under the Dawes Act to be in "excess" of Indian needs—"surplus land"—was made available for purchase or homesteading by non-Indians.

94. Abbott Seqequaptawa, tribal chairman when the Hopi challenged the expansion of the Arizona Snowbowl, argued that such an expansion would undermine the Hopi way of life: "We will not be able successfully to teach our people that this is a sacred place [and] the basis of our existence as a society will become a mere fairy tale to [our children]" (*Wilson v Block*, 708 F. 2d 735 [D. C. Cir., 1983], p. 740, n. 2).

95. "Cape Cod," in *The Writings of Henry David Thoreau* (Boston: Houghton Mifflin & Co., 1906), vol. 4, p. 43.

96. Felix S. Cohen, "Original Indian Title," *Minnesota Law Review*, 32 (1948): 59.

97. William Hart Blumenthal, *American Indians Dispossessed: Fraud in Land Cessions Forced upon Tribes* (Philadelphia: G. S. McManus Co., 1955), p. 43.

98. Felix S. Cohen, *The Legal Conscience* (New Haven: Yale University Press, 1960), p. 69. For a good brief summary of the various means by which the United States gained possession of these lands, see William T. Hagan, " 'To Correct Certain Evils' ": in Christopher Vecsey and William A. Starna, *Iroquois Land Claims* (Syracuse: Syracuse University Press, 1988), p. 17.

99. See *The Cherokee Nation v The State of Georgia*, 30 U.S. 1 (1831).

100. Ibid., p. 101.

101. Act of March 3, 1863; *Statutes at Large of the United States of America*, 12: 765.

102. In discussing a dispute over their treaty with the United States, as quoted in Peter Nabokov, ed., *Native American Testimony: An Anthology of Indian and White Relations from Encounter to Dispossession* (New York: Harper & Row, 1978), p. 172.

103. Despite positive intentions, the Act's major goal was, even according to the Indian Claims Commission's own historian, Harvey D. Rosenthal, to enhance governmental efficiency "by disposing of old claims and terminating Indian tribes" ("Indian Claims and the American Conscience: A Brief History of the Indian Claims Commission," in Imre Sutton, ed., *Irredeemable America: The Indians' Estate and Land Claims* [Albuquerque: University of New Mexico Press, 1985], p. 63).

104. *United States Statutes at Large*, 60, 79th Cong., 2d sess. (1946), ch. 959, pp. 1049–50.

105. The latter involved the Sioux Nation, which eventually won, in the Court of Claims, upheld by the Supreme Court in *United States v Sioux Nation*, 448 U.S. 371 (1980), the largest money award ever granted to an Indian tribe—$106 million, including interest.

106. See the United States Indian Claims Commission, *Final Report* (1978), especially pp. 5 and 125, for summaries of numbers of claims and awards. The Index of Indian Claims Commission Cases, pp. 23–106, is useful for details.

107. *United States Code*, 28, § 1362.

108. *Passamaquoddy Tribe v Morton*, 388 F. Supp. 649 (1975), affm'd, 528 F. 2d 370 (1st Cir. 1975).

109. "No sale of lands made by any Indians, or any nation or tribe of Indians within the United States, shall be valid to any person or persons, or to any state, whether having the right of pre-emption to such lands or not, unless the same shall be made and duly executed at some public treaty, held under the authority of the United States" (*Statutes at Large of the United States*, 1, 1st Cong., 2d sess. [1790], ch. 33, pp. 137-38. See Robert N. Clinton and Margaret Tobey Hotopp, "Judicial Enforcement of the Federal Restraints on Alienation of Indian Land: The Origin of the Eastern Land Claims," *Maine Law Review*, 31 [1979]: 17-90).

110. Paul Brodeur, "Annals of Law: Restitution," *The New Yorker*, Oct. 11, 1982, p. 150; but see Section 6, below.

111. The federal government had been involved in most of the Indian land transactions west of the Appalachians—or outside the final boundaries of the original thirteen states. Hence the western tribes could not readily resort to the Indian Trade and Intercourse acts for support of their own land claims. After 1946 their primary, if not sole, recourse was to the Indian Claims Commission.

112. For example, the Narragansett Tribe of Rhode Island, which had initially claimed some 3,200 acres within the town of Charlestown, reached a settlement in which they received 900 acres from the state and Congress appropriated $3.5 million to be used for the purchase of another 900 acres. In return, all tribal land claims within the state were extinguished (*Narragansett Tribe of Indians v Southern R.I. Land Development Corporation*, 418 F. Supp. 798 [D. R.I. 1976].

See also Thomas N. Tureen, "Afterword," in Brodeur, *Restitution*, p. 146). Hagan, "To Correct Certain Evils," points out that in most such cases Indian suits served mainly to stimulate out-of-court settlements.

The Oneidas, squeezed out of all but 32 acres of their land in New York State by virtual unilateral actions of that state, and denied access to either state or federal courts, won two major Supreme Court decisions in this period. In one (Jan. 21, 1974) the Supreme Court, holding that the Trade and Intercourse acts were applicable to the original thirteen states, opened the federal courts to suit by the Oneida. On March 4, 1984, the Court, in a 5-4 decision, held that Oneida and Madison Counties in New York were liable for damages caused to the Oneida by unlawful seizure of their ancestral lands (see Laurence M. Hauptman, "Iroquois Land Issues: At Odds with the 'Family of New York,' " in Vecsey and Starna, *Iroquois Land Claims*, pp. 70-74). The impact of these decisions on Indian-white relations in New York and elsewhere has been significant and continuous. It clearly demonstrates the importance of land issues in those relations. (On the eastern land claims see Clinton and Hotopp, "Judicial Enforcement . . . " and Robert N. Clinton, "Redressing the Legacy of Conquest: A Vision Quest for a Decolonized Federal Indian Law," *Arkansas Law Review*, 46 [1993]: 83-84.)

113. In Linda Hogan, *Mean Spirit* (New York: Ivy Books, 1990), p. 221, in explanation of Cree resistance to the Ghost Dance.

114. John Bodine, "Blue Lake: A Struggle for Indian Rights," *American Indian Law Review*, no. 1 (1973): 23. Bodine was perhaps the key non-Indian witness for the Taos. (See Robert Gordon-McCutchan, *The Taos Indians and the Battle for Blue Lake* [Santa Fe: Red Crane Books, 1991], for details in the Taos Blue Lake story.)

115. Twelve thousand acres on the slopes of Mt. Adams were returned to the Yakima Indians in 1972. This land had been lost to the Yakima through a surveying error in establishing tribal boundaries (O'Brien, *Tribal Governments*, p. 217). Also, through legislative acts the Havasupai Indians were guaranteed access to "sacred or religious places

or burial grounds" in the Grand Canyon National Park and the Zuni were enabled to take possession of certain lands in Arizona which are of religious significance to them (*United States Code*, 16, § 228i[c] [1975] and United States Congress. Senate. Select Committee on Indian Affairs, *Sen. Report* No. 98-411, 98th Cong., 2d Sess. [May 14, 1984]. Also *Zuni Indian Tribe Lands Bill. Hearings on S. 2201 before Select Comm. on Indian Affairs* U.S. Sen., 98th Cong., 2d Sess. [April 9, 1984]).

116. Socalled after the landmark Supreme Court decision in *Winters v United States*, 207 U.S. 564 (1908).

117. Quoted in O'Brien, *Tribal Governments*, p. 195.

118. The Commission intended to divest the Cherokee of their land by allotting it to individuals; quoted in Debo, *And Still the Waters Run*, p. 28.

119. "The Application of the Constitution to American Indians" in *Exiled in the Land of the Free: Democracy, Indian Nations, and the U.S. Constitution*, eds. John C. Mohawk and Oren R. Lyons (Santa Fe: Clear Light Publishers, 1992), p. 282.

120. Rennard Strickland, *et al*, eds., *Felix S. Cohen's Handbook of Federal Indian Law* (Charlottesville, VA: Michie, Bobbs-Merrill, 1982), p. 231; Court quotation from *United States v Wheeler*, 435 *U.S.* 313 (1978), pp. 322-23. Cf. *U.S. v Alcea Band of Tillimooks* 329 U.S. 40 (1946, plurality opinion), p. 54: "The power of Congress over Indian affairs may be of a plenary nature, but it is not absolute."

121. *Lone Wolf v Hitchcock*, 187 U.S. 553 (1903) p. 565. Clinton describes the decision in *Lone Wolf* as being as "devastating to Indians and their rights as *Plessy v Ferguson* (163 U.S. 537 [1896], overruled by *Brown v Board of Education*, 347 U.S. 483 [1954]) was to the cause of civil rights for African-Americans" ("Redressing the Legacy of Conquest," p. 99).

122. "Tribal Courts and the Federal Union," *1989 Harvard Indian Law Symposium* (Cambridge: Harvard Law School Publications Center, 1990), p. 27. Other authorities also regard the position stated by the Court in *Lone Wolf* as a gross misreading of what the framers of the Constitution had in mind. See, for example, Curtis G. Berkey, "United States—Indian Relations: The Constitutional Basis," and Laurence M. Hauptman, "Congress, Plenary Power, and the American Indian, 1870-1992," in *Exiled in the Land of the Free*, pp. 189-225 and 317-36. Both argue that the notion (or doctrine) of "plenary power" is a relatively recent invention of the Court. Berkey concludes, e.g., that "the historic loss of Indian land and sovereignty under federal law has no basis whatever in the intention of the framers" (p. 225).

123. Art. I, § 2, cl. 3.

124. Art. I, § 8, cl. 3.

125. Art. II, § 2, cl. 32.

126. Art. IV, § 3, cl. 2.

127. Art. I, § 8, cls. 1, 11, 12, 15-17.

128. The Major Crimes Act of Mar. 3, 1885, *United States Statutes at Large*, vol. 23, 48th Cong., 2d sess., ch. 341, sec. 9, p. 385; codified as amended at *United States Code*, vol. 18, sec. 1153.

129. See *Three Affiliated Tribes of Fort Berthold Reservation v United States*, 390 F. 2d 686 (1968), p. 691, in which the Court of Claims in attempting to reconcile the tension between trustee responsibility and the sovereign power of eminent domain, used the metaphor of the two hats.

130. ". . . nor shall private property be taken for public use, without just compensation."

131. *Tee-Hit-Ton v United States*, 348 U.S. 272 (1955), p. 372, et passim, appealing to *Johnson and Graham's Lease v McIntosh*.

132. Clinton compares this case with a similar case in Canada in which the Canadian Supreme Court found that the Royal Proclamation of 1763 protects property rights based on aboriginal possession and was also "a source of vested legal title for Indians" ("The Proclamation of 1763," p. 366). That Proclamation, important as it was historically, carries next to no weight in American court proceedings, however.

133. See Edward Lazarus, *Black Hills, White Justice: The Sioux Nation Versus the United States, 1775 to the Present* (New York: Harper, Collins, 1991) for an up-to-date and full account of the history and legal maneuvers that culminated in *Sioux Nation*. Lazarus is the son of one of the attorneys who shared in the ten percent fee awarded to Sioux attorneys in the case.

134. See Nell Jessup Newton, "Indian Claims in the Courts of the Conquerors," *The American University Law Review*, 41 (1992): 765, n. 62, citing an article in the Feb. 4, 1991 issue of the *Lakota Times*.

135. *United States v Sioux Nation*, p. 409. Cf. *Montana v United States*, 450 U.S. 544 (1981), which was decided shortly after *Sioux Nation*. See also Nell Jessup Newton, "Enforcing the Federal-Indian Trust Relationship after *Mitchell*," *Catholic University Law Review*, 31 (1982): 635–83.

136. See Newton, "Indian Claims in the Courts of the Conquerors," p. 765.

137. See *Oglala Sioux Tribe v the United States*, 650 F. 2d 140 (1981) and Stephen Cosby Hanson, "*United States v Sioux Nation of Indians*: Political Questions, Moral Imperatives and the National Honor," *University of West Los Angeles Law Review*, 13 (1981): 133–57.

138. Other Sioux tribes brought similar suits, all of which failed (see Newton, "Indian Claims in the Courts of the Conquerors," pp. 830–35). Following the Court decision in *Oglala v U.S.*, a group of Indians and others sought to lay claim to approximately 800 acres of National Forest land in the Black Hills for the establishment of a permanent camp for religious, cultural and educational purposes. On being challenged by the Forest Service, they appealed to, among other things, the free exercise clause of the First Amendment. They ultimately lost that appeal in a circuit court decision which used *Lyng v Northwest Cemetery Protective Association* as precedential: the Indians sought to impose "religious servitude" upon the land and by their religious practice they "could easily acquire de facto beneficial ownership of some rather spacious tracts of public property" (*United States v Means*, 585 F. 2d 404 [8th Cir. 1988], p. 407). It is noteworthy that, according to Jorgensen ("Land is Cultural, So is a Commodity," [cited in n. 25], p. 17), as of 1983, more than twenty Indian tribes or groups, because they claimed land not dollars, had rejected Indian Claims Commission and U.S. Court of Claims awards.

139. The treaty was made in 1855 and ratified by Congress in 1859.

140. *Brendale v Confederated Tribes and Bands of the Yakima Nation*, 492 U.S. 408 (1989), pp. 422–23. (For in-depth analyses of the implications of the Court's decision in *Brendale*, see Jessica S. Gerrard, "Undermining Tribal Land Use Regulatory Authority: *Brendale v Confederated Tribes*," *University of Puget Sound Law Review*, 13 [1990]: 349–75 and Joseph William Singer, "Legal Theory: Sovereignty and Property," *Northwestern University Law Review*, 86, No. 1 [1991]: 1–56.) Yakima sovereignty was further diminished in *County of Yakima v Confederated Tribes and Bands of the Yakima Nation*, 112 S. Ct. 683 (1992), which upholds State imposition of an *ad valorem* or property tax on fee-patented lands owned by Indians and permits foreclosure on such par-

cels. In this decision, as one commentator writes, the Court "has given the states power to diminish tribal land bases, further eroding what remains of tribal sovereignty and integrity" (Christopher A. Karns, "State Taxation as a Means of Diminishing the Tribal Land Base," *American University Law Review*, 42 [1993]: 1213-14. Cf. Deborah Jo Borrero, "They Never Keep But One Promise: State Taxation of Tribal Land," *Washington Law Review*, 67 [1992]: 937-57).

Tribal sovereignty has also been undermined by the Court's decisions in *Oliphant v Suquamish Indian Tribe*, 435 U.S. 191 (1978), in which the tribe was denied criminal jurisdiction over non-Indians who had committed crimes on tribal land, and in *Duro v Reina*, 110 S. Ct. 2053 (1990), in which such jurisdiction was denied over Indians who had committed crimes within tribal borders, but were not members of the tribe. Hence, tribal sovereignty appears increasingly to be understood as entailing control over tribal members as against control over territory.

141. *Cohen's Handbook of Federal Indian Law*, p. 522. (See American Indian Policy Review Commission, *Final Report* [Washington, D.C.: U.S. Government Printing Office, 1977], vol. 1, pp. 309-10.)

142. Preamble, Lac Courte Oreilles Band of Lake Superior Chippewa Indians (O'Brien, *Tribal Governments*, p. 221).

143. Ibid., p. 213.

144. Canada. House of Commons Standing Committee on Aboriginal Affairs, *Report*, 1991, p. 28.

145. Sec. 4. c.

146. Barsh, "Indian Land Claims Policy" p. 66. For details see Margot Kempers, "There's Losing and Winning: Ironies of the Maine Indian Land Claims," *Legal Studies Forum*, 13, no. 3 (1989): 267-99.

147. *The Return of the Native: American Indian Resurgence* (New York: Oxford University Press, 1988), p. 217.

148. *U.S. v. Gettysburg Electric Railway Company*, Supreme Court of the United States, nos. 599 and 629, October Term, 1895, pp. 680-82. See also Linenthal, *Sacred Ground: Americans and Their Battlefields* (Urbana: University of Illinois Press, 1991), pp. 113-14, et passim.

149. *Journals of the Continental Congress*, 32 (1787): 340-41.

150. *American Indians, Time, and the Law: Native Societies in a Modern Constitutional Democracy* (New Haven: Yale University Press, 1987), p. 4.

151. They could well continue for another century! The 1982 edition of *Cohen's Handbook of Federal Indian Law* comprises nearly 1,000 pages, including a 35-page Table of Statutes and a 25-page Table of Cases.

152. The pace of litigation of this type has increased exponentially in the last generation. The Cohen *Handbook* clearly bears this out. (See also Wilkinson, *American Indians, Time and the Law*, "Introduction.")

For a brief analysis which favorably compares American treatment of its indigenous minority with that of other nations, see Wilcomb E. Washburn, "Land Claims in the Mainstream," in Sutton, ed., *Irredeemable America*, pp. 28 and 36. Indian tribal sovereignty in America, Washburn argues, "extends beyond the wildest limits accorded other dependent, powerless peoples unable to assert their sovereignty in terms of their own power." And he concludes that "viewed in their totality, as one among many alternative routes that the course of Indian-white land history could have followed, the present status of Indian land claims presents an extraordinary spectacle of a variety of small cultural enclaves that have maintained better than anyone might have expected their culture, their aspirations, their land, and their autonomy after being overwhelmed by a tidal wave of foreign intruders." Cf. also Wilkinson's conclusion: "Federal Indian law is not what American Indians would choose. Their rights to land and political power are diluted, not pure. Nevertheless, for all of its many flaws, the policy of the United States toward its native people is one of the most progressive of any nation" (*American Indians, Time, and the Law*, p. 5).

Even Professor Hauptman, a sharp critic of recent Court decisions, points out that while the Court has been more than deferential to Congressional control over Indian affairs, it has also "frequently recognized Indian interests when they were not inconsistent or in direct conflict with federal interest" ("Congress, Plenary Power, and the American Indian," p. 321). He cites, e.g., decisions having to do with Indian fishing and water rights.

153. See Vine Deloria Jr. and Clifford Lytle, *The Nations Within: The Past and Future of American Indian Sovereignty* (New York: Pantheon Books, 1984).

154. The only just solution to the problem of American misappropriation and misuse of Indian land, Vine Deloria Jr. concludes, "would be an international forum or tribunal to which the United States and the Indian nations would submit their dispute" ("The Application of the Constitution to American Indians," p. 301). See Robert A. Williams, *Indian Rights, Human Rights: Handbook for Indians on International Human Rights* (Washington, D.C.: Indian Law Resource Center, 1984) for details on appeal to international tribunals.

155. Doig, *Dancing at the Rascal Fair*, p. 30.

3

RESACRALIZING EARTH
Pagan Environmentalism and
the Restoration of Turtle Island
Bron Taylor

Environmental Paganism and Environmental Conflict

T HE DARKNESS OF the high-desert night retreated immediately into the shadows as the FBI's flares launched skyward. The light signaled thirty heavily armed agents to descend on the three ecological saboteurs—and one FBI infiltrator—huddled below the giant electrical towers. Two of the saboteurs were quickly seized. The third disappeared into the shadows. Running with the wild abandon of all prey, when she paused to catch her breath, she began to feel herself mystically descend into Earth, sensing it merging with her, surrounding her, protecting her. She had become invisible—ghostlike. When the helicopters passed overhead, she hugged a tree or pressed herself into the ground, invisible. She had become like the ringtail cat, her totem animal. "The ringtail consciousness was in me that night," she recalls. "I ran through cactus gardens without getting stuck. I could feel the ringtail, like it was a part of me, encircling me. I felt its presence." Secure in this sacred mind-space they could never find her. Several hours later, still imperceptible, she slipped past her pursuers guarding a road on the edge of town. Back in the mundane world the next day, Peg Millett was seized and arrested at work—but she was not surprised, separated as she was from Earth's protective intention by the impermeable concrete of the building's foundation.[1]

Mark Davis had been quickly apprehended that night. He was soon charged with several different acts of "ecotage" (a term meaning sabotage defending ecosystems, also known as "monkeywrenching" in movement

parlance) including an effort designed to thwart the expansion of a ski resort in Arizona's San Francisco Mountains—an area considered sacred by
the Hopi and Navajo tribes (see Michaelsen's contribution in this volume).
In a letter from a federal penitentiary, he explained this particular action:

> Certainly there was some outrage involved at the blatant disregard of
> agreements with the Hopi and Navajo tribes, anger at the destruction of
> hundreds of acres of irreplaceable old-growth forest for the new ski runs,
> and indignation that the Forest Service was subsidizing a private company
> with public dollars. But the bottom line is that those mountains are sa-
> cred, and that what has occurred there, despite our feeble efforts, is a ter-
> rible spiritual mistake.[2]

When arrested in May 1989 in the Arizona desert, both Millett and
Davis were involved with Earth First!, the self-described "radical environmental" movement.

In 1990, a year after these arrests, while she was enroute to an organizing rally, a bomb exploded under the car seat of Earth First! activist Judi
Bari. She suffered permanent disabilities. Bari's pagan spiritual sentiments
are similar to those beliefs held by Millett and Davis, especially the belief
in the sacrality of natural landscapes.

Bari's paganism was not ignored by her adversaries.[3] Indeed, a letter pur-
portedly from her bomber quoted the Genesis "dominion" creation story
and, accusing her of blasphemous paganism, declared that "this possessed
demon Judy Bari . . . [told] the multitude that trees were not God's gift to
man but that trees were themselves gods and it was a sin to cut them. [So]
I felt the Power of the Lord stir within my heart and I knew I had been
Chosen to strike down this demon."[4] The rambling letter concludes warning other pagan tree worshipers that they will suffer Bari's fate.[5]

Perceiving the land as sacred, and being moved to defend that sacred
land through acts of sabotage, may seem strange and anomalous to many
Americans. But pagan religious sentiments leading to environmental activism are not a new phenomenon in America, nor is the hostile reaction
of those whose beliefs are based in the more dominant cultural monothe-
isms.[6] What is novel in recent events is the increasing boldness of the
movement I call pagan environmentalism, the intensifying alarm about
such militancy, and the escalating violence that is resulting as those with
different perceptions about what constitutes American sacred space collide in political battles over who controls the land, and for what end.[7]

The following pages provide an archeology of pagan environmentalism:
excavating spiritual perceptions of the sacrality of the natural world, un-

covering diverse acts of veneration and reconsecration in response to human pollution, illuminating hopes for the eventual reharmonization of people and nature, and describing the often hostile responses encountered by pagan environmentalists from those motivated by competing perceptions of sacred space. The study demonstrates that contemporary environmental conflicts are intertwined with disputes about the nature of sacred space and disagreements about the resulting human obligations.

Environmental paganism is an umbrella term for diverse spiritualities that, when combined with ecological understanding, lead to environmental activism. The spiritual tributaries contributing to environmental paganism include those traditionally labeled pantheism or animism (including shamanistic beliefs and experiences of interspecies communication)[8] and the holistic religions of the Far East, which tend to view the world as metaphysically interconnected and sacred.[9]

Most of those involved with the "deep ecology" and "radical environmental" movements can be called pagan environmentalists; they generally use these self-referents interchangeably, whether they find their primary spiritual home in Native American spirituality, neopaganism, Taoism, Buddhism, or some other nature-based spirituality. All such traditions are believed to express deep ecological sentiments.[10]

The experiences of Millet, Davis, and Bari show that the spiritual perceptions and radical tactics of Earth First! activists provoke those who do not share their spiritual presuppositions. Pantheistic and animistic spiritual perceptions animate the moral passions of many environmental activists in North America. Later we will scrutinize one excellent example of how mainstream religions in America react to the actions of environmental pagans, when we examine the case of the battle over the Mount Graham International Observatory in southeastern Arizona. This case illustrates the complex character of disputes over sacred spaces, especially when disputes about the nature of American sacred space collide in battles over who controls the land.

But first, without belaboring a point well made elsewhere,[11] it is important to the present interpretive task to remember that American religious nationalism holds a dominant conception of American sacred space as expressing a vision of America as a utopian space, which provides both a model for and a means to achieve God's purposes on earth. Such a worldview is naturally hostile to any competing worldview that either denies the premise that America constitutes sacred space or locates America's sacrality in the landscape itself rather than in the U.S. nation-state.

On the environmentalist side, this overall worldview conflict is grounded in the antipathy of most pagan environmentalists toward monotheistic religion, especially Christianity, which they blame (along with Western philosophy and science) for dualistic assumptions that have separated humans from nature, setting them free to assault the natural world.

These conflicts are further complicated because, just as monotheistic (and especially Christian) religion has co-existed in a reciprocally reinforcing relationship with American religious nationalism, so environmental paganism reinforces and is reinforced by political philosophies that hope to break down the barriers between humans and between humans and nonhuman entities. These competing clusters of religious worldviews—Christianity in league with religious nationalism (assuming the U.S. nation-state promotes a sacred mission), vs. paganism tied to ecological resistance movements defending natural landscapes considered sacred and attempting to overturn nation-state political domination—help explain the intensity of the escalating conflict over environmental issues in the U.S. → KEY PLAYERS | IDEOLOGIES IN ARTICLE

Paganism and the American Conservation Movement

From *The Mountains of California* to the Sierra Club

> When we try to pick out anything by itself we find that it is bound fast by a thousand invisible cords that cannot be broken to everything else in the universe. I fancy I can hear a heart beating in every crystal, in every grain of sand and see a wise plan in the making and shaping and placing of every one of them. All seems to be dancing to divine music. ... The clearest way into the Universe is through a forest wilderness."
> —John Muir[12]

This epigraph, a favorite among contemporary environmentalists, demonstrates the nascent pantheism of John Muir (1838–1914), the father of the nonanthropocentric wilderness preservation movement.[13] Although remnants of his theistic upbringing are still evident, and although he continued to use metaphors borrowed from Christianity, recent scholarship has well established Muir's pantheistic and animistic perceptions.[14] Until recently, Muir's religious sentiments remained largely unknown. Fox explains, "Muir lived in a Christian society and wrote for a Christian readership. Not wishing to offend, he generally kept the precise nature of his religious ideas to himself, confining them to journals, letters, and private discussions."[15]

Muir was more than a popularizer of Transcendentalism.[16] As his pantheism deepened through a variety of wilderness epiphanies, he articulated deep ecological sentiments long before the term was coined.[17] Many of his perceptions, and much of his rhetoric, set the tone and pattern for the militant wilderness conservation movement in subsequent decades.]

When speaking of wilderness, Muir often called his favorite wilderness places sacred, and referred to extractive enterprises as desecrations. He spoke of the Sierra Nevada as "mountains Holy as Sinai,"[18] and often analogized wilderness to the ultimate sacred place—the Garden of Eden:

> The very first forest reserve that I ever heard of . . . was located in the garden of Eden and included only one tree. The Lord himself laid out the boundaries of it, but even that reserve was attacked and broken in upon. The attacks then of sheepmen and lumbermen, unregenerate sons of Adam, on the Yosemite National Park are in the natural course of things.[19]

Muir often referred to specific wilderness places, mountains, groves, rivers as "cathedrals" or "temples," likening humans threatening them to agents of the devil. In response to a threatened dam on the Tuolumne River at Hetch Hetchy Valley, a righteous Muir railed against the "mischief makers and robbers of every degree from Satan to Senators."[20] "Dam Hetch Hetchy!," he wailed, "As well dam for water-tanks the people's cathedrals and churches, for no holier temple has ever been consecrated by the heart of man."[21]

For Muir, wilderness was a sacred environment where epiphanies could occur. Upon seeing a rare orchid, *Calypso borealis*, the young Muir wrote, "I never before saw a plant so full of life; so perfectly spiritual. It seemed pure enough for the throne of the Creator. I felt as if I were in the presence of superior beings who loved me and beckoned me to come. I sat down beside them and wept for joy."[22] Using today's terminology, this experience reveals Muir's biocentrism. After this epiphany, Muir "no longer defined the world in human terms. All species, no matter how outwardly useless, had their own purposes."[23] KEY – violence breaks this union

[Unitary consciousness (regarding the connectedness of all life) was the other central meaning Muir gained from his wilderness epiphanies.]From Yosemite's Cathedral Peak Muir felt "earth and sky [draw] together as one [making one feel] part of wild nature, kin to everything . . . the Cathedral itself [is] a temple displaying Nature's best masonry and sermons in stone."[24] Sacred wilderness promotes proper spiritual perception, "in our best times everything turns into religion, all the world seems a church and the mountains altars."[25]

Michael Cohen writes that in another case, Muir so cherished Yosemite's Shadow Lake that, fearing its destruction by sheep, he kept it secret,

> hoard[ing] its beauty as Indians before him had saved its sacred hunting grounds for times of hunger . . . Muir knew he could protect this sacred place [only] by keeping his silence. [But after an absence] he returned . . . to find his worst fears realized. [He wrote]: "all the gardens and meadow were destroyed by a horde of hoofed locusts, as if swept by a fire. The money-changers were in the temple."[26]

Muir viewed both humans and the creatures they tame as the primary agents desecrating paradise: "The beauty of the lilies falls on angels and men, bears and squirrels, wolves and sheep, bird and bees, but as far as I have seen, man alone, and the animals he tames, destroy these gardens."[27] But for Muir, domestic animals were not simply agents of despoliation, they were themselves desecrated. Humans had bred into oblivion their sacred, natural wildness. Muir glowed when describing noble, sacred, wild mountain sheep.[28] But tamed animals were not the only creatures defiled through domestication—humans were too—by their own civilization. "The gross heathenism of civilization has generally destroyed nature, and poetry, and all that is spiritual," including a proper humility.[29] The defiling influence of civilization, which improperly inflates human self-regard, needed to be purged from the body by "a good hard trip."[30] Indeed, "A little pure wildness is the one great present want, both of men and sheep."[31] As Max Oelschlaeger portrays Muir's thesis in "Wild Wool," "both human beings and sheep would be improved by an infusion of wildness."[32]

These ideas, that humans and their animals become degenerate when alienated from their wild natures, today permeate the sentiments of many ecological radicals. Following Muir, today's ecological radicals interpret Thoreau's phrase "in wildness is the preservation of the world" to mean that animals, including humans, are only authentic, only sacred, when undomesticated, living life wildly and spontaneously in harmony with, and when necessary in defense of, the natural world.[33]

Animism was embedded in Muir's pantheism—sacred voices were discerned in entities most Westerners do not believe can communicate.[34] In 1871 Muir sent a note to the famous Transcendentalist Emerson, who was visiting Yosemite valley, in Muir's opinion, too briefly to hear its sacred voices:

> Do not drift away with the mob while the spirits of these rocks and waters hail you after long waiting as their kinsman and persuade you to closer communion. . . . I invite you to join me in a month's worship with Nature in the high temples of the great Sierra Crown beyond our holy Yosemite. It will cost you nothing save the time and very little of that for you will be mostly in eternity. . . . In the name of a hundred cascades that barbarous visitors never see . . . in the name of all the spirit creatures of these rocks and of this whole spiritual atmosphere. Do not leave us *now*.[35]

On the occasion of an 1879 ascent in Alaska, Muir sensed all the entities surrounding him sharing his joy: "the plant people . . . rejoicing with me, the little ones as well as the trees, [as well as] every feature of the peak . . . seemed to know . . . the depth of my joy, as if they could read faces."[36]

Given Muir's animistic and pantheistic wilderness epiphanies, his primary missionary strategy was to get people to listen to earth's sacred voices: "Few are altogether deaf to the preaching of pine-trees. Their sermons on the mountains go to our hearts; and if people in general could be got into the woods, even for once, to hear the trees speak for themselves, all difficulties in the way of forest preservation would vanish."[37]

Here is the fundamental epistemological premise of the radical environmental movement, then and now. If people will only still themselves and listen to earth's sacred voices, they and the earth itself will be healed. This hope produced the tradition of Sierra Club outings, which attempted to bring people into proximity with such sacred voices, thereby enabling the development of proper earth ethics.[38]

Similar strategies underlie virtually all of this century's preservationist missions.[39] From the 1930s on, for example, the dissemination of landscape photographs of undefiled places, free from human artifice but slated for despoliation, has been a central preservationist tactic.[40] Within Earth First!, the arts, including photography and other visual arts, poetry, prose, music, and theater (both guerilla street theater and a host of currently evolving ritual practices) are used to evoke and deepen the human sense of the sacredness of the earth and one's embeddedness in it. Such arts, however, are believed at best to *remind* us of primary perceptions that ultimately derive only from direct experience in wild nature.[41]

In Muir's writings, a central irony emerges; while spiritual growth requires exposure to wilderness, civilized humans are not worthy of it. Their inability to perceive its sacrality leads them to destroy it. Toward the end of his life, Muir told an interviewer, "You say that what I write may bring this beauty to the hearts of those who do not go out to see it. They have no right to it."[42] This sentiment, that only the community of wilderness purists are worthy of the wilderness, has been common throughout the past century. As Linda Graber notes in her study of Muir's legacy in the mountaineering subcultures of the West, wilderness "purists resent the outsider's presence in sacred space because his 'inferior' mode of perception" and "inability to cope with distance and elevation" leads them to "desecrate wilderness."[43] And this sentiment is often tied to a belief that purification is needed before approaching natural places, which may include strenuous effort or physical danger.[44] *can explain the propensity toward danger*

For Muir, as for modern-day preservationists, dangerous excursions had a spiritual goal.[45] Mountaineering, for example, facilitated mystical unitary experiences, providing a Zen-like loss of self and experience of actionless action—motion without an individual actor involved.[46] Several times while climbing, Muir felt that neither he nor the mountain was moving, "but something beyond them" both.[47]

Fellow Travelers within the Preservation Movement

An essentially pagan spirituality motivated John Muir. The pantheistic experiences he described were in fact the central experience inspiring most preservationists prior to the 1960s (such as Bob Marshall, David Brower, Charles Lindberg, Alexander Skutch, Joseph Wood Krutch and Ansel Adams). Stephen Fox explains, however, that to express such ideas and "question the implications of Christianity, in an overtly Christian society, only complicated their efforts" so they, like Muir, tended to keep such sentiments to themselves.[48] Despite such reticence, one can find the above mentioned preservationists expressing interest in and affinity with Greek wood gods (Pan), Asian religions (especially Buddhism and Taoism), Native American spiritualities, and Spiritualism.[49] Even Aldo Leopold, who as a scientist was especially reluctant to sound mystical in his ecological writings, was deeply influenced by the Russian mystic Peter Ouspensky, who had thoroughly rejected Western dualism in his efforts to merge science and Eastern mysticism.[50]

The social and spiritual ferment of the 1960s brought greater tolerance for non-Western spiritualities. Meanwhile preservationist critiques of the negative environmental consequences of Western religion and science began to be more pointedly made, often with pagan or Eastern spiritualities offered as nature-beneficent alternatives. By the early 1970s the religious component of environmental controversies escalated in importance, with Christians counterattacking preservationist heresies.[51]

Although pagan spiritual sentiments animated John Muir and many preservationists prior to the 1960s, two writers signaled the emergence of a new and more militant form of pagan environmentalism, articulating a vision of communities engaged in direct-action resistance to the escalating destruction of wilderness places they considered sacred. They share many of Muir's spiritual sentiments and like him, their own contributions and rhetoric are often reflected within today's pagan environmental movement. Indeed, Edward Abbey and Gary Snyder are the two figures who most decisively set the stage for the emergence of Earth First!'s militant form of environmental paganism at the waning edge of the 1970s.

Desert Solitaire and *The Monkeywrench Gang*

Edward Abbey (1928–1989) was a Western writer who had periodically worked for the National Park and Forest Services, studied anarchist philosophy, taught writing for a Southwestern university, and whose nature writings, novels, and caustic essays reflected and captured the love many Westerners feel for their landscapes and their rage about its ongoing destruction. His writings are often credited with precipitating the radical environmental movement known as Earth First!. More accurately, Abbey wrote about a wave of illegal direct action against development schemes that began in the 1950s, and then fueled such ecological resistance by writing about and romanticizing it.

In this analysis, Edward Abbey represents those environmental pagans who are agnostic about metaphysical questions, but nevertheless believe that the natural world is ultimately valuable, and use metaphors of the sacred to convey spiritual experiences and perceptions. Writing in *Desert Solitaire* about his experiences during a mid-1950s stint as a ranger at Utah's Arches National Park, Abbey immediately struck a chord with many conservationists. Abbey considered desert landscapes, not mountains, to be the most holy, the most capable of fostering proper spiritual perception, but he shared Muir's contempt for tourists as agents of pollution, ridiculing their dependence on cars and other modern conveniences such as roads and "comfort stations." Like Muir, Abbey viewed citified humans as both perpetrators and victims of industrial culture—with a consequently flawed human character: "Mechanized tourists are at once the consumers, the raw material and the victims of Industrial Tourism."[52]

Abbey pled for reverent behavior in America's National Parks: "We have agreed not to drive our automobiles into cathedrals, concert halls, art museums . . . and the other sanctums of our culture; we should treat our national parks with the same deference, for they, too, are holy places."[53] Also like Muir, Abbey appropriated Eden as a metaphor to convey the sacredness of wilderness landscapes. "I saw only part of it," Abbey reminisced, reflecting on the canyon drowned behind Arizona's massive Glen Canyon dam, "but enough to realize that here was an Eden, a portion of the earth's original paradise. To grasp the nature of the crime that was committed, imagine the Taj Mahal or Chartres Cathedral buried in mud until only the spires remain visible."[54]

For Abbey as for Muir, it was the ability of wilderness places to convey spiritual truth that revealed their sacrality. Their wilderness epiphanies led to strikingly similar perceptions; a relativized sense of self, a recognition of one's place as embedded in all reality, and the experience and affirmation of the intrinsic value of all Earth entities. Abbey, for example, told of a wilderness epiphany when, during an extended stay in the remote canyons of Arizona's Havasu Indian Reservation, the boundaries blurred between himself and all else:

> I went native and dreamed away days on the shore of the pool under the waterfall, wandered naked as Adam under the cottonwoods, inspecting my cactus gardens. The days became wild, strange, ambiguous—a sinister element pervaded the flow of time. I lived narcotic hours in which like the Taoist Chang-tse I worried about butterflies and who was dreaming what. . . . I slipped by degrees into lunacy, me and the moon, and lost to a certain extent the power to distinguish between what was and was not myself: looking at my hand I would see a leaf trembling on a branch.[55]

Abbey knew he was not unique, mentioning several books whose spiritualities are based on desert experiences, including Joseph Wood Krutch's pantheist classic, *The Voice of the Desert*.[56] All this led Abbey to wonder,

> What is the peculiar quality or character of the desert that distinguishes it, in spiritual appeal, from other forms of landscape?
> The restless sea, the towering mountains, the silent desert—what do they have in common? and what are the essential differences? Grandeur, color, spaciousness, the power of the ancient and elemental, that which lies beyond the ability of man to wholly grasp or utilize, these qualities all three share. In each there is the sense of something ultimate, with mountains exemplifying the brute force of natural processes [but] . . . what does the desert say?
> The desert says nothing. Completely passive, acted upon but never acting, the desert lies there like the bare skeleton of Being, spare, sparse, aus-

tere, utterly worthless, inviting not love but contemplation. In its simplicity and order it [rejects the idea that] only the human is . . . significant or even . . . real.[57]

Thus the desert is sacred because no place has greater power to evoke a proper spiritual understanding of one's place in the universe. Abbey concludes from his desert-fostered perception of human insignificance, that an authentic death is dying and being eaten by other living entities. A proper death is one final means of being absorbed into the entire universe.

This idea seems to have been inspired by poet Robinson Jeffers, who was once temporarily mistaken for carrion by a vulture:

> I had walked since dawn and lay down to rest on a bare hillside
> Above the ocean. I saw through half-shut eyelids a vulture
>   wheeling high up in heaven,
> And presently it passed again, but lower and nearer, its orbit
>   narrowing, I understood then
> That I was under inspection. I lay death-still and heard the
>   flight feathers
> Whistle above me and make their circle and come nearer. . . .
>   how beautiful he looked, gliding down
> On those great sails; how beautiful he looked, veering
>   away in the sea-light over the precipice. I tell you solemnly
> That I was sorry to have disappointed him. To be eaten by that
>   beak and become part of him, to share those wings and
>   those eyes—
> What a sublime end of one's body, what an enskyment; what a
> life after death.[58]

Abbey's reflections on death are reminiscent of Jeffers, whom he admired; an authentic death is one unaccompanied by life-prolonging technology, when the body is left unpolluted by poisons so that it can properly reunite with and nurture the earth.[59] Reflecting on a tourist who died alone in the desert, Abbey mused,

> he had good luck—I envy him the manner of his going: to die alone, on a rock under the sun at the brink of the unknown, like a wolf, like a great bird, seems to me very good fortune indeed. To die in the open, under the sky, far from the insolent interference of leech and priest, before this desert vastness opening like a window onto eternity—that surely was an overwhelming stroke of good luck. . . . [Today], I think of the dead man under the juniper on the edge of the world, seeing him as the vulture would have seen him, far below and from a great distance. And I see myself through those cruel eyes . . . I feel myself sinking into the landscape, fixed in place like a stone, like a tree, a small motionless shape of vague outline,

desert-colored, and with the wings of imagination look down at myself through the eyes of the bird, watching a human figure that becomes smaller, smaller in the receding landscape as the bird rises into the evening.[60]

[Before his death in 1989, in his last act of desert consecration, Abbey arranged for his body, unpolluted by embalmer's artifice, to be spirited away and illegally buried in his beloved, sacred desert.]In death he would nourish the desert as it had him.[61]

Although Abbey articulated some of the meaning of his desert experiences, he indicated there was still something ineffable about them. The desert's wisdom is a "treasure which has no name . . . [Nevertheless], there is *something* about the desert . . . , there is *something there* which the mountains, no matter how grand and beautiful, lack; which the sea, no matter how shining and vast and old, does not have."[62]

As the desert vitiates our anthropocentrism, it also overturns our nationalist pretensions and fidelities. Abbey recounts an all-night discussion in which he confided his

desert thoughts to a visitor [and] . . . was accused of being against civilization, against science, against humanity. [After much discussion], with his help I discovered that I was not opposed to mankind but only to man-centeredness, anthropocentricity, the opinion that the world exists solely for the sake of man; not to science, which means simply knowledge, but to science misapplied, to the worship of technique and technology, and to the perversion of science properly called scientism; and not to civilization, but to [the United States and other] industrial culture[s].[63]

Both superpowers, Abbey concluded, "are essentially *industrial* cultures . . . and the more they compete the more alike they become."[64]

With such statements Abbey denied the special status of the U.S. nation-state, presaging his and his progeny's collision with religious nationalism and Christian fundamentalism, both of which usually assume that God has given the U.S. a special, earthly mission.[65]

Although Abbey eschewed nationalistic beliefs in some special divine U.S. purpose, he nevertheless maintained an eschatological hope in the reversal of human desecrating crimes and a reharmonization of life on earth. The primary agent for the restoration of Eden would be earth herself. "Glen Canyon will be restored eventually, through natural processes, but it may take centuries. (Pray for an earthquake).”[66] But humans also may have a role—if they resist the forces of ecological destruction. Although generally pessimistic about humans, Abbey thought that Americans were becoming "an increasingly pagan and hedonistic people (thank God!)" and asserted that "we are learning finally that the forests and mountains and desert canyons are holier than our churches. Therefore let us behave accordingly."[67] His hope was based in an ecological resistance movement that emerged in the 1950s, experimenting with tactics such as pulling up survey stakes and destroying advertising billboards. While on patrol in the Park he would sometimes find people with whom he could share "rumors from the underground where whatever hope we still have must be found."[68]

Indeed, wilderness was both means and end in Abbey's eschatological hopes, prerequisite to liberty, because it provides excellent guerilla habitat;[69] and also the ultimate end after the anticipated collapse of industrial society. Industrial collapse, Abbey hoped, would lead to

> the coming restoration of higher civilization [characterized by] scattered human populations modest in number that live by fishing, hunting, food-gathering, small-scale farming and ranching, that assemble once a year in the ruins of abandoned cities for great festivals of moral, spiritual, artistic and intellectual renewal—a people for whom wilderness is not a playground but their natural and native home.[70]

Despite his frequent allusions to the desert as a sacred place, Abbey remained agnostic about ultimate metaphysical questions. In *Desert Solitaire*, when marveling at a favorite desert landscape, he wondered,

> Is this at last *locus Dei?* There are enough cathedrals and temples and alters here for a Hindu pantheon of divinities. Each time I look up at one of the secretive little side canyons I half expect to see . . . the leafy god . . . a rainbow-colored corona of blazing light, pure spirit, pure being . . . *about to speak my name.*
>
> If a man's imagination were not so weak, so easily tired, if his capacity for wonder not so limited, he would abandon forever such fantasies of the supernatural. He would learn to perceive in water, leaves, and silence more than sufficient of the absolute and marvelous, more than enough to console him for the loss of ancient dreams.[71]

And in his farewell preface to the same volume, written while he was aware he would soon die, he urged his readers to eschew metaphysical preoccupations, addressing those who complain that *Desert Solitaire*

> does not reveal the patterns of unifying relationships that many believe form the true and underlying reality of existence, I can only reply that I am content with surfaces, with appearances. I know nothing about *under-*

lying reality, having never encountered any. I've looked and I've looked, tried fasting, drugs, meditation, religious experience, even self-mortification, but never seem to get any closer to basic reality than the lizard on a rock, a hawk in the sky, a dead pig in the sunshine. . . . Appearance *is* reality, I say, and more than most of us deserve. You whine and whimper for immortality beyond space-time? Come home for God's sake, and enjoy this gracious Earth of yours while you can . . .

Throw metaphysics to the dogs. I never heard a mountain lion bawling over the fate of his soul.[72]

Abbey believed that one can be unconcerned about metaphysics, but still perceive and act on the perception that wilderness places are sacred. For him, as for his Earth First! character/alter-ego Hayduke in *the Monkeywrench Gang* and *Hayduke Lives*, ecotage is the ultimate act of reconsecration.[73] The slogan "We stand for what we stand on" simply expresses Abbey's material brand of nature spirituality.[74] Abbey believes that one can know that the desert and other wild places are sacred—and that honor requires one to defend them—without speculating about why this is true.

Veneration and Gary Snyder's Labeling of *Turtle Island*

In Pueblo societies a kind of ultimate democracy is practiced. Plants and animals are also people, and through certain rituals and dances, are given a place in the political discussions of the humans. They are "represented." On Hopi and Navajo land, at Black Mesa . . . the cancer [of industrial civilization] is eating away at the breast of Mother Earth in the form of strip mining . . . to provide electricity for Los Angeles. The defense of Black Mesa is being sustained by traditional Indians, young Indian militants, and longhairs [hippies]. Black Mesa . . . is sacred territory. To hear her voice is to give up the European word "America" and accept the new-old name for the continent, "Turtle Island."

Calling this place "America" is to name it after a stranger. "Turtle Island" is the name given this continent by Native Americans based on creation mythology. The United States, Canada, Mexico, *are passing political entities*; they have their legitimacies . . . but they will lose their mandate if they continue to abuse the land.

For a people of an old culture, *all* their mutually owned territory holds numinous life and spirit. Certain places are perceived to be of high spiritual density because of plant or animal habitat intensities, or associations with legend, or connections with human totemic ancestry, or because of geomorphological anomaly, or some combination of qualities. These places are gates through which one can—it would be said—more easily be touched by a larger-than-human, larger-than-personal view . . .

The temples of our hemisphere [are] . . . the planet's remaining wil-

SUPER-
KEY!

derness areas. When we enter them on foot we can sense the *kami* or
(Maidu) *kukini* are still in force there.[75] —Gary Snyder

Gary Snyder emerged as an important counterculture figure during the
1950s "beat" literary movement, when a group of poets and writers, often
inspired by various religions originating in the Far East, posed a fundamental challenge to the dominant values of the post-war generation. Raised in
the Pacific Northwest, and influenced both by a love for the woods and by
an early dose of anti-industrial "wobbly" lore, Snyder left San Francisco in
1955, spending twelve years studying Zen Buddhism and taking vows as a
Zen monk. He introduced anti-anthropocentric ideas through his poetry
into the "beat" counterculture, and eventually played a major role in promoting the counterculture's appreciation of and experimentation with
communal forms of living beginning in the 1960s.[76] But it may be in his
role in promoting the counterculture, which in turn became the breeding
grounds for the radical environmental movement, that his most lasting impact will be felt.

America is a sacred place to Snyder—whose *Turtle Island* won the Pul-
itzer prize for poetry in 1975—especially its wilderness areas and places
inhabited by Indians and others who practice "the old ways" ("nature
based" practices including shamanism). Renaming America Turtle Island
is an act of veneration acknowledging the sacrality of the land by linking
it to sacred people—those still able to perceive its sacred voices and live
respectfully upon it. Such renaming is simultaneously an act of subversion,[77] questioning or repudiating any view that links the sacredness of the
continent to a presumed beneficent, divine "mission" carried forward by
the U.S. nation-state.[78]

The depth of Snyder's subversiveness is grounded in his animism and
concomitant critique of monotheistic nationalism. Recalling that he was a
"natural animist" as a child, Snyder asserts that other children are also
because, they are "so open to other creatures." He also believes that, even
today, animism and pantheism are more common than monotheism.[79]
Moreover, he adds, monotheistic perceptions should be subverted because
historically they promote and benefit from ecologically destructive nationalistic ideologies. Snyder believes that, viewed historically, monotheism
and nationalism are unnatural aberrations:

What's not common is the mind-body dualism that begins to come in
with monotheism. And the alliance of monotheism with the formation of
centralized governance and the national state, that's . . . unnatural, and
statistically in a minority on earth. The [majority of] human experience

has been an experience of animism. Only a small proportion of people on earth have been monotheists.[80]

In place of monotheistic religious nationalism, Snyder and a few others began developing, during the 1960s, an alternative vision—one infused with eschatological hope, but not always optimism—a utopian eco-political philosophy they labeled bioregionalism. Seeking to replace nation-state governance with an "ecological anarchism" characterized by widespread liberty, mutual aid, and collective self-rule, bioregionalists contend that governance systems should be limited in size to specific ecosystem types.[81] Most bioregionalists also believe that by "reinhabiting" and defending a specific region one can eventually discern its sacred voices and learn appropriate lifeways from them.

Such bioregional epistemology, assuming that one must long remain in a place in order to learn the birds, plants, weather, and eventually its sacrality, can be seen when Snyder quotes a Crow Elder, "I think if people stay somewhere long enough—even white people—the spirits will begin to speak to them. It's the power of the spirits coming up from the land. The spirits and the old powers aren't lost, they just need people to be around long enough and the spirits will begin to influence them."[82]

In bioregional thought, political philosophy, paganism, and ecological resistance converge. Often Snyder has alluded to wilderness epiphanies where animistic experiences of interspecies communication occur, or where one experiences a pantheistic sense that the entire earth is alive and sacred. Recalling in 1968 an earlier experience while working on a trail crew in Yosemite National Park, "I found myself being completely there, having the whole mountain inside of me, and finally [I had] a whole language inside of me that became one with the rocks and with the trees."[83] Although reluctant to discuss such experiences specifically for fear of trivializing them, Snyder insists that "you can hear voices from trees" and recalls that "I have had a very moving, profound perception a few times that everything was alive (the basic perception of animism) and that on one level there is no hierarchy of qualities in life—that the life of a stone or a weed is as completely beautiful and authentic, wise and valuable as the life of, say, an Einstein."[84]

Snyder has been reluctant to discuss the specific experiences he has had of interspecies communication because words are inadequate to convey such experiences. But during a long discussion, he gave an idea of how these perceptions occur:

Do you know how things communicate with you? They don't talk to you directly, but you hear a different song in your head. In fact, I knew an old Irish mystic lady in the bay area in the 50s, Ella was clear about this. Once while walking in Muir woods (near Mt. Tam), Ella said, 'that yellow crown warbler gave that to me'and I said, 'you mean that one that just sang just now' and she said 'yes that was a special song, I heard it . . . ' It's not that animals come up and say something in English in your ear. You know, it's that things come into your mind. . . . Most people think that everything that comes into their mind is their own, their own mind, that it comes from within. It may come from someplace deep within or less deep, but everybody thinks it comes from within. That's modern psychology. Well, some of those things that you think are from within are given to you from outside, and part of the trick is knowing which was which—being alert to the one that you know was a gift, and not think, 'I thought that.' Say [instead], 'Ah, that was a gift!' . . . I have a poem about Magpie giving me a song (Magpie's song). That's just one [example].[85]

Snyder thinks such experiences are available when actively pursued.[86] Muir, Abbey, and Snyder are united by the conviction that wilderness is sacred, at least partly because it is the locus of sacred experience. Snyder believes, for example, that wilderness pilgrimages and backpacking are especially good rituals of transformation. They "bring a profound sense of body-mind joy," he writes, that "take us . . . out of our little selves into the whole mountains-and-rivers mandala universe."[87] But private wilderness experiences are not enough; since the natural world is never totally ruined, resistance and restoration are morally obligatory, reconsecrating acts.[88]

These convictions lead Snyder to view most extractive industry as desecration demanding resistance. He may have been the first to refer to industrial civilization as a "cancer" on earth. And in his valorizing of the Black Mesa and other ecological resistance movements, Snyder joins Abbey in providing some of the earliest published approval of extralegal ecological resistance. They diverged on the issue of monkeywrenching, however; Abbey enthusiastically endorsed it, while Snyder generally cautions against such practices, warning that its practitioners counterproductively cede the moral high ground and fail to recognize that all extra-legal activism is theater and must play well to the public audience.[89]

Snyder also deviates from Abbey's penchant to deride metaphysical speculation: "the world is nature, and in the long run inevitably wild, because the wild, as the process and essence of nature, is also an ordering of impermanence."[90] Although he is inspired by crosscultural expressions of shamanism as well as animistic and pantheistic religious experiences,

Snyder's primary spiritual home remains Zen Buddhism, partly because he thinks ancient Zen teachings express deep ecological ethics with unsurpassed philosophical sophistication.[91] He calls himself a "Buddhist-Animist."[92]

Despite disagreeing about the value of thinking about ultimate metaphysical questions (Abbey once told Snyder that he liked everything in *Turtle Island's* "Four Changes," "except the Buddhist bullshit"), Snyder and Abbey both believe that wilderness and wildness are essential to a spiritual epistemology capable of fostering a "larger-than-personal" insight. "Only the early Daoists," Snyder writes approvingly, recognized "that wisdom could come of wildness."[93] This epistemology of wildness is reminiscent of the sense among many environmental pagans that the earthly process of eating and being eaten is sacred.[94] Snyder's own spiritual perceptions parallel Abbey's here: "Countless men and women . . . have experienced a deep sense of communion and communication with nature and with specific nonhuman beings. Moreover, they often experienced this communication with a being they customarily ate."[95] "To acknowledge that each of us at the table will eventually be part of the meal is . . . allowing the sacred to enter and accepting the sacramental aspect of our shaky temporary personal being."[96] For Jeffers, Abbey, Snyder, and their soulmates, the vulture serves as metaphor for physical and ultimately spiritual union and reharmonization with all reality.

Snyder has been sympathetic to militant bioregionalists including Earth First! activists (themselves substantially inspired by Abbey). (Earth First!ers often discuss bioregional ideas, sometimes considering themselves the bioregional militia.)[97] Snyder has also promoted the bioregional strategy known as "watershed organizing," and is considered by many bioregionalists and radical environmentalists to be a movement "elder."

Snyder is also responsible for inspiring many within the pagan environmental movement to view and use the arts, especially poetry and song, as a tactic. Poetry and song are among "the few modes of speech that [provide] access to that other yogic or shamanistic view (in which all is one and all is many, and many are all precious)."[98] Indeed, using the arts as a weapon in ecological struggle has become a central strategy within contemporary pagan ecological resistance.[99]

Back to the Pleistocene: The Primitive as Paradise

Snyder almost surely coined the slogan "back to the pleistocene!", subsequently appropriated by Dave Foreman, one of the founders of Earth

First!, as a rallying cry. Although Snyder later clarified his reflections in this area, speculating that people lived most harmoniously with nature during the Upper Paleolithic, and although he acknowledges that we cannot go back in time, this nostalgia for an earlier paradise parallels Muir's and Abbey's metaphorical references to Eden as a sacred place. In the last two decades, much debate has occurred within the pagan environmental movement regarding where humans went astray, and how we can live in a way that respects the earth and her creatures. Whatever the diagnosis about what humans did to leave Eden, Muir, Abbey and Snyder all helped set the stage for movements to follow, reconsecrating land and striving to resacralize human attitudes toward it.

Earth First!: Vanguard of the Pagan Environmental Movement[100]

Since its founding in 1980, partly due to its high-profile tactics, Earth First! has surged to the forefront of what I am calling the pagan environmental movement. Although characterized by great pluralism, three central convictions are almost universally shared within the movement: (1) The natural world is morally valuable apart from its usefulness to human beings. The various labels for this idea, deep ecology, "biocentric," or "ecocentric" ethics, underscore the rejection of anthropocentric moral systems, whether theistic or humanistic. Related to this conviction are ubiquitous descriptions of the Earth and her natural processes as sacred, and exhortations that we resacralize our perceptions of her. Most Earth First!ers believe industrial agricultures went awry when they abandoned forager lifeways, losing the primordial perception that the earth is sacred. (2) We are in the midst of an unprecedented, anthropogenic, extinction crisis. (3) Corporate power prevents democratic processes from responding adequately to the crisis. Grounded upon these convictions, Earth First! activists have pioneered diverse means of ecological resistance, including illegal tactics such as civil disobedience and ecotage (or monkeywrenching).[101]

The actions of Peg Millet and Mark Davis, described earlier, may seem sensational. Yet similar experiences and sentiments to theirs underlie the moral passions of most ecological radicals practicing civil disobedience or ecotage. Such activists view wilderness defense as a sacred vocation, for in wild places yet undefiled by development, humans can still experience the sacred and discern how to live harmoniously on the planet.

Most Earth First! activists believe that today's environmental crises are rooted in our current spiritual dysfunction—by paving over the earth's sacred voices we can no longer recognize or learn from the sacrality of Earth. (Indeed, my own interviews with activists confirm further, that animistic or pantheistic religious experiences undergird the ecocentrism of nearly all Earth First! activists.)[102] The defense of wilderness is essential if humans are to "resacralize" Earth and avert an apocalyptic, global ecological collapse.

Given the heritage of Muir, Abbey, Snyder and others, it is obvious that Earth First!ers are not expressing new sentiments when they rage against human despoilation of nature—but they have extended that outrage to an increasing number of human activities. I cannot detail every form of earth defilement perceived by Earth First!ers nor enumerate each consecrating response, but an overview of typical Earth First! perceptions of and responses to the destruction of nature is possible. I will follow this with a more detailed discussion of the battle over efforts to build telescopes on Mount Graham, a site in Arizona considered sacred, in differing but related ways, by Earth First!ers and many Native Americans.

Perceiving the Sacrality and Desecration of Earth

Earth First!ers perceive many forms of human-caused defilement, including commercial developments (and the accompanying pavement); most forms of tourism (following Abbey, especially industrial tourism including developed campgrounds involving habitat destruction); human efforts to "manage" nature (by replacing natural, biodiverse forests with tree farms, for example); and suppressing fires (thwarting sacred natural processes). Also defiling is the pollution of land, water, and sky (including aviation vapor trails) and flush toilets (robbing earth of sacred, regenerating compost). Indeed for most Earth First!ers, few corners of modern society have not profaned Sacred Earth, from the laboratories of vivisectionists to zoos and aquatic parks.

The human enclosure and privatization of land escalating with the emergence of industrial societies is often thought of as the central, arrogant, desecrating crime. One reason enclosures are abominating acts is that they destroy the earth's sacred peoples—those indigenous "nature peoples" who know how to live in a way that recognizes and venerates Sacred Earth. (Several groups led by Earth First!ers include "Sacred Earth" in their organization titles or charters.)

Earth First!ers generally share the conviction of their predecessor preservationists, that the defilement of earth is exacerbated by the desecration of wild animals by humans, who breed into oblivion the wildness and free-dom originally inherent in all creatures.

Of course, sacred and profane animals are not new in the history of religion. What is novel is the suggestion that *domestication* profanes sa-cred animals. Earth First!ers, for example, share Muir's contempt for do-mesticated sheep, sometimes quoting his description of them as "hooved locusts." In an interesting contemporary innovation, Earth First!ers but-tress their analysis of the process of desecration with ecological science. Domestic sheep defile land (by overgrazing and displacing authentic, wild creatures), water (by polluting it with their excrement), and sky (by belch-ing and farting enormous amounts of ultimately anthropogenic green-house gases).

Consequently, many Earth First!ers wish to purify sacred places of unauthentic domestic animals. Some even suggest that domestic cows and sheep should be clandestinely shot or poisoned. Reports of such incidents have been increasing in the Western U.S.[103] Sacred places also need to be purified of human despoilers, whether developer, government lackey, off-road vehicle fanatic, religious fundamentalist pro-natalist breeders, or eager immigrants lusting after unsustainable consumer lifestyles.[104]

From Perception to Reconsecration:
Responding to the Desecration of Earth

Awareness of this part of the radical environmental worldview explains why veneration and consecration takes many forms, including *rituals of resistance* such as political protests, civil disobedience, ecotage, and elec-toral politics; *rituals of healing* designed to purify the earth from human defilement (e.g., through ecological restoration projects) and human con-sciousness from delusions of separation (e.g., through meditative work-shops); and *rituals of worship* such as neopagan ritual circles at Earth First! gatherings.

Much creative energy goes into such ritualizing. A ritual process known as the "Council of All Beings" provides a context where devotees grieve for the loss of wild creatures and seek empowerment from them for ecological struggles.[105] Since at least 1986 the liturgical ritualizing unfolding at Earth First! wilderness gatherings has been designed to foster group cohesive-ness (one night, for example, is devoted to the "tribal unity dance"), and to deepen these activists' spiritual connections with nature.

One form of ritual worship that particularly illustrates the present con-cerns of Earth First! are "road shows." These events typically weave ecology lectures with slide-show pictures of undefiled wilderness, contrasting these with landscapes devastated by clear-cuts or overgrazing. The itinerant road show "prophets" sometimes exhort the assembly to "learn to listen to the land"—reflecting an animistic presupposition—while urging repentance from ecological destruction and the restoration of wilderness places to their original purity.[106]

Pictures of undefiled sacred places are believed able to touch natural, but societally suppressed, connections humans have to nature. Alice Di-Micelle, a long-term Earth First! musician from the northwestern U.S., was designated a special role during a 1992 European road show. She was to bring her audience *experientially* into the forest: through her slides and music, she was expected to awake in them a mystical experience of the wild. Illustrating her own feelings about the sacrality of wilderness, she exclaimed, "that was fine with me, [the wilderness] is my church."[107]

Earth First! worshipers sometimes express devotion to the earth explicitly, referring to her as the Goddess or Gaia. Certainly Earth First! ritualizing is designed to focus attention on the sacredness of earth and foster in neophyte and mainstay the pagan religious experiences and sentiments that undergird the movement.

Although I have delineated three kinds of rituals—resistance, healing, and worship—these are often intertwined. Sacred songs learned during wilderness gatherings are regularly sung at demonstrations. Acts of ecological resistance, such as being buried in a logging road or doing a multiday "tree sit," sometimes produce altered states of consciousness involving experiences of unity with earth or a tree, or communication with the spirit of some nonhuman entity or earth herself. Acts of worship or meditative processes such as "eco-breath" workshops, designed primarily to alter consciousness and deepen one's empathy toward and connection with the sacred natural world, are also thought by some to actually facilitate planetary healing.[108] (The metaphysical basis for this belief is the conviction that, since all entities are interrelated metaphysically, the transformed consciousness of one or more beings can have a salutary healing impact upon the whole.)

The above typifications show that the pagan environmental movement exhibits diverse strategies of venerating land. By looking at the specific events at Mount Graham, we can better see the impact pagan environmentalists are having, particularly when their spiritual sentiments collide with incompatible ways of understanding sacred places.

The Battle for Mount Graham:
Earth and Outer Space as Sacred Space

At every Earth First! rendezvous, different groups lobby to host the next year's Earth First! gathering. The lobbying typically centers around arguments about which wilderness is the most pristine and threatened, and thus worthy of pilgrimage and defense. In 1992 several groups made impassioned pleas, arguing that their preferred place was the most biologically diverse, with the most fragile ecosystem; had many endangered species; and represented a crucial, precedent-setting battle. (The arguments became so repetitious that several advocates humorously recited this litany of claims as a prologue before advancing their specific cases.) The decisive factor in the group's decision turned out to be whether *people* they considered sacred—namely North American Indians with their nature-based religions—were also imperiled and whether the campaign could promote a desired alliance with them.

Earth First! chose to meet during the summer of 1993 in eastern Arizona where, since the mid-1980s, environmentalists and Earth First!ers had been fighting plans by astronomers at the University of Arizona and other cooperating research institutions, including the Vatican Observatory, to construct the Mount Graham International Observatory, a complex of advanced technology telescopes. (The Vatican astronomers moved to Arizona in the early 1980s in order to flee Rome's light pollution.) As the battle unfolded, it increasingly had been characterized by an environmentalist alliance with traditional Apache Indians who considered the peak sacred and viewed the observatory project as a threat to their freedom of religious practice. Predictably, there were religious tensions between this resistance and the Vatican's proponents of the telescope project.

The Mount Graham controversy provides what may prove to be an archetypal example of conflicts over American sacred space tangled with environmental disputes. The central characteristics of this controversy can be quickly summarized. Earth First!ers view Mount Graham as sacred because it is a special, ecologically fragile, "sacred island ecosystem" (according to Earth First! movement tabloids) that since the last Ice Age has been isolated biologically by the surrounding desert. Consequently, it provides habitat for several unique species of flora and fauna that evolved only there, including the Mount Graham red squirrel.

Earth First!ers generally wish to support indigenous nature peoples wherever they are found, believing they provide the remnant of human knowledge and spirituality needed for the reharmonization of humans and sacred natural processes. Consequently, Earth First!ers also view Mount Graham as sacred in deference to traditional Apache who also venerate the mountain and oppose the telescopes. Various Apache believe that the mountain is the chief (or one) among four (or two) sacred mountains, is an important pilgrimage site, a secret burial site for their medicine people, the home of important spiritual beings (sometimes called the Gaahn, Lightning People or Crown Dancers) to whom they pray for life giving water, and the locus of sacred plants essential to the practice of their healing arts.[109] Apache opponents fear the telescopes will block their prayers to the creator, which travel to the heavens via Mount Graham.[110]

Resistance to the Mount Graham telescopes began when both pagan and mainstream environmentalists declared that it would contribute to the extinction of the endangered red squirrel. About the time the prospects for this strategy declined, traditional Apache came forward with their claims about Mount Graham's sacredness. Environmentalists quickly championed these assertions, partly as a strategy to open a second front in the battle, but also out of sympathy for the nature spirituality and cultural integrity of the Apache. By the early 1990s the two strategies had merged into complementary expressions of the sacrality of the mountain, well encapsulated in the heading of a publicity flyer: "Mt. Graham—Sacred Mountain, Sacred Ecosystem."[111]

The beginning of the resistance can be traced back to mid-1985 with the formation of the Coalition for the Preservation of Mount Graham. A year later $20,000 of equipment was stolen from the University of Arizona's Steward Observatory on Mount Graham's High Peak. In 1987 a civil disobedience campaign began with the arrests of Earth First!ers blockading road construction for the project. On 30 August 1988, Dave Foreman vowed that, if built, the telescopes would be destroyed. In another act of defiance, on 5 May 1989, microwave dishes and telescope housing were sabotaged at the University of Arizona in Tucson.

In November 1988, however, when Congress passed the telescope-sympathetic Arizona-Idaho Conservation Act, the University of Arizona gained permission to construct three telescopes immediately through an exemption from federal environmental laws. A second phase would include four more, if the red squirrel population did not decline as a result of the first phase.[112] By September 1993 the first two telescopes, including the Vatican observatory, had been completed, and it appeared that the act was the deathknell to the *environmental* strategy against the observatory complex.[113]

Much of the *environmentally* based opposition to the project has been based on the perception, often not articulated for strategic reasons, that Mount Graham is a sacred wilderness ecosystem. About the time of the enabling legislation and the waning of hopes that ecological rationales would thwart the telescopes, an opposition *explicitly* based on the sacredness of the mountain reignited the controversy.

This phase of the opposition was foretold by several letters sent in January 1987 to the United States Forest Service during the National Environmental Policy Act comment period. The authors claimed that Mount Graham was sacred to the Apache; one suggested that Mount Graham was currently utilized by the San Carlos Apache for religious purposes. But these claims went largely unacknowledged until 4 October 1989, when Ola Cassadore Davis, the great-granddaughter of Apache Chief Cassadore, went public in the *Tucson Citizen* protesting the scopes as a desecration.[114] Environmentalists soon established a coalition with Davis and other Apache spiritual leaders who shared Davis's perceptions, forming the Apache Survival Coalition in May 1990.

Soon the Coalition had presented its claims to a congressional oversight committee dealing with Mount Graham and secured a 10 July 1990 resolution by the San Carlos Apache Tribal Council asserting that "for generations our elders have instructed us on the sacredness of Dzil nchaa si an (Big Seated Mountain, aka Mount Graham)," labeling the project "a display of profound disrespect" and proclaiming "firm and total opposition to the construction of a telescope."[115] About a year later, in a 6 June 1991 letter signed by all nine members, the Tribal Council threatened the Forest Service with a lawsuit for violating several federal environmental and religious freedom laws. Shortly afterward (on 19 August 1991) the coalition filed a lawsuit versus the U.S. Government (and its Forest Service) for permitting the telescopes; the University of Arizona joined the lawsuit to gain standing to defend their interests. The Tribal Council reaffirmed its support for the Coalition's legal effort on 10 December 1991.[116] Also, during 1990 and 1991 several letters were written to U.S. government agencies by prominent Apaches protesting the desecration of Mount Graham;[117] and a variety of Native American tribal associations and solidarity groups in the U.S. and Europe went on record opposing the telescopes.[118] Meanwhile, direct action by Earth First! activists and other environmentalists against the road building and site preparation, and civil disobedience at the University of Arizona, led to increasing numbers of arrests and substantial regional awareness regarding the controversy.

Although the resistance had gained momentum during the early 1990s, telescope opponents suffered a major setback in September 1993 when the San Carlos Apache Tribal Council, on a 4–4 vote that Council Chair Harrison Talgo refused to break, withdrew its opposition to the telescopes (Salerno 1993).[119] Moreover, by this date, prospects for a legal victory by either environmentalists or the Apache Survival Coalition appeared remote.[120] Nevertheless, the tenacity of the opposition had created a public relations nightmare for the University of Arizona and the Vatican, who are now seen by many to be insensitive or racist toward Native Americans and their religions. In May 1992 Apache and other U.S. opponents of the telescopes traveled to Europe, winning resolutions opposing the telescopes by many members of the German and Italian parliaments.[121] An audience with the pope that had been scheduled to discuss their concerns was abruptly cancelled, further bolstering accusations of Vatican insensitivity and "bad faith." On 16 December 1991 Belgian activists pulled a bulldozer up to a Catholic cathedral, symbolically threatening its desecration, protesting by analogy the Vatican's bulldozing of Apache sacred ground.[122] And on 18 August 1992, in a "sacred run" for Mount Graham, Apache ran from Mount Graham to Tucson to publicize the importance of Mount Graham to their religious traditions.[123]

Negative publicity contributed to the withdrawal of all U.S. participants in the telescope project, including the Smithsonian Institution and several prestigious universities, leaving only the Vatican Observatory, Germany's Max Planck Institute, and Italy's Arceti Observatory as collaborators. Dr. Steve Emerine, spokesperson for the University of Arizona's Steward Observatory, claimed that it was impossible to have predicted how fierce and relentless the opposition would be. He might not have been so surprised had he recognized that people fight the hardest when defending values or places they consider most sacred.

Proponents of the telescope have done their best to deflect opponents' accusations. The Vatican and its observatory personnel in particular have been vulnerable to the charge of religious insensitivity.[124] This has been complicated by Pope John Paul II's pronouncements supporting Native American efforts to preserve their heritage.[125] Such pronouncements have been used by telescope opponents to accuse the Catholic church of hypocrisy. Opponents cite, for example, the name originally given to the third telescope permitted by the enabling legislation, "the Columbus project," as evidence of Vatican and University of Arizona insensitivity.[126] To diffuse such perceptions, the project was given a simpler, more descriptive label, the "Large Binocular Telescope."[127]

The Vatican Observatory's astronomers faced a conundrum. They would either have to withdraw from the project, abandoning professional prestige, years of effort, and probably their sole chance to control a high-quality (but not unusually powerful) telescope.[128] Or, they would have to reject claims by the coalition and others that they were desecrating the mountain and promoting cultural genocide. The observatory's response has been led by two Jesuits, George V. Coyne, the observatory's director, and Charles W. Polzer, curator of ethnohistory at the Arizona State Museum in Tucson, Arizona. Their strategy has been to insist that they respect Native American religion and to acknowledge that the mountain is considered sacred by some Apache, while denying that there is any "credible evidence" from "authentic Apache" that the telescope project violates Apache religious freedom.[129]

In spite of their efforts to appear sympathetic to those who revere the mountain, a review of Coyne and Polzer's defense of the observatories reveals ambivalence and even hostility toward the pagan perceptions animating many of their opponents; these Jesuits reject the conception of sacred space articulated by their opponents.

Coyne and Polzer have argued that there is no historical or archeological evidence proving that the telescopes are incompatible with Apache religious practice: since no shrines were found at the telescope site on Emerald Peak, for example, the project cannot desecrate sacred sites. Moreover, they assert that since an anthropologist who studied the Apache in the 1930s did not mention Mount Graham as a pilgrimage destination, it must not have been an important ceremonial site.[130] They conclude that Apache religious practice is not dependent on physical access to the mountain and that thus the telescope does not threaten Apache religious freedom.[131]

Polzer and Coyne have made these assertions despite their acknowledgment that "the field notes of Grenville Goodwin, archived at the Arizona State Museum [demonstrate] that the Apaches did revere Mt. Graham." Coyne argued that "none of the references single out either the summit or the range itself as unique," insisting that "the Vatican Observatory offers no opposition to the continuance of Apache religious practices or the preservation of traditional Apache religious sites on Mt. Graham." He goes on to suggest that, not only is there is no evidence "Mt. Graham possesses a sacred character which precludes responsible and legitimate use of the land," but that "responsible and legitimate use of the land enhances its sacred character."[132]

Coyne's assertions have been sharply disputed by two contemporary anthropologists specializing in Apache culture, Keith Basso of the University of New Mexico and Elizabeth Brandt of Arizona State University at Tempe. They contend that Coyne and Polzer inappropriately exclude or misinterpret the ethnographic evidence, and that both the field notes of Goodwin (who studied the Apache in the 1930s) and contemporary ethnography demonstrate that Mount Graham is vitally important for Apache religion and practice.[133]

Coyne has gone especially far in his effort to appear sympathetic to Apache religion, virtually adopting his opponents' rhetoric of sacrality, while still insisting that the telescopes will not defile the mountain: "We wish, frankly, to preserve the sacred character of Mount Graham by assuring that public access associated with the Observatory will not contribute to the degradation of the mountain. We are dedicated to assuring that the platform from which we observe the heavens will not become a staging area for the destruction of the earth." Coyne even invited "our Apache brothers and sisters to join [us] in finding the Spirit of the Mountains reflected in the brilliance of the night skies."[134] Such statements seem to concede the sacredness of the mountain, and even to contradict Coyne's monotheistic tradition. They also reveal that, underlying much of the controversy, there are irreconcilable conceptions regarding what actually constitutes sacred space.

Indeed, it is plausible to suggest that for Coyne, outer space is the ultimate sacred space. Space is sacred partly because it is the place where divine mysteries are still being revealed—today through the miracle of astronomical technology. Upon such an premise, astronomy itself assumes the character of a sacred calling. Evidence for this interpretation can be found in Coyne's assertion that the Mount Graham International Observatory will eventually "contribute to both . . . the conservation of the environment and the knowledge of its ultimate origins" as well as fulfill human "curiosity to know where [the environment] and human civilization came from."[135] The implied goal here is to find God, or at least deepen human understanding of God's creation and character. One might even surmise that the sites of such missionary activity—in this case telescope complexes—like any epiphany site, would also assume a sacred character. It is not surprising that Coyne, whose Catholicism has traditionally located

God outside the biosphere, would still conceive of space, of the heavens, as the ultimate sacred place, nor that the practice of his religion and the deepening of his understanding would supersede in importance the religious practices of a relatively small number of traditional Apache and environmental pagans.

Other statements illustrate the incompatibility between the worldviews of Coyne and his opponents. Accusing environmentalist "ideologs" of manipulating American Indians into opposing the telescopes, Coyne declared "No mountain is as sacred as a human being and there is no desecration more despicable than the use of a human person for self-serving purposes."[136] Here Coyne's anthropocentrism is clear, quietly grounded in those biblical passages assuming that humans alone are sacred because only they are created in God's image. Certainly such assumptions collide with the pantheistic or animistic perceptions of many pagan environmentalists; and also with the perceptions of those Native Americans who speak of other creatures as kin and reject Chain-of-Being hierarchies.

Even more telling are statements in Coyne's "Personal Reflections upon the Nature of Sacred in the Context of Mount Graham International Observatory." He begins, "I have a profound respect . . . for the resolutions of the San Carlos Apache council" declaring that Mount Graham is sacred. But when people claim a public place is sacred and deserves protection, he continues, such protection would have "civic effects [and] . . . they must offer reasonable arguments. To my satisfaction they have not." Coyne next assails the worldviews of many of his opponents, criticizing those who "claim that the features of our land (nature, if you will), . . . the earth transcends our existence." The earth has only been around 4.5 billion years, he reasons, and given the life span of the sun, will last only another 5 billion years. "There will come a time when . . . Nature and the earth . . . will not be there. . . . They are beautiful . . . but passing, expressions of the sacred relationship I have with God."[137]

Coyne clearly believes the earth itself is not really sacred because it is not eternal; at most it can "express" the sacred human-divine relationship. But the earth is not sacred or valuable intrinsically as it is for environmental pagans and traditional Native Americans. Again, Coyne resists the metaphysical holism of his opponents, arguing that "We must distinguish between earth, nature, cultures, and [eternal] human beings." He concludes with words reminiscent of the Inquisition, "As both an environmentalist and a religious person I find that it is precisely the failure to make the distinctions I mention above that has created a kind of environmentalism and a religiosity to which I cannot subscribe and which must be suppressed with all the force that we can muster."[138]

One further statement helps clarify why for Coyne, the evangelical mission of the Church takes precedence over fears of earthly desecrations. Coyne envisions asking extraterrestrials contacted through the sub-millimeter radio frequency technology (built in phase one) if they had "ever experienced something similar to Adam and Eve, in other words, 'original sin'," and "Do you people also know a Jesus who has redeemed you?" A reporter interviewing him concluded that, "The Roman Catholic Church is look[ing] for life in outer space [in order to] spread the Gospel to extraterrestrials."[139] Apparently the sacred calling of the Mount Graham International Observatory extends beyond the quest for epiphanies to a willingness to spread the Gospel's universal message.

Some Catholics have been appalled at the statements by Coyne and Polzer, forming a group they called Catholics for Ethics and Justice to fight the telescopes and persuade the Church to withdraw from the project.[140] Coyne views this group as a nefarious front for the Apache Survival Coalition, accusing them of "stealthy, cowardly, unethical, and unjust" tactics and falsehoods, threatening them with a lawsuit in a 19 May 1992 letter. Their attorney responded by threatening Coyne with a defamation lawsuit.[141]

Communication between adversaries in this conflict has become intensely vitriolic. In one of the ugliest moments in the conflict, Charles Polzer attacked a group that, ironically, shares his monotheistic presuppositions. Polzer accused two Phoenix medical doctors, leaders of the mainstream environmentalist opposition to the telescope project, of spearheading a "Jewish Conspiracy" designed to "undermine and to destroy the Catholic Church."[142] One of the two doctors is Lutheran.[143]

A Sacred but Fragile Alliance[144]

If differing perceptions regarding the sacredness of Mount Graham have fueled the conflict between proponents and opponents of the Observatory complex, the perception that the mountain is sacred, shared by most opponents of the project, has not led to unity among the resistance. There remains enough diversity of opinion about Mount Graham's sacredness that internal bickering periodically threatens to undermine the opposition's fragile alliance.

This became apparent shortly after Mount Graham was chosen as the

3.1 Editorial cartoon by Mike Ritter. Reprinted by permission of
Tribune Newspapers of Arizona, all rights reserved.

pilgrimage site for the 1993 Earth First! rendezvous. Several close associates of Earth First! founder Dave Foreman expressed dismay that the rendezvous would be on, rather than near, Mount Graham.[145] Fearing that five hundred people would damage the fragile ecosystem, one said with disgust, "they think because they are nature-loving hippies that their shit doesn't stink. If they think the place is sacred, they should stay off the mountain." Jaspar Carlton, founder of the Biodiversity Legal Foundation, an important legal arm of the radical environmental movement, complained "If it's sacred to the Apache and sacred from an ecological perspective, then it's hypocritical to tramp 500 people through there."[146]

Fears that such a gathering would itself desecrate the site were raised at the 1992 site selection meeting. The assembly had been assured that ecologically sensitive places would be avoided, and that Apache elders would be consulted to insure their sacred places were respected.[147]

Despite assurances that the mountain would be respected, several prominent Earth First!ers did not attend the 1993 meeting, and their criti-

3.2–3.5 Demonstration at the University of Arizona in July of
1993 protesting the Mt. Graham International Observatory. All
photographs © Bron Taylor. Used by permission.
All rights reserved.

cisms eventually were passed on to the rendezvous organizers. One organizer responded to these criticisms by arguing that the precautions taken to protect the mountain, and the direct action resistance, meant that "in many ways, we were resacralizing the place."[148] Thus the Earth First! pilgrimage was seen as *both* desecration *and* reconsecration among those very people who *agree* that Mount Graham is sacred and should be defended.

Extensive precautions were taken at the rendezvous, including plastic tape strung to bar access to red squirrel habitat, signs urging devotees to remove their shoes before entering the meadow where the daily meetings and workshops were held (for some, going barefoot has the additional epistemological benefit of enhancing one's contact with earth's sacred voices), and solar power was used to amplify music during the major rendezvous rally, maintaining the purity of the sacred, ritual space. Additionally, restoration efforts followed the rendezvous. That such rules and precautions were adopted without controversy is striking given the rebellious and anarchistic predispositions of most Earth First!ers.

One proposed rule, however, led to dissension. As early as the 1990 rendezvous in Vermont, activists worried that the rendezvous' alcohol-fueled party atmosphere could alienate Native American activists who link such drink to cultural genocide. On Mount Graham the issue came to a boil.

After an evening where revelers encroached upon an "alcohol-free campfire" complaints were raised at the next morning's "circle" (begun after the passing of smoldering, purifying sage) and the assembly was reminded that the Apache elders wanted no alcohol on the Mountain. The ensuing discussion lasted several hours, partly because Earth First! tries to operate by consensus, talking until agreement is reached or opponents "stand aside" and remove their "blocks" to the group will.

A majority were willing to quickly pass a resolution disapproving of alcohol consumption. The outnumbered opposition, however, was difficult to budge. Virtually all of the debate centered around whether alcohol consumption was compatible with respect for the sacred people (the Apache and other indigenous nature peoples) and the sacred mountain itself.

The morning's discussion began calmly, with a respected Sea Shepherd activist (known for successfully sinking whaling vessels), urging everyone to think carefully about the "sound bites" they might give the press. He suggested "we're here because this place is sacred." The discussion devolved. A woman responded, "but they'll think we're desecrating this place, especially if they see drugs and alcohol." A man from the rendez-vous committee responded defensively, missing her point, but implicitly responding instead to the criticisms that the rendezvous itself was a hypocritical defilement, "We're not desecrating [it], we're off the site itself."

A brief digression followed, during which a woman objected to allowing the press to attend evening fire circles. She didn't want them to see the "spiritual stuff" that happens in that sacred space-time, likening this to "invading a church." At this point a young American Indian Movement (AIM) activist appealed for abstention from alcohol, articulating two arguments often repeated thereafter: drinking is disrespectful to the mountain itself, and it is disrespectful to the indigenous peoples of this continent whose cultures are threatened with extinction by the dominant European culture. "In our hearts we don't want you to drink," he entreated, "look to your heart. Look to respect these natural places." If your family is into the bottle, "you'll respect that by not drinking . . . You're supposed to be our allies, not our enemies, and you can't be our allies if you don't help us here."

A woman spoke next, asserting that refraining for two days out of respect for the mountain was not asking too much. Angel responded, "We don't want two days set aside for Indian people, for this sacred mountain." We should have respect every day, he insisted.

At this point, the debate went back and forth. "As an anarchist" a woman wanting to block the resolution against drinking explained, "I don't want any restrictions. Even if we make restrictions, they will be ignored." Several agreed loudly, clapping and exclaiming "ho," ironically using a mode of agreement borrowed from Native American cultures. Passionately, and on the verge of tears, a man expressed his dismay at such sentiments, "There are lots of Native nations watching us. Many won't come here because of the alcohol, because of their fear [of us due to our reputation about alcohol]. We're talking about [risking an alliance with] six million indigenous people in North America!"[149]

This plea did not convince those ideologically opposed to any official position: "We don't want to make laws about this stuff. It should come from the heart." Disagreeing, another voice expressed disbelief at what he was hearing, making a passionate appeal, "We're arguing about whether or not to respect a mountain. What's going on here? Are we going to respect the mountain or not? Or are we going to be butt-heads?" To this a woman shouted out, "If we disgraced the mountain, we did it by *driving* here."

Another confessed to feeling bad that she drank alcohol the previous night, "I've prayed and asked the Mountain for forgiveness" she exclaimed, "we can learn a lot from this mountain—and alcohol gets in the way."

To all this another woman replied incredulously, dismissing the notion that the mountain has an opinion, "The mountain doesn't care if we drink or not." Later, when given a chance to respond, another woman claimed that to deny the mountain has a perspective is "a white view," arguing that "we also have people in our tribe hurting themselves with alcohol" and concluding that "out of respect for the mountain we should not drink."

Despite occasional interjections opposing the preference of the majority to pass a resolution against alcohol consumption, the majority relentlessly mounted their case. A Wiccan woman involved in the development of various forms of ritual practice in the movement began by expressing her empathy for those who want to drink, "I come from a Catholic and a pagan perspective. In both, drinking is sacramental." And "normally, I'd be a rebel" against those who want to make rules. "But here, this is some one else's church. It's right for them, in their church, to ask us not to drink. Just as I would ask them not to use tobacco, their sacrament, in many of our pagan ceremonies." She also reminded the assembly that Ola Cassadore Davis, the Apache elder leading the opposition to the telescopes, had requested that each morning and night everyone take a moment alone to listen to the Spirit of this mountain. "If we do that," she suggested to much clapping and more "Ho!s" "that voice will make the decision for us."

A man who often leads neopagan sweat ceremonies at Earth First! retreats argued similarly, "It seems to me that, despite the fact that the entire Earth is sacred, this place is especially sacred. We must remember why we're here, what our duty is. Respect is not too much to ask." A woman agreed, noting that "We've drawn inspiration from their cultures—it's the least we can do—we're talking about helping them to survive." Another woman argued that there had been too much talking about what "I" want, not enough about what's good for the Earth or what's good for "the sacred alliance with the Native peoples here." These appeals were greeted with expressions of approval by at least ninety percent of the gathering.

After a dissenter again inveighed against more rules, a long-term AIM activist stepped forward, mentioning how his people have substances like peyote to alter consciousness, but "the bottle symbolizes the destruction of our people. If you want to help the family, you have to be in solidarity" with us in this struggle too, he insisted. He concluded by grounding his antidrinking argument in the sacrality of the Mountain, reasoning "If we are to respect this mountain you have to respect our bodies that come from it."

Perhaps the turning point came when Dana Lyons, a musician who has been particularly active in promoting the alliance, and who has emerged as a spiritual leader whose role is to focus the tribe on the sacred and their corresponding duties, walked into the center of the circle. This was an unusual move, symbolically asserting his spiritual authority, "With all due respect, we are warriors," he began, pausing for emphasis, "Every society has warriors who are working for the community." This issue can be looked at two ways, he asserted, we can view it simply, like the Indians, "No fucking consensus—its sacred, [pausing again for emphasis], this should be enough." A secondary rationale for not drinking, he continued, is strategic. "We're talking about the most important alliance ever formed to fight for the Earth. At what other rendezvous have we had AIM people here?," he asked rhetorically. Then raising his voice to emphasize his conclusion, "The warrior sometimes must rise above his personal needs for the good of the community." His speech was greeted with the most "Ho!s" and cheers to occur during the debate.

Shortly thereafter, an AIM activist from Oregon exclaimed, "I don't want to have to go home and report that we spent so much time talking about chemical dependence [and] respect for Native Americans. I want to talk about strategies to make respect for the land happen." Expressing pantheistic and animistic reverence for the land, he made a variety of observations: the tree people, the bird people, are listening, "These peoples have to decide if they want you back . . . " "Think about, when you're leaning against a tree, you're leaning against a relative . . . I came here to promote community; to pray; to understand that its all alive. We love this land so much that we leave it alone. That's why we [Indians] don't hike so much [as white people]."

After a wide-ranging discourse he returned to the central debate: "To be warriors you have to do the [ceremonies] to purify your body. Keep in mind that you are teachers," he urged. "We need powerful minds and spirits to be real warriors. . . . The trees don't need [alcohol, you don't] either." Ominously, he warned them that alcohol jeopardizes the alliance, "I'll oppose you coming to sacred mountains if I know you bring alcohol here." He then offered them hope, describing a vision he has had of Indians and Earth First!ers united in a massive occupation defending a sacred site.

Toward the end of the debate, a well known Earth First! spiritual leader who regularly facilitates the Council of All Beings tried to diffuse the dissension by stating "Respect is a matter of the heart. It can't really be defined. I don't want people battling over different views of respect." Of course, this is precisely what the entire controversy was about, not only between opponents and proponents of the telescopes, but within the opposition itself. It is difficult to find unity when disputes remain about the nature of the sacred and the concomitant duties toward it.

Eventually the facilitators realized that a consensus could not be achieved (several blocks remained to a resolution "opposing alcohol on the mountain out of respect to the mountain and the native peoples here").[150] A vote was then taken. (Voting is considered a last resort that has become necessary in large part because, it is believed, the movement is disrupted by authorities who purposefully sow discord.) The vote made clear that at least ninety percent of the assembly felt strongly that alcohol should be removed out of respect for the sacred mountains and the indigenous nature-peoples of the region. Through the rest of the rendezvous, although still present, alcohol-fueled revelry was significantly reduced from the levels at previous rendezvous.[151]

From Dissension to Resistance

Despite such tensions as the ones described above, most Earth First!ers and Indian activists expected their shared reverence for Mount Graham to unify them in resistance to the observatories. Lone Wolf Circles, an Earth First! spiritual leader, expressed the view that both Indians and Earth First!ers were tribes, with differing customs, and that both groups must learn to respect each other's traditions if the alliance were to flourish. Several ritual processes on the mountain served to foster such respect, building solidarity between the two groups.

Several of the Indian activists stayed with Earth First! allies while on the mountain, attending evening fire-circles, which involved diverse forms of merriment interwoven with reverent periods of nature-revering poetry and song. One song that speaks passionately about defending Mother Earth was rewritten to embrace the Apache in their struggle; to its previous chorus "this is our land, this is our home" (explaining their willingness to fight to defend it), was added "Apache land, Apache home." At another evening's fire, a carefully planned "neopagan" ritual was performed, beginning with a ritual leader leading the assembly in chanting the Apache name for Mount Graham, Dzil nchaa si an. (Like Gary Snyder, Earth First!ers often use the Native American names for places as a form of veneration.)

The climax of the rendezvous began when more than a dozen Apache and several Earth First! runners completed an 18 mile "sacred run" up the mountain to the Rendezvous site, carrying sacred eagle feathers that had been blessed by a medicine man. The run was both an astute antitelescope publicity event, and a transforming pilgrimage; as explained by a woman prior to the run, "each footstep is a prayer, an intense spiritual connection with the Earth."

Before the arrival of the runners, the sacredness of the event and the ending place was underscored when the assembly was told not to take pictures or audio recordings of the ceremony. After the run, Franklin Stanley, an Apache medicine man, explained that the mountain has "always been a sacred place," and that their medicine men are buried there. He performed a blessing, dusting the assembly with yellow powder (probably corn pollen, which is used in many Native American ceremonies), and gave a long prayer in his native language.

Interestingly, Stanley drew on Christian notions, referring to God and Christ, suggesting that "we're all equal in the eyes of the Supreme Being." Stressing again that "this is holy land," he proudly reminded everyone that his people were the last Indians fighting the U.S. army; then he urged unity for the coming struggle: "We're blossoming again. You [Earth First!] people are too. We're no different. Every people, each of the four colors, are given special powers. When we meet other people, look at their eyes to see if they have respect. We have to teach those who don't have respect. The prophesies say that someday we will all sit down together. That time is coming."

Stanley then planted a stick with three sacred Eagle feathers in the earth (the fourth carried on the run would return to the reservation). "You're purified to be here," he told the crowd. "There are visions here. Your fight is critical" and "this unity means a lot to us. . . . It's all of our fight to protect Mother Earth."

The demonstrations following the rendezvous also furthered unity between the groups. The Indians seemed moved by the nature-spirituality present at the demonstrations. Before the gate to the telescope construction they sang earth-revering songs borrowed from North American neopaganism. One such song, "The Earth is Our Mother" had been sung as early as 1989 during blockades on Mount Graham. The song was sung reverently, repeating many times the verses,

> The earth is our mother; we must take care of her;
> the earth is our mother, we must take care of her.

Her sacred ground we walk upon, with every step we take;
her sacred ground we walk upon, with every step we take.

The chorus is apparently inspired by a Native American song, "Hey yunga, ho yunga, hey hung yung" (repeated several times).

A similar song, "Ancient mother," reveres the earth as goddess and empathizes with her pain as she experiences her own defilement:

Ancient Mother, I hear you calling,
Ancient Mother, I hear your song.
Ancient Mother, I hear your laughter,
Ancient Mother, I taste your tears.

When sung before the gate of the construction site, the song spontaneously transformed the demonstration into a powerful ritual of mourning and commitment. Reminded by the song of the earth's suffering, most present gathered into a circle, many already weeping. A young woman who had grown up in the Church of All Worlds, a neopagan commune in Northern California, spoke about how the consciousness of the tribe comes from the Goddess. She then broke down crying as she thought about having no children. (Many Earth First!ers remain childless hoping to preserve the earth and her creatures from the ravages of overpopulation.) Someone thanked her for considering that level of commitment. She responded that it was not her, but the Goddess working in her.

The grief was palpable, and this led to a mourning ritual usually reserved for the Council of All Beings. A man who regularly facilitates the council at Earth First! gatherings placed a stone in the center of the circle, as is commonly done in the council's "mourning" phase.[152] He then told those in the circle that he wanted to say goodbye to the possibility of grandchildren, recounting that with his blessing, both of his children recently decided against having children. At this point, all the protesters were huddled together, crying freely.[153]

After a time, the grief was transformed to rage as an activist reminded the group that grief was not enough, and that those destroying the earth "have names and addresses." Another approached the locked gate shaking it in fury, tears still streaming down his face, setting the stage for the arrests to come. One of the AIM activists who earlier in the week had been offended by the stubbornness about alcohol confided to the group "I used to hate all white people, but today, you people showed me something."[154]

Demonstrations continued the next day as activists picketed the mirror laboratory at the University of Arizona in Tucson. They chanted "Sacred

Mountain, Sacred site, telescopes are not alright," "Squirrels first, Pope last," and displayed signs such as "Mt. Graham = Church," "Crucify the Pope Scope," and "Pope, come back to earth."

After demonstrators occupied the office of the University of Arizona's president, many Earth First! songs were sung, including "the Earth is Our Mother," "Ancient Mother," and another with lyrics reminiscent of Muir's attitude that tourists needed but were not worthy of wilderness: "the Mountain is open to the righteous." Twenty-two people were eventually arrested and dragged out of the administration building by police using eye-socket-pain compliance techniques. Earth First!ers, along with perhaps a dozen Apache and AIM activists, locked arms and sat down in the road-ways attempting to block the departing arrestees. In a symbolic egress, the blockade was circumvented as the police drove their vans off-road, crushing the plants adjacent to the blockade.

Despite the shaky start, the rendezvous and the action afterward had furthered the alliance between the devotees of these two nature religions. It should be noted, however, that the growing alliance depended on previous efforts by Earth First!ers and Indians in various regions. As individuals from these groups become better acquainted, they realize similarities in their spiritual perceptions.

To illustrate this with just one example, a woman calling herself "Sage" was first drawn to Native American spirituality through her interest in the holistic health movement. After connecting with Earth First!ers who shared similar interests, she learned to pick sage in the traditional way, so that "the spirit would come with the sage." She recalls how the sage spoke to her, calling her to give her own life back to the plants. In a discussion that reminded me of Gary Snyder's reflection on how one "hears" nature spirits, she said that when the sage speaks, "You don't hear a voice," but have a growing awareness. "For me, when the awareness came, the sage fields looked beautiful—they were alive to me. I was communicating to them in prayer and I was open to their spirits."[155] As with Snyder, openness is the prerequisite to discerning nature spirits.

She also explained that traditional Gabrielino elders recognize "what's happened between me and the sage. They say the sage called me." Moreover, these elders now vouch for her authenticity, so she has not been harassed by AIM members who sometimes ridicule New Age "wannabes." This is one example where Earth First!ers have gained credibility with spiritually traditional Native Americans by revealing their own connections to nonhuman entities. I have heard many times from Indian activists and spiritual leaders that spiritual insight is a matter of openness, not ethnicity; they also uniformly add that many Indians have been severed from their spirituality. Many such leaders also welcome non-Indian interest in Native American spirituality as a hopeful sign of the prophesied reharmonization of lifeways on Turtle Island.[156]

Conclusions

Since the days of John Muir, increasing religious pluralism and rising environmental anxiety have provided fertile ground for pagan environmentalism, a small but growing movement that is inspiring a militant environmental activism increasingly in alliance with Native American activists. The increasing militancy of pagan environmentalists, combined in many quarters with distaste for and fear of such pagan religiosity, is further escalating the intensity of social conflicts surrounding the development of America's remaining wilderness areas.

Pagan environmentalists generally believe that the entire earth is sacred. Practically speaking, however, it is difficult to act consistently as though this were true. Thus they are forced to prioritize the defense of those areas most important for the preservation of biological diversity (which are usually the most pristine areas) and the places considered sacred by the planet's remnant nature peoples. I have been struck, for example, by how Earth First!ers usually do not hold their gatherings in true wilderness, due to their conviction that they should not subject these holiest of places to the impacts of large numbers of humans. Their gatherings are usually held not in wilderness "holy of holies" but at nearby "tree farms" or clear-cuts created by monocultural forest management practices.[157] (Had the Mount Graham gathering been held in a more obviously desecrated place, discord over the site would have been avoided.)

These gradations of holiness support Chidester and Linenthal's contention in the introduction to this volume that Eliade's distinction between the sacred and the profane has been overdrawn; field-level observations suggest that such distinctions are often muddy. Indeed, for Earth First! and other environmental pagans, the mundane-ordinary is not opposite to the sacred; the mundane *is* the sacred.[158] It may be that, *a significant part of all environmental conflicts boils down to disputes between those who feel that the sacred is beneath their feet and those who think it is above or beyond the world. As we have seen, the political battle over Mt. Graham was fueled by a more fundamental dispute over the location of the sacred.*

Did the sacred reside in the earth or sky? Was the sacred ultimately situated in natural space or outer space?[159] Perhaps conflict is not inevitable between those who locate the sacred on earth and those who perceive it to be beyond this world—but it seems likely. In this case, those like Coyne, who locate the sacred in outer space, had to look to the skies from the earth; this positioned the battle between warriors of earth and sky on contested ground.

Finally, parallels can certainly be found between the dynamics I have described and those found in contests over other sacred places. For example, Linenthal's description of disputes over American battlefields as involving processes of veneration, defilement, and redefinition (a term referring to the struggle to maintain control over or to redefine public perceptions about the nature of the sacred and concomitant human obligations)[160] reveals patterns found again in the present analysis. Certainly a good example of redefinition is the attempt by environmental pagans to define the sacred as a landscape "without borders"—namely—to delegitimate nation-states, redefining them as defiling monstrosities.[161] In movement literature the U.S. is often called "Amerika." Likening the U.S. to a totalitarian regime certainly contradicts an understanding of the U.S. nation-state as an exceptional, American sacred space. Thus environmental paganism erodes religious nationalism. It decenters the national state from the sacred center, repositioning currently marginalized tribal societies to the center of the desired ecological utopia, the future-eden. Environmental paganism thereby wages a sacred battle against the most powerful form of religious sentiment and expression in U.S. culture.[162]

Beyond the struggles related to veneration, defilement, and redefinition, a fourth and fifth dynamic can be discerned in the environmental conflicts under scrutiny, namely efforts at restoration and reharmonization.[163] Restoration is the act of healing damaged ecosystems, thereby resacralizing, reconsecrating despoiled landscapes; reharmonization involves reuniting humans with the rest of nature in complementary lifeways.

Restoration and reharmonization both move beyond the struggle to define or redefine the conception of the sacred; they also raise eschatological questions. How will the desired healing, the restoration, of natural processes come to pass?[164] And how should we envision, build, sustain, and ultimately reharmonize, human lifeways on the planet?

As the heirs of Muir and other pagan preservationists, most of today's pagan environmentalists believe that, whether through human agency or following human extinction, the original, edenic natural paradise will be restored. The more optimistic among them still hope that tribes of human nature-peoples will populate that earthly, sacred place.

Notes

The author gratefully acknowledges the documentary assistance of Dr. Robin Silver and the astute comments on earlier drafts of this paper by the editors, Matthew Glass, Kathleen Dahl, Lauren Bryant, and Jean Crawford.

1. Interview with Peg Millett, San Gabriel Mountains (Southern California), 6 February 1994.

2. Letter to the author, received summer 1992.

3. When I first met her, at a spring 1991 community meeting in Philo, Cal., she musingly excused herself, in Rastafarian fashion, for "prayer"—namely, a few puffs of marijuana—consenting to talk afterward. Later, she told me that hallucinogens have had a decisive role in fostering in her, and in other Earth First! activists, the perception that the entire natural world is interconnected and sacred; many Earth First!ers make similar observations.

4. The letter's authenticity is in doubt. Initially I thought it looked like a difficult-to-fabricate synthesis of Christian fundamentalism and mental illness. American Indian Movement activist Ward Churchill and some Earth First!ers believe, however, that the letter is an FBI hoax—patterned after similar letters authorities received subsequent to abortion clinic bombings—designed to cast suspicion away from law enforcement agencies involved in the assassination attempt and/or its cover-up. Whether authentic or a ploy designed to divert attention from the actual perpetrator(s), this letter underscores how for some, sacred values are at stake in such environmental conflicts.

5. It is easy to multiply examples of hostility toward environmental pagans. Charles Cushman of the pro-development Multiple Use Land Alliance thinks that preservationists are promoting "a new pagan religion, worshipping trees and animals and sacrificing people" and in battles over the forests he envisions "a holy war between fundamentally different religions" (quoted by Michael Satchell, "Any Color But Green," *U.S. News and World Report* [21 October 1991]: 76). Such sentiments can also be found among utilitarian conservationists. Alston Chase, for example, criticizes the "mindless pantheism" and "clandestine heresies" of radical environmentalists in *Playing God in Yellowstone* (Boston: Monthly Review Press, 1986), 309, ch. 16 & 18, and rejects the now common charge, first articulated by Arnold Toynbee in "The Religious Background of Our Present Environmental Crisis," *International Journal of Environmental Studies*, 3 (1972): 141–46; and popularized by Lynn White, "The Historical Roots of Our Ecological Crisis," *Science*, 155 (1967):1203–07, that by repressing animism and pantheism, monotheistic religions are responsible for much of the West's devaluation and destruction of nature.

6. Stephen Fox, *The American Conservation Movement: John Muir and His Legacy* (Madison: University of Wisconsin Press, 1981), 358–73.

7. Violence against all types of environmentalists has been increasing. The Center for Investigative Reporting documented in 1991 104 violent attacks on environmental-

ists; see Carl Deal, *Greenpeace Guide to Anti-Environmental Organizations* (Berkeley, Cal.: Odian, 1993), 12. How much of this is animated by religious passion is unknown.

8. By most people discussed in this article, such notions are commonly called animism. As David Chidester recently explained to me, however, the term animism originated with E. B. Tylor's *Primitive Culture: Researches into the Development of Mythology, Philosophy, Religion, Art and Custom* (London: J. Murray, 1871), who used it to refer to what he considered to be the inferior perception of "primitives," whom he believed incapable of distinguishing between dreams and reality. I use the term here in a nonpejorative way, to refer to the belief that the natural world is inspirited and that communication with nonhuman entities is possible.

9. By "sacred," a few movement participants seem to mean as little as "ultimately real" and "ultimately valuable"; more often they also have in mind an explicitly religious dimension of "holiness" when using the term, perceiving that the natural world is part of all divine reality, or part of a universal divine Being. The discussion of Edward Abbey's spirituality will illustrate the former conception.

10. In personal correspondence dated 29 December 1993, in response to an earlier draft of this manuscript I had sent to him, Gary Snyder suggested that I replace the phrase "pagan environmentalism" with "deep ecology environmentalism" because of the problematic nature of the term pagan and the bad image that paganism has in U.S. culture. He suggested that the term "deep ecology" was developed to avoid the negative connotations of this term, while still expressing essentially the same sentiments. I have demurred from his suggestion for the following reasons. First, the term pagan carries a strong religious connotation, which is not true of the term deep ecology. Secondly, the term can be defined nonpejoratively as I am doing in this article. Thirdly, many in the movement are trying to redeem the term by using it in a positive way and are attempting to counter the negative associations that now accompany it in Western culture.

Interestingly, Snyder's suggestion helps make one of my central points, that conservationists are often animated by essentially pagan perceptions, but often fear expressing their sentiments in a culture they consider hostile.

11. E.g., in this volume. See also several other important studies: John Sears, *Sacred Places: American Tourist Attractions in the Ninteenth Century* (Oxford University Press, 1989); Edward Tabor Linenthal, *Sacred Ground: Americans and their Battlefields* (University of Illinois Press, 1991); and Wilbur Zelinsky, *Nation into State* (University of North Carolina Press, 1988).

12. Quoted in Fox, *American Conservation Movement*, 291 and Max Oelschlaeger, *The Idea of Wilderness* (Yale University Press, 1991), 177.

13. Muir is best known as the founder of the Sierra Club, but his foremost legacy is the National Park System, where his preservationist ideals found institutional expression. He was raised on a Wisconsin homestead by a strict Scotch Calvinist father, against whom he rebelled, and a mother who would sing him old Celtic songs, which may have helped shape his love of nature.

14. Michael P. Cohen, *The Pathless Way: John Muir and American Wilderness* (University of Wisconsin Press, 1984); Fox, *American Conservation Movement*, 80; Oelschlaeger, *Idea of Wilderness*, 172-204.

15. Fox, ibid.

16. Oelschlaeger, *Idea of Wilderness*, 172.

17. By Norwegian philosopher Arne Naess, "The Shallow and the Deep, the Long-Range Ecology Movement" *Inquiry*, 16 (1973).

18. Cohen, *Pathless Way*, 65.

19. Ibid., 289-90.

20. Fox, *American Conservation Movement*, 141.

21. Cohen, *Pathless Way*, 330.

22. Fox, *American Conservation Movement*, 43.

23. Ibid., 45, 52-53. Oelschlaeger plausibly argues that, although "at this time it cannot be fairly said that Muir was a pantheist . . . , he was now passing from an orthodox theism through a panentheistic zone of transition toward pantheism." *Idea of Wilderness*, 177. Borrowing from Barnhart, Oelschlaeger well defines these terms; ibid., 414, n. 35.

24. Cohen comments that he has been on this summit perhaps twenty times, and "Each day on Cathedral Peak that I remember seems sacred. The world seems to flow about that granite altar in all its wholeness," *Pathless Way*, 359. Given such sentiments, it is not surprising that Cohen was drawn to Earth First! in the 1980s, and currently retains a qualified sympathy for radical environmentalism.

25. Ibid., 359-360.

26. Ibid., 192.

27. Oelschlaeger, *Idea of Wilderness*, 197.

28. Cohen, *Pathless Way*, 173-75; compare page 23 and also his discussion of Muir's blurring of the line between domestic and wild animals in his children's stories, pp. 342-50.

29. Fox, *American Conservation Movement*, 13-14.

30. Ibid., 14.

31. Oelschlaeger, *Idea of Wilderness*, 200.

32. Ibid.

33. Cohen concludes that Muir did not fully develop his view, or the logic, of sacred animals as wild creatures—especially with regard to predation *(American Conservation Movement*, 179-81).

34. Oelschlaeger correctly notes that "virtually all of Muir's later works (beginning in 1868, during his first summer in the Sierras) manifest [an] animistic vision" (*Idea of Wilderness*, 185).

35. Fox, *American Conservation Movement*, 5.

36. Oelschlaeger, *Idea of Wilderness*, 185.

37. Cohen, *Pathless Way*, 303.

38. Although largely satisfied with the results of these outings, Muir felt they could also desecrate the wild, even complaining that campfire jokes "profane the Sierra night" (quoted in Fox, *American Conservation Movement*, 120).

39. Many environmentalists would not call themselves preservationists because ecological change is inevitable. Nevertheless, the term can refer to preserving habitats and ecologial processes, and this is what I mean by the term.

40. Fox, *American Conservation Movement*, 318; Linda Graber, *Wilderness as Sacred Space* (Washington, D.C.: Association of American Geographers, 1976), 58-67. Cohen cogently critiques the use of photography in the preservation movement, *Pathless Way*, 236-52.

41. Bron Taylor, "Evoking the ecological self: art as resistance to the war against nature" *Peace Review*, 5 (2 June 1993): 225-30.

42. Fox, *American Conservation Movement*, 366.

43. Graber, *Wilderness As Sacred Space*, 28, 81.

44. Johnathan Z. Smith, *To Take Place: Toward Theory in Ritual* (University of Chicago Press, 1987), 56.

45. Fox, *American Conservation Movement*, 350.

46. Cohen, *Pathless Way*, 66, 68.

47. Ibid., 70. While on another dangerous climb, Muir had another one of his most profound spiritual experiences, this time, of interspecies communication with a small dog accompanying him, deepening his understanding of the intrinsic value of all creatures: see Fox, *American Conservation Movement*, 69–70. Pantheistic experiences have also been reported by other twentieth-century mountaineer-preservationists, including Bob Marshall (see ibid., 208).

48. Ibid., 362.

49. Ibid., 359–71. Another factor obscuring public knowledge of these sentiments has been press self-censorship. When "Thoreau declared his faith in the immortality of a pine tree and its prospects for ascending to heaven . . . the *Atlantic* ran the piece without the offending sentence, thereby eliciting a furious letter from the author," ibid., 363.

50. Ibid., 367.

51. Ibid., 371–73.

52. Edward Abbey, *Desert Solitaire* (Univerity of Arizona Press, 1968), 47.

53. Ibid., 50.

54. Ibid., 135.

55. Ibid., 176.

56. Ibid., 209. Abbey was also taken by the example of "the lad Everett Reuss, author of *On Desert Trails*, who disappeared at the age of twenty-one into the canyon country of southern Utah, never to return . . . For all we know he is still down in there somewhere, living on prickly pear and wild onions, communing with the gods of river, canyon and cliff" (ibid.).

57. Ibid., 209–10.

58. Robinson Jeffers, *Rock and Hawk*, ed. Robert Hass (New York: Random House, 1987).

59. Abbey, *Desert Solitaire*, 74–75.

60. Ibid., 186, 190.

61. Earth First! musician Darryl Cherney's song "free the dead" epitomizes pagan environmental sentiments about an authentic death; its lyrics deal with poison-free decomposition.

62. Abbey, *Desert Solitaire*, 212.

63. Ibid., 213.

64. Ibid., 214.

65. E.g., Abbey contrasted civilization, which he viewed as compatible with sacred places, with culture, which was not, due to its multifaceted defiling engines. "Civilization is mutual aid and self-defense, culture is the judge, the lawbook and the forces of Law and Ordure [sic]; Civilization is uprising, insurrection, revolution; culture is the war of the state against the state, or machines against people. . . . Civilization is tolerance, detachment and humor, or passion, anger, revenge; culture is the entrance examination, the gas chamber, the doctoral dissertation and the electric chair," ibid.,215.

66. Ibid., 135.

67. Ibid., 50.

68. Ibid., 205.

69. Ibid., 117, 137–38.

70. Edward Abbey, "A Response to Smookler on Anarchy," *Earth First!*, 7 (1 August 1986).

71. Abbey, *Desert Solitaire*, 155.

72. Ibid., xii.

73. Edward Abbey, *The Monkeywrench Gang* (New York: Avon, 1975); and *Hayduke Lives* (Boston: Little, Brown and Company, 1990).

74. This phrase Abbey speaks through his character Bonnie Abbzug. See the epigraph at the outset of *Hayduke Lives*.

75. Gary Snyder, *Turtle Island* (New York: New Directions, 1974), 104 and *The Practice of the Wild* (San Francisco: North Point Press, 1990), 40, 93.

76. For an excellent description of the influnce of Snyder and the "beats" in American culture, see Michael Davidson, *The San Francisco Renaissance: Poetics and Community at Mid-Century* (Cambridge University Press, 1989).

77. Snyder concludes: "the State itself . . . is inherently greedy . . . entropic, disorderly, and illegitimate," and quoting Cafard, "The region is against the regime—any Regime. Regions are anarchic," *Practice*, 41.

78. Other examples of such naming-veneration and naming-subversion include Snyder's claim that "You have to get rid of the name Cincinnati. . . . After all its the Ohio River Valley . . . [And] Ohio means *beautiful* in Shawnee," *Turtle Island*, 5. Furthermore, "We're consciously reinventing a language for North America." Using "Turtle Island . . . is part of reinventing a language for our time here. Its a political act." From interview with Gary Snyder, Davis (Putah-toi), Cal., 1 June 1993.

79. Snyder, interview.

80. Snyder claims that Jews and Muslims are the only pure monotheists, because Christians hold to it in "a very qualified and tricky way." "Everybody else in the world is a multi-faceted polytheist, animist or Buddhist, who sees things in the world" not as dead matter, valuable for its utility only, but as having continuity with all life. Snyder, interview.

81. Kirkpatrick Sale, *Dwellers in the Land: the Bioregional Vision* (Santa Cruz, Cal.: New Society, 1985); and Van Andruss, C. Plant, J. Plant, and E. Wright, *Home!: A Bioregional Reader* (Santa Cruz: New Society, 1990).

82. Snyder, *Practice*, 39.

83. Gary Snyder, *The Real Work: Interviews and Talks 1964–1979* (New York: New Directions, 1980), 8.

84. Snyder, *Real Work*, 17. Such allusions to the land as alive are common in Snyder's writings, e.g.: "Inhabitory peoples sometimes say 'this piece of land is sacred' or 'all the land is sacred.' This is an attitude that draws on an awareness of the mystery of life and death; of taking life to live; of giving life back—not only to your own children, but to the life of the whole land" in *The Old Ways* (San Francisco: City Lights, 1977). 59–60.

85. Snyder, interview.

86. Snyder, *Real Work*, 67.

87. This experience is not just available to backpackers: "the same happens to those who sail in the ocean, kayak fjords or rivers, tend a garden, peel garlic, even sit on a meditation cushion. The point is to make intimate contact with the real world, real self," in *Practice*, 94.

88. Snyder, *Practice*, 94.

89. Snyder, interview.

90. Snyder, *Practice*, 5.

91. Snyder, interview.

92. Gary Snyder, letter to author, 29 December 1993.

93. Snyder, *Practice*, 6.

94. Snyder calls this process "the real work" and gives a book of interviews this title, *Real Work*, 82.

95. Snyder, *Old Ways*, 13–14. Snyder also is fond of Jeffers's "vulture" poem (interview).

96. Snyder, *Practice*, 19.

97. Dave Foreman, "Reinhabitation, biocentrism and self defense" *Earth First!*, 7 (1 August 1987). He is also critical of many tendencies within Earth First! which are not relevant to the present analysis.

98. Snyder, *Old Ways*, 13–14.

99. Taylor, "Evoking the Ecological Self."

100. Unless references are cited, the material on Earth First! has been gathered by means of interviews and personal observation since 1990.

101. Ecological sabotage, now abbreviated "ecotage" or "monkeywrenching" in movement parlance, had begun at least as early as the mid-1950s in the southwestern United States, according to Edward Abbey in *Desert Solitaire*. Abbey's novel *The Monkeywrench Gang* celebrated the heroism of ecological saboteurs and helped inspire the development of Earth First! ecotage tactics such as "tree spiking" (hammering objects into trees to hinder logging), and bulldozer "decommissioning."

102. I will detail descriptions of these experiences in *Once and Future Primitive: The Spiritual Politics of Deep Ecology*, forthcoming from Beacon Press.

103. Bruce Hills, " 'Ecoterrorists' may take aim at lifestock," *Deseret News* (8 October 1990).

104. The logic here, combined with antianthropocentric ethics, might lead one to think that at least in some cases, human desecrators should be shot like other domesticated despoiling agents. Some Earth First!ers are bold enough to express such sentiments, but to the best of my knowledge, thus far such sentiments remain theoretical.

105. Bron Taylor, "Earth First!'s Religious Radicalism" in *Ecological Prospects: Scientific, Religious, and Aesthetic Perspectives*, ed. C. Chapple (State University of New York Press, 1994); John Seed et al., *Thinking Like a Mountain: Towards a Council of All Beings* (Santa Cruz, Cal.: New Society, 1988).

106. Taylor, "Evoking the Ecological Self."

107. Interview with Alice DiMicelle, Oshkosh Wisc., 9 October 1992.

108. I will detail such experiences in future work.

109. Keith Basso, Declaration, Apache Survival Coalition et al. vs U.S. et al., University of Arizona, Intervenor, CIV. No. 91-1350-PHX-WPC. Declaration on Mt. Graham (Dzil nchaa si an), prepared for Patricia J. Cummings, Attorney at Law, and Apache Survival Coalition (31 March 1992); John P. Wilson, Apache Use of the Pinaleno Mountain Range, II, Report No. 57, prepared as defendant's exhibit for the Safford Ranger District, Coronado National Forest. Las Cruces, N. Mex. (January 1992); Tim McCarthy, "Apache Tribe Lives New Vision in Fight to Save Mountain," *National Catholic Reporter*, 27 (36, 2 August 1991).

110. Franklin Stanley, grandson of Apache Chief Bylas, and a full-blooded Apache medicine man, testified against the telescopes:

"I know the songs that are sung at our holy ground, and there are songs about Mt. Graham that are an important part of our religious practice. There are herbs and sources of water on Mt. Graham that are sacred to us. Some of the plants on Mt. Graham that we use are found nowhere else. These plants are important to our spirtual practices and healing. . . . The Apache relationship with the mountain includes showing respect to the natural things found on the mountain, the things we have discovered in revelations, or that the mountain has given us."

"The mountain is part of spiritual knowledge that is revealed to us. The mountain gives us life giving plants and healing . . . Our prayers go through the mountain, to and through the top of the mountain . . . There is also very sacred plants on top of the mountain and very, very important trees . . . The mountain is like a gateway or river and putting the telescopes on top of the mountain is like putting a dam on the river . . . The construction would be very detrimental because our prayers would not travel their road to God . . . God is the Almighty, the 'Ruler of Life.' There are very serious consequences, to us, if we act with disrespect. [Moreover] The 'Gaahn' [spirit beings] live on Mt. Graham. Mt. Graham is one of the most sacred mountains. The mountain is holy. It was holy before any people came, and in the mountain lives a greater spirit . . . If you take Mt. Graham from us, you will take our culture . . . If you desecrate Mt. Graham it is like cutting off an arm or a leg of the Apache people." Declaration of Franklin Stanley Sr. in support of preliminary injunction, Apache Survival Coalition et al. vs. U.S. et al., University of Arizona, Intervenor, CIV. No.91-1350-PHX-WPC (31 March 1992).

111. The undated flyer is from "Friends of Mount Graham" (P.O. Box 41822, Tucson, AZ 85717-1822). For strategic purposes, cognizant of their negative image in many sectors, Earth First! activists often form "front" groups with names obscuring their Earth First! roots. Some such groups do not obscure their pagan spiritual sentiments, such as Minnesota's "Sacred Earth Network."

112. Charles Bowden, "How the University Knocked Off Mount Graham. *City Magazine (Tucson, Arizona)*, 4 (1 January 1989): 28–36; John Dougherty, "Star Whores: The Ruthless Pursuit of Astronomical Sums of Cash and Scientific Excellence," *Phoenix New Times*, 24 (25, 16 June 1993): 2-11.

113. The June 1989 Sierra Club Legal Defense Fund lawsuit against the United States lost when the courts ruled that Congress intended to exempt the project from these laws, and has the discretion to do so. However, the University of Arizona, with the approval of the U.S. Fish and Wildlife Service and the U.S. Forest Service, decided in 1993 to move the location of the third and most powerful telescope (the Large Binocular Telescope) outside the area permitted by the Act. They then enraged environmentalists by cutting 250 trees from the new site on 7 December 1993, only hours after gaining these approvals. This led to another lawsuit, this time by a coalition of eighteen environmental groups. This lawsuit produced the first legal victory against the International Observatory, when on 28 July 1994 a Federal judge ruled that moving the telescope violated the Endangered Species and National Environmental Policy Acts. This ruling was upheld in September 1994 by the 9th U.S. Circuit Court of Appeals in San Francisco, delaying indefinitely the completion of the third (and most important) telescope.

114. While on a 1989 vision quest, Davis consulted a medicine woman on the reservation. "Praying in a wickiup, the traditional Apache shelter, Davis saw herself dangling off the east side of Mount Graham. A dangling man faced her from the west, their hands joined at the summit as if to harbor the entire range in their gigantic embrace. She thought the man was white. The medicine woman told her to push on with her opposition to the observatory," quoted by McCarthy. This vision helped inspire the Indian-environmentalist alliance against Mt. Graham.

115. San Carlos Apache Tribal Council resolution opposing Mt. Graham telescopes. San Carlos Reservation, Arizona (10 July 1990).

116. The first vote was 6-0, the second 9-0.

117. For example, on 31 Aug 1990, San Carlos Tribal Council chairperson B. Kitche-yan wrote to the USFS criticizing them for violating Apache sacred beliefs, protesting their failure to contact the tribe about the telescope project. (The USFS disputed his contentions, claiming that in August 1985 they sent letters to the tribal council about two rock cairns and a shrine found on the mountain, asking the Apache for comments or concerns about the cultural or religious significance of these finds.)

After his dismissal as tribal chair in the middle of 1991 for misusing tribal funds, Kitcheyan reversed himself, claiming Mount Graham was not sacred to the Apache, eventually testifying in this way before the University of Arizona's Board of Regents. Kitcheyan was convicted of embezzlement on 7 July 1994. See Ann-Eve Pederson, "Former San Carlos Apache Chairman Pleads Guilty to Embezzling $63,312," *The Arizona Daily Star, Tucson* (8 July 1994).

118. E.g., on 18 July 1991 a unanimous resolution against the telescopes was passed at a European meeting of groups in solidarity with North American Indians.

119. Telescope opponents interpreted this as evidence that university promises of economic and educational assistance eroded opposition within the council. But disputes about the religious significance of Mount Graham among the Apache were nothing new. This was partly due to divisions between religiously traditional Apache and those who are not, and also because of significant differences between clans. It was federal action against the Apache that placed different clans in close proximity on reservations; uniformity of worldview has not been a characteristic of all the different bands. For details, see Basso, Declaration on Mt. Graham.

120. The reasons cited by the district court for rejecting the ASC's lawsuit has been the failure of Apache opponents to register their claims at an earlier date, and the ruling that Congress does have the discretion to override their own environmental laws. The ASC appeal was rejected by the 9th U.S. District Court, No. 92-16288, D.C. No. CV-91-1350 PHX WPC (8 April 1994). The first two telescopes, including the Vatican's, were completed in September 1993.

121. Sal Salerno, "Apache Delegation Returns from European Tour of Protest," *The Circle (News from a Native Perspective)*, 13 (6, June 1992): 28.

122. Sal Salerno, "Vatican Denies Sacred Ancestry of Mt. Graham," *The Circle*, 13 (4 April 1992).

123. Sacred runs from the San Carlos Apache reservation to Mount Graham again protested the desecration of Mount Graham in 1993 and 1994. They included non-Indian solidarity activists, see "San Carlos Elders Thank Runners" in *The Navajo-Hopi Observer* (6 July 1994).

124. This is due in part to increasing public discourse, accompanying the recent 500-year anniversary of Columbus's journeys, about the Catholic Church's role in suppressing indigenous Americans.

125. Theresa Schuelke, "Indians Told to Keep Culture," *The Catholic Sun* (24 September 1987): 24-27.

126. Vatican Observatory proponent Charles W. Polzer, in stark contrast to Gary Snyder, who emphasizes the spiritual value of renaming this continent Turtle Island, refers to the region of southern Arizona, including Mount Graham, as "Northern New Spain." See affidavit of Charles W. Polzer, responding to Apache Survival Coalition lawsuit (6 April 1992).

127. Telephone interview with University of Arizona spokesperson Steve Emerine, 3 December 1993.

128. The Vatican's telescope received a relatively small mirror (six meters long) that

was fabricated as the test for the larger mirrors to go into subsequent scopes. For example, the Large Binocular Telescope has two 8 m × 4 m mirrors, and will be able to explore areas of the Universe previously unseen. The second project also was designed with unique capabilities; the "sub-millimeter" technology allows astronomers to measure radio frequencies at levels never before heard.

129. These arguments were made in affidavits by both Coyne and Polzer in response to the Apache Survival Coalition lawsuit and in other forums. See, e.g., George V. Coyne, "Statement of the Vatican Observatory on the Mount Graham International Observatory and American Indian Peoples" (5 March 1992), also submitted as University of Arizona, Exhibit "B," Apache Survival Coalition et al. v U.S. et al., University of Arizona, intervenor, CIV. No.91-1350-PHX-WPC (6 April 1992).

130. For example, "Mt. Graham itself was subject to only the most casual and ephemeral use by the tribe, as documentary and archeological evidence clearly shows." Affidavit of Charles W. Polzer, responding to Apache Survival Coalition lawsuit (6 April 1992).

131. See Coyne, "Statement on American Indian Peoples" and Polzer, affidavit.

132. See Coyne, "Statement on American Indian Peoples."

133. See Basso, Declaration, and Elizabeth A. Brandt, "Executive Summary of the Preliminary Investigation of Apache Use and Occupancy and Review of Cultural Resource Surveys of the Proposed Mt. Graham Astrophysical Area, Pinaleno Mountains, Arizona," prepared for the Apache Survival Coalition (28 May 1991). Taking an intermediate view is John P. Wilson, a USFS employee, in "Apache Use of the Pinaleno Mountain Range," II, Report No. 57, defendant's exhibit for the Safford Ranger District, Coronado National Forest, Las Cruces, New Mexico (January 1992). Focusing only on the Goodwin papers, he concluded that "the mountains are a minor element in the exercise of Apache religion" and "while this range has some symbolic importance, traditional Apache religious practices do not require visits to [it]." This study begs the question about whether the Apache would view the telescopes as a desecration; its focus was very narrow, assuming that only historically demonstrable "traditional" practice is authentic religion. Thus it ignores other relevant evidence. Moreover, much of the material Wilson quotes from the Goodwin papers could easily be used to argue against his conclusions: that Mount Graham was of central religious significance to the Apache during the period of Goodwin's research.

134. See Coyne, "Statement on American Indian Peoples".

135. See George V. Coyne, "Statement of the Vatican Observatory on the Mt. Graham International Observatory, the ecology of the Pinaleno mountains, and related political issues" (22 April 1992).

136. See Coyne, "Statement on American Indian Peoples." Interestingly, in a hearing on Mount Graham before the University of Arizona's Board of Regents, a member of a pro-telescope group calling itself the San Carlos Apache Tribe People's Rights Coalition testified using language nearly identical to Coyne's: "*No mountain is as scared as a human being.* Therefore I believe that we as a people will survive [the telescope construction]. I believe that *responsible and legitimate use of the land enhances its true purpose*" (testimony of Karon Long before the Arizona Board of Regents Mount Graham Open Forum, 27 March 1992, my emphasis). This parallel rhetoric suggests that Coyne may be employing the very strategy he accuses his opponents of using, in his case, exploiting an Apache as a means to defend his telescope.

137. George V. Coyne, "Personal Reflections upon the Nature of the Sacred in the

Context of the Mount Graham International Observatory," Castel Gandolfo, Italy (25 May 1992).

138. Coyne, "Personal Reflections." In a newspaper article appearing after these "personal reflections" were made public by Coyne's opponents, he claimed that his statements were not a call to suppress Apache religion but "a condemnation of 'an extreme environmentalist tendency toward the worship of nature.'" See Jim Erickson, "Astronomer-Priest Contends that Science, Religion Don't Clash," Arizona Daily Star (11 November 1992). Coyne reiterated this explanation in a 14 January 1992 letter sent to signatories of a statement protesting his comments about suppressing nature religion. In this letter he says that the controversial quote was taken out of context, and that his statement "refers [only] to false worshippers of the Earth as described in the immediately proceeding paragraph." He then states that, since "my statement about suppression of religiosity has led to ambiguities and to maliciously false interpretation, I have removed it in the revised version."

According to Coyne's own logic, however, to the extent that Native American spirituality involves reverence for nature itself, it must be "false," and he would wish it suppressed; certainly some Apache spirituality would qualify (see, for example, Franklin Stanley's testimony in endnote #110). Logically, Coyne cannot desire to suppress environmental but not Native American paganism. (I wish to thank Dr. Coyne for sending his above-mentioned letter and other related documents.)

139. Bruce Johnston, "Vatican Sets Evangelical Sights on Outer Space, "London Daily Telegraph (28 October 1992); see also Dougherty.

140. Another group of Catholics appealed to the President of Italy to resist Italian participation in the project, see Marla Donato, "Come One, Come All to the Telescope Feud," Chicago Tribune (11 January 1992).

141. May 1992. No lawsuit followed.

142. Steve Yozwiak, "Priest Calls Telescope Foes Part of 'Jewish Conspiracy,' " The Arizona Republic (14 August 1992).

143. Polzer admitted making the statements, which were also acknowledged by his religious superiors, see Yozwiak, " 'Jewish Conspiracy'." Polzer apologized for the pain his comments had caused, while claiming he had been ambushed by an Apache interviewer who had intended to set him up.

144. The following analysis is based primarily on field observations and interviews during the 1993 Earth First! rendezvous on Mount Graham and subsequent demonstrations, 28 June through 7 July 1993.

145. Foreman, who disassociated himself from Earth First! in 1990, retains great influence within the pagan environmental movement. From as early as the mid-1980s, he proclaimed that humans should "resacralize" their perceptions of the natural world.

146. Interview with Jaspar Carlton, Oshkosh, Wisconsin, 22 May 1993. Carlton is often frustrated with what he sees as the ecological ignorance of many Earth First! activists, which he thinks leads them to desecrate places they should be protecting. During a 2 July 1992 interview at the Earth First! rendezvous in the San Juan Mountains of southeastern Colorado, he complained about activists walking disrespectfully in the meadow, stepping on blue lupine, a threatened meadow flower. "I cannot respect those who unthinkingly are trashing these plants," he said. "We are in a sacred area here. All this stuff is sacred." Adding that we must be sensitive to smaller life forms, he emphasized that humans should ask "biologically, legally, morally, how ought we to manage our sacred wilderness ecosystems."

147. Within the Native American and pagan environmental communities, "respect" and "disrespect" are ubiquitous terms that serve as verbal proxies: respect denoting "veneration," disrespect indicating "defilement" or "desecration."

148. Interview with Jean Crawford, Mount Graham, Arizona, 5 July 1993.

149. This figure is exaggerated. Census figures indicate that about 1.5 million self-identify as Indians in the U.S.; tribal enrollment is smaller still.

150. The remaining "blockers" were anarchists apparently from a "punk" subculture; one of the most vocal expressed a hyperindividualistic anarchism that illustrates one extreme boundary of the social philosophies undergirding some of those drawn to Earth First!. He asserted, "from my worldview this is not a sacred mountain. And there is no connection between booze and respect. Alcohol is fun. Its a good thing." Revealing a naivete that seems absurd for one presumably involved in an extremist form of political activism—that no idea is morally preferable to another—he concluded, "I'm against this proposal, it says [that] one view is better than another." Three individuals applauded this sentiment, prompting the facilitators to move toward a vote. (Later that evening two Earth First!ers justified their alcohol consumption by discussing how the Apache traditionally made their own alcohol.)

151. Still, drunken revelers did impinge on the sacred ritual space of the fire-circle at least one evening after this discussion, causing one ritual leader to tell them to "fuck off" as he drove them back into the shadows. (The ritual space is defined roughly by the penumbra of the fire and those encircling it; mere observers, as well as revelers and inebriates, are expected to stay outside of this space. This expectation often remains unfulfilled, sometimes intentionally by those who think the ritualizers are taking themselves too seriously.)

One common response to complaints about the drinking and partying is that rendezvous provide the major time each year for this extremely hard-working tribe to cut loose with their tribal family, and have some fun. Sometimes the pressure of being an outlaw group resisting great powers is cited. Few Earth First!ers appear to be alcoholics, however, perhaps because alcoholism tends to militate against political activism and environmental concerns.

152. Taylor, "Earth First!'s Religious Radicalism."

153. I wish to thank Charles Rothschild for describing this scene to me, since at this moment I was being denied access to the site by the police.

154. I wish to thank Jean Crawford for this anecdote and for the description of how mourning was transformed to rage at the demonstration.

155. Interview with Leona "Sage" Klippstein, Pasadena, Cal., 17 August 1993.

156. For more about the borrowing of Native American spirituality by Earth First!ers and the diverse reactions such borrowing engenders, see Bron Taylor, "Empirical and normative reflections on Deep Ecology's appropriation of Native American spiritualities," a paper presented to the North American Religion Section, American Academy of Religion, Washington, D.C., November 1993, author's files.

157. This was stated explicitly in "Midwest Rendezvous Upcoming," *Midwest Headwaters Earth First!* newsletter (2 August 1992). After directions are given, the gathering site is described: "The forest there has been logged but is recovering, there's plenty of firewood, space for tents, etc. It is not actually in the Wilderness but is very close. We might not feel so bad about leaving a bit of a trace (unavoidable) in an area already logged than in the designated wilderness."

158. Of course, as we have seen, it is possible for the sacrality of a place to be eroded

and even lost. In the cases where Earth First! gatherings are held in places of lesser sacrality, at least the potential for restoring the sacrality of the place is embodied, either symbolically by the pilgrimage itself, or practically, through acts of restoration ecology or political resistance. In the worldview of most Earth First!ers, if left alone for a long enough time, desecrated places can heal themselves.

159. Acknowledging that such conceptual disputes are important variables in environmental conflicts should not be mistaken for idealism. This analysis purposefully begs the question about whether material conditions or human conceptualizations have been most decisive in creating today's environmental and cultural realities. For an introduction to such disputes see John Bodley, *Anthropology and Contemporary Human Problems*, 2nd ed. (Mountain View, California: Mayfield, 1983); Roderick Nash, *Wilderness and the American Mind* (Yale University Press, 1967); and Oelschlaeger, *Idea of Wilderness*.

160. See Linenthal, this volume.

161. At the 1989 Earth First! rendezvous the U.S. flag was burned—the ultimate symbol of U.S. religious nationalism and of the U.S. *nation* as a sacred place. Only a few were offended since most disdain modern nation-states.

If it is true that the shopping mall can also be considered a sacred center of the U.S. culture of consumption, as Ira G. Zepp argues in *The New Religious Image of Urban America: The Shopping Mall as Ceremonial Center* (Westminster, Md.: Christian Classics, 1986), then another effort at decentering was an Earth First! "puke in" against shopping in the late 1980s, and plans to disrupt shopping at the Mall of America.

162. A good example of the collision between the antinationalist sentiment of most environmental pagans and the patriotism of religious nationalists can be found in the Greenpeace/Earth First! act of "symbolic guerilla warfare" which desecrated Mount Rushmore, described in this volume by Matthew Glass. (Mount Rushmore is an especially good site for anti-nationalist veneration of the land, since its construction depended on the violent appropriation of the Black Hills from the Lakota.) For the term see Edward T. Linenthal, *Sacred Ground: Americans and Their Battlefields* (Urbana: University of Illinois Press, 1991), p. 163.

163. David Chidester reminds us that efforts at reharmonization provide one of the few universals in religious ethics, *Patterns of Action: Religion and Ethics in a Comparative Perspective* (Belmont, Cal.: Wadsworth, 1987). Of course the conceptions of the cause and nature of the dis-harmony vary widely, as do the prescriptions for reharmonization.

164. Catherine Albanese suggests that "New Age [spirituality is] a new healing religion [and] a planetary dimension is intrinsic to that healing," in "The Magical Staff: Quantum Healing in the New Age," in *Perspectives on the New Age*, ed. J. R. Lewis and G. J. Melton (State University of New York Press, 1992), 75. This emphasis on planetary healing in the New Age movement parallels the sentiments of many environmental pagans. New Agers *tend* to conceive of this healing in more mystical terms, and environmental pagans, in more political terms, although one can find both emphases among devotees of either spiritual subculture.

4

"ALEXANDERS ALL"
Symbols of Conquest and Resistance
at Mount Rushmore

Matthew Glass

> No one has sung, painted or carved adequately the story of this
> irresistible God-man movement that fled its ancient moorings,
> comprising Alexanders all in their quest for new worlds to con-
> quer; following the sun into the unknown west—into the night!
> —Gutzon Borglum, sculptor

Introduction

IN DECEMBER 1935 A. N. Demaray, associate director of the National Park
Service (NPS), begrudgingly attended another in a continual series of congressional budgetary hearings, seeking further appropriations for construction at Mount Rushmore. Asked about the meaning of the slowly
progressing project, Demaray admitted he did not know what it meant.[1]
Demaray's admission underscores a perpetual problem within the cultural
history of the memorial, its inherent ambiguity as a prominent symbol on
America's patriotic landscape. In this chapter I want to examine some of
the tensions arising out of various efforts to fix the meaning of the "Shrine
of Democracy," as it is often called.

Rushmore's distinction among the many symbols of patriotism marking the American landscape stems precisely from the lack of interpretive
clarity surrounding the memorial since its earliest days. Just what does it
mean? This ambiguity has insured the memorial a lasting history of interpretive conflict as Americans of various groups struggle with each other to
impose a meaning on the mountain as clear as the outlines of its presiden-

tial faces. In particular I want to focus here on the processes of symbolic creation, appropriation and rejection stemming from the interpretive struggles visible at the memorial.

To understand these interpretive conflicts, however, we can find little help within the customary discussion of mountains as sacred places. The conflicts at Mount Rushmore, and their temporal proximity to our own day, make it difficult to analyze the memorial in ways that dovetail readily with the scholarly treatment of other sacred mountains. In Mircea Eliade's classic formulations mountains are sacred because they are the sites of "hierophanies," revelations. Accordingly, people "are not free to choose the sacred site, they only seek for it and find it by the help of mysterious signs."[2] Eliade's emphasis on revelation, and his well-known equation of modern times with the "desacralization of the cosmos" would seem to militate against considering as sacred a mountain chosen by a sculptor during the modernist heyday of the 1920s.[3] Nor would we gain much insight from the long history of wilderness appreciation in America. The reverence or aesthetic wonder cultivated by John Muir and numerous others also tends to locate the symbolic power of a mountain in its "sublimity" or its great remove from human manipulation.[4]

Further, there is the basic problem of interpretive ambiguity and conflict. Eliade does admit that a sacred site may be the place of conflict, as when he says "by occupying [foreign territory] and, above all, by settling in it, man symbolically transforms it into a cosmos."[5] However, there is a permanence and an absoluteness in this process of settlement which makes it sound as though the previous occupants of the site were removed once and for all.

When we consider Mount Rushmore, however, this finality appears to dissolve into the smoke of incessant symbolic creation, destruction, and reinterpretation. As will become apparent in what follows, each attempt to fix Rushmore's sacred significance by one group results in countermoves of resistance by another group. That is, as Rushmore comes to be sacralized concern arises that the sacred meanings emplaced there by one group are threatened by another. Consequently, there is a seesawing of symbolic reversals. Those interpretations advanced as pure expressions of the memorial's essential meaning trigger others to raise the specter of profanation. Increasingly in recent decades, interpretive conflict over the memorial has taken the form of political protest, most especially as Native American activists fastened on to Rushmore as an important site at which to attack the impact of American nationalism on native lands and traditional modes of life.

Rushmore sits in the middle of the Black Hills, an ancient mountain range near the center of North America, rising abruptly from the surrounding plains, catching the eye of the traveler, spurring on the imagination. With their vivid contrast between dark slopes covered in yellow pine and spruce and the surrounding world, bifurcated into two equally vast tiers of plains and sky, the Black Hills have drawn people for several thousand years. In the course of that long span of time, many cultures have left their marks on the Hills. Mount Rushmore, America's "Shrine of Democracy," is simply the most noticeable. Indeed, to understand Rushmore's functions as a patriotic shrine in American culture, it is necessary to lay out the symbolic backdrop against which it stands in relief. Viewing the memorial as part of a multitude of efforts to portray the Black Hills as sacred indicates the important religious creativity characterizing modern American use of sacred space, and forces us to abandon Eliade's own emphasis on antiquity as a basic indicator of the presence of the sacred.

Foregoing for the moment the lengthy Native American presence, the Hills also reflect Christian labor to construct meaningful parallels between the symbolic world of biblical religion and the American landscape. In addition to numerous church and Bible camps, there is the little town of Bethlehem, begun by Benedictine monks in 1956 at the northern edge of the Hills. Intending to establish a shrine for peace, the monks built a nativity scene inside Crystal Cave, in Elk Creek Canyon. According to Bethlehem's founder, Father Gilbert Stack, the rationale for establishing the shrine follows from the symbolic significance of caves within the history of Christianity. As he told an interviewer: "Christ was born in a cave and the church first took hold in the Rome of catacombs during 300 years of persecution. Saint Benedict, patron saint of cave explorers, lived in a cave for three years before he founded the famous order of Monte Cassino Abbey."[6] To fulfill Benedictine requirements monks at Bethlehem established a Christmas and greeting card business in order to be self-supporting and successfully petitioned for a post office from which thousands of Christmas cards are postmarked annually. Within the shrine, candles representing all the world's nations are kept lit continually, services held twice a day, and a litany for world peace offered at the end of daily tours.

In the late 1960s Sen. Francis Case and Lincoln Borglum, son of Rushmore's sculptor, undertook a campaign to erect a three-hundred-foot statue of Jesus atop a mountain in the northern Hills above Spearfish, home to the Black Hills Passion Play since 1932. Supposedly visible up to eighty miles away, the statue was based on a model constructed by sculptor Gutzon Borglum for the city of Corpus Christi, Texas. Promoters hoped to face the statue either southward, establishing a symbolic link between the Christ in North America and a smaller Christ statue overlooking the city of Rio de Janerio, or else eastward, where the upraised arm of Jesus would wave back to the Statue of Liberty.

According to Dr. Ray E. Lemley, chair of the project's board of directors and a major financial contributor, the statue would become "the largest symbol in the world to the greatest Being that ever influenced the world and whose influence is surely needed in these perilous times." For Lemley and other contributors, financial pledges commemorated the pioneering spirit of their Black Hills ancestors.[7] Local chambers of commerce enthused over the idea, and a church advisory council formed in 1966 assured that the inspirational qualities would stand to the fore. Although, as board member Jim Shea stated to reporters: "We realize, however, that the impact on the entire state of such a monument can be tremendous. It could attract pilgrims from all over the world."[8]

In addition to these Christian efforts to establish sacred places in the Black Hills, their great remove from urban centers also triggered efforts to portray the Hills' inspirational qualities as capable of reforming political as well as personal life. When World War II drew to a close and the nascent dream of a United Nations took hold, a number of visionary Westerners looked to the Hills as the ideal location for the UN's headquarters (just as members of an earlier generation sought to move the Vatican). In a 1946 brief submitted to the UN Interim Site Committee by governors Dwight Griswold—Nebraska, M. Q. Sharpe—South Dakota and Lester C. Hunt—Wyoming, the authors argued the Hills afforded the new international organization an unparalleled opportunity to establish a base of operations.

Promoters portrayed the Hills as an idyllic environment, remote from global hot spots in Europe, Asia, and Africa, but also a potential center of global travel. According to maps provided by the governors, the Hills were equidistant from most national capitals, assuring the new headquarters would not favor particular nations at the expense of those more remote. Promoters also claimed this centeredness in the midst of the sparsely populated Great Plains would foster a new level of global cooperation, comparable to the impact on human consciousness of other great spiritual and moral developments. Pointing specifically to the historic examples of

Buddha, Jesus, Mohammed, the Treaty of Westphalia, and the Council of Trent, promoters emphasized an apparent correlation between irruptions of world-reforming humanistic values and remoteness from metropolitan life. To mark the Hills as a source of cooperative, cosmopolitan inspiration in the postwar climate, some advocated construction of a giant sculpture commemorating allied leaders Franklin Delano Roosevelt, Josef Stalin, and Winston Churchill.[9]

Thus to make sense of Mount Rushmore's status as a sacred mountain within the context of the Black Hills as a whole, it is necessary to acknowledge that the most vexing issue will likely be the multiplicity of interpretations and outright conflicts over the mountain's symbolic definition. Since these interpretations are generally part of the political efforts of groups to mark out the Hills in general, and Rushmore in particular, as a crucial symbolic center of American life, it is important to see the various interpretations of the mountain as strategic efforts.[10] Consequently in what follows I want to focus on the most notable strategic symbolic configurations visible at the memorial, configurations used by different groups to advance their own interpretive claims about the mountain's meaning.

I. Dreamer and Sculptor

Originally the memorial was Doane A. Robinson's idea. South Dakota's official state historian and a prolific poet, Robinson strove to preserve the legacy of the pioneering generation, the romance of the West, and what he saw as the passing of Indian culture. In 1923, eager to increase the flow of tourists on the federal highway running from Chicago to Yellowstone National Park Robinson contacted sculptor Lorenzo Taft, broaching the idea of a gigantic carving in the Hills to commemorate the West's heroic figures. Robinson went public with his proposal in 1924, at a meeting of the Black and Yellow Trail Association. The regional association of business owners built campgrounds and maintained the dirt, gravel and partially paved route. Competing for hearty cross-country travelers and their dollars along with other western trail associations in the years after World War I, supporters of the Black and Yellow sought ways to improve the volume of traffic. Robinson's idea seemed a likely hook to pull Yellowstone travelers off the road and into the restaurants, gas stations, and hostelries of Rapid City.[11]

Robinson's early promotional efforts revealed a self-conscious ambiguity over purpose and meaning. On the one hand Robinson envisioned a serious work of art, a monument to the American myth of frontier expansion and conquest. Robinson's own telling of this myth, in a poem called "Religion," underscores the depths to which he saw the frontier saga energized by a divine force.

> Mystic dynamic of the universe,
> Immeasurable, inscrutable,
> Whose potent fires flame the the hearts of men,
> Compelling them to do deeds of miracle:
> Brave trackless seas, thread jungle wilderness,
> Transforming ruthless, pagan savages
> To mild, benignant servants of the Lord.[12]

In the body of the poem he goes on to eulogize the spiritual labors of early explorers, missionaries and the pioneer denominations taking root in Dakota Territory. For Robinson the history which he sought to preserve was sacred history, the stories of men and women acting as agents of a divine civilizing process.

At the same time however, his vision of giant sculpture in the Hills also played up the enormous commercial potential for local and state businesses. As he put it in a letter in 1924, "While my native tendency is to stress the artistic and sentimental, the practical extension of the proposition has its appeal. . . . Every automobile ought to be induced to tour the entire Hills district." Writing to J. B. Green, secretary of the Rapid City Commercial Club, Robinson said, "Scenery alone will not sell the Black Hills to the world. . . . Tourists soon get fed up on scenery, unless it has something of special interest connected with it to make it impressive. . . . Having passed through Rapid Canyon, they would not go far to see another of equal beauty, but they would drive a hundred miles to see Wild Bill's grave. We must have definite things to play up and work upon the imagination of the tourists."[13] Over the years promoters and supporters have struggled continually with the tension between the commercial and inspirational appeal of Mount Rushmore, present from the very beginning.

When Lorenzo Taft proved unable to take on the project in 1924, Robinson sought out Gutzon Borglum, at the time amazing many across the country with his bas-relief monument to Robert E. Lee at Stone Mountain, Georgia. Under commission by the Daughters of the Confederacy, Borglum's work became embroiled in controversy, and he viewed Robinson's idea as not only a greater aesthetic challenge—carving on multiple surfaces, but also an escape from a legal thicket.[14]

The sculpture's proponents found it necessary to link patriotic appeal with commercial potential, in large measure as a result of the explosive opposition surfacing within the region as news of the proposed sculpture spread. While Rushmore's supporters often sought to downplay the ire of the local population, numerous letters and editorials from Black Hills residents attacked the idea as itself an unthinkable desecration. As Hills resident Maude Hoover wrote Robinson, "*Why* should we add to, or rather, desecrate, the work of nature with the puny work of man? What if we do have a great cliff face 'with nothing on it' among those towering peaks? . . . Please Mr. Robinson, do not use your influence against us Black Hillers in this matter. We love our Black Hills with a love that grows with acquaintance. Leave them to us as nature left them, deep, quiet, majestic, natural." J. B. Townsley, editor of the *Dakota Republican*, told Robinson that while he did not object to statuary sculpture, "it is distinctly out of place in the wilds of the Black Hills, where God's statuary surpasses any possible conception of mere man."

Robinson himself had to resort to religious language in order to castigate the sculpture's opponents, rebuking one naysayer with a biblical accusation: "ye would not," and chastising another Dakota editor, "God only makes a Michelangelo or a Gutzon Borglum once in a thousand years." As to the idea that such a carving was desecration, Robinson retorted "Of course God made the Needles [initially proposed for the memorial's location] as he made everything else that man has taken to himself and improved and beautified. That is what God made men and things for. There is no logic I am sure in the desecration suggestion." Robinson's theology of divine/human co-creativity required human participation, as he put it in another letter from 1925. "God did not quite complete his job in the Harney district [the Hills south of Rushmore], but left it for man to come into that section and create Sylvan Lake, the very jewel of the section. God always leaves it to man to finish his work—that's why we have Burbanks and Hansens developing the seed of beauty which God planted."[15] In light of his eulogy to missionaries, Robinson seems to have viewed the artistic and scientific transformations of nature as an embodiment of an essentially religious task.

While the form of the original vision was Robinson's, Borglum gave it substance. Robinson's initial idea for western heroes such as Gen. George Armstrong Custer, Meriwether Lewis and William Clark, Jedidiah Smith, or even Sacajowea and Red Cloud would have sacralized the myth of western expansion and the heroism of the pioneer. But Borglum saw the unique potential for a "monument so definitely and dominatingly national that we will arouse interest in every American."[16] In Borglum's eye the monument lost its regional focus and would instead serve to inspire national patriotism. Borglum evidently had wanted to carve Washington and Lincoln for some time, and the final choice of figures was his. In a 1924 telegram to Robinson following his return to Atlanta after first visiting the Hills, Borglum dashed: "Let us hold to that unbeatable and inspiring thought of those two lone giants, standing on top of America, George cloaked and Abe hatless, their figures rising out of the mother ledge. That may be enough."[17]

Like Robinson, Borglum also saw a divine force at work in the world, which he saw most directly evident in the contrast between the New World promise of America and the decay of Europe. As he put it in a newspaper article written in 1934: "It took ten years in the ruins and ashes of Europe to teach me how limitless and great our opportunity is, and that by some new awakening, some new understanding and great courage, man's great adventure in America would find expression." For Borglum the carving at Rushmore was a test of the American mettle, a reckoning with the sacred, world-historical task bestowed upon America since the days of Columbus. "In the fullest sense the great trek of the old world into the new, following that great child of the Renaissance, Columbus, meant more to the mind and soul-freedom that resulted than all the discoveries of lands or continents and their commercial value to men and civilization."

In Borglum's estimation, Americans had not yet properly weighed the full measure of their contribution to history. Art thus played a valuable prophetic role, calling the people back to their heritage. "Too little has been written on the wide freedoms secured, the virgin worlds offered—unpeopled, untitled, ungoverned—the nomads incapable of resisting even this unorganized aggression of the invaders. No one has sung, painted or carved adequately the story of this irresistible God-man movement that fled its ancient moorings, comprising Alexanders all in their quest for new worlds to conquer; following the sun into the unknown west—into the night!"[18]

Borglum first viewed Rushmore in 1924 as he reached the summit of nearby Harney Peak, surveying the Hills, a "garden of the gods," for a rock surface suitable for carving. Staring north towards Rushmore he proclaimed, "American history shall march across that skyline." Consciously using the mythic theme of Prometheus storming heaven to depict the fundamental meaning of American history, he envisioned a sculpture in which god-like beings placed "as close to Heaven as we can," could inspire the American, and the world's, population to continue their self-divinizing task.[19]

And yet Borglum, like Robinson, was prudent enough not to cast the pearls of artistic or patriotic sentiment before swine. He also took every opportunity to trumpet the sculpture's commercial appeal. The editors of *Specialty Salesman Magazine* recognized Borglum's booster qualities in a 1935 interview, which proclaimed him to be one of "the outstanding salesmen of America." According to the author of "But First He Had to Sell It!": "Borglum did not dwell on the value of colossal art in making the lives of the men and women who saw the great figures . . . more liveable . . . Instead he compiled figures showing an estimate of the number of people who could be expected to visit South Dakota as a result of the Memorial." Borglum told the interviewer: "I realized that the average person in South Dakota, when he was approached in regard to financing Mount Rushmore Memorial, would think of it in terms of dollars and cents. . . . We tried to talk to the people of that state in just those terms."[20]

Historian John Bodnar claims a tension exists within the politics of public memory in American society, as elites struggle with the masses for control of public symbols.[21] It would be tempting to see a similar cleavage between patriotic inspiration and commercial appeal working at Mount Rushmore. However, the willingness of Rushmore's two creative sources to draw on the commercial, and the memorial's own genesis as a promotional scheme, undercut any attempt to mark a rigid boundary between elite and what Bodnar calls "vernacular" cultures. Even though Robinson and Borglum were always ready to use the commercial to advance their sense of the sacred potential of the mountain, they also voiced some uneasiness with this conflation, as if it might give rise to inappropriate views of the memorial's significance. Borglum offered a biting critique of the same American public he earlier seemed willing to address in terms of dollars and cents. In a 1939 letter to Robinson, Borglum wrote that "not a tenth of one percent of the thousands who come long distances to see this work—mainly because it is big—contribute a single profound thought on either the effort to build the soul and character of men in such dimensions, or do they see much beyond the dimensions, and very little, if at all, of why it was done."

Robinson also complained about the American population's view of the mountain, though with more attempted understanding than voiced by the aristocratic Borglum. For Robinson the problem lay primarily in the memorial's newness, which kept modern people from grasping its sacred significance easily. Accordingly Robinson wrote "were we as simple-minded as most primitives, it would take no more than a single generation to create a tradition that the portraits on Rushmore were carved by lightning handed down from heaven . . . and from it would spring a mecca of devotion." In spite of their slow response, Robinson nevertheless admitted that he had "observed a growing tendency on the part of the public to confer upon the project a sort of mystical, semi-religious connotation, and I have no doubt that in due course that will involve a worshipful reflex from those Americans who in mounting numbers assemble here to make obeisance before this shrine of patriotism."[22]

For Robinson and Borglum the sculpting of gigantic human profiles in the Black Hills was an unquestionably appropriate way to memorialize their triumphalist reading of the American experience. Both men shared theological assumptions about divine guidance of American history found among many Protestants of the time. Their passion for monuments was also common across America during the 1920s. Individuals in numerous communities sought to preserve an authoritative, inspirational interpretation of the past in the midst of a rapidly modernizing social order.[23] More importantly, both were also disposed to see the same divine influence on American history embodied in the creative process whereby art transforms matter into spirit. Thus, the poet/historian and sculptor envisioned a memorial to American history in which the artist's creation, the transformation of silent stone into heroic testimonies, was itself symbolic of the creative power exerted by the American people on the landscape of North America.

At the same time, however, their theological rationale triggered mixed reactions. Some Dakotans rejected outright the effort to carve a memorial to nationalism. Others were evidently more enthused by the carrot of potential profit dangled by Robinson and Borglum in their appeals to the public. As both men recognized, their own rationales for monumental sculpture in the Hills did not always cohere in the years ahead, giving rise to interpretations they themselves might well have disavowed.

II. Patriotic Inspiration and Commercial Appeal

Both Robinson and Borglum seemed to recognize that control over the memorial's meaning would prove tenuous. One important way in which the memorial's promoters have managed to emphasize a particular reading of the memorial was to initiate frequent public ceremonies commemorating some aspect of the memorial's sculpting. To a great extent, these have been held in conjunction with important dates in national history, particularly the Fourth of July. These ceremonies provide the clearest examples of efforts to produce patriotic sentiments at Mount Rushmore, but their very scope, extending from Calvin Coolidge's appearance as carving began in 1927 to George Bush's official dedication of the memorial on July 4th, 1991, makes them difficult to summarize.

However, close attention to one illustrates some of the basic ritual and symbolic framework present at the memorial. Ceremonies of dedication or commemoration simultaneously focus on the achievement of the memorial's construction, the achievement of the nation symbolized by the presidential faces, and the needs of the present generation for inspiration and guidance in facing the problems of the day, although at any particular ceremony one focus might override the others. Consider for instance, the ceremony dedicating the completion of the memorial's night-lighting system, held June 25, 1950, attended by a vast crowd waiting "in awed silence" according to the announcer from radio station KOTA.

As with many ceremonies held in relation to the construction, a major theme in the speeches and prayers of the participants was the relationship between technology and nature, sacralizing the processes by which Borglum transformed stone into art. Master of ceremonies Van Heflin, in the Hills to play famous western scout Jim Bridger in the movie *Tomahawk*, expressed the need for night-time lighting at the memorial in terms of overcoming the constraints of nature and its limits on the expression of patriotic spirit. "Today the Mount Rushmore Memorial welcomes visitors by the thousands. But what of those who pass this way at night? They too should be given the opportunity to see this magnificent memorial." Previous unsuccessful attempts to light the memorial included army surplus floodlights, theater spotlights, and starshells bursting briefly five hundred feet above the memorial. Heflin relayed the history of artificial lighting in heroic terms: "The granite faces that were fashioned by the removal of five hundred thousand tons of stone still were cloaked in darkness. But the men who loved the shrine hadn't given up."

Rev. Carl Locke, of the local Keystone Congregational Church, gave the lighting ceremony a further symbolic definition in his invocation. His prayer turned the lighting into spiritual metaphor. "Prosper us in the event tonite and grant that this stone may be as the LIVING GRANITE of life's great program in our American way of life." Locke connected the task of lighting the mountain to the Cold War tasks facing the nation: "that Christian America may lighten the world and enlighten its people to a program of PEACE ON EARTH and GOODWILL TOWARD ALL MEN—as from this Sacred Shrine may the darkest hour turn into the Sunrise of a bright morning star of everlasting Peace."

Following a performance of Beethoven's "Nature's Adoration" by bass-baritone Deseri Ligeti, syndicated columnist Drew Pearson addressed the evening's theme. Earlier speakers had emphasized the task of turning what Pearson called "the modern miracle of electricity on the [four] faces." By contrast, Pearson, although seeking to find inspiration for the present in the illumination of the presidential faces, hesitated over the equation of technology and divine force. Pearson began by noting that modern technology creates problems unimaginable to a Washington or Lincoln. "How would they face the atom bomb, the hydrogen bomb, the jet-propelled plane, germ warfare, the mechanical brains that calculate mathematical problems for men. Would it be too much for them?" However Pearson's real point was not to discount the past in light of the present. He used historical distance instead to make judgments about the American character. According to Pearson Americans had been "living in an age of fear" in the months since "President Truman announced that Russia had the atom bomb." But, he claimed, Washington and Jefferson actually had far more reason to fear in the uncertain years following the Revolution. For Pearson, technological accomplishments were sapping the spirit of a once-courageous "pioneering people."

To reinvigorate a nation paralyzed by Cold War fears and hot war setbacks in Korea, Pearson urged Americans to recapture the faith and courage of the four granite faces. "I do know that if Washington, Jefferson and Lincoln were alive today they would throw their great pioneering spirit into working for new goals." For Pearson, a world federalist, these new goals were global democracy, obtained not through armed struggle, but persuasiveness, of a market-oriented form. "We are letting Russia win the battle of creeds, without even giving our own creed a good display in a big show-window. We are supposed to be the world's best salesmen. We've sold ice-boxes to the Eskimos, sun-lamps to Hottentots. Yet we, a nation of crack salesmen, let the Communists out-sell us." "If we hold up a goal of ideals that are broad enough and sell it hard enough, we can penetrate that [Iron] curtain."[24]

Many public ceremonies at Rushmore have been coordinated by groups such as the Mount Rushmore National Memorial Society (MRNMS), a voluntary organization established in the 1930s to help promote the memorial, and to insure that patriotic expression remains nonpartisan. Pearson's own controversial world federalist prespective is proof that various political viewpoints can emerge in the course of such ceremonies. Thus it is not politics per se that produces interpretive conflict at Rushmore. Instead, problems arise because of a perceived tension between pure patriotic devotion and creeping commercialism.

Even though key official players at Rushmore, such as Borglum, Robinson, and the Mount Rushmore National Monument Society (MRNMS), exhibited some ambivalence about their own linkage between the commercial and the patriotic, many entrepreneurs have seized the opportunity to fuse their own commercial efforts with the memorial's attractive qualities. In the 1930s, promotional literature prepared for the separate unveilings of the presidential faces by the MRNMS contained full-page advertisements by companies such as Standard Oil and the Chicago and Northwestern Railroad. These companies conflated the possibility of finding patriotic inspiration at Rushmore with purchase of their own products and services. A gasoline ad from the period speaks of a visit to the memorial as "a wonderful gift you can give your children: a personal involvement in their country's past, the discovery that learning can be an adventure. And it's so easy."[25] In this ad, patriotic inspiration and education come easy because of the antiknocking compounds which make for smooth sailing over the Black Hills' many up-grades.

This process of equating patriotic inspiration with consumer purchases produced some notable campaigns over the years. In many cases, however, Rushmore's supporters have attacked these advertisements, complaining that they are actually sacreligious. A recent proposed Seagrams whiskey ad, which showed three presidents sipping, read, "George went out to get another fifth." The MRNMS was successful in getting this ad pulled before it went to press.[26] Such advertisements have a long lineage. In 1941, the year of Borglum's death and the cessation of work, the Rushmore faces appeared in beer ads, and in a Walt Disney cartoon, leading to heated arguments among many South Dakota editors. The cosmopolitan *Sioux Falls Argus Leader* contended that such commercial use of the mountain did not hurt its symbolic power, but brought greater visibility and visitation. The editor of the more parochial *Brookings Register* countered by exclaiming that "profanity doesn't hurt God any, but I don't like it."[27]

In addition to countless commercial campaigns linking the memorial with a product or service, there also have been efforts to make connections between the heroic, often divine, moral virtues associated with the presidents by Borglum and Robinson, and the qualities necessary for more typical forms of success in American society. Interestingly, while the virtues found reflected in the presidential faces are political, in their translation into moral models for ordinary Americans they become economic. Thus Kemper National Insurance Company used Rushmore as a "mark of excellence" in a booklet urging its employees to increased productivity and competitiveness.[28] In a similar vein, during the Bicentennial a Minneapolis firm marketed a plaque for sales companies bearing the face of their choice of "salesman of the year." The promo called the plaque a "unique symbol of recognition and a great conversation piece."[29] This particular campaign sparked an exchange of letters between Hoadley Dean, president of the Memorial Society and Harvey Wickware, the memorial's superintendent, in which they agreed that the award "amounts to desecration."[30]

In recent years the MRNMS embarked on an extensive capital raising campaign to fund restoration and expansion of the visitor facilities. Several corporations have been able to use the memorial as a backdrop in exchange for contributions to the renovation fund. A Roundup pesticide commercial shown in the spring of 1993 features a suspended figure spraying a weed poking through a crack in stone. The camera pulls away, revealing the stone to be Teddy Roosevelt's nostril. Surely there is a fundamental ambiguity at work here. A symbolic nose-cleaning is given approval, yet an equation of individual enterprise with presidential virtue is termed desecration.

The tension between commercialization and patriotism has a parallel in the efforts of Rushmore's federal caretakers, the National Park Service (NPS), which has administered the memorial since 1933. Since a comprehensive history and analysis of the strategy of federal administration at Mount Rushmore would take up enormous space, I simply want to highlight an issue which affects federal involvement at the memorial. Given the First Amendment considerations that constrain any federal agency, the NPS walks a delicate line in administering all its units. In recent decades at units with historical or cultural significance, the NPS has sought creative means to tell the stories of the American people's history, becoming especially sensitive to cultural diversity. As several studies have recently shown, this task has been far from easy. Nevertheless the agency has played an important educational role in the politics of racial, ethnic, and gender identity in American culture.[31] This delicate effort to respect the pluralism of American life has been particularly difficult at Mount Rushmore, however, where patriotic faith has been articulated in unadultered form, without benefit of a battle, a homestead, a president's place of birth, or a factory to provide interpretive focus.

Rushmore is first and foremost a symbol designed to trigger intense emotional reactions from visitors, and the NPS there has the frequently unenviable job of dealing with the memorial's wide range of cathartic effects. To focus on just one instance, consider the controversy over the placing of the American flag during the 1976 Bicentennial celebration. To emphasize Rushmore's status as a national shrine, the NPS erected an avenue of state flags leading up to the memorial, each flag receiving two days of commemorative activity. Crowning the avenue, a large American flag was flown from the top of Lincoln's head. As a symbol, bicentennial planners at the memorial thought the flag had historical precedent, since one had been flown by Borglum at the site's initial selection in 1925, and throughout the years of construction. However, superintendent Harvey Wickware began receiving complaints from visitors shortly after the flag was first raised. One visitor said "I was appalled at the sight of the flag pole atop the Mt. Rushmore carving. It seems to me that this is going too far with the Bicentennial theme. To me, the sight of this flag pole is a desecration of the majestic work of the Mt. Rushmore carving." Other visitors spoke of the flag detracting from the "simple majesty of the sculpture itself." One, a landscape architect, wrote NPS director Gary Eberhardt that he found it "not only a distraction, but in very, very poor taste." The architect was dismayed "that such defacing of a national monument was actually perpetrated by the National Park Service itself."[32]

In response to these complaints, superintendent Harvey Wickware initially argued that the flag was an important aspect of the patriotic spirit necessary for the Bicentennial celebration.[33] However, a memo issued a week later by Wickware says, "The scope of the concern was beginning to have the overtones of a controversy, therefore I have decided to avoid the growth of such conflict by having the flag lowered," a move which he thought "should in no serious way affect our spirits in this Bicentennial year."

Unfortunately for Wickware, his conciliatory move toward those who saw the flag as desecration or in poor taste only aroused the ire of many other patriotic Americans. In their letters Wickware appears guilty of far more than bad taste. One woman wrote the MRNMS: "Personally I cannot understand how a few people can decide that the flag should not be there permanently—do we have to listen to these few? Why are Communists allowed to dictate in our Black Hills?"

Many letter writers also noticed an unhealthy connection between the NPS lowering the flag while at the same time allowing panhandling by members of the International Society for Krishna Consciousness, Inc. For one visitor the Hare Krishnas were a threat, leading him to write Sen. George McGovern that "this places the Shrine of Democracy on the street level and opens it to all forms of BEGGARS." Such linkage forced Rushmore's superintendent and regional director Lynn Thompson to claim that under First Amendment law the Hare Krishna group's practices were recognizably religious in intent. But such arguments themselves sounded to many Americans as if the government was more eager to please extremists, "radicals" and the quasi-religious, than the majority. As one pastor put it, "I do not know what all was involved in such a decision but it would be grounds for the christian and patriotic community to rise up in protest for such cowardly and regressive action during our Bicentennial year, or any other time. After all, what is the Shrine of Democracy saying about our Nation, our Flag, and our freedoms?"[34]

Such controversies are common at Rushmore, and the tenor of this one serves to emphasize the sort of dilemma historically faced by the NPS. As others have noticed, government itself is often a problem at American public monuments and memorials.[35] At Mount Rushmore the NPS has always fought against an anti-government bias, extending back to Borglum himself, who distinguished the divine energy which had been incarnated in the American people and their enterprising spirit from the governing institutions which worked to constrain that spirit. Indeed during the present campaign for renovation, during which new parking lots, visitor and administrative facilities are being constructed, the NPS designs have been challenged by the Sierra Club, which threatened to bring suit. An officer for the Black Hills chapter of the Sierra Club told me that the new facilities themselves would be a desecration, primarily because their size would make for an overshadowing bureaucratic presence.

III. Conquest and Conflict

The protracted interpretive contest visible at Mount Rushmore reveals the difficulty modern Americans face in reaching consensus about the memorial's sacred status. However in the last few decades another set of conflicts has grown even more intense as activists from the American Indian Movement (AIM) and other groups have turned Rushmore into the symbolic focus of their critique of American society, frequently reversing the symbolic associations made by the memorial's promoters and defenders. AIM's militancy gave political activism among Native Americans a new form in the wake of the civil rights movement of the 1960s. The Black Hills as a whole, however, hold a long history of contention between tribal groups and the dominant American culture. Indian/white conflict over the Hills dates back to the Plains Wars of the 1860s and 1870s, if not earlier. Lakotas reacted strongly to the expedition led by George Armstrong Custer in 1874 and the consequent invasion by hordes of miners. Subsequent legal conflicts over ownership of the Black Hills throughout the twentieth century enmeshed the Lakota nation in the most protracted litigation in American history. Their case eventually resulted in a Supreme Court decision in 1980 compensating them for an illegal taking of the Hills by the United States in 1877. (The United Sioux Tribes have consistently refused to accept the resulting award, which totaled, by 1990, over $350 million with interest).[36]

As indicated earlier, many cries of desecration arose in response to the carving of Rushmore begun in 1927. These came not from Lakotas (or at least there seems to be no record of Lakota protest) but rather from white residents who recoiled at the disturbance of the Hills' tranquil beauty. Instead, several prominent Lakota leaders took steps to show their support for Borglum and his project. At the most pragmatic level, this simply may have been because Borglum had Washington connections. On several occasions Borglum used his influence to bypass the miasma of Office of Indian Affairs paper channels that made Lakota reservations micro-managed colonial islands.[37] At the same time however, some Lakotas viewed the project as an incomplete symbolic expression. In 1931 Henry Standing Bear approached Borglum about carving "an Indian head" in the Black Hills to complement Washington and the other presidents. While Standing Bear initially wanted white people kept out of the project, the idea behind it was not to deny the appropriateness of the carving, but to add to its legitimacy. Writing in 1933, Henry's brother, Luther Standing Bear, also voiced some resentment at the Rushmore carving, along with a desire to see a testimony to the Lakota experience. "Two lovely legends of the Lakotas would be fine subjects for sculpturing—the Black Hills as the earth mother, and the story of the genesis of the tribe. Instead the face of a white man is being outlined on the face of a stone cliff in the Black Hills. This beautiful region, of which the Lakota thought more than any other spot on earth, caused him the most pain and misery."[38]

Borglum himself, in spite of his nativist genetic theories and philosophy of history, and his participation in the Ku Klux Klan, portrayed himself as a supporter of the "noble" Indian. While in South Dakota a Pine Ridge family adopted him and gave him the name Inyan Wanblee (Stone Eagle). James H. Red Cloud, son of the great Oglala leader, and himself tribal chair at Pine Ridge during the early 1930s, wrote Borglum that "we believe the Great Spirit has brought you to the Hills to be our friend." For Red Cloud, Borglum's project caused no alarm; he speaks of both Borglum's providential presence in the Hills and the need to uphold the 1868 treaty recognizing the Hills as Lakota territory.[39] While Borglum was unable to take on the Indian project, Henry Standing Bear eventually succeeded in enlisting the efforts of Borglum's assistant, Korczak Ziolkowski, whose family has been carving a gigantic memorial to Crazy Horse not far from Rushmore since the late 1940s. Like Rushmore, this sculpture also creates intense controversy in both the Lakota and white communities.[40]

As for the memorial itself, other Lakota leaders have taken steps to incorporate it within the sacred landscape of the Black Hills. In 1936, two days prior to President Franklin Delano Roosevelt's visit to mark the unveiling of Jefferson's head, Nicholas Black Elk, the holy man popularized in poet John Neihardt's book *Black Elk Speaks*, ascended the mountain in the workers' gondola, accompanied by a small group of Oglalas and reporters. According to his son, atop the mountain Black Elk prayed to the *Tunkasila*, the six grandfathers, "that Borglum and his men be protected in their work" and for the "preservation of the greatness of the memories of the men whose granite likenesses are being carved on the mountain, and asked that their greatness be carried on through 'changes in nations and races.' "[41]

Black Elk himself received a vision as a boy, in which the *Tunkasila* brought him to nearby Mount Harney. In recounting his life to Neihardt, Black Elk later said of Mount Harney that it was the "center of the earth." At this point, in the harsh decades following the 1890 Wounded Knee massacre, Black Elk still hoped to find the power to renew the Lakota nation in the Black Hills. In a 1931 climb to the top of Harney Peak, he prayed: "You [the *Tunkasila*] have set me here and made me behold all things, the good things, and at this very place, the center of the earth, you have promised to set the tree that was to bloom. But I have fallen away; thus causing the tree to never bloom again; but there may be a root that is still alive."[42] Black Elk, who spent many of his adult years as a devout Catholic, tried to reconcile the newly dominant American worldview with that of his ancestors. As with his contemporaries James Red Cloud and the Standing Bear brothers, Black Elk sought to find points of harmony between Lakota traditions regarding the Black Hills and the sacralizing of the memorial noticed by Doane Robinson. These points of agreement would keep Lakota sacred memories from disappearing as the whites altered the traditional landscape.

Beginning in 1941 Black Elk's son Ben made a career at the memorial out of his distinguished face, posing for hundreds of thousands of tourist photos. One highpoint from his 27-year stint at Mount Rushmore came in 1963 with the launching of the Telstar satellite. Ben Black Elk's face was the first image carried on transcontinental TV, followed by the Mormon Tabernacle Choir singing "A Mighty Fortress Is Our God" at the base of the memorial. Like his father, Black Elk sought to find harmony between traditional Lakota values and those American values symbolized at Mount Rushmore. Legends have grown up that Black Elk's face is actually visible on the mountain, and in 1977 an Italian photographer captured an image to the left of George Washington that he said was Crazy Horse; though many Lakotas believe it really was Black Elk's.[43]

For many Native Americans the first several decades of the twentieth century were times of severe cultural stress. Until passage of the Taft Howard Act in 1933, reorganizing tribal government, native religions remained outlawed by the federal government. The Office of Indian Affairs regulated nearly all aspects of Indian life, and the intrusive gaze of government peered through a nearly nonexistent curtain of personal privacy. Consequently, native people spent considerable energy on keeping sacred traditions hidden from government view. Or else, as with Black Elk, those stories and ceremonies made public required harmonization with white values in ways that might still preserve elements of Indian culture. According to anthropologist James Scott, such strategies are the necessary "weapons of the weak," providing members of subordinate cultures with the means to resist a colonizing culture at a time when social conditions hamper more overt forms of resistance.[44]

By the late 1960s however, the nationalizing American culture which had come to dominate the landscape between the Civil War and the New Deal was itself under strain. If Lakotas such as Ben Black Elk were able to incorporate their own views of the sacred into the memorial's patriotic symbolism, for many in the last twenty-five years this has become increasingly difficult. Many younger Native Americans, influenced by the goals and tactics of the civil rights and antiwar movements, reacted bitterly to continued federal efforts promoting assimilation. In response to the government's termination policy and urban relocation programs, young Indians looked back to reservation life and traditional lands as key elements necessary for the preservation of their own identity. While a growing number of college-educated tribal leaders throughout the 1950s had been turning to the avenues of law and public administration in order to achieve goals of tribal sovereignty suggested by the New Deal, other young people adopted more direct forms of protest.

Mount Rushmore, the shrine of democracy erected on Lakota land, provided AIM with a powerful symbol of the American spirit of conquest. The myths enshrined at Mount Rushmore came to embody for AIM members the legitimation of their own cultures' subjugation. While AIM's membership was national in scope, the most powerful elements within the organization came from Lakotas and Anishenaabegs (Chippewas) whose families had been relocated to nearby cities such as St. Paul and Minneapolis. Rushmore was thus also a convenient point at which those in the heartland might attack American values.

AIM's members relied on several tactics in order to reorient public perceptions of the memorial, including reoccupation, symbolic inversions of dominant patriotic interpretations, desecration, and purification. Drawing on the approach also used at Alcatraz Island and the Bureau of Indian Affairs offices in Washington, D.C., Indian activists occupied Mount Rushmore several times during the 1970s. Protesters linked together a variety of themes in their occupations of Rushmore. Initially, however, two issues stood out in their public discourse. The first attacked the government's refusal to return nearby Pine Ridge land taken during World War II for a gunnery range and since then incorporated into Badlands National Park. Activists also hoped to focus national attention on the Lakota Black Hills case, at the time being heard by the Indian Claims Commission.[45]

The most sustained occupation began late in the summer of 1970. On August 23rd several carloads of Lakotas arrived at the memorial for what became a three-month occupation. The Indian presence at the memorial was often quite shaky, as national activists came and went from one media event to another, and as the resources of local people stretched thin. But the symbolism of Indian takeovers of federal property excited the concerns of many Rushmore supporters. In the wake of Yosemite's Stoneman Meadow riot on the Fourth of July, anxieties rose over the potential for violence within the national parks.[46] One Rushmore visitor complained of the sidearms carried by NPS personnel. He also reported a conversation in which a Yellowstone ranger spoke of a new day of "Indian fighting," as did Dinosaur National Monument superintendent Cecil D. Lewis.[47] Rushmore superintendent Wallace McCaw noted in a letter to the Mount Rushmore National Memorial Society, whose members were disturbed at the low-key approach taken by NPS rangers, that the Lakotas had gathered "in protest to the many injustices they felt had been imposed on all Indians over the past couple of centuries." McCaw said he viewed the situation as peaceful, until the arrival of "out-of-State, professional Indian agitators" from the national AIM group, including Dennis Banks, Russell Means, and Lehman Brightman, from United Native Americans.[48]

The press conveyed the disapproval of the activists' tactics. As the occupation wore on, an editorial appeared in the Los Angeles *Herald Examiner* expressing the concerns of the Hearst family (whose fortune was made mining Black Hills gold). According to the editor, "Rushmore brings out the best in people." However, "Rushmore did not bring out the best in these people (the outside agitators). Like the minority radicals everywhere, nothing seems to inspire decency or good. They were only interested in destruction. Kooks are kooks the world over."[49] Papers within the region struck the same note in response to the takeover, accusing the NPS of negligence in allowing the Indian encampment. According to the Sioux Falls *Argus Leader*: "Those who feel that the suggestion of damage to Rushmore is too farfetched to deserve attention overlook the odd and weird events of recent times."[50] The NPS eventually took steps to increase security at the memorial: hiring a bomb expert, requesting overwhelming support from other enforcement agencies during Indian demonstrations, arresting protesters at the bottom of the memorial prior to their climb to the top.[51]

The social turmoil shaping perceptions of the Native American threat also colored the reflections of the activists themselves. The calls to solidarity issued by Rushmore's occupiers sounded an apocalyptic note: "Perhaps before it is too late, the rest of the Nation will awaken to the greatness of our way of life, and all men will be brothers. If not, then we will all succumb to complete annihilation at the hand of the whiteman's greed and ignorance." The cataclysmic expectations surrounding the initial occupations increased in the following years. Dennis Banks wrote of government plans to control demonstrations at Rushmore in 1973, in the wake of the recent occupation at Wounded Knee: "It appears now that Government and State Law Enforcement elements are laying the blueprint for mass execution. The Indian and non-Indian public should respond immediately to what we believe can only result in total Civil War."[52] NPS officials often sought to downplay the Indian presence at the memorial, as when Superintendent McCaw told reporters in 1970 that the demonstration was becoming "more entertaining" as the days went by.[53] Still, the threats and dangers eventually proved more than hypothetical. On June 27, 1975, a bomb detonated at the visitors' center, the day after the killing of two FBI agents and a Lakota on the Pine Ridge reservation.[54] Given the tension of the times, it is worth examining AIM's symbolic tactics.

As can be seen from above, AIM's very presence at the memorial was cause for alarm in the press, in government channels, and among Rushmore's visitors and supporters. Such a presence registered as an invasion of public space. The NPS frequently answered charges from critics accusing the staff of failing to uphold their duty to protect the memorial. Park officials, however, worked to incorporate the Indian protests within the framework of free speech and access mandated by the public nature of the facility. Thus NPS staff had to diffuse the symbolic sense of danger posed by Indian occupants. Indeed one AIM member, who had come down from the mountain to attend a conference on the Winnebago reservation in Nebraska, claimed that park staff were "thinking of mutinying in terms of the federal government, because they believe in the Indian people."[55]

Protesters heightened this sense of invasion by advancing claims of ownership. Russell Means told the press following his arrest after the June occupation of 1971: "We were not trespassing. In fact the federal government is trespassing as are all individuals not authorized by the Indians."[56] Signs hung across the amphitheater in 1970 reflected the problem of ownership. "Christians—Wakantanka gave the Lakota the Paha Sapa. The wasichu came and took the Paha Sapa from the Lakota. Now the Lakota say the wasichu must make a fair payment for the Paha Sapa." "Wasichu—how did you gain possession of the Black Hills? When will you start treating your fellow men as brothers?" Most simply, "Yankee, go home."[57]

As a corollary to the challenge of ownership, protesters renamed the mountain "Mount Crazy Horse" and referred to themselves as the "Crazy Horse Movement." One AIM member, Darlene Flynn, put to verse the activist interpretation of Crazy Horse.

> The beautiful Paha Sapa
> So sacred to the SIOUX,

Was trampled by foreign feet,
White man that was YOU!

You desecrated our sacred land
and showed us where to go
you mined our hills and streams
in search of yellow gold

You carved upon our mountain
heroes of your own
Our own great CHIEF forgotten
in some lonely grave alone

BUT now HE has returned again
in many forms we've seen
to guide his people once again
NO more to mourn and dream

This MOUNTAIN that is Holy
we named for OUR great CHIEF
the faces of your heroes
look down with shame and grief

OUR GREAT CHIEF LIVES AGAIN
white men shake with fear
when LIGHTNING lights the sky
CHIEF CRAZY HORSE IS NEAR.[58]

Within the worldview of AIM members and other activists in South Dakota during the 1970s, Crazy Horse thus became a redemptive figure. As this poem suggests, his return from the dead took on millennial overtones, and according to some reports, he was seen here and there across the landscape, encouraging AIM members to continue their fight to resacralize traditional Lakota lands.

In promoting Mount Crazy Horse as the more appropriate name, AIM members had to deflate the symbolic values associated with the four presidential faces, and valorize the figure of Crazy Horse.[59] Deflation took several forms, some verbal, others involving acts of intentional desecration—although AIM leaders insisted they would avoid defacing the memorial. One noticeable form of deflation consisted of retelling the stories of the four presidents. Borglum and the memorial's supporters always sought to stress the virtuous, or even divine, qualities possessed by Washington and the others.

Within AIM's worldview, however, the faces did not recall the sacred history of American expansion, but rather crimes against native people. Thus, each face was associated with a specific set of injustices. Winnebago

AIM member Reuben Snake detailed these injustices in a letter to the editor of the Los Angeles *Herald Examiner*. According to Snake, "what ever mythical virtues 'White America' has endowed Washington, Jefferson, Lincoln and Roosevelt with, to erect a Shrine of Democracy in their likeness is beyond the ken of many, many non-white Americans. Washington and Jefferson were slave owners, striving to totally annihilate Redmen from the face of the earth. Lincoln signed an executive order for the execution without trial of over thirty Santee warriors in Minnesota. Also . . . the infamous Trail of Tears might never have happened if Lincoln had truly been the godlike character as which is now memorialized. Teddy 'the ole rough rider' Roosevelt nationalized the park service by taking Indian land for White America's playground." Snake observed that "Rushmore is the White Americans' sacred cow," a place where they could "stand in reverent awe of their own greatness," ignorant of the fact that Indians and other minorities "continue to suffer and die under the iron heel of the white-man's form of democracy."[60] While such historical reconstruction is less than accurate, it effectively served to trigger sentiments opposite to those sought by the memorial's creators and underscored what activists saw as a hypocritical expression of white democratic ideals.

In addition to such verbal forms of symbolic deflation, activists chose more visual means as well. Those arrested at the beginning of the 1970 occupation carried cans of red paint, used to coat rocks near the sculpture. In addition activists also covered the bust of sculptor Gutzon Borglum located by the old studio with strips of red paint. Banners proclaiming "Sioux Indian Power" hung from the mountain.[61] John Fire Lame Deer, a Lakota *wicasa wakan* (holy man) who allied himself with AIM during this period, tells of another form of deflation, involving a conscious effort to defile the space of the memorial. In his autobiography Lame Deer told of a friend involved in the 1970 occupation, "a Santee Indian who . . . climbed up here one night a few years ago with a few friends just to pee down on the nose of one of those faces. He called it a 'symbolic gesture.' The way he told me it was quite a feat. They had to form a human chain just to make it possible for him to do it."[62] Lame Deer expressed the logic which makes intentional desecration possible at any sacred place, saying "one man's shrine is another man's cemetery."

Rushmore frequently becomes the site for concern over symbolic forms of desecration, but, as can be seen from the controversies surrounding the memorial's commercial appeal, very little of that has been of conscious origin. However, within the strategy of symbolic resistance developed by

Indian activists, desecration itself became a necessary means to deflate the memorial's power. Perhaps the most notable incident of desecration was the bombing of the visitors' center in June 1975 mentioned above. While this appears to have been the only incident of violence during these years, Rushmore's law enforcement officers heard a constant string of rumors about AIM plans to blow up the memorial itself. An NPS memo on the 1975 blast noted the logic in AIM's choice of symbolic locations, and concluded that their intention was evidently "to stop the flow of tourism."[63]

If Native American activists were attempting to deflate the symbolic power of the memorial, it certainly was not because they were only interested in destruction, as they were sometimes accused by the press and public officials. Rather, these acts of deflation and defilement required AIM to restore what they saw as the mountain's original sacred character. To that end, activists focused their efforts on ritual acts of purification. In addition to the regular performance of songs and dances as part of public demonstrations, many of which drew enthusiastic responses from visitors, other less visible ritualized actions helped cleanse the mountain. Lame Deer planted a prayer staff at the top, "in order to make the mountain sacred again." He explained the staff's significance to a curious reporter.

> The lower part of this staff is painted black. That stands for night. It stands for black face paint in war. It also represents people praying, either with their eyes closed or in the dark. It also means that I am putting a blanket, or shroud, over the mountain by planting this staff, and the Presidents' faces shall remain dirty until the treaties concerning the Black Hills are fulfilled. The upper part of the staff is red, which represents the day and the sun, the red face paint of gladness. It means when the government's promises to the Indians will be fulfilled the Black Hills will be covered with brightness again, but this could take some time."[64]

AIM also sought to use more public rituals to purify the new Mount Crazy Horse. During the summer of 1973, with national attention still focused on the lengthy, violent standoff between armed AIM members and government forces at Wounded Knee, AIM announced plans to hold a Sun Dance (*wiwanyang wacipi*) at Rushmore. The Sun Dance played a prominent role in AIM's efforts to build a "pan-tribal" movement. As Dennis Banks put it in a release issued by AIM, the Sun Dance is "the most sacred of all Indian religious events." For many AIM members the Sun Dance, historically a part of many Plains cultures, was important because it gave dramatic visual form to their understanding of the nature of being truly "Indian" in modern America. Accordingly, its performance at the memorial would further the effort to reframe the memorial as native sacred space. With its classic themes of purification and sacrifice for the good of the community, the Sun Dance could well have been the ritual vehicle sufficient to mobilize support among the Lakota population, as well as among other nearby tribes. With the publicity attendant upon such a spectacle, the performance was likely to increase support among other Americans. This performance, however, would not come to pass, since the NPS refused to issue the necessary permit.

AIM members were still able to use this prohibition in furthering their cause. Banks and Russell Means released documents to the press detailing the authorities' coercive efforts to proscribe the dance. According to Banks, the FBI falsely claimed to have "tracked convoys of trucks bearing arms to the Sun Dance area. The FBI further stated that they observed the trucks being unloaded and explosive elements." In addition, FBI agents meeting other officials at the memorial sought to initiate a campaign of harassment and brutality against the Crazy Horse Movement. For Banks, the government effort to curtail the dance even involved laying "the groundwork to commit mass murder." Russell Means, following a meeting with Lakota holy man Chief Frank Fools Crow, who had agreed to lead the dance, also attacked official overreaction. Noting the history of government efforts to suppress native religions, Means said the FBI and South Dakota's Governor Richard Kneip were "preventing the Traditional Lakota People from worshiping in *our* sacred Paha Sapa which is guaranteed to remain ours forever by the treaty of 1868."[65] In the end Leonard Crow Dog Jr. held the dance on his family's land on the Rosebud reservation. From there a caravan made its way to Rushmore for a briefer demonstration.

In subsequent years, the AIM effort to reorient patriotic interpretations of the memorial has had some success. The militancy of the period brought AIM much condemnation from Lakotas and others. Their attempt to negotiate a critical interpretation of Rushmore's symbolism, however, enabled a number of other Lakotas to take a public stance attacking the memorial.[66] Indeed Lame Deer's conclusions in the wake of AIM's occupation of the summit in 1970 seem truer now than they did then.

> A million or more tourists every year look up at those faces and feel good, real good, because they make them feel big and powerful, because their own kind of people made these faces and the tourists are thinking 'we are white, we made this, what we want we get, and nothing can stop us.' . . . This is what conquering means. They could just as well have carved this mountain into a huge cavalry boot standing on a dead Indian."[67]

What has changed dramatically in the last twenty years is the extent to which such a perspective no longer serves simply to promote solidarity among dissidents. Supporters celebrated the memorial's fiftieth anniversary in 1991, and used the occasion to dedicate it officially, a task not performed in the wartime climate of 1941. Noticeably absent in the group of celebrities and officials brought together with President George Bush for the ceremonies were the tribal chairs of South Dakota's various Lakota reservations.[68]

Another indication of the extent to which the radical critique offered by AIM has spread beyond the bounds of militant dissent can be found in the journalism of Tim Giago, editor of the largest Indian newspaper in the country, the *Lakota Times*. In the years since the 1973 occupation of Wounded Knee, Giago and AIM leaders have engaged in a long-running verbal battle over the legitimacy of AIM and the wisdom of its tactics. In spite of such ideological division, Giago offered a trenchant statement of the perspective AIM offered during its occupations in the 1970s, in an editorial appearing two days before the July 4th, 1991, celebration. "In the 50 years since Gutzon Borglum completed desecration of the Sacred Paha Sapa (Black Hills) of the Lakota Nation by carving the faces of four white presidents who were largely responsible for the death, destruction and humiliation of countless (some extinct) Indian people and nations, dual systems of justice, theft of Indian lands, desecration of sacred sites, the attempted subjugation of a free people, and failed efforts to assimilate, acculturate and destroy a unique culture have been the rule, not the exception. These barbaric acts of hostility have been the legacy of Mount Rushmore."[69]

IV. Rushmore's Place in America's Sacred Landscape

This examination of interpretive conflict over the significance of Mount Rushmore is far from exhaustive. The efforts to frame Rushmore's meaning considered here are, however, representative of the range of strategies and issues which might arise in the course of a more detailed cultural history of the memorial. Consequently, my efforts to interpret Mount Rushmore do prompt a number of observations which might sharpen our understanding of sacred space in America.

It might be tempting to interpret the numerous conflicts over the memorial's meaning within the dominant culture as an indication of Rushmore's lack of stature as sacred space. However, this would depend upon

Interesting definition of sacred space

the assumption that "real" sacred places are the object of uniform interpretation within a given culture. Surely a better clue to a place's status as
sacred is whether people think it is worthwhile to fight over its symbolic
significance. Consider how the patriotic spirit which is enshrined at
Mount Rushmore differs from partisan politics or ideologies, at least
within the framework of the dominant American culture. Americans used
Rushmore to mobilize for the Cold War, for instance; as when Drew Pearson sought to call upon the faith of the presidential figures during his comments at the 1952 night-lighting dedication ceremony. Pearson, however,
used the memorial's patriotic appeal to buttress a world federalist critique
of Harry Truman's containment policy.

The interpretations of Rushmore as a sacred shrine considered here
comprise a fairly representative range of twentieth-century American political ideologies. Borglum's Anglo-Saxon nativism and the Park Service's
own commitment to cultural diversity conjure up very different visions of
the values undergirding American society. The fact that Americans of various political commitments seek to draw support from appeals to the symbolic power of the memorial seems strong evidence for its status as a sacred
place in American culture. → *relates to cultural redefinition of sites*

As a patriotic symbol, Rushmore is fluid; it cannot be fixed to a particular political ideology. Nor can we find an easy way to distinguish a sacred
from a profane usage of the memorial. The memorial blends together the
religious and the economic. Robinson and Borglum intentionally envisioned a heroic sculpture that could have both patriotic and commercial
appeal. These two forms of public appeal appear at times to be linked together by necessity. Such confusing of the religious with the economic
runs counter to "the separation of spheres" that sociologists such as Tal-
cott Parsons say characterizes modern societies. At the same time, it
seems consonant with the work of others who have studied shrines and
pilgrimages, as well as the enterprise of modern tourism.[70] What is surprising is the extent to which conflict over commercialization continues
at Rushmore, as if it were an endless task to delimit, define, and protect
the memorial's ability to inspire patriotic sentiment. Like obscenity, crass
commercialism and its patriotic opposite seem very difficult to define.

Consider also the memorial as a human artifact, a piece of sculpture.
Rushmore took on sacred qualities through the self-conscious acts of those
who blasted and chiseled the granite away from the mountain. Robinson
in 1939 claimed to observe "a growing tendency on the part of the public
to confer upon the project a sort of mystical, semi-religious connotation"

Sacrality covers up the physical work being done here

and confided he had "no doubt that in due course" Rushmore would prompt "a worshipful reflex from those Americans who in mounting numbers assemble here to make obeisance before this shrine of patriotism."[71] There are no hierophanies here, no actions by supernatural beings. Rushmore gains its sacred qualities solely on the basis of human modification of the landscape, the same sort of effort which transformed the American continent, although Borglum and Robinson believed this human effort embodied divine will. Thus, accounting for Mount Rushmore forces us to acknowledge that places deemed sacred within the dominant American culture will likely be places of human construction. The memorial undercuts the expectation that a real sacred place has to be something like Mount Sinai, where human memory recalls an original divine action.

The deepest conflicts at Mount Rushmore have arisen out of the contest over ownership stemming from the United States's appropriation of the Black Hills in 1877. In the ensuing years Lakotas, and more recently other Native Americans, have engaged in a number of strategies to reorient the dominant culture's vision of the memorial. These strategies range along a continuum. At one end is the effort to find points of harmony between native symbols and values and those of the dominant American culture; at the other end, a variety of efforts to subvert the dominant interpretations. Further study of Lakota efforts to reorient public perception of the memorial might well reveal a number of other strategic approaches.

American Indians engaged in the strategy of harmonization most frequently during the politically repressive decades of the early twentieth century, although it continues to play some role in the present as well. Lakotas such as the Standing Bear brothers or Nicholas and Ben Black Elk strove to incorporate some form of Indian presence within the symbolic horizon of the memorial, a strategy which the elder Black Elk hoped would prevent traditional Lakota values from being forgotten in a rapidly changing social environment. Many other Lakota leaders also took steps to preserve important aspects of Lakota culture during the years between Wounded Knee and the New Deal.[72]

To some extent this strategy proved successful, in part at least because of a growing infatuation with things Indian by many in the dominant and increasingly urban American culture. Thus, business leaders in the area were able to draw upon the past association of the Hills with native cultures in their efforts to stimulate the tourist trade.[73] As Brian Dippie and others have pointed out, receptiveness to things Indians during this period was carefully circumscribed and generally apolitical. The figure of the Indian provided Americans with a symbolic connection to a more ancient past, especially when that figure appeared as an emblem of a vanished way of life.[74] Indeed the *Rapid City Journal* stressed this in a 1935 editorial applauding Congress for appropriating money to carve the head of Lincoln. "Years and years ago, according to old Indian legends, the Black Hills were held sacred by the Indians. . . . Its mild climate and scenic beauty appealed to the hidden religious beliefs of the savages. . . . Now, that the Black Hills have come into the hands of the white men, their value is becoming known more and more. As they served the Indians, so will they serve the folk of modern times. Many persons will find solace and comfort there after the stirring struggles of commerce."[75]

Given the ambiguous results greeting those Lakotas who attempted to preserve their culture by harmonizing it with the symbolic power of the memorial, it is perhaps not surprising that activists adopted the apparently opposite strategy of symbolic resistance during the late 1960s. Like earlier Lakota concerns about the memorial, AIM's efforts to reorient perceptions of Mount Rushmore were also often less than successful. On the basis of the various interpretive efforts examined in this chapter, however, this is apparently true for all who have taken a role in providing the mountain with a symbolic definition. If American sacred space is conflictual, it is likely inevitable that no group ever succeeds in completely framing a place according to its conception of the sacred.

In spite of limited success—stemming from both the deliberate federal campaign to discredit AIM and varying degrees of support for AIM from within the American Indian community, AIM's strategic efforts have had some success. By subverting the patriotic narrative provided by the memorial's supporters and caretakers, by engaging in symbolic acts to defile the growing aura of sacredness surrounding the memorial, by physical occupation and a recurring threat of violence, and by their efforts to purify a damaged part of the Lakota landscape, Native American activists were able to offer a long-term challenge to American self-understanding at one of the symbolic centers of its civil religion. As a by-product of AIM's rejection of more institutional forms of pursuing a political agenda, numerous non-militant Indians also took up the themes of AIM's challenge to Rushmore's sacred status.

The interpretive conflicts at Mount Rushmore reveal the social tensions evidently inherent in making space sacred. At Rushmore claims advanced by some in favor of the sacred are rebuffed by others. Efforts to embody such claims in a physical way call forth various forms of resistance by those who see such embodiments as profanation of their own views of the sacred. Whether such conflict is limited to American efforts to sacralize the landscape or occurs on a far broader scale is worth pursuing. In any case, it seems clear that the sacred awareness which Rushmore's promoters hoped would advance national unity has been far from successful.

Notes

1. Gilbert C. Fite, *Mount Rushmore* (Norman: University of Oklahoma Press, 1952), p. 167.

2. Mircea Eliade, *The Sacred and the Profane* (New York: Harper and Row, 1959), p. 28.

3. Eliade, *Sacred and Profane*, p. 51.

4. For extended treatments of the wilderness aesthetic in American life see Michael P. Cohen, *The Pathless Way: John Muir and American Wilderness* (Madison: University of Wisconsin Press, 1984); Stephen Fox, *The American Conservation Movement: John Muir and His Legacy* (Madison: University of Wisconsin Press, 1985); Roderick Nash, *Wilderness and the American Mind*, 3rd edition (New Haven: Yale University Press, 1982); and the chapter by Bron Taylor in this volume.

5. Eliade, *Sacred and Profane*, p. 31.

6. "Benedictine Monks Spend Busy Hours in Black Hills of Dakota" n.d, n.p., South Dakota State Archives, vertical files.

7. *Rapid City Journal*, 2/14/68; *Edgemont Herald*, 11/22/67.

8. *Belle Fourche Tribune*, 1/6/68.

9. On the UN proposal see "Brief on the Subject of Location of the Permanent Headquarters of the United Nations Organization," 1/31/46, South Dakota State Archives, vertical files. On FDR/Stalin/Churchill see Fern Erskine to Doane Robinson, 6/19/45. Doane A. Robinson Papers, Box 9, #149. South Dakota State Archives, hereafter cited as Robinson Papers.

10. See David Chidester, *Salvation and Suicide: An Interpretation of Jim Jones, the Peoples Temple and Jonestown* (Bloomington: Indiana University Press, 1988) for a good treatment of religion as strategic effort.

11. See John E. Miller, *Looking for History on Highway 14* (Ames: Iowa State University Press, 1993), pp. 9-13; and Rex Alan Smith, *The Carving of Mount Rushmore* (New York: Abbeville, 1985), pp. 24-29.

12. Robinson Papers, Box 9, #240.

13. Robinson to Lee Marford, 2/11/24 and to J. B. Green, 3/7/24. Robinson Papers, Box 9, #149.

14. Howard and Audrey Schaff, *Six Wars at a Time: The Life and Times of Gutzon Borglum, Sculptor of Mount Rushmore* (Sioux Falls: Center for Western Studies, 1985), pp. 143-53.

15. Maude Gardner Hoover to Robinson, 1/17/25. J. B. Townsley to Robinson,

12/26/24. Robinson to F. W. Myers, 12/4/24. Robinson to Mrs. Maude Gardner Hoover, 1/20/25. Robinson Papers, Box 9 #149.

16. Borglum to Sen. Peter Norbeck, 8/28/25. Robinson Papers, Box 9 #149.

17. Borglum to Robinson, 11/21/24. Robinson Papers, Box 9 #149.

18. *San Francisco Examiner*, 2/22/34.

19. Smith, *Carving*, p. 33.

20. Ruel McDaniel, " . . . But First He Had to Sell It!: An Interview with Gutzon Borglum" *Specialty Salesman Magazine*, April 1935.

21. John Bodnar, *Remaking America: Public Memory, Commemoration and Patriotism in the Twentieth Century* (Princeton: Princeton University Press, 1991).

22. Borglum to Robinson, 7/5/39. Robinson, undated note. Robinson Papers, Box 9 #149.

23. See generally Michael Kammen, *Mystic Chords of Memory: The Transformation of Tradition in American Culture* (New York: Alfred A. Knopf, 1991); and Bodnar, *Remaking America*.

24. "Dedication of Mount Rushmore Monument Lighting" 6/25/50. National Park Service, Mount Rushmore National Memorial Archival Collection (hereafter NPS) 1030, Box 21.

25. The national park movement, and the very idea that such parks were an important source of inspiration for modern, urban Americans was developed by various segments of the American transportation industry. For a useful history see Alfred Runte, *National Parks: The American Experience* (Lincoln: University of Nebraska Press, 1987).

26. Personal conversation, Tom Griffith, Mount Rushmore National Memorial Society, Rapid City, S.D., 11/5/92.

27. *Sioux Falls Argus Leader*, 12/13 and 12/23/41.

28. South Dakota State Historical Society, vertical files, "Mount Rushmore."

29. Mount Rushmore National Memorial Society archives, Mount Rushmore Society—1976 (hereafter MRNMS).

30. Harvey Wickware to Hoadley Dean, 6/10/76; Hoadley Dean to Harvey Wickware, 6/21/76. MRNMS, 1976.

31. See Bodnar, *Remaking America*, ch. 7 and, generally, Edward Tabor Linenthal, *Sacred Ground: Americans and Their Battlefields* (Urbana: University of Illinois Press, 1991).

32. Jerome J. Pisney to Harvey Wickware, 5/22/76; Gerald Holst to Harvey Wickware, 5/25/76; and Theodore J. Wirth to Gary Eberhardt, 5/25/76. NPS Box 57, 1081, folder 1.

33. Harvey Wickware to Jerome J. Pisney, 5/25/76; Harvey Wickware to Gerald Holst, 5/25/76. NPS, Box 57, 1081, folder 1.

34. Memo to staff from Wickware, 6/2/76. Nell Doering to Hoadley Dean, 7/2/76. Paul Mueller to George McGovern, 7/7/76. Lynn Thompson to Hoadley Dean, 7/9/76. Harvey Wickware to Georgia Mae Clough, 9/3/76. Burnell A. Lund to Harvey Wickware, 7/15/76. NPS, Box 57, 1081, folder 1.

35. See Kammen, *Mystic Chords*, ch. 14.

36. Although marred by personal concerns, Edward Lazarus's *Black Hills/White Justice: The Sioux Nation versus the United States, 1775 to the Present* (New York: HarperCollins, 1991) details the long-standing conflict over ownership of the Hills.

37. For an extended treatment of this period, see Thomas Biolsi, *Organizing the*

Lakota: the Political Economy of the New Deal on the Pine Ridge and Rosebud Reservations (Tucson: University of Arizona, 1992).

38. Luther Standing Bear, *Land of the Spotted Eagle* (Lincoln: University of Nebraska Press, 1978), p. 43.

39. Schaff and Schaff, *Six Wars*, pp. 281–82.

40. For a celebrational account, see Robb DeWall, *Crazy Horse and Korczak: The Story of an Epic Mountain Carving* (Crazy Horse, S.D.: Korczak's Heritage, 1982).

41. Quoted in Raymond DeMallie, *The Sixth Grandfather: Black Elk's Teachings Given to John G. Neihardt* (Lincoln: University of Nebraska Press, 1984), pp. 65–66.

42. John G. Neihardt, *Black Elk Speaks: Being the Life Story of a Holy Man of the Oglala Sioux* (Lincoln: University of Nebraska Press, 1932, 1979 reprint), p. 271; DeMallie, *Sixth Grandfather*, p. 295.

43. *Lakota Times*, 9/8/77.

44. See Biolsi, *Organizing the Lakota*, as well as Stephen Cornell, *The Return of the Native: American Indian Political Resurgence* (New York: Oxford University Press, 1988) and James Stuart Olson and Raymond Wilson, *Native Americans in the Twentieth Century* (Urbana and Champaign: University of Illinois Press, 1984). On forms of resistance to colonialism, see James Scott, *Weapons of the Weak: Everyday Forms of Peasant Resistance* (New Haven: Yale University Press, 1985). Biolsi, "The Political Economy of Lakota Consciousness" in John H. Moore, ed. *The Political Economy of North American Indians* (Norman: University of Oklahoma Press, 1993, pp. 20–42) considers the symbolic dynamics of the American flag erected at contemporary Lakota powwows.

45. See Lazarus, *Black Hills/White Justice*, pp. 315–27.

46. Runte, *National Parks*, p. 176.

47. Lewis's comment appears in a memo commending MR's staff in its handling of the 1975 demonstrations. Memorandum A7615 (D), Superintendent, Dinosaur to Regional Director, Rocky Mountain Region, 7/8/75. NPS 1081 Box 57 "AIM misc-1975."

48. Wallace O. McCaw to Hoadley Dean, 2/10/71. MRNMS, "Annual Meeting," 1972.

49. *Los Angeles Herald Examiner*, 11/25/70.

50. *Sioux Falls Argus Leader*, 10/27/70.

51. Wallace O. McCaw to National Bomb Data Center, 7/28/72. As an example of the threats faced by the NPS, consider a memo alerting officials to a plan "calling for a trenching machine behind the sculpture, into which was to be placed 300 cases of dynamite." Memorandum W-2630, Benson V. Holmes, Acting Superintendent to Director, Midwest Region, 8/9/72. NPS 108, Box 57, folder 6.

52. "Crazy Horse Movement" n.d. NPS 1081, Box 57, folder 5. American Indian Movement communication #1, 8/25/73. NPS 1081, Box 57, folder 11. See Ward Churchill and Jim Vander Wall, *Agents of Repression: The FBI's Secret War against the Black Panther Party and the American Indian Movement* (Boston: South Bend, 1990).

53. *Rapid City Journal*, 9/1/70.

54. Memorandum W34(RMR)MP Regional Law Enforcement Officer to Regional Director, Rocky Mountain Region, 8/1/75. NPS 1081, Box 57, "AIM Misc-1975." For an extended, though controversial treatment of the 1975 murders and the surrounding events, see Peter Matthiessen, *In the Spirit of Crazy Horse* (New York: Viking, 1991).

55. Interview with Twila Martin, 9/11/70. American Indian Research Project, tape #0594, South Dakota Oral History Center, University of South Dakota.

56. *Sioux Falls Argus Leader*, 6/10/71.

57. Clipping, n.d. n.p., NPS 1081, Box 57, folder 4.

58. NPS Box 57, 1081, folder 4.

59. The mountain received the name Rushmore in a rather arbitrary way. The lawyer Charles Rushmore, checking titles in the area in 1885, apparently asked a local man the peak's name. Replying that it had none, the local said "we'll call the damn thing Rushmore." Gilbert C. Fite, *Mount Rushmore* (Norman: University of Oklahoma Press, 1952), pp. 52–53.

60. Reuben Snake to Donald Goodenow 12/1/70. NPS 1081, Box 57, folder 5.

61. Memorandum from Director, Midwest Region to Director, National Park Service, 8/31/70. NPS 1081 Box 57, folder 4.

62. John Fire Lame Deer and Richard Erdoes, *Lame Deer, Seeker of Visions: The Life of a Sioux Medicine Man* (New York: Simon and Schuster, 1972), p. 91.

63. Memo from Regional Law Enforcement Officer to Regional Director-NPS, 8/1/75. NPS Box 57, 1081, "AIM Miscellaneous, 1975."

64. Lame Deer and Erdoes, *Lame Deer*, p. 94.

65. Dennis Banks, press release 7/25/73; Russell Means, press release 7/25/73. NPS 1081 Box 57 folder 11. For a biography of Fools Crow, widely regarded as a spiritual leader by AIM members, see Thomas E. Mails *Fools Crow* (Lincoln: University of Nebraska Press, reprint 1990).

66. I conducted personal interviews with several Lakotas of various occupations and cultural perspectives in 1990, and all of them were more inclined to view MR's symbolic power as summed up in the phrase "the faces of killers."

67. Lame Deer and Erdoes, *Lame Deer*, p. 93.

68. *Rapid City Journal*, 7/6/91.

69. *Lakota Times*, 7/2/91.

70. See, for instance, John F. Sears, *Sacred Places: American Tourist Attractions in the Nineteenth Century* (New York: Oxford University Press, 1991); and Victor and Edith Turner, *Image and Pilgrimage in Christian Culture* (New York: Columbia University Press, 1978).

71. Robinson, undated note. Robinson Papers, Box 9 #149.

72. For example, many of the elders interviewed by James Walker, Pine Ridge physician from 1896 to 1914, expressed their concern that traditional language, rituals and sacred stories were in danger of being forgotten. Given the heavy assimilationist policies in effect at Pine Ridge during the period, such concerns were well-founded. See James R. Walker, *Lakota Belief and Ritual*, Raymond J. DeMallie and Elaine A. Jahner, editors (Lincoln: University of Nebraska Press, 1980); and *Lakota Myth*, Elaine A. Jahner, editor (Lincoln: University of Nebraska Press, 1983).

73. Consider Nicholas Black Elk's participation for many years in Duhamel's Sioux Indian Pageant, held along the highway to Mount Rushmore, still under construction. On summer afternoons the pageant, which introduced tourists to various aspects of Lakota culture and religion—including the pipe and the Sun Dance, moved to downtown Rapid City, in front of Duhamel's Trading Post. Rapid City's premier hotel, the Alex Johnson, across the street, featured an interior decorated in numerous Lakota motifs. See DeMallie, *Sixth Grandfather*, pp. 63–65.

74. See Brian J. Dippie, *The Vanishing American: White Attitudes and U.S. Indian Policy* (Middletown: Wesleyan University Press, 1982); and Robert F. Berkhofer, *In the*

White Man's Indian: Images of the American Indian from Columbus to the Present (New York: Alfred A. Knopf, 1978).

75. *Rapid City Journal*, 5/13/35. For more information on the appropriation of Indian images at the memorial see Matthew Glass, "Producing Patriotic Inspiration at Mount Rushmore," *Journal of the American Academy of Religion*, 57, no. 2 (Summer 1994).

5

CREATING THE CHRISTIAN HOME
Home Schooling in Contemporary America
Colleen McDannell

These words, which I command thee this day, shall be in thine heart; and thou shalt teach them diligently unto thy children, and shalt talk to them when thou sittest in thine house, and when thou walkest by the way and when thou liest down, and when thou risest up. —Deuteronomy 6:6–7

Education is not preparation for life; it is life itself.
—John Dewey

◊ check other articles

IN 1869 Catharine Beecher and her sister Harriet Beecher Stowe explained in their book, *The American Woman's Home: Or, Principles of Domestic Science*, that "a small church, a school-house, and a comfortable family dwelling may be all united in one building."[1] The Beecher sisters then produced an architectural plan that integrated, within one cost-efficient space, worship, education, and domesticity. During the second half of the nineteenth century, evangelical Protestants elaborated an ideology which placed the home at the center of the creation of religious and patriotic values. By adapting Gothic revival architecture for house construction, they emphasized the connection between the design of homes and the designs of churches. Making and displaying religious artifacts created a properly pious environment in the household. Family worship brought the Christian rituals of prayer, hymn singing, and preaching into the space of the home. This enabled the "Christian family," and the "Christian neighborhood," according to the Beechers, to "become the grand ministry, as they were designed to be, in training our whole race for heaven."[2]

By the beginning of the twentieth century, however, social and cultural changes in America weakened the common assumption that home was a sacred space.[3] Both secular and religious forces attacked the Victorian attitude that private morality created public virtue. Liberal theologians and social reformers urged Americans to look beyond their homes to view the whole world as needy of care and concern. At the same time, modern design trends criticized the decorative and overstuffed Victorian home. Wax crosses, needlepoint pious sayings, and elaborate family Bibles stopped being fashionable.[4] By the 1930s, domestic Christianity no longer functioned as a unifying force transcending Protestant denominational differences. Home Bible reading, sentimental religious art, Victorian notions of gender roles, and the belief in the saving forces of the family marked one as a conservative Protestant who was critical of modern perspectives on Christianity.

The Victorian perspective on the home as a distinctly sacred space did not die with the coming of Progressive Era reforms, increasing divorce rates, and changes in architectural styles. Historians Betty DeBerg and David Watt have shown that domestic ideology was essential to the fundamentalist and evangelical religious message.[5] Fundamentalists agreed with Billy Sunday's 1916 statement that the home was "the most sacred spot on the globe."[6] According to David Watt, in the 1940s and 1950s "Evangelical leaders frequently asserted that making sure America's homes were strong was the most important task facing the American people—more important than fighting poverty, or crime, or Communism."[7] As conservative Christianity revealed a more public and strident voice in the 1970s, it carried with it a pro-family message that had its roots in Victorian culture.

The Home as School

Crucial to the Beecher sisters' 1869 vision of the Christian home was that it contained not merely a house and a church but also a school. During the week, the family's work would center in the kitchen, and the main room of the house would be converted into a school and eating-room. "Here the aim will be," the sisters wrote, "to collect the children of the neighborhood, to be taught not only to read, write, and cipher, but to perform in the best manner all the practical duties of the family state."[8] While informal academic and religious instruction was encouraged by Victorian writers, the Beecher sisters were unique in emphasizing that formal education was natural to domestic space. It would not be until the late twen-

tieth century, however, that their vision of a home that included religion
and education would be come a part of the American religious landscape.

It is estimated that almost a half a million children currently are being
educated, not in public or private schools, but at home.[9] Of those children,
the vast majority are being taught at home for religious reasons. Protestants, Catholics, Mormons, and adherents to New Age philosophies have
decided that the public schools lack appropriate religious values, inculcate
a suspect humanism, and fail on academic standards. Parents, rather than
placing their children in private schools, educate them at home. From the
perspective of home-schooling parents, it is only within the confines of
domestic space that they can control what values their children learn and
what information they are taught.

Home schooling typically is discussed as an *educational* reform. This
is a critical oversight of scholarship because home schooling is basically
a *religious* reform. Recent scholarship on conservative Protestants—Fundamentalists, Evangelicals, Pentecostals, Charismatics—has focused on
their challenges to American political life and their restructuring of the
Protestant theological agenda.[10] Even those who write on evangelical education concern themselves exclusively with the Christian school and not
domestic education.[11] With only a few exceptions, the importance of the
private dimension of conservative Christianity has been neglected.[12]

My intention is to move the discussion of conservative Christianity
away from the current focus on the public spaces of churches, legislatures,
schools, and seminaries and toward the private realm of the home. While
scholars and the media have highlighted the conservative political agenda
of the "New Religious Right," they have failed to recognize the internal
and perhaps more extensive ways that Christians are developing alternative cultures for themselves. To understand fundamentalism's impact on
both American society and religion, we must recognize that the conservative fascination with the home is not merely a result of political choices. It
is rooted in a long tradition of Protestant domestic Christianity. Home
schooling falls within the tradition of domestic Christianity, articulated
by Victorian ministers, novelists, reformers, and theologians. As with their
Victorian counterparts, contemporary Christians understand the creation
of an alternative Christian culture as beginning in the home.

Conservative Protestants, through home schooling, articulate a domestic ideology that shapes their Christian piety, political orientations, and attitudes toward their local churches. This essay examines not the ideology
of Christian domesticity, but how Christians use a particular strategy—

speaks to exclusio? *white racial issue?*

home schooling—to create a Christian space within the home. Home schooling is used by contemporary Christians to achieve the Beecher sisters' goal of creating neighborhoods to train "our whole race for heaven." My focus is on how this "training" comes about and what impact it is having on the lives of individual Christians and their churches. I am convinced that conservative Protestantism will undergo significant changes in the future as parents take seriously pro-family ideology. Home schooling does not merely socialize children. It teaches their parents how to be Christians. By emphasizing the fundamentally religious nature of their private lives, home schooling empowers the family.

instructive for parents too. *SPACE & COLLECTIVE PoWER*

Who Home Schools?

In every state in the union, parents may legally withdraw their children from public school and teach them at home. Home schooling received the tacit support of the Supreme Court when Amish parents claimed the First Amendment's "free exercise" of religion clause permitted them to exempt their children from compulsory high school (Wisconsin v Yoder 1972).[13] States independently establish their own regulations to monitor home education. In 1988, the state of Pennsylvania passed Act 169, which "allows any non-felon with a high school diploma or GED to teach his or her child at home."[14] A certified evaluator reviews the child and the curriculum annually. At grades three, five, and eight, children are tested with nationally recognized achievement tests. In Texas, on the other hand, any parent regardless of educational level may home school. Texas requires no registration of home-schooling families, no oversight by local authorities, nor testing. State requirements for home education are typically in flux and court cases over regulations abound. In general, however, both the courts and local school districts are becoming more and more sympathetic to home schoolers.[15]

The largest home-schooling promotional organization, the Home School Legal Defense Association (HSLDA), is decidedly Christian. Its publications are punctuated by biblical quotations and Christian sentiments, but it does not require its members to hold Christian beliefs. HSLDA sponsored the largest study of home schooling families that was conducted by educator Brian D. Ray.[16] It was based on 1,516 families, all of whom were HSLDA members. Of those families, 93.8 percent of the fathers and 96.4 percent of the mothers described themselves as "born-again" Christians. It is clear that the percentage of Christians in this sample is exceedingly high because of how the survey was conducted. However, educators and newspaper reporters also acknowledge that the majority of home schoolers are Christians. In a newspaper article on home schooling in Pennsylvania, Michelle Rizzo noted that, "The backbone of the home-schooling movement is evangelical, fundamentalist or charismatic Christian."[17] Specialists estimate that between sixty-five and ninety percent of those who home school are Christian.[18]

According to opinion polls, somewhere between one-fifth and one-third of Americans consider themselves to be "born again" into a new and personal relationship with Christ.[19] Scholars of religion place these "born-again Christians" within a conservative Protestant tradition that includes fundamentalist, evangelical, charismatic, Holiness, or Pentecostal churches.[20] While members of such churches acknowledge their denominational affiliations, they tend to call themselves "Christians." Obviously other Protestants and Catholics also understand themselves as Christians, but in this essay I will use the term "Christian" to refer to those Protestants who base their beliefs and behavior on literal readings of the Bible and support a conservative political agenda to enact those religious commitments. I prefer their terminology because it emphasizes their tendency to devalue denominational differences, to reject media and scholarly appellations (e.g., "Born-Agains," "New Religious Right," "fundamentalists," "evangelicals"), and to claim for themselves a direct lineage to the New Testament. Randall Balmer is quite correct when he writes that, "Some evangelicals draw a careful distinction between being (merely) Christian and being a Christian; therein lies the difference between hell and heaven."[21] For these conservative Protestants, the word "Christian" is not merely a denominational affiliation or a scholarly category. It is the source of their religious and communal self-identification that separates them from other religious people.

Christians seek to create a society and culture based on their understanding of the biblical principles of "love, joy, peace, long suffering, gentleness, goodness, faith, meekness, [and] temperance." (Gal. 5:22) Toward this end, they have increasingly formed political and institutional organizations to pressure the government and the non-Christian society to enact their religious goals. Since they believe it is impossible to attain a perfect life on earth due to humanity's sinful nature, a series of compromises must be made with the "world." They strive to develop a society based on Christian ideals while realizing that non-Christian culture impinges on every aspect of their lives. According to sociologist Melinda Wagner, what

PVRITY

Interesting idea for black/white relations

they create is a "transition culture" made up of Christian and secular ideas and behaviors. One strategy that an increasingly large number of Christians use to create a transition culture is home schooling.

As an alternative to schooling that takes place in the public sphere, home schooling utilizes the private space of the home and the teaching abilities of family members. According to the HSLDA-sponsored report, 88 percent of the instruction is given by mothers to their children. Over 67 percent of the families include three or more children. The average household income, educational level of the parents, and scholastic achievement of the children are somewhat greater than the corresponding national averages.[22] Mothers spend an average of three hours a day in direct instruction with the remainder of the day being spent with the children doing household chores, field trips, and religious activities. Educational styles and curricula vary by family.

Educators and media experts display a cautious nervousness about Christian dominance in home schooling. Although newspaper reporter Michelle Rizzo noted that most home schoolers are Christians, and that there has been a rapid increase in the numbers of home-schooled children (in Pennsylvania a 37 percent increase between 1989 and 1990), she failed to include any other mention of religion in her essay. One of the largest studies of home schooling families did not include any questions about religious affiliation.[23] In spite of that lacuna, the authors who wrote up the study of the Washington families included the comments of one home-schooling father who explained that "because we love our children, and because we feel that it is the command of God, we home school them."[24]

Educators have a difficult time acknowledging that those who currently home school are not part of a tradition of liberal educational reform. While there certainly are home schooling parents influenced by Ivan Illich's *Deschooling Society* or John Holt's *How Children Fail*, the majority of home schooling parents are conservative Christians who are not sympathetic with such humanistic orientations. Educators discuss home schooling as if religion is not significant, assuming that as many parents home school for pedagogical reasons as for religious ones.[25] While some scholars include the Christian rhetoric used by parents, none analyze it. If specialists in religious history neglect the domestic dimension of conservative Christianity, then educators and media experts reveal their discomfort with religion by ignoring the obvious fact that home schoolers are committed to a specific religious world view.

Most publications on home schooling focus on either educational or legal issues. In order to gain a fuller understanding of the religious dimension of home schooling, over a one-year period I visited with five home-schooling families in Austin, Texas.[26] The families I interviewed are not unlike those in Nancy Ammerman's study of the fundamentalist "Southside Church."[27] They were white, middle-class, and the parents were college educated. Although Austin is known as a liberal university town, these families supported a conservative political agenda. My visits were informal. They were not intended to document a community of home schoolers. My intentions were to discover how Christian commitments shaped the educational activities of a few families. Rather than use these families as sources for an ethnographic study, I have chosen instead to pick from our conversations comments that illustrate wider themes and ideas concerning the home as a sacred space in contemporary Christianity.

Why Christian Home Schools?

Rather than reflecting the liberal trends familiar to historians of education, contemporary home schooling arises out of the struggle to create Christian homes. Christian parents home school their children for the same reasons they place their children in private schools. They want to shape strong Christians who are academically trained. Both private Christian schools and home schools have increased rapidly since the early 1960s. Christian schools are the fastest growing sector of nondomestic education in the United States. Since 1960, it is estimated that two new Christian schools open somewhere in the United States every day.[28] Enrollment doubled between 1965 and 1975, so that by 1990 approximately 1.5 million children were taught in Christian schools.[29] Conservative Christians control 35 percent of the nation's private schools and make up 3 percent of all students. While the overall number of children in Christian schools is small, the magnitude of the increase in both schools and students is significant.

Private Christian schools promote many of the same values found among home schoolers. Christian education assumes that all truth is God's truth and so teaching must be Christ-centered. While teachers most likely have been trained in secular colleges and universities, it is assumed that they are committed Christians. Parents know that in private schools their children will receive biblical as well as academic training. A private school, however, is still a school situated in a public space.

Advocates of home schooling point out that Christian schools are just not Christian enough. They explain that too many private schools merely tack on a period of Bible study to standard public education.[30] Such observations are supported by academic studies that point out that religious convictions are not always the primary factor motivating parents to enroll their children in Christian schools and that extra-curricular activities are surprisingly similar to those in the public schools.[31] Children still are asked to compete for the teacher's time and attention. The brightest student easily becomes bored, the slower student frustrated. Classes that are divided by age, according to one home schooling advocate, "undermine wisdom and maturity" and encourage negative peer pressure.[32] Since private schools are usually eager for enrollment increases, they often accept students who have discipline problems and cannot cope with public schooling. There also is the real problem of cost. Where do families, who often rely financially on only the father's income, find the tuition for several children? While advocates of home schooling agree that Christian private schools are certainly preferable to public schools, private schools have their limitations.

In addition to such practical criticisms of private schools, advocates of home schooling argue that both private and public education is wrong because it occurs in the wrong place. As Christians who interpret the Bible literally, advocates of home schooling quickly point out that God intended education to take place at home. From their perspective, the Bible places education within the family and in the private space of the home. Schools are a compromise with non-Christian society. Christians who truly seek to follow the Deuteronomic command to teach children "when thou sittest in thine house, and when thou walkest by the way and when thou liest down, and when thou risest up" should not give their children over to strangers for the bulk of their education. Home schooling, then, becomes the God-given method of education.

In the World but Not of It

Perhaps the most distinct quality of Christian worldview is that good and evil exist and that the definition of what is good and what is evil is not determined by personal experience or opinion. The Christian worldview is a worldview of judgment and division. Ideologically, there is a fundamental division between the Christian and the non-Christian. Spatially, there is a division between the home and the world. Through home schooling, Christians demonstrate their commitment to separating themselves from

[handwritten margin note: Important: the other is always determined in regard to... something/someone else. Non-Christians... Christians need in order to call themselves Christian.]

evil and constructing the good. By not sending their children to either public or private schools, they privilege the private space of the home as the place where true virtue can be cultivated. And yet this separation can never be fully completed. In spite of their desire to withdraw, I will argue that home schoolers find it difficult to stop looking to the non-Christian world for direction and affirmation. *[handwritten: → They could not be Christian without the non-Christian]*

Home schooling advocates use a military rhetoric to vividly portray the battle that divides the forces of good from those of evil. "The enemy army has already made its intentions clear," writes Gregg Harris in *The Christian Home School*, "This is a declaration of religious war. We are not overreacting. We are simply taking our enemy at his word. He wants our children."[33] Proponents of home schooling who use military rhetoric echo the same sentiments found in popular Christian novels, inspirational literature, and music. All of these cultural forms are based on apocalyptic imagery drawn from selected passages from the epistles and the Book of Revelation.[34] When I asked a home-schooled teenager about whether or not she agreed with the military metaphors, she replied that "the battle is the Lord's battle" because "Satan would destroy godly children." No one I spoke to underestimated the seriousness of the battle. A home-schooling father explained that a friend told him that sending children to public school and expecting them to "witness" was like sending a soldier to Vietnam without any previous training or weapons. In a world divided between good and evil forces, home schooling becomes an essential battle strategy.

The enemy is sin in "the world"—a world devoid of Christian values and spirit, ignorant of the biblical message, and determined to turn people against God. As a part of that world, public schools do not follow God's intentions and instead support humanistic education. Teachers use values clarification, engage in sex education, accept diverse lifestyles, and criticize the American economic and social system. Christians point out the results of such human-centered learning: classroom disorder, extensive drug use, teen pregnancy, lack of personal discipline, and poor educational achievement. Advocates of home schooling do not have to go far to find support for their condemnation of public schools. They can choose from a myriad of governmental reports and anecdotes from disgruntled parents to make their case.

The chief weapon in the battle against the world is the home. Gregg Harris sees the immediacy of this battle in graphic terms. Children become "arrows" that will be "mighty weapons in the hand of God." God calls Christians "to establish our homes as embassies of His Kingdom and

[handwritten margin note: Space as a cultural weapon — is this rhetoric too strong?]

to train up families that will be powerful weapons in God's hands for years to come."[35] In order to survive the spiritual warfare that Christians sense every day, the home has to function both as a refuge and as a training center. The more Christian culture portrays a non-Christian world populated by demons who successfully tempt and pervert humanity, the more the home must become a source of refreshment, order, and safety. While parents might have no control over the public sphere of government, schools, and business, they do feel that they can use their homes as a "weapon" against ungodliness.

The Manichean division between Good and Evil has a long tradition in Christian history. It is easy to employ a rhetoric of war because biblical language can be dramatic and colorful. The actual battle, however, is more complicated and nuanced than the language used to describe it. Spiritual warfare, in fact, is not a battle where the enemy is easily spotted and objectified. Rather it is more like a civil war with neighbors facing other neighbors. Evil is manifested in the human behavior of people one knows. Christians interact on a daily basis with non-Christians where they shop, where they work, and in their movements through their neighborhoods. Because Christians are called to witness and convert the non-Christian, they cannot ignore these people. Christians continuously negotiate between the calls of isolation and interaction. At the same time, within the growing Christian community, problems arise. Self-help books flood Christian bookstores, pointing out solutions for the personal and family disorders of committed Christians.[36] Sin and weakness are not the monopoly of the non-Christian. Christians themselves must negotiate between their own socialization (that most likely includes the non-Christian attitudes of ambition, self-pride, competition, and independence) and their acceptance of Christian goals that call for a remaking of their lives.

We can see the difficulty in drawing clear battle lines between the good space of the Christian home and the evil space of the non-Christian world in the writing of Gregg Harris. Harris, a major spokesman for the Christian home-schooling movement and the founder of his own series of Christian Life Workshops, presents his readers with two contradictory messages. On the one hand, he freely uses battle rhetoric to fire up his readers over the menace of secular forces in American society. Harvard and Yale, he explains, were once a religious colleges but "now, sadly, [are] bastions of anti-Christian humanism."[37] As with many Christian writers, he condemns modern, secular education, placing it firmly in the enemy's camp.

However, when he wants to reassure his readers that home schooling will not leave their children educationally disadvantaged, he resurrects the Ivy League and secular education. In a later part of his book, he tells the story of a California family who educated three boys at home. The parents shared the fears of many home-schooling families that they would not be able to give the boys a competent high school education. The boys, however, did so well in science at home that one was accepted to Harvard. "As of this writing," Harris boasts, "he is preparing to graduate with honors in biology from Harvard. His brother now attends Harvard as well. So much for their parents' fears."[38] The enemy has now been transformed into a usable standard of success. Not only has a boy been accepted into the bastion of anti-Christian humanism, he majored in a field which surely demanded the study of evolution. → *Manipulation of Christian narrative*

Harris does not explain this apparent inconsistency in his text. Perhaps he assumes that proper Christian home schooling will prepare the boys to withstand the pressures of Harvard and biology. Or perhaps he thinks the boys will be able to witness at their college and use their knowledge of evolution to support creationism. Harris, however, did not tell a story about boys going off to a Bible college or to Oral Roberts University. When symbols of success are needed, Christians frequently draw not from their own culture but from the non-Christian world. → *Example of how Christians rely on non-Christians*

When I discussed this passage with family members, they recognized the problem. They saw that getting accepted to Harvard is a sign of academic accomplishment, and that Christian parents are not free from such pressures.[39] A mother explained to me that although she places spiritual achievement above academic achievement, "when my child does well in the SAT, it is hard not to call Grandma and brag." Although home-schooling Christians have removed their children from the physical space of the public school, they have not eradicated their own expectation of achievement. If the battle lines were so clearly drawn, and Christian space separated from non-Christian space, then why would children be taking college entrance exams designed by non-Christians for non-Christian schools? Even Christians who separate themselves from non-Christian society by teaching their children, monitoring their intake of popular culture, and providing a strong Christian alternative culture, face the problem of the permeability of boundaries. The families I visited tended to follow the Austin public schools' schedules of vacation times, buy their children treats from Toys R' Us, and follow the trials and tribulations of their favorite football teams. While they would probably agree with Gregg Harris that "the torch of God's Truth is passed from one generation to another, not during the good times, but in the heat of battle," they also know that they are "doing the pioneer thing."[40] The struggle is not only with the non-Christian world but also with their own socialization that unconsciously accepts the standards and definitions of non-Christian society.

"Doing the pioneer thing" means recognizing that one learns to be a Christian not through going to church but through continuous, daily interaction with other Christians. Removing the standards of the world and replacing them with Christian goals cannot be accomplished by merely meditating on the problem. Home schooling provides a distinct method of inculcating new values and standards. The parents I spoke with consider their lives to be more "Christian" than their own parents, not because their parents did not go to church and profess Christian beliefs. They differ from their parents because they attempt to instill Christian attitudes in every aspect of their daily lives. For these home-schooling Christians, Christianity is less an organized belief system and more a means of spiritual orientation and social behavior. Consequently, families who home school carefully supervise with whom their children socialize. Support groups made up of home-schooling families provide time for children to play with other Christian children. These support groups sponsor field trips, art demonstrations, and even ways that mothers can take a "night out" with other home-schooling moms. Rather than joining the Boy Scouts or Girl Scouts, children join Christian equivalents like "AWANA" (for boys and girls) or "Stars" (for girls). These are not church youth groups but Christian parallels to scouting, complete with uniforms and badges. Home-schooled children are not isolated in their houses with their mothers because parents supplement Christian domestic education with Christian extracurricular activities.

The most obvious element of home schooling is that children are moved from the public space of the school and are taught in the private space of the home. By removing their children from public schools, and frequently from the company of non-Christians, parents draw boundaries between a domestic good and a worldly evil. It is significant that Victorian writers understood the home as a "nursery" of "patriotism and piety," while contemporary Christians see the home as "powerful weapons in God's hands."[41] The mood within the Christian community is one of embattled resistance. The home is no longer portrayed as a society writ small; now it must be a forceful alternative. At the same time, however, Christians struggle to continually define how their society should relate to the non-Christian world. To what extent, for instance, can children "minister" in the neighborhood? How seriously should parents take their children's performances on standardized tests? Is it right for a home-schooled boy, gifted in science, to attend Harvard? Responses to such questions seriously cannot be answered by battlefield rhetoric.

The Integrated Home

In my research on the Victorian Christian home, I concluded that one of the goals of domestic housing reformers was to present the home as a "mediating and unifying sacred symbol."[42] The home served to bring together contrasting and diverse realities that on the surface were incompatible. I pointed out that one set of opposites that reformers ignored was the opposition between work and leisure within the home. The ideology of domesticity said that within the home the dichotomies of: public/private; nature/culture; child/adult; male/female; and old/young could be harmoniously resolved.

Contemporary Christians attempt to do the same type of mediating in their homes through a process of integration. They are particularly concerned about resolving the tensions between: religious truth/scientific truth; objective knowledge/character formation; professional teacher/committed mother; and learning child/teaching parent. Unlike the Victorians, Christians have also developed ways to integrate work into domestic space. To the extent that families perceive that these dichotomies (which they would call false and attribute to a wayward American society) are diminished in their homes, the home becomes "sacred," or "holy." For contemporary Christians, the godly nature of the home is defined by how well the sacred can be embedded in the profane.

Home-schooling Christians are acutely aware of the isolation of religion from everyday life. American society prefers the world to be divided, segregated, and isolated. Christian symbols are not to be displayed in public places. If religion is taught in the schools, it should be taught in an objective manner that does not present one religious idea as more true than any other. Churches create clubs, prayer groups, social committees, and charitable organizations, but these do not reach into the home. They also barely affect the world outside the church. Sunday Schools mimic public schools by dividing children by age and separating them from their families. Outside work, that once claimed only fathers, now claims mothers as well. Work removes parents from the home and places them in public spaces for most of the day. Grandparents live in retirement villages. Children go to day-care. The home becomes an isolated space, often not occupied at all during the day.

While all Christians would see their lives as God-centered, home-schooling Christians act on those beliefs in a practical and systematic way. Home-schooling Christians seek to integrate faith, morality, and knowledge to such an extent that religion becomes a total way of life, not merely a belief system. Christians see public schools, as they do their own schools, as agents of socialization.[43] Public schools integrate knowledge with life-style, just as home schools do. In the words of John Dewey, "Education is not preparation for life, it is life itself." Public schools then, are not condemned by Christians merely because they are disorganized, dangerous, and academically suspect. While Christians discuss public schools as being secular and irreligious, what they really mean is that public schools present an alternative religious system to their own. Public schools promote a humanism that asks the child to see his or her well being as the primary foundation for behavior. "Public schools and Christian schools," summarized Gregg Harris, "are religious rivals."[44] For Christian home schoolers, the life instilled by the public schools is not the life they want for their children.

Consequently, if one seeks to teach children proper behaviors and attitudes, then the best way to do this is to follow the path laid out by God in the Bible. In spite of a paucity of explicitly supporting biblical texts, home-schooling parents insist that the Bible accords the responsibility for the education of the children to the parents, not teachers.[45] In one family, above the school books and globe hangs the motto: "Be it known to all who enter here that Christ is the reason for this school." For this family, God is the controlling force in their everyday lives, including their intellectual lives. Home schoolers are quick to point out that home schooling is not new, that it was how most people were educated until modern times. While Christians will vary on the extent to which they take the Scriptures literally, all will agree that the ultimate sacred source that directs their home life is God's word as revealed in the Bible. Personal growth or family stability does not serve as the foundation of the home. Education is not a goal in itself but is intrinsically bound to religious goals.

Christians and liberal educators both agree that education is not value-free but rather carries with it a powerful socializing force. Christians want to make that force a religious force. For them, education must stress the biblical message and every aspect of home school should have an underlying religious principle. On the most obvious of levels, the curricula which home schoolers use are explicitly Christian. On one afternoon, a family who uses the Weaver curriculum for their science lessons, did an experiment in their backyard. The purpose of the experiment was to introduce to third grade children how the biblical Flood created various types of rocks. The children took a jar, filled it with dirt and debris, and planted match sticks in it to symbolize trees. Then they poured water in the jar, shook it up, and watched as the dirt settled into different layers. Their text explained that, "After Noah and his family and the animals were in the ark, the rain began. At this time, the 'fountains of the deep' also opened, meaning that there was a great shaking of earth as the earth's crust itself opened in various places to spend forth a powerful release of pressurized water."[46] The animals which were trapped between the layers of settling dirt after the flood eventually became the fossils that some scientists wrongly date to be millions of years old.

For this home-schooling family, there is no discontinuity between the scientific divisions of rocks into igneous and sedimentary types and the biblical account of the Flood. Christians use contemporary science as long as it does not conflict with biblical truth. Children, for instance, do not have to give up loving dinosaurs. They just learn that dinosaurs and people lived at the same time about ten thousand years ago and dinosaurs were destroyed during the flood. Those who use the Advanced Training Institute of America (ATIA) curriculum found nothing odd in the sentence, "How does the Second Law of Thermodynamics come from prophecy?"[47] From the Christian perspective, God created the laws of nature as well as those of the moral order and religion. Home schooling curricula freely combine religion and academics. The Weaver curriculum, for instance, is based on the explication of a series of Bible verses. When students study Josh. 5:10–12, they also study: walls in a social science lesson, volcanoes in science, and biographies in language arts. Home schooling curricula, which direct the daily studies of children, reinforce the conviction that biblical truth is the foundation for all truth.

The fluidity between Bible and education appears in every subject, not just science. In one family, children perfect their handwriting by writing out biblical quotations. In an other, a math game is played where players move around a board that contains squares explaining, "the bugs are feasting on your garden, spend $3.00 on insect killer. I Samuel 30:16." Children create colorful time lines that begin with Adam and Eve and include biblical and other historically famous figures. In *Old World History and Geography*, a text published for home schoolers, the origins of the "black

This exclusion also relates to other races, meaning this is a majority WHITE practice

race" is explained as the descendants of "people who traveled from the tower of Babel to the part of Africa south of the Sahara Desert." When discussing India, the book concludes that "the superstition of the Hindu keeps them living lives of fear. Their gods stand in the way of the people's health, the country's progress, and the people's knowledge of the one true God who promises to take care of all those who follow and trust Him."[48] While public school children might be encouraged in their studies to accept the diversity of the world's cultures, Christian home schoolers only acknowledge that diversity. Diversity itself is not a value. Only the Bible presents both the correct information on the origins of humanity and the way to achieve a society in harmony with God's laws. The illustration and explanation of those laws, and not some type of abstract knowledge, is the purpose of education.

As we have seen, home-schooling parents stress that there is no fundamental difference between religious principles and academic subject matter. All learning should be integrated. At one point, when I asked a child what she was studying in school, she responded: "termites, Pharisees, and the court system." Curricula not only juxtapose religious themes with academic subjects, they strive to bring the two together so that all knowledge forms a seamless cloth. For non-Christians the connections can seem bizarre and contrived. In one unit, children are taught "How the Holy Days of Israel illustrate the development of a child in the womb." According to the lesson, Passover occurs on the fourteenth day of the first Jewish month, just like ovulation occurs fourteen days into the mother's "birth calendar." The unit integrates the sacred time of a community with the birth process. In doing so, it transforms the birth process from being an objective, biological change with no religious significance to being a sacred event ordained by God. The lesson concludes with a chart that lists the "Holy Days of Israel," the "Pre-Birth Event," and the "Steps for Wise Parents." It seeks not only to sacralize pregnancy but to spell out how parental behavior can instill those beliefs. Thus the unit removes the standard educational barriers between: what children learn (the growth of the fetus), religious meaning (the holy days), and adult behavior (how parents should behave during pregnancy).

While playing Bible games or writing out biblical verses has obvious religious connections, home schoolers also employ more subtle teaching techniques to instill values. Christians believe that there is a God-created order and pattern that structures the world. Nothing is random or coincidental because God has a plan for people, nature, and society. Consequently, parents try to create a planned, ordered, domestic environment for their families. Mothers who teach are particularly responsible for making sure that tasks are clearly stated and lesson plans carefully written down. ATIA expects parents to fill out weekly reports on their children which are mailed to their headquarters and evaluated. Children have lists of chores and academic responsibilities. Paperwork, which includes listing goals and accomplishments, structures the home school.

Home schoolers, as do other Christian educators, prefer the phonics method of reading to the "look and say" method. Phonics assumes that language is built on a series of patterns that can be translated into a set of defined rules. The "look and say" method, used by other educators, assumes that language can best be learned through the mastery of a variety of words. There is less emphasis on the memorization of rules of word formation. Phonics, however, makes more sense to Christians because it implies that like the world, language has a decipherable pattern that can be mastered if one learns the proper rules. Christian home schooling emphasizes the God-given structure and order of the world rather than presenting a universe of meaningless diversity.

Home schooling also tends to emphasize the importance of memorization. Children memorize grammar rules, mathematical principles, the capitals of the world's nations, and the Gettysburg Address. They read their social science books knowing they will be quizzed on specific terms by their mothers. The emphasis on memorizing academic materials accompanies an emphasis on Scripture memorization. Parents take pride in listening to their three-year-olds recite chapters from the Bible. "Memory work" is understood as the way to "put God in your heart." Several parents told me that once texts are memorized, then children can always compare their behavior to the biblical ideals. Memorizing Scripture helps children spot that which is not "helpful and wholesome." Memorization also implies that the text is fixed and unchanging. Where humanistic education and liberal Christianity stress the importance of interpretation and discussion of texts, home schooling relies on the memorization of information. The text, like the world, is fixed and determined. Mastery of the text, like mastery of the world, comes about when one knows "in one's heart" what the ideal is and then strives to become a reflection of that ideal.

Memorization is a formal way to learn the biblical ideal and the principles of knowledge. Character development, another important goal, is achieved through less specifically religious means. Academic achievement, while important to home schoolers is not their end goal. The end

Memorization takes the place of thought development & discussion, feeding into an unquestionability, but accurate memorization of Christian doctrine.

goal is the goal of salvation. Forming the character of children becomes a critical task and serves as a backdrop for many intellectual exercises. The popular ATIA curriculum structures its whole academic program around the development of a set of "life principles." Children are taught to value kindness, peace, unselfishness, obedience, helpfulness, submission, neatness, orderliness, politeness, courage, and determination. They read stories about animals, like the otter who "turn routine tasks into enjoyable experiences." Mothers frequently design their own games to impart values. In one, fruit are given various character traits. A picture of a pear ("self control, Proverbs 16:32") needs to matched with: "You feel tired and mom asks you to help her." Mottos are placed on kitchen cabinets: "Train don't React." Place mats on the kitchen table describe "Guidelines to Strong and Happy Christian Families." Children are asked to role-play situations where they might be tempted to disobey or act in an un-Christian manner. One mother bakes bread (starting with grinding the unmilled wheat grains) with her sons. Her goal is to shape her sons' abilities to work together and refine their business sense since some of the bread is eventually sold. Nothing that children do is left to chance or mere pleasure. Parents intend for even enjoyable play activities to support character building.

Home schooling seeks to erase the boundaries between biblical truth and scientific truth. It also intends to imbue academic learning and character building. In a less explicitly educational manner, home schooling rejects the divisions between professional teacher and devoted mother. By having mothers teach their children in the private sphere, home schooling attacks the notion that education is best done by specialists in public spaces. The concerned mother, even if she is not an expert on every academic subject, is better prepared to teach her children because God wills it. In my discussions with home-schooling parents, all hoped that they could school their children through high school. None felt that they should give over teaching to experts when the materials got too difficult for them. By de-emphasizing the importance of purely academic knowledge, and by placing the emphasis on creating good Christians who could function in the world, parents reject the professionalization of education with its boundaries between child, parent, and teacher.

By teaching children of various ages and abilities together, home schoolers stress the importance of children learning from one another in small groups. For them, learning in distinct age groups does not facilitate education. They feel that the peer learning (peer pressure) found in the public schools destroys family cohesiveness. Christians encourage their children to bond first with family members. Children should learn from their siblings, parents, and respected adults. In one family, a great-grandmother made weekly visits to the home to be with the children during their lessons. Other parents expressed concern when their own parents criticized their home schooling since this isolated the nuclear family from the extended family.

The integration of children of various ages into one home-learning environment is perhaps the most difficult goal for mothers to achieve. A toddler is cajoled on his mom's lap while she gives mathematic instructions to her two sons. A fussy four-year-old is taken into the bedroom to be paddled for disobedience while his sisters work on essay writing. An eight-year-old practices the violin in the kitchen while mother helps her eldest daughter with a geography lesson. To facilitate household learning, every room in the home is used and children seem to be on an endless march from one space to another. Even when special schoolrooms are created, the sheer number and diversity of the ages demand that all of the house be used.

Teaching three or four children of different ages means that children can learn from their mothers, their lessons, or from each other. Or, if they are so disposed, they can be sufficiently distracted and not learn anything. Domestic education, however, is not limited to the children. Parents also gain from this shift from teacher learning to family learning. Mothers frequently told me that they learned along with their children. They described how "we" were learning Greek or "we" were studying about barometers. Mothers along with their children learn how the Second Law of Thermodynamics comes from prophecy. Although the educational materials are geared for the children, mothers must master the concepts that are being presented. As one mother told me, "I gain more [from the lesson] because I'm the teacher and the adult, far more [than the children]."

Unlike the Victorians, contemporary home schoolers consciously strive to integrate work into education and home life. Christian home schoolers reject the notion that the home is solely a place of leisure and emotional fulfillment. Seeing the home as a space for education already adds an additional element to the domestic environment. Children not only maintain their own space (e.g., making their beds), they also are expected to contribute to the running of the household (e.g., by cleaning the bathrooms or vacuuming the living room). They participate in money-earning activities like pet-sitting or bread baking. The daughters of a family living outside of Austin raise sheep and goats. Mothers supplement the family budget by

> Parents are equally doctrinated

tutoring neighborhood children or sewing. In one family, a father started his own business and worked out of his home office. The practice of having children working in the home not only inculcates responsibility and provides for additional income, it challenges the notion that work must take place in a nonfamilial, public space.

While home schooling certainly is successful at integrating education and religion and attempts to integrate age groups and work, it has difficulties integrating men into the domestic sphere. Since the nineteenth century, the middle-class home has been a place dominated by mothers and children. Even the Beecher sisters eliminated the male presence by saying that their church-home-school could be run by "two ladies" who would adopt two orphans and manage several servants.[49] Contemporary Christians, however, reject the feminizing trend of Protestantism that leaves the religious nurture of children to their mothers. Following the patriarchal traditions of the Bible, Christian families are told that men are the leaders of the household. They not only are required to support the family financially but are to direct it spiritually.

Parents underscore the importance of the father in education but admit that in reality the father does not take part in the daily education of the children. Paternal involvement is difficult to achieve even for home-schooling families. Mothers and fathers must counter their own socialization that associates home with women and does not give men clear roles in child raising. They also face the reality that single-income households economically are more unstable than those where the wife also earns a salary. In all the home-schooling families I visited, the fathers realized the importance of their roles in the education of their children and struggled to keep actively involved.

The problem of the feminization of domestic education was remedied in a variety of ways by the Austin families. Some fathers tried to come home for lunch as well as dinner. Most families had morning prayers or Bible study led by the father. Or they ended the day with father-led prayers and hymn singing. In the AITA "family report," one section is "to be completed by father only," and asks questions such as: "Did you listen to your children recite their Scripture memory this week" and "Do you have accurate records of your children's progress for this week?" Fathers design special weekend science experiments and field trips. Mothers told me that they discussed their weekly lesson plans with their husbands, sometimes going as far as to schedule "dates" with him to confer about household education. I was told that families that try to home school without the active input of the father face significant obstacles. These families recognize that in this country both education and religion tend to be feminized, but their goal was to refute this unbiblical trend. They strive not to re-establish a distant male authority figure in the home, but rather to integrate the father into the educational and spiritual life of the home.

Creating Domestic Christianity

Home schooling typically is discussed as an educational alternative to the public schools. Depending on one's commitment to public schooling, domestic education may be seen either as a dangerous inward orientation that will undermine American communal spirit or as the only natural response to a collapsing academic system. Typical discussions of home schooling pit family interests against the interests of the state.[50] Home schooling also provides a fundamental challenge to another public institution that many hold dear: the church. Because of its religious nature, the Christian home school shifts the attention away from the public space of the church as the defining religious space. Home schooling produces what I will call a "domestic Christianity" that has its own unique characteristics. The very process of home schooling becomes a method of Christianizing the family in a particular way. Domestic religion (reflecting the power of the family) has frequently threatened public religion (reflecting the power of the community).[51] In this final section, I want to explore some of the possible ways that home schooling is challenging and modifying conservative Protestantism.

While the purported reason for home schooling is the education of children, what really happens is the religious education of the whole family. Christians who home school frequently are "first generation" Christians. Their parents were churchgoers and perhaps believed in the literal truth of the Bible, but they did not attempt to bring biblical principles into every aspect of home life. Prayers might have been said before meals, but children did not drink from cups imprinted with "Give Thanks to the Lord." Several hours during the week might be spent in church, but home-schooling mothers spend at least three hours *a day* teaching lessons with strong religious messages. Home schooling, by insisting that parents teach religious principles along with academic subjects *every day*, systematically instructs the parents, especially the mothers. Mothers told me that they

(1) Interesting notion that the home shifts attention / power away from the church. This is sacred space reinterpreted.

(2) Domestic religion vs. public religion

had changed their viewpoints and developed their own spirituality through teaching their children. Home-schooling curricula helped them "keep their priorities straight." Mothers manage to keep up the daily routine of schooling because they learn and develop at the same time as the children. Fathers are asked to review weekly lessons and to provide guidance for their families. They, too, are forced to think about their Christianity in intense and pragmatic ways. While an initial, powerful conversion experience might motivate an adult to instill his or her life with religious enthusiasm, it is through the continuous and daily instruction of children that religion is embedded into the fabric of their lives.

The type of religion that is embedded is also different from that experienced at church. Home schooling promotes a domestic Christianity that does not separate the sacred from the profane, the extraordinary from the ordinary, the pious from the trivial. From the perspective of domestic Christianity, there is nothing about religion that need be separated from the everyday life of the family. Families who I talked with did not find it sacrilegious or in bad taste to wear baseball caps with "Jesus Christ, He's the Real Thing" stitched on their rims. Nor did they think paper napkins with blue ducks and the phrase "Praise the Lord" inappropriate for a ladies' luncheon. Children received combs imprinted with "Can't bear to be without Jesus" as party favors. When I pointed out that baseball caps get sweaty, napkins are thrown in the trash, and combs get coated with dandruff, it did not change their attitude. The objects—caps, napkins, combs—were good in themselves. The phrases were excellent Christian sentiments. Sweat or dirt or dandruff could not profane either the object or the ideas.

Home schooling reinforced the idea that biblical truth must not be separated from academic knowledge and, in the same way, Christianity need not be separated from popular culture. Studying "termites, Pharisees, and the court system" or wearing T-shirts printed with "We are the fragrance of Christ," moves Christianity out of the space of the churches and into the everyday life of learning, family, and consumerism. For domestic Christianity, the dualism is not between the sacred and the profane, but between good and evil. The home is sacred space when it is a space where people act in accordance with God's laws. Sacrality is accomplished through behavior and not through the intrinsic meaning of an object.

Home schooling promotes a domestic Christianity that insists that there is no fundamental separation between religious knowledge and academic knowledge, between religious object and commercial object, between

(1) But isn't the mere act of home schooling creating those differences?

(2) Great example of how ACTIONS create a space as holy or sacred..

Cool
connection

the child as learner and the parent as learner. Its emphasis on integration rather than separation reasserts the long-standing religious assertion that God is intimately involved with every aspect of life. Christians see God as directly influencing as well as watching over them. I would argue that God becomes, in effect, a home-schooling mother. Home schooling mothers, unlike their public school counterparts, are always interacting with their children. Children rarely work on their own, without interrupting their mothers, for more than ten minutes at a time. Although parents will describe how their children work independently, the reality is that children constantly interact with their mothers. Whereas public school teachers have thirty or forty children to supervise and their attention can be drawn away from their class, home-schooling mothers oversee fewer children with far more intensity. This constant monitoring and interaction by the all-pervasive mother is a human reminder of the God from whom there is no escape. → too much!

The Christianity that emanates from home schools can at times threaten the public traditions of the church. Domestic Christianity can be a challenge for churches because it defines private space as the most significantly religious space. It is there that everyday life becomes filled with the Christian spirit. Churches, on the other hand, possess a rarified atmosphere of piety. In domestic Christianity, the natural family is better able to reflect Christ's saving power than the church family. Fathers, in domestic Christianity, are the spiritual leaders of their families, not the minister. Children, rather than being noisy distractions, become the focus of religious life.

Although home schoolers see the church and communal worship as necessary, they frequently point out that churches work against families. Sunday schools, for instance, divide children by age groups and separate them from their families. Modeled after the public schools, Sunday Schools typically ignore the family. In their Sunday School classes, home-schooled children find that their knowledge of the Bible and religious issues far exceeds the knowledge of their classmates. In many Protestant churches, children do not even stay with their parents through the whole service but go instead to a "children's church." Fathers do not assert their spiritual authority at church, but instead give over their leadership to a series of assistant ministers, deacons, and Sunday School teachers. Church activities themselves draw family members away from the home and each other. Home-schooling parents express dismay over churches that boast they are a "family church," when the first thing they do is split up the family.

① Interesting perspective on church & its activities

Several home-schooling parents told me that they are trying to change this situation. They want to instill in their churches the same integrative orientation that they have in their homes. Why, they ask, can't Sunday School be an activity for the family as a group? Why is it that children are screened from prayer groups where "real" issues are being coped with by Christians? The problem then becomes to what extent the church service should be geared to the needs of children. If sermons discuss adult topics of sexuality or societal violence, should children be exposed to such matters? As one father told me, "sometimes the sermons are more vivid than what is on TV."

Other home-schooling families avoid the whole issue by creating "home churches." As evangelical, fundamentalist churches flourish, they tend to get larger and larger, causing some Christians to feel that they are merely a cog in a large church wheel. Home churches, made up of a small number of families, forego the institutional benefits of a large church for the intimacy of meeting with a small group of like-minded Christians. The issues raised in home schooling and the development of a domestic Christianity are having a direct impact on church life. The private sphere is not merely a passive recipient of theological and social changes begun in the public spaces of the churches and seminaries. Home schooling empowers parents to make demands on their churches based on experiences at home.

Home schooling is also helping to rewrite conservative Christian gender relationships. As historian Betty DeBerg has argued, early twentieth-century fundamentalism continued to uphold Victorian gender stereotypes in spite of social changes in American family life. To be a fundamentalist meant to believe that God placed women in the family (with the children) and men in the workplace. While such ideology still exists, home schooling complicates the simple dichotomies set up by fundamentalist writers and preachers. Women still are in the homes with the children. However, because they teach, they assume a professional attitude regarding their domestic activities.

Being the sole provider for their children's education not only increases a mother's responsibility, it gives her a respectable career. Mothers read home-schooling magazines, exchange advice on teaching techniques with other mothers, try to find outlets to buy science equipment, and study the personality types of their children. They put together weekly lesson plans, survey the variety of academic curricula available, and attend summer teaching seminars. Teaching becomes their profession. They no longer see themselves as simply housewives or mothers. They have found an occupation that is fully acceptable within their religious and cultural milieu and that also places them within the wider profession of educators. Not only those mothers with degrees in education, but all home-schooling mothers express their creativity, skill, and academic interests. Through home schooling the home becomes a workplace; a "school" where a "teacher" performs her professional duties.

As mothers become transformed into professionals, fathers are expected to become more domesticated. Christian ideology expects men to be the spiritual, social, and economic leaders of the home. Home schooling not only expects the father to lead Bible study, it expects him to oversee the education of his children. Popular curricula like ATIA insist that men do their part in domestic education. Home-schooling mothers accept the fact that day-to-day schooling is their responsibility, but they also assume the support and guidance of their husbands. While Christian advice books encourage men to become more caring and committed to their families, home schooling provides them a structured way to express that commitment.

For grown men who have been raised in families where their fathers had little influence on the lives of their children, the impact of home-schooling may be ineffective. Or, men may feel stifled in their desire to be with their children because of their work responsibilities. As one mother summarized when I asked her about her husband's role in their home school, "we definitely need to improve in that area." For sons, however, the situation is different.

Home-schooled sons and daughters do not see the home as either an empty place populated by parents only on the weekends or as a place for leisure. The home is a place of school work, character building, and communal responsibility. Because housework and schoolwork are integrated, both boys and girls learn domestic skills. Boys learn how to take care of their younger siblings, how to clean the bathroom, and how to bake bread. One mother proudly told me that her young sons managed the household for several days while she was sick in bed with the flu. When I asked if her sons' domestic skills would be shared by the males in her family or her church, she replied in the negative. This mother felt that other Christians did not involve their boys in the details of homemaking. Boys mowed the lawn or set the table but did not learn the intricacies of baby diapering and laundry. By seeing the home as a place of work, home schooling "domesticates" the male worker by introducing him to traditionally female-gendered activities. Homework is not devalued. It is seen as a critical aspect of the training of both boys and girls.

Home schooling also serves as a means for Christians to redefine humanistic, secular values so that they can be fit into their religious culture. Freedom, individuality, and empowerment—words that are bantered about in the media and in academic circles—are not ignored by Christians. Christians, for instance, reject the notion that freedom in itself is a virtue. People who equate freedom with self-interest place their own personal wills above God's. True freedom comes about when the Christian harmonizes his or her intentions with God's will. By accepting the idea that God intended families to teach their children, parents point to the freedom home schooling provides them as indicative of God's blessing. Unlike public school children, their children have a flexible schedule that can be molded to their own family's needs. If Grandma is visiting, school can be halted for a few days to take advantage of the occasion. Or, more significantly, weekly lessons can be altered to integrate Grandma into the domestic educational routine. Whereas public school children are locked into a rigid schedule that parents and children cannot alter, home-schooling families feel they are free to find their own educational rhythm.

Christians also reject the notion that the public schools encourage individuality and that their own religious orientation stresses conformity. Just as true freedom is accomplished only by submission to God's will, true individuality comes about only when the person develops in the manner God intended. Children in the public schools, from the Christian perspective, are mass-produced. They blindly follow the dictates of American culture expressed both by their teachers and inculcated in their interactions with other students. Peer pressure makes children not into individuals but into clones of each other. Home schooling, on the other hand, is understood to eliminate the standardization rampant in the average public school classroom. It also reduces the corrosive effects of peer pressure. Children are free to go at their own pace and mothers match their teaching lessons to their children's personalities."[52] Home-schooling parents commented on the number of books and resources available to them. They see diversity in their resources rather than conformity. For them, freeing their children from the control of television and peer pressure is how true creativity is formed.

Home schooling is used by Christians as a means of empowerment. While the non-Christian world might be all-pervasive and seemingly impossible to control, the home and family can be managed. Home schooling provides a strategy for parents to control their household. Parents become invested in controlling what goes in and what goes out of their homes. They monitor the food their families eat, their access to television and other entertainments, and what their children are taught. By "investing" in the home, a mother explained, "one looks at things from a different perspective. You're the one responsible."

In *The American Woman's Home* the Beecher sisters seem somewhat unclear about exactly *where* the Christian home will be built. On the one hand, we are led to believe that every home should be a Christian house: "a house contrived for the express purpose of enabling every member of a family to labor with the hands for the common good, and by modes at once healthful, economical, and tasteful."[53] On the other hand, they tell us that such a house should be built in missionary territory. Then "the most self-sacrificing men and women" would not have to give up the benefits of a Christian community and "commence the family state amid such vice and debasement that it was ruinous to children to be trained in its midst."[54] However, once Christian families established a Christian neighborhood "in any destitute neighborhood" a critical change could occur. "A central church would soon appear," with its accompanying social and cultural services, and the "school-house would no longer hold the multiplying worshipers."[55] In the long run the Beechers, the members of a family of noted Protestant ministers, could not permit Christianity to be detached from the public space of the church and sequester itself in the home.

Catharine Beecher and Harriet Beecher Stowe stood firmly among the Protestant elite of Victorian America. Their family, and families like them, controlled the cultural and economic forces of the Republic. They defined what was "American" and what was not. Today the Protestant hegemony of 1869 no longer exists. In spite of the conservative Reagan years, America is a secular country that tolerates a diversity of cultures and lifestyles. Prayer has not been put back into the public schools, abortion is still legal, and evolutionary biology is still the accepted standard. A desire to Christianize the public spaces of schools, hospitals, work places, and legislatures might be an admirable goal for some, but it is a unrealistic social strategy. However, given secular society's approval of personal choice and privatized religion, Christianizing the family will face few outside obstacles. Teachers and psychologists will argue over how "normal" or "educated" home-schooled children are, but there is no indication that the state will be able to stop this trend. Home schooling, rather than the more flashy TV evangelists or Eagle Forum leaders, will shape how future conservative Christians understand their religion.

Sociologist Pierre Bourdieu has argued that "inhabited space—and above all the house" is where we learn the divisions, hierarchies, and classification systems that define our culture. "One of the fundamental effects of the orchestration of habitus," Bourdieu wrote, "is the production of a commonsense world endowed with the *objectivity* secured by the consensus on the meaning (*sens*) of practices and the world . . . "[56] While Bourdieu speaks in the language of a French social scientist, he shares with the Victorians the understanding that the home (however defined) is a powerful space, rich in materials for the scholar's interpretive skills. In a similar way, Gaston Bachelard and Gerardus van der Leeuw have also provided provocative and often poetic discussions of "house and universe."[57] Their writings reveal that their understanding of sacred space was conditioned by their own personal sense of "home" as constructed in nineteenth-century Europe. When Van der Leeuw wrote that, "House and temple, still further, are essentially one" he would receive agreeing nods both from Victorian Americans like Catherine Beecher and contemporary home schoolers like Gregg Harris.[58] Those who understand the home as a sacred space often speak of it in similar ways: It is a domain of purity in a defiling environment. It is a place of empowerment in a disempowering world.

GOAL —] And yet, what I hope that this essay has introduced is the idea that domestic sacred space is not merely an abstract category. Homes are places where real people interact with one another in the hopes of promoting specific religious and cultural values. Domestic religion is experienced differently by men, women, and children. The "unitary power" of the home is as much an ideological position as a phenomenological model. As residents in a post-Freudian world, we know that the "unquestioned reality" of domestic sacred space of which Van der Leeuw wrote is filled with both spoken and unspoken conflict.[59] Perhaps it is our own disenchantment with family life that leads us to question the easy association of house and temple. This essay has attempted to challenge some of the broad generalizations about domestic sacred space by showing how one group of Americans attempt to make their homes schools of faith. While the dream of a Christian home for many evangelicals may resonate closely with Van der Leeuw and Bachelard, the political, educational, and theological beliefs of evangelicals may be repugnant to certain Christians and liberal scholars.

The home, like all space, is contested space that changes meaning over time. Future studies will further refine how the sacred space of the home is created and maintained across shifting religious, political, and social boundaries.

Notes

1. Catharine Beecher and Harriet Beecher Stowe, *The American Woman's Home: Or Principles of Domestic Science* (New York: J. B. Ford & Co., 1869), p. 455.

2. Ibid., p. 459. On the nineteenth-century Christian home, see Colleen McDannell, *The Christian Home in Victorian America, 1840–1900* (Bloomington: Indiana University Press, 1986); and A. Gregory Schneider, *The Way of the Cross Leads Home: The Domestication of American Methodism* (Bloomington: Indiana University Press, 1993).

3. This change is described in Colleen McDannell, "Parlor Piety: The Home as Sacred Space in Protestant America," in Jessica Foy and Thomas J. Schlereth, *American Home Life, 1880–1930* (Knoxville, University of Tennessee Press, 1992), pp. 162–89.

4. For a discussion of the material culture and religion, see Colleen McDannell, "Interpreting Things: Material Culture Studies and American Religion" *Religion*, 21 (1993), pp. 371–87; and *Material Christianity: Kitsch, Bodies, and Rituals in America* (New Haven: Yale University Press, forthcoming).

5. Betty A. DeBerg, *Ungodly Women: Gender and the First Wave of American Fundamentalism* (Minneapolis: Fortress Press, 1990); and David Harrington Watt, *A Transforming Faith: Explorations of Twentieth-Century American Evangelicalism* (New Brunswick, N.J.: Rutgers University Press, 1991).

6. Billy Sunday, "Home," *Trenton Evening Times*, 15 January 1880. As cited in DeBerg, *Ungodly Women*, p. 61.

7. Watt, *Transforming Faith*, p. 84.

8. Beecher and Beecher Stowe, *American Woman's Home*, p. 457.

9. The exact number of children in home-schooling situations is impossible to determine. Since there are no national requirements for education, states and school districts determine where, when, and how children are placed in educational settings. Most states do not collect statistics on home schooling. In states which require home schoolers to register, some families may not register. Even determining who is home-schooled is difficult. Is a three-year old who is taught along with her brothers and sisters to be counted?

   This number is based on research done by Patricia Lines from the U.S. Department of Education. She based her estimate on how many people were enrolled in academic curricula and adjusted to account for the large numbers of families who do not enroll. She concludes, "it seems likely that roughly 10,000 to 15,000 school-aged children were schooling at home in the early 1970s, 60,000 to 125,000 by fall 1983; 122,000 to 244,000 by fall 1985; and 150,000 to 300,000 by fall 1988." Patricia Lines, "Home Instruction: The Size and Growth of the Movement," in Jane Van Gallen and Mary Anne Pitman, *Home Schooling: Political, Historical, and Pedagogical Perspectives* (Norwood, N.J.: Ablex, 1991), p. 20. In a later study (Working paper OR91-537 U.S. Dept. of Education), she estimated that the numbers in 1991 ranged from 248,000 to 353,000. If we assume the same growth from 1991 to 1994 as between 1988 and 1991, and add an estimated 100,000 children to account for those under 5, then the numbers would approach 500,000.

10. Recent works that describe the political and public activities of Conservative Christians include: Peggy L. Shriver, *The Bible Vote and the New Right* (New York, Pilgrim Press, 1981); Randall Balmer, *Mine Eyes Have Seen the Glory: A Journey into the Evangelical Subculture in America* (New York: Oxford University Press, 1989); and Walter H. Capps, *The New Religious Right: Piety, Patriotism, and Politics* (Columbia, S.C.: University of South Carolina Press, 1990). On theological and institutional struggles, see George M. Marsden, *Reforming Fundamentalism: Fuller Seminary and the New Evangelicalism* (Grand Rapids, Mi.: William B. Eerdmans, 1987); Nancy Tatom Ammerman, *Baptist Battles: Social Change and Religious Conflict in the Southern Baptist Convention* (New Brunswick, N.J.: Rutgers University Press, 1990); and *Southern Baptists Observed: Multiple Perspectives on a Changing Denomination* (Knoxville, Tenn.: University of Tennessee Press, 1993).

11. On Christian schools, see Alan Peshkin, *God's Choice: The Total World of a Fundamentalist Christian School* (Chicago: University of Chicago Press, 1986); Paul F. Parson, *Inside America's Christian Schools* (Macon, Ga.: Mercer University Press, 1987); Susan D. Rose, *Keeping Them out of the Hands of Satan: Evangelical Schooling in America* (New York: Routledge, 1988); and Melinda Bollar Wagner, *God's Schools: Choice and Compromise in American Society* (New Brunswick, N.J.: Rutgers University Press, 1990).

12. The major exception to this conclusion is Nancy Tatom Ammerman's ethnographic study of fundamentalists in a middle-class, Northeast suburb. See *Bible Believers: Fundamentalists in the Modern World* (New Brunswick, N.J.: Rutgers University Press, 1987).

13. Michael S. Shepherd, "Home Schooling: Dimensions of Controversy, 1970–1984," *Journal of Church and State*, 31 (1989), pp. 101–114 at 106.

14. Michelle Rizzo, "Home Ed," *Philadelphia Inquirer Magazine*, 25 October 1992.

15. For example, see Krista Ramsey, "Home Is Where the School Is," and "Home Schooling: A Choice the Cupertino District Supports," both in *The School Administrator*, 49 (1992), pp. 20–27 and Virginia Seuffert, "Home Remedy: A Mom's Prescription for Ailing Schools," *Policy Review*, 52 (1990), pp. 70–75.

16. Brian D. Ray, *A Nationwide Study of Home Education: Family Characteristics, Legal Matters, and Student Achievement* (Salem, Oregon: National Home Education Research Institute, 1990).

17. Rizzo, "Home Ed," p. 21.

18. Discussion with Brian Ray, president of National Home Education Research Insitute, Salem, Ore., April 1992.

19. Wagner, *God's Schools*, p. 7. The frequently cited figure of 22% of the adult population as being evangelical comes from a 1978 survey done by the Princeton Religious Research Center for the private use of the Evangelical periodical *Christianity Today*. A discussion of those findings is in James Davison Hunter, *American Evangelicalism: Conservative Religion and the Quandary of Modernity* (New Brunswick, N.J.: Rutgers University Press, 1983), pp. 142–44.

20. Wagner, *God's Schools*, p. 11.

21. Balmer, *Mine Eyes Have Seen the Glory*, p. 4.

22. "A Nationwide Study of Home Education," *Home School Court Report*, December 1990, is a synopsis of "A Nationwide Study of Home Education: Family Characteristics, Legal Matters, and Student Achievement" conducted by the National Home Education Research Institute and published in 1990. It was commissioned by the Home School Legal Defense Association in Paeonian Springs, Va., and was directed by Brian Ray, a professor of science and education at Western Baptist College in Salem, Ore.. The study received information from 1,516 randomly selected families, all of whom were members of the Home School Legal Defense Association.

23. Maralee Mayberry, "Home-based Education in the United States: Demographics, Motivations and Educational Implications," *Educational Review*, 41 (1989), p. 173.

24. Ibid., p. 174.

25. Ivan Illich, *Deschooling Society* (New York: Harper Colophon, 1970) and John Holt, *How Children Fail* (New York: Pitman, 1964). Other educational reformers cited include Paulo Freire, *The Pedagogy of the Oppressed*, trans. M. B. Ramos (New York: Herder & Herder, 1970); Alan Graubard, *The Open Classroom: Radical Reform and Free School Movement* (New York: Pantheon, 1970); and Jonathan Kozol, *Free Schools* (Boston: Houghton-Mifflin, 1972).

In a review essay by J. Gary Knowles, Stacey E. Marlow, and James A. Muchmore, "From Pedagogy to Ideology: Origins and Phases of Home Education in the United States, 1970-1990," *American Journal of Education*, 100 (February 1992), pp. 195-235, the authors acknowledge that "when contemporary home schools are examined, it becomes clear that they are *not* closely tied to the liberal roots of home education," yet they still insist that, "the modern emergence of home education has its roots in the philosophies of the educators who wrote on the issues of reform during the late 1960s and early to mid-1970s" (p. 227). See also Jane A. Van Gallen, "Ideology, Curriculum, and Pedagogy in Home Education," *Education and Urban Society*, 21 (1988), pp. 52-68.

26. All quotes come from interviews with the five families. Each family is a member of CHEA, the Christian Home Education Association. They live throughout the Austin area, one residing in the countryside. Four of the five own their own homes. The fathers are white-collar workers (optician, family therapist, businessman, salesman, hospital administrator). One family has two daughters (ages 7 and 9); two families have three children (one one-year-old daughter, sons 10 and 7; two daughters 10 and 7 and a son 4); and two families have four children (three daughters, ages 9, 11, 13 and a son 4; four daughters, ages 21, 18, 14 and 12). Two families belong to a Reformed Presbyterian church, one to an independent Charismatic congregation, and one to a Church of Christ.

27. Ammerman, *Bible Believers*, pp. 25-31.

28. Rose, *Out of the Hands of Satan*, p. 34.

29. Wagner, *God's Schools*, p. 19.

30. Gregg Harris, *The Christian Home School* (Brentwood, Tenn.: Wolgemuth & Hyatt, 1988), p. 39.

31. Rose, *Out of the Hands of Satan*, p. 33; and Peshkin, *God's Choice*, p. 148.

32. Harris, *Christian Home School*, p. 42.

33. Harris, *Christian Home School*, p. 7.

34. The clearest description of spiritual warfare is Eph. 6:10-18, where the reader is commanded to "put on the whole armor of God" so as to contend "against the world rulers of this present darkness, against the spiritual hosts of wickedness in heavenly places." The image of the Christian as a soldier battling in the struggle between good and evil has a rich history dating from the early Christian depictions of Christ as a

Roman centurion through the familiar hymn, "Onward, Christian Soldiers" (text 1865; music 1871). Contemporary Christians can read Frank E. Peretti's novel *This Present Darkness* (Winchester, Ill.: Crossway Books, 1989) about a family battling both evil people and demons, and Praise Unlimited manufactures plastic suits of toy armor so children can play as soldiers for Christ. Other biblical passages that reflect this battle rhetoric include: Ex. 15:3; 2 Sam. 22:32–51; Matt. 10:34; 2 Cor. 10:3–6; 1 Tim. 1:18; 2 Tim. 2:3–4; 1 Tim. 6:12; 2 Tim. 4:7; Rev. 12:17; Rev. 18:21; Rev. 19:14–16. See also Ammerman, *Bible Believers*, pp. 99–101.

35. Harris, *Christian Home School*, pp. 151; 13.

36. Christian advice books exist on every possible subject from masculinity to divorce to incest. A selection of those on family life include: Ray E. Ballmann, *How Your Family Can Flourish: A Guide to Christian Living in a Post-Christian Culture* (Wheaton, Ill.: Crossway Books, 1991); John MacArthur Jr., *The Family* (Chicago: Moody Press, 1982); Steve Farrar, *Family Survival in the American Jungle* (Portland, Ore.: Multnomah, 1991); Mike Yorkey, *Growing A Healthy Home* (Brentwood, Tenn.: Wolgemuth & Hyatt, 1990); Mary Pride, *All the Way Home: Power for Your Family to Be Its Best* (Westchester, Ill.: Crossway Books, 1989).

37. Harris, *Christian Home School*, p. 30.

38. Ibid., p. 49.

39. The issue of what home-school children do after high school is becoming increasingly important as the movement ages. See the dissertation by Lesley Taylor, "At Home in School: A Qualitative Inquiry into Three Christian Home Schools," Stanford University, 1993.

40. Ibid., p. 74.

41. Henry W. Cleveland and Samuel Backus, *Village and Farm Cottages* (New York: Appleton, 1956), p. 3; Harris, *The Christian Home School*, p. 13.

42. McDannell, *Christian Home*, p. 45.

43. That public schools teach children more than objective facts is discussed in David Nasaw, *Schooled to Order: A Social History of Public Schooling the United States* (New York: Oxford University Press, 1979); Charles Leslie Glenn Jr., *The Myth of the Common School* (Amherst: University of Massachusetts Press); David B. Tyack, *Managers of Virtue : Public School Leadership in America, 1820–1980* (New York: Basic Books, 1982); and Richard Sennett, *Hidden Injuries of Class* (New York: Knopf, 1972).

44. *Christian Home School*, p. 8.

45. Home schoolers consistently cite Deut. 6:7 and a parallel text 11:18–21. The text, however, appears to refer to teaching to children the Great Commandment: "to love the Lord your God with all your heart, and with all your soul, and with all your might." It does not mention teaching skills or even literacy. Other texts which are cited as proof texts, such as 2 Cor. 10:5 refer to "knowledge of God," not knowledge of the natural or human order. In 2 Tim. 3:14–16 Paul assumes that Timothy has learned the Scriptures from early childhood, but does not mention if he learned them at home or someplace else. The gospels are notably silent on children.

46. Rebecca Avery, *The Weaver Curriculum: Grade Three* (Riverside, Ca.: Weaver Curriculum, 1992).

47. "Wisdom Booklet," Advanced Training Institute of America (Oak Park, Ill.: Institute in Basic Youth Conflicts, 1987).

48. *Old World History and Geography*, teacher's edition (Pensacola, Fl.: A Beka Books, 1992), p. 38 and 221.

49. Beecher and Beecher Stowe, *American Woman's Home*, p. 457.

50. Arguing over who teaches/controls children has a long history. In the fourth century B.C.E., Plato argued that the ideal state should begin to be built by sending all of the parents out of town and raising those children who were under ten years of age (*Republic*, Book VII, end). For an excellent discussion of the fight over the control of the modern family, see Jacques Donzelot, *The Policing of Families* (New York: Random House, 1979).

51. For a brief discussion of the conflicts between domestic religion and public religion, see McDannell, *Christian Home*, pp. 3-4; and Colleen McDannell and Bernhard Lang, *Heaven: A History* (New Haven Yale University Press, 1988), pp. 2-7.

52. Books that discuss personality types are popular among Christians. See Tim La Haye, *Understanding the Male Temperament* (Old Tappan, N.J.: Fleming H. Revell, 1977). An example of how this is used in home schooling is found in Cathy Duffy, "Choose Curriculum to Fit Learning Styles," *The Teaching Home* (1987), pp. 12-15.

53. Beecher and Beecher Stowe, *American Woman's Home*, p. 24.

54. Ibid., p. 453.

55. Ibid., p. 458.

56. Pierre Bourdieu, *Outline of a Theory of Practice*, trans. Richard Nice (Cambridge: Cambridge University Press, 1977), pp. 89, 90. Other scholars who emphasize the home as a defining category are Juan E. Campo, "Shrines and Talisman: Domestic Islam in the Pilgrimage Paintings of Egypt," *Journal of the American Academy of Religion*, 55 (1987), pp. 285-305 and *The Other Sides of Paradise: Explorations into the Religious Meanings of Domestic Space in Islam* (Columbia: University of South Carolina Press, 1991); Joel Schwartz, "Home as Haven, Cloister, and Winnebago," *American Quarterly*, 39 (1987), pp. 467-73; David E. Sopher, "The Landscape of Home: Myth, Experience, Social Meaning" in D. W. Meinig, ed., *The Interpretation of Ordinary Landscapes: Geographical Essays* (Oxford: Oxford University Press, 1979), pp. 129-49.

57. Gaston Bachelard, "House and Universe," *The Poetics of Space* (Boston: Beacon Press, 1969), pp. 38-73; Gerardus van der Leeuw, *Religion in Essence and Manifestation*, trans. J. E. Turner (Princeton: Princeton University Press, 1986), pp. 395-99.

58. Van der Leeuw, ibid., p. 395.

59. Van der Leeuw, ibid., p. 396.

6

LOCATING HOLOCAUST MEMORY
The United States Holocaust Memorial Museum
Edward T. Linenthal

THE OFFICIAL GROUNDBREAKING for the United States Holocaust Memorial Museum in Washington, D.C., located adjacent to the Washington Mall and within the "monumental core" of the nation, took place on October 16, 1985 at ten o'clock in the morning. The nation's most sacred soil—home of the monumental expressions of central national narratives—would now be ceremonially comingled with "holy soils" from European concentration and death camps and venerated cemeteries: Auschwitz, Bergen-Belsen, Dachau, Theresienstadt, Treblinka, and the Warsaw Jewish Cemetery. Elie Wiesel, death-camp survivor, American icon, and chairman of the United States Holocaust Memorial Council, remarked that through the act of groundbreaking "we begin to lend a physical dimension to our relentless quest for remembrance." Mark Talisman, the vice chairman of the Council, called the audience's attention to the significance of the location and the ceremony. "We stand not 1500 yards away from the monument to our first President. We are at the very heart and soul of our beloved country. We gather in this hallowed place to break this earth together, to consecrate this place as a memorial to the victims of the Holocaust."[1] WHAT % ARTICLE ...

This chapter tells the story of how those responsible for locating Holocaust memory in American sacred soil struggled with a variety of questions deemed crucial to the appropriate spatial context for official Holocaust memory. In what city should the memorial be? And, even after the choice of the nation's capital, at what site within the city should it be located? Other issues, some of them having to do with the demands of Washington regulatory agencies—acting as "guardians" of the Mall—were hotly contested. How large should a museum/memorial building be in order to house adequately Holocaust memory? What kind of architecture could do justice to an event that resists profound aesthetic expression? What should be the appropriate "demeanor" of a building that is to be a permanent part of the nation's memorial showcase, albeit one that tells an indigestible story of horror? And once built, how should the museum's interior exhibit space appropriately frame the narrative told in the permanent exhibition? Throughout the work of locating Holocaust memory "on" the Mall, constructing Holocaust memory in a building, and interpreting Holocaust memory in a museum exhibition, there were two crucial tensions: first, the manner in which the museum was to participate in both the prestige of American memorial space and the visceral reality of European Holocaust sites; and secondly the fact that every place of memory is also a place of forgetting.

As we will see, the decision to build the museum adjacent to the Washington Mall was a controversial one. For some, it properly indicated the significance of remembering the Holocaust. For others, it was memory "out of place." And, for museum architect James Ingo Freed, American space, while proper space in which to locate a building, was not the appropriate aesthetic context within which to tell the story. His building was designed to remove visitors from Washington through a whole range of architectural strategies. Further yet, for those who designed the permanent exhibition, Freed's strategies of removal were not sufficient. Not only would architecture have to create foreign space, so too would the interior design of the permanent exhibition have to embody the "feel" of the Holocaust. Part of creating this atmosphere was a decision to bring to the museum the material reality of the Holocaust, to remove visitors even more from American space and create vestiges of the world of the Holocaust in the suspended space of the museum.

Ironically, for many survivors and others who had provided much of the political and financial impetus for the museum, the realization that their wish was soon to be a reality, that the Holocaust would be remembered from such significant space, brought concomitant fears. Who, exactly, would be remembered? Would the pluralistic imperative of a national museum contribute, unwittingly, to the diminution of what was to them, a unique Jewish tragedy? Once the story of the Holocaust was no longer owned and operated by one ethnic community, the appropriate status of that community—as having the right to tell the story in traditional ways, and the prestige of being "first" among victims—was endangered, as others sought to gain public status through claims as Holocaust victims. Such claims threatened to displace Jews and threatened the understanding of the

① SPACE functioning to remove visitors from the actual PLACE

- Movies   museums
- music
- art

Holocaust as "unique." Such arguments took place with regard to the museum's space, as arguments about who "owned" the Hall of Remembrance—the hexagonal memorial space facing the Mall—revealed how difficult it was to appropriately locate victims through construction of an agreed upon hierarchy of victims.

Centering Holocaust Memory in American Culture

[Before the museum could be built, the Holocaust itself had to assume the status of an important memory in American culture] The Holocaust had to move from periphery to center. Impetus for the museum appeared as part of a massive revival of interest in the Holocaust in American culture in the late 1970s, strikingly different from the neglect of the subject in immediate postwar years. "In the beginning," wrote historian Raul Hilberg, "there was no Holocaust. When it took place in the middle of the twentieth century, its nature was not fully grasped."[2] What came to be known as "The Holocaust" was often indistinguishable in the immediate postwar years from the millions of non-combatant casualties due to terror bombing of civilian populations, epidemic illness, or starvation. It was considered by most as simply part of the horror of war[And, if the Holocaust "lived" at all in American culture, it did so in survivor memories, the displaced memories of those who had been characterized as "displaced persons" in American culture.]

The Holocaust emerged gradually as a significant cultural memory in the 1960s with the widely publicized trial of Adolf Eichmann in Israel beginning in April 1961. In 1967, the Six-Day War seemingly threatened Israel with annihilation, the announced goal of Egyptian President Gamal Abdul Nasser. Another Holocaust seemed in the making, and the Holocaust became the backdrop against which many American Jews perceived this crisis.

The year 1978 was important in the development of Holocaust consciousness. The highly publicized threat by American Nazis to march through Skokie, Illinois, home to many Holocaust survivors, brought the principle of free speech into conflict with survivor sensibilities. The Office of Special Investigation was created to bring to trial Nazi war criminals living in the United States. NBC's nine-and-one-half-hour miniseries "The Holocaust," aired April 16–19, 1978, with an estimated audience of one hundred twenty million. And it was in 1978 that President Jimmy Carter announced his intention to create the President's Commission on

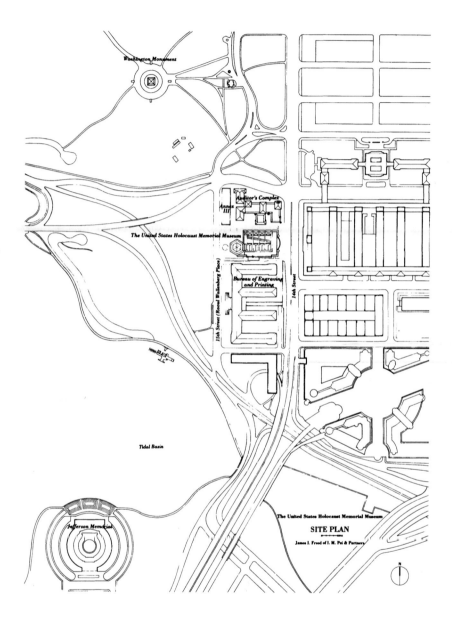

Within the image (labels):

Washington Monument

Auditor's Complex

Annex III

The United States Holocaust Memorial Museum

15th Street (Raoul Wallenberg Place)

14th Street

Bureau of Engraving and Printing

Tidal Basin

Jefferson Memorial

The United States Holocaust Memorial Museum

SITE PLAN

James I. Freed of I. M. Pei & Partners

N

6.1. The location of the United States Holocaust Memorial Museum, immediately adjacent to the Washington Mall. (© Pei Cobb Freed & Partners *Architects*. Used by permission.)

the Holocaust, in the White House Rose Garden on May 1, 1978, during a reception in honor of Israel's thirtieth anniversary. Formally established by Executive Order 12093 on November 1, 1978, and made up of twenty-four members and a twenty-seven person advisory group, the Commission was asked to submit a report to the President and the Secretary of the Interior within six months containing "recommendations with respect to the establishment and maintenance of an appropriate memorial to those who perished in the Holocaust."[3]

The formation of the Commission signaled that the Holocaust had moved not only from the periphery to the center of American Jewish consciousness, but to the center of national consciousness, as well. It was a story too important to be bounded by ethnic memory. It was, by virtue of its awesome impact, worthy of inclusion in the official canon that shaped Americans' sense of themselves.

The Site of Holocaust Memory

At their first meeting on February 15, 1979, members of the President's Commission argued whether New York or Washington, D.C., was the most appropriate location for official Holocaust memory. Historian Lucy Dawidowicz argued in favor of New York City. It was, she said the "center of the Jewish population in the United States and the cultural crossroads of the modern world. A site facing or near the United Nations would be particularly suitable." At a meeting of the subcommittee on museum and monument on March 22, 1979, Benjamin Meed, Warsaw ghetto survivor and organizer of the annual New York City Holocaust commemoration, and Yaffa Eliach, founder of Brooklyn College's Center for Holocaust Studies, and herself a survivor of the extermination of the Lithuanian village of Ejszyszki, also argued for New York. It was, Eliach said, "a harbor of safety and a cradle of liberty to all coming to America. It was the place where most of the survivors came when they left the Displaced Persons camps."[4]

Many others, like Hyman Bookbinder, Washington representative for the American Jewish Committee, believed that since this was to be a "national" memorial, Washington, D.C. was the essential location. Irving Bernstein, executive vice chairman of the United Jewish Appeal, agreed that "a Washington site would give this institution a unique character and a special opportunity to contribute to national life. It would make clear that the commemoration of the Holocaust is a concern of the entire American population." Members of the Commission were persuaded that Holocaust memory would be most effective if located in the nation's capital. Consequently, at their June 7, 1979 meeting, the Commission accepted the subcommittee's recommendation that a museum be built in Washington. It would have to be, deputy director Michael Berenbaum said, "of symbolic and artistic beauty, visually and emotionally moving in accordance with the solemn character of the Holocaust."[5]   —7 AESTHETICS

The choice of the nation's capital would prove fortuitous. A museum built in New York, even if national in intent, would clearly be perceived as a Jewish museum built in the heart of the Jewish community in America. Memory of the Holocaust would remain the province of American Jews. A national museum in Washington, on the other hand, made a more expansive—and controversial—claim on memory. Representatives of those lumped together as "other victim groups"—Poles, Gypsies, Ukrainians, homosexuals, for example—who may not have sought inclusion in a Jewish museum in New York felt empowered to claim what they saw as their rightful place in an institution housing national memory to the Holocaust in the capital city. —7 Not, blc I'm America, is the holocaust now my story, too?

This decision made the work of the United States Holocaust Memorial Council—created in 1980 to implement the recommendations of the Commission—infinitely more difficult. It had to contend not only with the imperatives of American pluralism—that, in this case, many are entitled to make their case for inclusion in Holocaust memory—but it had to contend as well with the choice of and justification for a particular site. Furthermore, it had to decide upon an architectural form of Holocaust memory aesthetically and politically acceptable in Washington, architecture that would contain and express the enormity of the event to the satisfaction of survivors, many of whom felt that locating the museum in Washington must not dilute the centrality of the Jewish core of the Holocaust. Their custodianship of Holocaust memory had developed in the intimacy of their postwar memorial services, and in the recognition that they had undergone experiences unfathomable to the outside world. Their experiences and their guardianship of the story gave them, many survivors believed, the right to determine the essence and the boundaries of the narrative to be developed in the museum. As one Commission member stated, "Jewish people are entitled to such a reminder of their tragedy and sorrow . . . and it should be in our nation's capital."[6]

Following the formation of the Council a subcommittee on site selection considered twelve locations in Washington, eventually choosing a site just adjacent to the Washington Mail, next to the Bureau of Printing and

Key ①

① SPACE, and the pre-conceived cultural context & social context behind it, as the part creator / gatekeeper of NARRATIVE & MEMORY FORMATION.

Engraving, between Fourteenth and Fifteenth Streets. The extant buildings were called the Auditor's Complex, consisting of a main Auditor's Building and three annexes. They had been designed around the turn of the century for the Bureau of Agriculture. By 1980 the annexes were unused and in poor repair. The low, crumbling, red brick buildings, however, reminded some Council members—survivors and nonsurvivors alike—of barracks at Auschwitz, and therefore seemed an appropriate house of Holocaust memory. What was most attractive, of course, was the site's location. Here, not only would there be a national museum to the Holocaust in the nation's capital, but, by virtue of its location just off the Mall, the museum would gain the prestige of a *central* national memory. Council member Bookbinder, echoing general Council sentiment, said, "If we had been told 'select a place' . . . I think we would have chosen that very spot. It is part of what all the tourists go to. . . . Secondly . . . if I were going to design . . . I would want it to look exactly like that. . . . There's a feeling about that structure that seems to me to be absolutely ideal for what it's going to be." Elie Wiesel remarked, "I feel it's probably the best that we could get. Really, the best. The possibilities . . . are extraordinary."[7]

The General Services Administration—the government's "real estate agent"—transferred annexes 1 and 2 to the Council on August 12, 1981. Monroe Freedman, the Council's executive director commented, "It's the kind of providential thing that I really still have difficulty believing has happened. One can go to Washington literally with hundreds of millions of dollars . . . and not be able to purchase that building. And there is nothing like it. On the tourist route, next to the Bureau of Printing and Engraving, perhaps the most popular tourist attraction in Washington, right near the Mall, right near the Washington Monument, with space, enormous amounts of usable space." The exact transfer involved .80 acres of land, and annexes 1 and 2.

For survivors, a museum within the monumental core was especially important. They worried about the preservation of Holocaust memory after their passing, particularly given the threat they perceived from Holocaust deniers. Victimized by the Holocaust, survivors believed they faced a second victimization: the murder of their memories. A museum at the heart of American commemorative space was viewed as an eternal insurance policy. It was, in the words of Council Executive Director Seymour Siegel, "at the most prestigious spot for a museum in the Western world, perhaps in the whole world . . . [That location] puts on a scientific and unshakable basis the truth of our story and the accuracy of the events."[8]

② SPACE as creator of TRUTH or POWER (SACRALITY as NARRATIVE AFFIRMATION)

When the official announcement was finally made in 1983 that the government had donated the land to the Council, controversy arose among Jews and non-Jews alike regarding the appropriateness of a Holocaust museum located "on the Mall." There was fear that resentment about Jews "pushing their way onto the Mall" would spark a new wave of antisemitism. Others believed that if the museum was to be in the nation's capital, it had to speak more universally about genocide. "Where are the Native Americans and the black slaves represented?" "First we need a monument to blacks and Indians." Some argued that the museum would be contaminated by the nation's hypocrisy during the Holocaust. One respondent to the museum's direct-mail fund-raising efforts said angrily, "imagine a Holocaust museum in the town whose political sages refused to lift a finger to halt the Holocaust or open our shores to the few survivors! How offensive to any informed individual!" Likewise, Benjamin Hirsch, Holocaust survivor and Atlanta architect, worried that the museum would "subvert history" by honoring President Franklin D. Roosevelt—guilty, said Hirsch, of inaction with regard to Europe's Jews—since other presidents were traditionally glorified on the Mall. Others argued, conversely, that any memorial on this space should celebrate American heroism and sacrifice during the war. A letter to the *Washington Post* in 1987 called for Holocaust victims to "build a memorial to the American dead who gave their lives to free them."[9] The argument heard most often declared the museum misplaced because the Holocaust was not an American event. A 1983 letter to President Ronald Reagan said that the celebratory nature of the institutions on the Mall should not be "confronted by a morbid reminder of genocidal crime committed by an alien tyranny on another continent." And, as planning for the museum progressed in 1987, a World War II combat veteran argued that "it is the wrong place, wrong country, wrong time." Arguing that it was the right museum in the wrong place, a letter in *Time* declared the building "highly appropriate in Jerusalem, where it would be more relevant." A member of a Philadelphia focus group organized by Peter D. Hart's Research Associates polling firm—hired by the Council to analyze public reaction to the museum and its permanent exhibition in 1992—said that "it should be in Germany or Austria, where these things happened. That doesn't belong there" [in Washington, D.C.]. A response in *Jewish Week* in August 1987 to Hebrew University professor Shlomo Avineri's claim that the museum was misplaced suggested a novel solution. It called for a portable "Exodus Museum," a ship that would sail "from port to port, hosting seminars, teaching Jewish history."[10]

Others understood the museum's location as an example of the politicization of the Holocaust. The Kennedy School's Howard Husock perceived it as a regrettable example of the "use of ethnic power politics in the American political system." He was convinced that it would be seen as a Jewish museum intruding into American sacred space, functioning as a "surefire way to spotlight day in and day out the historic justification of a Jewish state before Congress and the White House." Another member of Hart's focus group expressed a related oft-heard fear, that the museum would be "pro-Israel . . . as far as the discussions going on in the Middle East right now."[11]

These arguments were countered by those who believed that the significance of the Holocaust—often characterized as "unique," a "watershed" event, a "turning point" in history—made it a crucially important story to tell within the memorial core. The maintenance of Holocaust memory was, in this view, a responsibility of the United States, and a centrally located, official Holocaust memory would function as both warning and lesson. →7 SPACE as EDUCATOR (similar to McDonnell)

Political columnist George Will, for example, said that the Mall told a variety of stories, not all of them pleasant, and, in any case, America had a special responsibility for Holocaust memory. "No other nation has broader, graver responsibilities in the world . . . no other nation more needs citizens trained to look life in the face." For Will, writing in 1983, the peak year in the revival of the "second cold war," and an intense period of nuclear anxiety, the lessons of the Holocaust were cold war lessons. The museum would teach Americans that the world was dangerous, "a mind-opening reminder of the furies beyond our shores . . . an antidote to our innocence."[12]

The museum was seen as a potential storehouse for a whole variety of other lessons. It would remind Americans of the dangers of being bystanders, it would teach Americans where Christian antisemitism could lead, and it would impress upon Americans the fragile relationship between technology and humanistic values. Some supporters insisted that the museum would provide a crucial lesson in individual responsibility. Hillel Levine, professor of sociology at Boston University, and former deputy director of the Council, hoped that Washington bureaucrats, some of whom would see the building every day, would be moved to "reflect on the way bureaucracy fragments responsibility and perspective." He hoped that they would learn from the museum that Germans who ran the railroads taking millions to their deaths "were not just random workers throwing a switch, but part of a murderous bureaucracy, an organized evil."[13]

Several focus group members spoke of a Mall location impressing upon visitors the need to take on personal responsibility for issues usually deemed affairs of state. "It's time we say 'no' to genocide as a country, as a nation. . . . And I'm saying 'Why not start with something that we all know took place'? I don't see it ever really stopping just with the Holocaust of the Jewish people. What about the Cambodian genocide; what about other types of genocide. . . . To me, we have not learned our lesson." Several others in the focus groups also spoke of the need to connect lessons learned from the Holocaust museum to contemporary situations, from the plight of the homeless to the boat people.[14]

The Council also claimed that the Mall was an appropriate place to tell cautionary tales. A space for lessons was also a space for warning about the consequences of not appreciating the lessons. In 1983, *Time's* Lance Morrow viewed such a museum as the "moral equivalent of impaling heads on spikes by the roadside; it rules the attention of the passers-by and leaves them with a memorable warning." The late civil rights activist Bayard Rustin, a former member of both the Commission and Council, believed that from the "center of our democracy," the museum would stand as a "warning against hatred and dehumanization whoever is the victim." And, a letter accompanying Rustin's editorial to the *New York Times* argued that "genocide is a crooked finger . . . pointed at any race or creed." The museum, the writer declared, should remind visitors that "no one is immune from inhumanity."[15]

Nowhere has the physical *site* of an American Holocaust monument been as controversial as that of this museum. Those who argued against it often assumed that the Mall was a place of celebration, that the museum would contaminate the cheerful patriotism of visitors, or they assumed that the Mall was an unchanging repository of primal national stories, symbolizing the seemingly unchanging nature of American identity.[16]

Curiously, however, few supporters of the museum pointed out that Mall was an ever-changing, dynamic site. From the original vision of Major Pierre Charles L'Enfant, hired by George Washington to design the capital city in 1790, to the Mall's current status as a repository of American identity, it has undergone radical change. L'Enfant, who came to America in 1777 as a military engineer, had envisioned an impressive capital city, including a "Grand Avenue, 400 feet in breadth," lined with rows of trees, much like the Champs Elysees in Paris. While some of L'Enfant's plan for Washington was realized—the geographical expression of the separation of governmental powers represented by the President's House and the Capitol, the street grid and diagonal boulevards that created both private neigh-borhoods and public spaces—his plan for the Mall would not be recalled until the beginning of the twentieth century.[17]

Before the Civil War, the Mall was either swamp or commercial space. Pamela Scott noted that "ad hoc private use is recorded as early as 1804 and 1805 when fairs were held near Center Market. Even as late as 1850 the Mall was used for private cultivation of 'grain or vegetables' and for storage of 'lumber or firewood and occasionally for rubbish of an offen-sive and unsightly kind.'" During the Civil War volunteers drilled and bivouacked on the Mall, and the grounds of what would become the site of the Washington Monument were used as a cattleyard. At the end of the war, this area became known as "murderer's row . . . the hangout of escap-ees, deserters, and other flotsam of the war."[18]

The Mall had also been the site of slave pens, and not until slave trading in Washington was outlawed in 1850 were they removed. Jesse Torrey's *Portraiture of Domestic Slavery in the United States* (1815) described a view from the Capitol of "men, women, and children, resembling that of a funeral . . . bound together in pairs, some with ropes, and some with iron chains."[19]

In 1851 President Millard Fillmore hired New York landscape architect Andrew Jackson Downing to develop a plan for a unified Mall area. He proposed transforming the Mall into a huge public garden "to be traversed in different directions by graveled walks and carriage drives and planted with specimens properly labelled, of all the varieties of trees and shrubs which flourish in this climate." Downing believed that if his plan were carried out, the Mall would "undoubtedly become a Public School of In-struction." Downing's plan did not survive his death in 1852, and the Mall was fragmented into seven gardens, administered by different government bureaus.[20]

The Smithsonian castle—whose cornerstone was laid in 1849—was completed in 1855, and the cornerstone of the Washington Monument was laid in 1848. Both projects altered the character of the Mall, although it would be some time before the Washington Monument was completed. Lack of funds delayed construction, and in 1855 the Know-Nothing party, angry that Pope Pius IX had contributed a monument stone, vandalized the construction site and threw the stone into the Potomac. By the begin-ning of the Civil War in 1860 the monumental stump, had risen only 150 feet. The project would not be completed until 1876, the nation's centen-nial year.

Each of these events is significant for our story. The location of the Smithsonian Institution helped transform the Mall from a pastoral environment into a place where cultural institutions could help shape an enlightened citizenry. This pedagogical ideal would be associated with the eventual proliferation of museums on the Mall and provided one of the most popular arguments for the value of a Holocaust museum. The Washington Monument served as the center point for future monumental development of the Mall, and the lengthy controversy that attended its conception and construction foreshadowed future memorial controversies.

The present character of the Mall as a "shrine-like corridor of monumental dimensions" is credited to the McMillan Plan of 1901 and 1902. In the early years of the century, the Mall was still a series of parks and gardens, and the Baltimore and Potomac Railroad's depot had been located on the Mall since 1872. Beginning in 1898, President McKinley considered various memorial proposals as part of the centennial celebration of the move of the nation's capital from Philadelphia to Washington in 1800. Several of these proposals—the construction of a memorial hall and a memorial bridge across the Potomac—affected the city's landscape. Senator James McMillan (R-MI), chair of a joint congressional committee to evaluate these proposals, sponsored a resolution calling for the appointment of a park commission to report to the Senate on the state of the city's park system.[21]

Their report dealt not only with parks, but with a unified vision of the Mall. Even though the Commission was dismissed in 1902, its influence remained. Congress passed legislation to remove the railroad depot and relocate the new Union Station off the Mall. Despite bitter objections, the Potomac site of the Lincoln Memorial was approved and construction completed in 1922. This location continued the Mall axis to the Potomac and the Commission's report also extended the White House axis to what would be the site of the Jefferson Memorial. The influence of the Commission was felt in architecture as well. "No public building was erected in the capital city that did not conform to the ideals of the plan, and . . . to specific sites and locations. A long generation of artistic dominance extended to the building of the Jefferson Memorial and the National Gallery of Art in the mid-thirties."[22]

Even though the ceremonial core of Washington seems to exude a sense of permanence, the Mall's government buildings, national monuments and memorials, and stately museums that inhabit and surround it have been produced in space that has been reshaped to fit various intellectual impulses: the neoclassical ideal of L'Enfant, the pastoral ideal of Andrew Jackson Downing, and the Progressive vision of the McMillan Commission. There are layers of meaning at the ceremonial core, each altering the topography of this space. The widespread contemporary desire to be memorialized on the Mall bears witness to its role as a significant ceremonial center, a place where various groups of Americans now seek to tell particular stories laden, they believe, with universal import.

As with the Washington Monument, other memorial proposals to follow—particularly the Lincoln Memorial, the Jefferson Memorial, and the Vietnam Veterans Memorial—became the subject of bitter debate over location, style, and meaning. Controversy over the appropriate site and function of the Holocaust museum was not unique. The buildings on the Mall were, as Charles Griswold remarked, a "species of recollective architecture," and the nature and content of national memorial recollection had always been subject to debate, given the malleability of the Mall.[23]

Building Holocaust Memory & NARRATIVE

Just as earlier advocates of monuments and memorials on the Mall struggled with appropriate forms of memory, so too did the Council. In 1983 and 1984, while technical studies of the annex buildings were going on, the clock was ticking on what is popularly known as the "sunset clause" of the Council's enabling legislation (P. L. 96–388, October 7, 1980). The Council had until October 7, 1985, to satisfy the Secretary of the Interior that it was making adequate progress in both raising the private funds necessary to build the museum and in the design of the building. However, beginning in 1982 and continuing for several years, there was concern that the annexes were too small to serve as a home for a permanent exhibition, a research center, an educational outreach center, and a memorial space. The Council faced a problem that historian and Council member Raul Hilberg expressed in 1981: "The size of the building must be large enough to permit us to do the things that we have talked about during the last few years. Our principal theme was that of a 'living' memorial. . . . Above all we must remember that the building will be our statement about the Holocaust. If it is too small, so is our memory."[24]

Hilberg expressed a common concern: any new building would be measured against American memory preserved on the mall housed in a monumental obelisk (Washington), temples (Lincoln and Jefferson), and the haunting space of the Vietnam Veterans Memorial. If the building containing this "new" central memory did not measure up, it would not only

Sam hit on this comment last week; but what about when space is anthropomorphized & places like Monticello (modest outside & expansive inside) are valued?

6.2.The Enav design. In December 1984, the Council received permission from the Advisory Council for Historic Preservation to tear down the two annex buildings and design a new building. One unsuccesful proposal was from an Israeli architect, Zalman Enav. Unlike James Ingo Freed's buiding, which sought to be a "good neighbor" to adjacent buildings, this exterior was black granite, designed to contrast with its surroundings. Visitors entered by descending into a "deportation court." (Used by permission of Zalman Enav.)

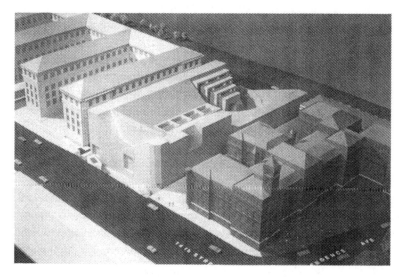

6.3. The Finegold design. Maurice Finegold's graceful and evocative building proposal was designed to draw visitors into a vortex in which the Hall of Remembrance was shaped like a large oval. The exterior of the building was to be dark-red and gray stone. (Used by permission of Maurice N. Finegold.)

reduce the impact of the memory, it would be an act of defilement, an act of architectural trivialization of the Holocaust.

The danger of insufficiently housed Holocaust memory loomed over attempts to fit memorial space, a library and archive, administrative offices and the permanent exhibition into the approximately 50,000 square feet of the two annexes. The job of trying to fit Council aspirations into this space fell on Anna Cohn, the first museum professional hired by the Council, and the architectural firm Notter, Finegold, and Alexander, chosen by the Council as project architects because the firm had already been doing restorative work on the Auditor's Building for the Bureau of Agriculture. Cohn had been Director of the B'nai B'rith's Klutznick Museum in Washington, D.C., for seven years, until she left in 1982 to become Project Director of the Smithsonian Institution's "Precious Legacy" exhibit, which brought to the United States the rich collection of Judaica housed in the State Jewish Museum in Prague. Cohn gradually became involved in the Holocaust museum's planning, first as consultant while still at the Klutznick, and eventually as the Council's director of museum planning until her return to the Smithsonian in 1985.[25]

None of the Council members had any idea of what it took to build a museum, she recalled, and they talked in grandiose terms of how to concretize a story of such epic proportions appropriately. "They had an endless list of needs, which required an enormous amount of space," said Cohn. "Space for records, artifacts, a commemorative space, exhibition space to tell the story, and space for a learning center. Their frustration at not being able to do all of this in the annexes was the first time that their aspirations clashed with the reality of the space available."[26]

After energetic attempts to squeeze Council plans into the limited space of the annexes were unsuccessful, it was widely recognized that the annexes were simply too small, and that the Council needed to enter into the laborious work of having the buildings "delisted," removed from the Historic Register—a necesssary step toward tearing them down—and construct a new building. Cohn recalled that Wiesel and some other survivors did not want to lose the annexes. "These buildings were already perceived by some as essential, as sacred, given their evocation of the feel of Auschwitz barracks." The museum, however, needed at least twice as much room, 100,000 square feet, and Cohn recommended that the Council demolish annex 1, retain annex 2 for offices, acquire annex 3, which had *not* been transferred, and build a "full-fledged museum building."[27]

By December 1984, the Council had received permission from the Ad-

6.4. Drawing of the original Kaufman design. (Used by
permission of Maurice N. Finegold.)

visory Council for Historic Preservation to tear down the two annex buildings. Micah Naftalin, the Council's deputy director, commented, "whatever symbolic significance was first seen in the buildings has always been
secondary to the site [near] the Mall and what we want to do. Now we have
an option of making an architectural statement about the Holocaust, starting from scratch." The way was now paved for deliberation on an architectural design appropriate for national memory of the Holocaust.[28]

On May 10, 1985, the Council made public its new building proposal in
which the Hall of Remembrance, the museum's memorial space, was suspended 20 feet above the main entrance to the building. Benjamin Forgey,
architectural critic for the *Washington Post*, was already worried about the
intrusion of the museum on the Mall. The building, he thought, must take
a "distinctly secondary position" to other memorials on the Mall. He
called for a smaller building, a change from dark red to a color matching
neighboring buildings, and an alignment on the site line of the Bureau of
Printing and Engraving.[29]

The plan also ran into trouble at a meeting of the Commission of Fine Arts, an advisory body directed to rule on the aesthetic appropriateness of public buildings in Washington. Several commissioners spoke of it as too "massive," noting that the Vietnam Veterans Memorial proved that "simplicity and delicacy are more provocative." Commissioner Edward Stone, worried about its appeal, remarked that the building exuded "foreboding, almost so severe that it may not welcome you with open arms." Also worried about the building's "feel" was commissioner John Chase, who argued that the function of memorial architecture was to provide an "emotional backdrop." This museum, he said, needed "some real feeling . . . some love and understanding."[30]

Some commissioners were clearly disturbed by the aesthetic discord that Holocaust memory would bring to the monumental core. There were calls to soften its impact—and therefore soften the impact of the Holocaust—through a building that would be welcoming and loving. In his letter to Secretary of the Interior Donald P. Hodel, Fine Arts Chairman J. Carter Brown wrote, "the Commission has serious concerns. . . . The sheer massiveness of the elements . . . tends toward an inhuman scale and an overstated emphasis on physical strength, both questionable characteristics in a memorial that is to reflect the human dimensions of the Holocaust." An angry letter to the Washington Post on June 6, 1985, put the matter more bluntly, "from the front, the building looks like a huge oven. From the side it looks like a huge coffin. Apart from that, it is pompous— the last sentiment I would associate with a proper memorial to Hitler's civilian victims." On June 28, 1985, Fine Arts unenthusiastically approved a revised concept, but there remained significant opposition to the design.[31]

There were also disagreements over symbolic ownership of interior space. In 1979, the President's Commission had already discussed the need for the memorial institution to have three parts: a museum, a monument, and an educational center. The "monument" was soon understood as a clearly distinct memorial space, the Hall of Remembrance, to be joined by a Hall of Witness to tell the story of the Holocaust, and the Hall of Learning, to confront the contemporary implications of the Holocaust through education. From the days of the President's Commission, however, there were arguments between Jews and non-Jews about who was to be memorialized in this space. There was a suggestion that those of different religions—perhaps belonging to different victim groups—should have separate chapels. "While the Holocaust should be depicted in a manner which certainly emphasizes its particular significance for our Jewish people, it should also reflect the destruction of . . . non-Jews. . . . There may be chapels where one can pray and seek solace and they would represent different faiths."[32] After the introduction of the new building plan in 1985, the arguments intensified. Was the Hall of Remembrance to be contemplative space for everyone, or just for Jews? Albert Abramson, a prominent Washington developer who had taken control of the building project, reminded people of the hexagonal shape of the Hall of Remembrance, and thought that the agreement had been that this was "essentially a memorial for the six million Jews." Fr. John Pawlikowski, professor of social ethics at the Catholic Theological Union in Chicago and longtime Council member, argued that the space was for all victims. "I think it's very crucial that the non-Jews who visit the museum feel impelled to go there and remember too, after having seen this and contemplate not only what happened, but perhaps even more importantly, why it happened and . . . since the overwhelming majority of them would be Christian—why the Christian churches had a pivotal role in the process." Holocaust survivor Sam Bloch countered, "We . . . have no intention of creating the Jewish ghetto. Don't look at this that way. But we are entitled in this museum to one area that should be specifically Jewish. We owe it to the memory of our six million people."

Council member and Holocaust survivor Kalman Sultanik, vice president of the World Jewish Congress, also made it clear that the HOR was only for commemoration of the six million, and that there were bitter feelings toward treating those who might have been killers—one could be a murderer of Jews and also fight against the Nazis—as victims worthy of commemorative respect. "Jews," he said, "they [were] killed not only by Germans." Ideas were floated for separate rooms, a room with a Jewish center, a commemorative hall of national patriots. Council member Franklin Littell asked Sultanik if Daniel Trocmé could be remembered in the Hall of Remembrance. Trocmé was the second cousin of Andre Trocmé, the heroic pastor of the French village of Le Chambon, which, under the leadership of Trocmé and his wife Magda, saved many Jews. Captured by the Gestapo in a raid, Daniel Trocmé was murdered in Majdanek's gas chamber on April 4, 1944. Israel declared him a Righteous Gentile in 1976 and planted a tree for him, as they had done for Pastor Trocmé, at Yad Vashem. Sultanik responded negatively to Littell's question. No, he said, he couldn't be honored in the Hall of Remembrance because "he didn't die as a Jew. . . . The six million Jews . . . died differently."

Mark Talisman, chairing the meeting, sensed how tenuous were the bonds of civility, and said, somewhat desperately, "no need to get angry over this because we are friends. We have come too far to have this dissolve." Attempting to resolve the situation, Abramson said, "I think we will specify that it is a non-religious memorial; that we want no religious symbol; it's a place for creative design." Of course the problem was not "religion," but rather issues of inclusion, exclusion, and the clash of victim group memories. Interestingly, for some survivors, claiming symbolic ownership of space near the Mall was not enough. Memory was first to be legitimated through emplacement of the museum in the monumental core; then boundaries had to be defined and hierarchies clearly constructed in its interior space. Here, the issue was not who got "wall space" in the permanent exhibition, but what space was appropriately "owned" by what group, who was at home in certain space, and who was a visitor in another person's memorial place.[33]

Questions of ownership of interior space were accompanied by bitter remarks about potential defilement of this space. The Council's 1982 fundraising plan recognized the need to honor donors in a "dignified way consistent with . . . practice in the great museums of the world." The plan envisioned naming for generous donors facilities within the museum. Such facilities might be "a theatre, kosher dining pavilion, library . . . education, research, and archival center." In addition, by the late 1980s, as fund-raising, called "A Campaign to Remember," moved into high gear, a glossy brochure described various space in the museum which would honor donors. Museum "Founders," givers of one million dollars or more, would have their names engraved on a "Founders Wall" near the elevators to the permanent exhibition. Near the Fifteenth Street entrance there would be a "Donors Lounge" with dark granite panels listing donors on four separate levels, in keeping with the amount of their gifts. There would also be two leather-bound books with names of those giving more modest donations, and a computerized "Scroll of Remembrance," listing all who gave smaller amounts. Joseph M. Brodecki, national director of the campaign and a son of a survivor, said that these names would all be placed in "non-sacred" places, and Michael Berenbaum, the museum's former project director, now director of the museum's research institute, said "no amount of money would get your name on the Hall of Remembrance."[34]

For some, however, the *whole* museum building was a sacred environment, and it was inconceivable that any part of a building devoted to Holocaust memory could be characterized as non-sacred. Naming facilities and

6.5. The Hall of Remembrance. (Photographs © Jeff Goldberg/Esto. All rights reserved.)

honoring donors in this manner was, in this view, a form of defilement. At a Fine Arts meeting in 1987, for example, Warner Hausenberg, a survivor of Westerbork and Bergen-Belsen, voiced his opposition to "the notion of permitting generous donors to . . . have parts of the monument named after themselves or their designees." This would he said, "desecrate the memory of millions of nameless persons who were victimized by the holocaust." Emma Andrea Kolodny, a founding member of a group of Jewish child survivors also objected, declaring before Fine Arts that "the idea is inappropriate, because a Holocaust Museum should commemorate the fate of the millions of nameless holocaust victims."[35]

By early 1986 Albert Abramson was getting the message from a number of people that the proposed building design was simply not appropriate. Deeply troubled was consulting architect Maurice Finegold, who characterized it as "neoclassicism worthy of Albert Speer." From several sources, including Finegold, both Elie Wiesel and Albert Abramson were told that a new architect would better design what the council wanted, a "world-class" museum building. The Council turned to architect James Ingo Freed, who was introduced at a Council meeting in December 1986.[36]

Freed was born in Essen, Germany in 1930, and emigrated to Chicago in 1939. He attended the Illinois Institute of Technology, whose school of architecture was directed by Ludwig Mies van der Rohe. After he graduated, he joined with Van der Rohe in New York in 1955, and I. M. Pei the following year. As Freed, who designed the Jacob Javits Convention Center in New York, the First Bank Place Tower in Minneapolis, and the Los Angeles Convention Center, struggled with early drawings for a building with little success, he began to recall his childhood years as a German Jew, particularly *Kristallnacht*, spent riding the streetcars with his father to avoid the violence. Freed escaped when he was nine with his sister and went first to France, then to Switzerland, and finally to the United States. His father and mother arrived in 1941 on one of the last refugee ships. In 1945, Freed's mother learned that most of her family—parents, brothers, sisters—had been murdered. His family stopped speaking German at home. "There was a conspiracy of silence about the Holocaust and about our being Jewish," Freed recalled. "Only since I've been working on this project have I really thought about my childhood. I did what a lot of people, a lot of my friends did—we just forgot about it, took it out of our minds."[37]

Freed immersed himself in Holocaust literature and documentary films, but every time he began a design, "I just froze." Freed soon realized that he had to go to Eastern Europe to visit the camps before he could successfully create a design. In October 1986, Freed, museum director Arthur Rosenblatt, and Finegold visited a variety of Holocaust sites in Europe. Finegold spoke of walking with Freed through Auschwitz. They had arrived on All Hallows' Eve, to a camp shimmering in candlelight and full of people. They walked through the Auschwitz museum's permanent exhibition—barracks housing displays made brutal by their sheer mass—of victims' hair, eyeglasses, shoes, and personal belongings—walked to the ruins of the crematoria in Birkenau, and went upstairs into a guard tower that overlooked the massive city of extermination that was Birkenau, where, Finegold said, "the enormity of the Holocaust became apparent." Freed recalled being grasped by the power of the place. "When I walked into this, some archaic memories must have been stirred, because emotionally this was a turning point for me. As we walked to the crematorium, there were scuffed-up little bones everywhere that had never turned to dust. I stood in a time warp, realizing that, except for good fortune, I would have been brought to such a place to die." He also remembered struggling to detach himself *from* the place. "I retreated into a more analytic [mode] where I look[ed] at things and I began to speculate how one would do a building that might . . . incorporate some of these techniques of construction." He started to sketch his building that evening.[38]

Freed decided that this could not be a neutral container, or a "black box," which only held a meaningful story inside, but "had nothing to tell you, neither outside nor inside." Such a building, would say, "I give up." It would indicate that there could be no adequate architectural statement about the Holocaust. Nor could he envision a high-tech building "that would not fit into Washington, would not fit into this subject matter." His building had to be "expressive of the event." It would have to communicate through its raw materials and its organization of space the feel of inexorable, forced movement: disruption, alienation, constriction, observation, selection.[39]

Freed paid attention to the tectonics of the camps, the way buildings were put together. His use of raw materials: steel, brick, glass, evoked what architecture critic Herbert Muschamp called the "hard industrial forms" of the Holocaust. The museum, he observed, "is a place quarried from the memory of other places." For example, at Auschwitz Freed studied the banded steel strapped around the crematoria because brick was exploding due to the intense heat of burning bodies. And, while this steel strapping is evident in the museum, Freed insisted that these symbols must be "sufficiently ambiguous and open-ended so that others can inhabit the space, can imbue the forms with their own memories." Discussing his formidable towers, read often as watch towers, Freed declared "I don't want to [tell] anybody these are towers and towers are bad. Towers may be good. . . . I wanted to do this . . . so that you are forced to acknowledge your separation from . . . Washington, from the world that you're in."[40] → Key!

Freed's building, from its outward appearance to its interior mood and insistence on certain ways visitors inhabit and move through space, is designed as a place of disorientation, a building that will force visitors to "leave" Washington, D.C. Ironically, then, while the location of the museum in the monumental core was deemed crucial for those who believed that Holocaust memory should be an integral part of the nation's memory, Freed's building has as its object the removal of visitors from Washington, so that they might be receptive to the story told in the permanent exhibition. The location of the museum asks visitors to "pay attention" to a crucial memory, and the attributes of the building inform you that you must, in order to pay attention, leave Washington. "I don't think you just

Key!

Wonderful point . . .

ever walk into the door and there is just the Holocaust," Freed remarked. "You can't do it. You have to prepare yourself psychologically for it." Evocative architecture and the manipulation of interior space served as Freed's agent of spiritual preparation for the journey into the Holocaust.[41]

This reorientation of priorities begins even before visitors enter the building. No longer is the Fifteenth Street side of the museum merely a city street. On October 8, 1986, it was renamed Raoul Wallenberg Place, and a plaque was dedicated to the Swedish diplomat credited with saving thousands of Hungarian Jews in 1944–45. (Wallenberg was captured by the Russians, and his fate has remained a mystery ever since.) Visitors encounter the redeeming memory of Raoul Wallenberg, and walk into Dwight D. Eisenhower Plaza on their way into a story in which acts of resistance and rescue are minor, albeit important, themes. And, even as Freed's building seeks to take visitors out of American space, they are reminded that as they make this symbolic journey their purpose is to remain firmly rooted in American ideals. On exterior walls of the Hall of Remembrance appear statements by Presidents Carter, Reagan, and Bush, about the importance of remembering the Holocaust, and in the hallway of the Fifteenth Street entrance is George Washington's famous statement that the government of the United States "gives to bigotry no sanction, to persecution no assistance," and a statement from the Declaration of Independence about the "unalienable rights" of humankind.[42]

Visitors enter the building on either Fourteenth Street or Raoul Wallenberg Place. The *Washington Post's* Benjamin Forgey and *New York Times's* Herbert Muschamp described their entrance at the museum's opening. Forgey wrote, "the entry sequences themselves are disorienting. Directions are not clearly labeled. The visitor must choose—go left, go right, go down, up, forward. Passing through the revolving door of the monumental west facade [Raoul Wallenberg Place] one confronts a slablike wall of black granite with a single, square window that opens onto a cavernous atrium, a space one can get to only by going down and then up again." And Muschamp, entering on Fourteenth Street, "visitors walk toward a monumental portico, a turret-shaped bulge of limestone that provides a frame for three tall rectangular arches. . . . The arches do not welcome. They gape. Four large square holes, set just above the arches, are fitted with stone grids that contradict the concept of opening. These openings are closings. They are windows that warn: Don't look. Once beyond the arches, we find that we're still outside the building. The limestone bulge is a screen, a mask of state, but no less intimidating for being merely a mask. . . . In-

6.6. The 14th Street entrance. (Photograph © Jou Min Lin.
Used by permission.)

stead of issuing an invitation to enter, the building exerts a repulsive force."[43]

Having made the initiatory journey, visitors enter the Hall of Witness, a space Muschamp called an "atrium from hell, a room purged of every pleasure that large indoor spaces often provide." Once again, Freed wanted his raw materials to create appropriate space in which to negotiate the museum: "brick walls, exposed beams, boarded windows and metal fences and gates will let visitors know they are in a different place—that the Holocaust is an event that should disturb and be felt as well as perceived." Visitors may have an uncanny sense of being watched, as people move on glass-bottom walkways on the floors above, hinting, architectural critic Joseph Giovannini remarked, "at inaccessible, anonymous presences in control." The walkways themselves call into question what Freed understood as a misplaced confidence in the beneficence of technology. "It failed us once," he said, "yet we have more faith in it than anything else."[44]

The Hall of Witness is not comfortable space to inhabit. From the skylight cutting across the space diagonally, held in a warped, twisted metal truss, to the cold and inhuman crossbracing under the skylight to the steel bands that seemingly hold the brick walls together, there is a sense of a space that is twisted and tortured in the effort to contain the story of the Holocaust, a space that screams as it seemingly strains to rip itself apart. It is also a space perceived from various vantage points as visitors work their way from the beginning of the permanent exhibition on the fourth floor, across bridges to tower exhibits, to the end of the exhibit on the second floor. "You circle down," Freed remarked, "gathering information as you come." And, from bridges on the fourth and third floors, visitors glimpse the Hall of Witness through glass panes etched with names of destroyed communities, and first names of murdered people.[45]

Before returning to the Mall, Freed wanted visitors to linger in the Hall of Remembrance, which contains an eternal flame under which is buried more soil from Holocaust sites and soil from American military cemeteries spread *over* victims' soil, "because their soil symbolizes the end of darkness and the beginning of new hope." This building, facing the Washington Mall, would prove to be the most contentious space in the museum, as Freed's design began its journey through Washington's bureaucracy.[46]

At a May 22, 1987 meeting of the Commission of Fine Arts, Freed noted that his building was designed to be a "good neighbor" to both the limestone building of the Bureau of Printing and Engraving and the brick Auditors Building, and he said that his Hall of Remembrance would have to be reasonably sized so as "not to compromise the other institutions or monuments." He also noted, however, that the Hall of Remembrance needed to protrude beyond the site line of the Bureau of Printing and Engraving, because when lined up, his commemorative space was swallowed by the Bureau's monumental size. "There is a complex, spiritual side to this," said Freed. "Set back in line with the other buildings, this could never be a monument; it will always be a building." At a June meeting, the Fine Arts gave approval to the design, although it made Freed pull back the Hall of Remembrance five feet eight inches to the exact site line with the Bureau of Printing and Engraving. This reduced the building almost 10 percent, about 26,000 square feet, and the height was cut by 5 feet to 70 feet.[47]

Impressed yet ambivalent about Freed's design was the *Washington Post's* Benjamin Forgey, who characterized it as "difficult and uncompromising." Forgey was at first "deeply troubled" by the building's relationship to the Mall, since in his opinion, the Holocaust was not an "American story." He walked around it a good deal, realized it had an oblique relationship to the Mall, and decided, in his words, "not to take it on." He agreed, however, that the Hall of Remembrance must be moved back to the Bureau of Printing and Engraving's site line in order to avoid competition with the other memorials. Forgey *was* willing to join with Washington preservation forces to oppose the Council's latest request that annex 3 be torn down. While some argued for the architectural value of this building, Forgey was more direct and more honest about his reasons for opposing its demolition. He argued that by removing the annex, the Council was "insisting that the museum building be more a part of the Mall, less a part of the city. . . . If Annex 3 is destroyed to make a plaza-park, the . . . Museum and its striking Hall of Remembrance will forevermore exist in direct sightline with the Washington Monument as well as the Jefferson Memorial, and will rival both. This, I submit, is wrong." (The Council withdrew its request, and in December 1990 the annex was transferred to the Council and now houses its administrative offices.)[48]

Embedded in these discussions is an important disagreement regarding the essence of the museum. Was it merely a museum building occupying prime location in downtown Washington near the Mall, its primary architectural mission that of a "good urban neighbor?" In this case, annex 3 served well as a shield, protecting a portion of the Mall from the disruptive aesthetic presence of the Hall of Remembrance. Or, was the museum, as the Council understood it, a new national monument whose presence in the monumental core was essential to the civic health of the nation? If so, its architectural mission was not primarily to be a good neighbor, rather, its mission was to evoke the "indigestibility" of the Holocaust through a building steeped in Nazi methodologies of construction and to proclaim the importance of this story for the Mall.

Whether urban building or integral part of the monumental core, the museum's visual presence bothered some on the Commission of Fine Arts. In 1988 Freed faced calls for minor building alterations that appeared to be merely aesthetic concerns, but were in essence requests for Freed to create a preferred architectural narrative which would soften and dilute the building's strong visual statement. "When we write of martyrs instead of victims; focus on resistance instead of mass murder; celebrate the human spirit and bypass the human body; invoke the dignity of the self and ignore its humiliation—we are," said Holocaust literary analyst Lawrence Langer, "initiating the evolution of preferred narratives that use embattled words to build buffers of insulation against the terrors of the Holocaust, without bringing us any closer to its complex and elusive truths." The desire for such "buffers of insulation" was certainly at work in the CFA's reaction to Freed's design.[49]

Key Theme

Meeting on February 18, 1988, several commissioners declared that Freed's building should somehow resolve or redeem the Holocaust. Vice Chair Neil Porterfield asked, "is there any part of this memorial that gives hope and gives joy about the future? Commissioner Diane Wolf said, "with a gate and a forbidding entrance I doubt whether people will want to enter and the whole idea of a Holocaust Memorial is to teach people so it doesn't happen again." Also conflicted about how—or if—a message of hope should emerge from the building was Robert Mendelsohn, vice chairman of the Council's building committee, who wondered aloud whether the Hall of Remembrance *should* provide "an uplifting experience?"[50]

At a March 17, 1988 meeting, Commissioner Diane Wolf focused on a new issue. She said that she was bothered by the bricked-up windows in the Hall of Remembrance. These had been characterized by Benjamin Forgey as an "eloquent, understated suggestion of the extraordinary tragedy that is being memorialized within." "You have done," Wolf said, "an awfully persuasive job of showing us that humanity has been awful. . . . I would like to ask my fellow Commissioners if they don't feel that perhaps those windows, which are now blocked up . . . shouldn't be opened to reflect some light and to reflect some hope. After all, the western facade faces our nation's greatest memorials . . . four of them." Freed noted that at each corner of the free-standing walls there were slits of glass to let in sun as a sign of hope. This was not enough for Wolf, who said the windows "were blocking those symbols of America. Don't block the symbols. Incorporate them in your building." Hope, she said, "means open arms, it doesn't mean closed, blind windows."[51]

These closed, blind windows served a particular purpose: they kept American space from contaminating memorial space. Freed worried about visitors having a full view of the Mall anywhere in the museum. In the Hall of Witness, for example, he altered a window at the top of a set of narrowing stairs—reminding some of receding train tracks—because he did not want the Mall to be a "player" in the museum. It was there, partially visible, however, and served a crucial function. "Why," asked Freed, "do you consciously make openings where you can see the various American icons on the Mall? Because these are the things that save you." It is, he said, "very important to bring into play these monuments, not to be seen as an equal to them, but to glimpse them, just barely glimpse them." Freed's architectural strategies were designed to alter the way in which visitors perceived the Mall, just as the permanent exhibition was designed to alter perception of citizenship in a modern state.[52]

KEY!

6.7. The Hall of Witness. (Photograph © Jeff Goldberg/Esto.
All rights reserved.)

In response to Wolf's call for further "study" of the bricked-up windows, Freed spoke of the Hall of Remembrance as a space betwixt and between the story of the Holocaust, told in the Hall of Witness, and American Mall space. Visitors *must* go through the Hall of Remembrance before emerging from the museum, he argued. "I think that memorials are not gazebos. . . . I am fanatically convinced that we don't want people walking to a window looking out on the Mall. . . . We want people to have a moment of concentration, because after you have seen all of this, I don't think you are ready to go out." Commissioner Roy Goodman also took issue with commissioners who wanted the building to resolve the story of the Holocaust and provide a redemptive ending. "There really are a substantial number of people in the world . . . who believe that the lessons of the holocaust are not lessons which involve the vanquish[ing] of evil and the emergence of hope. . . . The returns, in the view of some of us, are not yet in." Fine Arts Commission Chairman J. Carter Brown asked that in the interest of collegiality, Freed think about the issue, but, he said, he could not imagine a design improvement. "It has," Brown remarked, "a kind of indescribable

① resolution of narrative

poetry . . . which you could easily destroy by fussing with it." For his part, Freed remarked that he found the discussion "very disturbing." He did not know, he said, how to "design hope."[53]

At the next meeting on April 21, 1988, Freed brought a modified plan, in which brick had been removed from the windows and limestone inserted, making them match the rest of the building. He sacrificed brick, and with it the resonance of the ghetto, but remained adamant in his refusal to transform the Hall of Remembrance into American space. He argued, "If we made the interiors visible from outside, that would dissipate energy and sacrifice discovery. We need to help people make the transition from official Washington into a world of shifted values unlike anything they have ever perceived." Visitors would, he hoped, occupy the mediating space of the Hall of Remembrance before returning, albeit in altered condition, to the Mall.[54]

Freed's building "means" in a number of important ways. Its very location and existence—quite apart from its architectural attributes—was a triumph for those who believed the Holocaust an event apart, deserving of a prestigious location in American memory. The building itself can be perceived as a "code," a collection of Holocaust symbols that need to be identified and "read." In 1992, for example, museum staff taking donors and other VIP's on tours of the unfinished building occasionally used a four-page guide to the "architectural symbolism and other features of the . . . museum," which decoded the symbols in a straightforward manner: "the curved entranceways leading off the Hall of Witness are reminiscent of the shape of the crematoria doors, while the massive brick towers on the north side of the HOW [Hall of Witness] represent chimneys." The building "means" as a part of "official Washington," especially in the way its outer skin of limestone and brick pays attention to its neighbors. In this way, Herbert Muschamp stated, the building's outside "vocabulary," its civilized relation with other buildings, existed in contrast with its interior vocabulary, the world of ghettos and death-camps. "We see," Muschamp wrote, that these faces are not cleanly separated from each other, but . . . dissolve into one another, as though the official body of the State were slowly revolving to face us with a gun. We see that the brick that seems to harmonize so happily with [the Bureau of Printing and Engraving] is in fact derived from the barracks at Auschwitz."[55]

The building "means" in at least one other way. Just as the Lincoln Memorial is associated with the advancement of civil rights and has been the site of famous protest gatherings, so too is the Holocaust museum associated with American democratic tradition, albeit in complex ways. For some, the story it expresses and contains can be seen as so radically different, so alien to American life, that the museum and its story become an anomalous place housing an anomalous event. In this case, the museum reinforces the boundaries of American experience by graphically revealing what America is not. For others more readily willing to recall genocidal impulses in the nation's history, the museum may serve as a warning beacon, a contemporary commentary on the ever-present dangers of racism, antisemitism, or the classification of people as members of a "surplus population." In 1979 the Commission's *Report to the President* noted that while various Smithsonian museums "represent the accomplishments of civilization, the Holocaust illuminated an alternate dimension of human experience," adding "a somber dimension to the progress of humanity celebrated by the Smithsonian." Finally, whether visitors understood the Holocaust to be an alien story or expressive of tendencies found in every culture and individual, the museum aimed to be associated with faith in the so-called "lessons" of the Holocaust. It sought to function, as we have seen, as space for civil enlightenment, contributing to the wisdom of the body politic.[56]

For many observers, Freed's building successfully negotiated the maze of taboos and imperatives that govern Holocaust representation. For Raul Hilberg, the building itself was more significant than the permanent exhibition. Freed, Hilberg said, had accomplished something quite extraordinary, he had "built a concentration camp on the Mall." The museum, Hilberg thought, "rewrites the ground rules about what Americans should be concerned about," as Americans incorporated something done to Europeans into "the fabric of our national memory." It was this promise of a radical alteration of the boundary of memory that had convinced Hilberg the project was a worthy one.[57]

Interior Space: The Mood of Memory

The design team had to shape the exhibition within the confines of the space that Freed provided, for building construction preceded the design of the permanent exhibition, and museum designer Ralph Appelbaum often felt constrained by these limitations. Believing that "a museum functions from the inside out," Appelbaum understood that part of the design team's challenge was to make Freed's set of complex spaces work, to create a "whole environment that supported the interpretive story." They

6.8. The Hall of Witness. (Photograph © Jeff Goldberg/Esto.
All rights reserved.)

decided to present, in Appelbaum's words, "a play in three acts". "Nazi Assault-1933–1939," "Final Solution-1940–1945," and "Last Chapter." Bridges on the fourth and third floors that connected large exhibition space with tower exhibits were designed to be transitional spaces. Here, visitors viewed the Hall of Witness through glass covered with names of destroyed communities and people. The bridges provided, wrote architectural critic Adrian Dannatt, "a double sigh, of relief from the pressures of history on either side and of sadness at the tale that continues before and after. It is also only from these bridges that the full crookedness and distorted proportions of the main hall below can be understood . . . [which] reveals itself as a distorted, ruptured, structure, just as the classical foundations of fascist society seen from the overview of history appear as barbarism, insanity, chaos." The towers, containing volatile exhibits, were places of special intensity, power points in the exhibition.[58]

Appelbaum and the rest of the design team believed that the interior mood had to be "visceral" enough so that visitors would gain no respite from the narrative. "The permanent exhibition," he remarked, "has a vocabulary much like Freed's building. We built it in glass and steel and stone. There is no wood or plexiglas. We wanted to emphasize that the story was a permanent one." Appelbaum thought that one reason former exhibition designers had failed to satisfy the Council was their belief that some kind of singular design would make this museum memorable. "We tried to bleach out the idea that a designer's style was important. We used basic abstract concepts of style: contrast, proportion, scale, within a modular matrix."[59]

The feel and rhythm of space and the setting of mood were important. Appelbaum identified different qualities of space that helped to mediate the narrative: constrictive space on the third floor for example, where, as visitors enter the world of the death camps, the space became tight and mean, heavy and dark. Indeed, walls were not painted, pipes were left exposed, and except for fire exits and hidden elevators on the fourth and third floors for people who, for one reason or another had to leave, there is no escape. Slanted glass was used in exhibit cases to draw visitors in.[60]

Just as Freed provided an aesthetically appropriate building for a Holocaust narrative at the center of American commemorative space, so too did an appropriate interior environment provide the proper setting for taking visitors through the story. "We knew early on," said Appelbaum, "that one of the extraordinary parts of the event was that Europe was in flux and the victims were in flux because the perpetrators were moving rapidly throughout the countries. We realized that if we followed those people under all that pressure as they moved from their normal lives into ghettos, out of ghettos onto trains, from trains to camps, within the pathways of the camps, until finally to the end. . . . If visitors could take that same journey, they would understand the story because they will have experienced the story."[61]

Visitors, then, are *twice* removed from Washington, D.C. Recall Freed's desire that his building take people out of the city as visitors negotiate oppressive space and are to be spirited away from the Mall through his

Key!

architecture of suggestion. For a journey through the world of the Holocaust planned by the design team, this was not enough. Visitors had to be even further removed from American ground—on elevators taking visitors to the opening of the exhibit on the fourth floor—and then immediately introduced to exhibition space that would both house the experience and suggest with what kind of spirit they should approach it. The mood of exhibit space offered not only aesthetic but also moral direction. Visitors were to take this journey with a heart and soul "heavy and dark," like the space itself.

"Touching the Holocaust": Transforming American Space

British Emmy-award winning filmmaker Martin Smith, who became director of the permanent exhibition in 1988, agreed with museum designer Ralph Appelbaum that film, photographs, and small artifacts alone could not carry the museum's planned story line. Traveling together in 1988 to various Holocaust sites—Mauthausen, Auschwitz, Treblinka, Lodz, Warsaw—led them to appreciate the power of the material evidence of the Holocaust. Appelbaum recalled that while walking in Warsaw he glanced at an area excavated for phone lines, and saw, clearly, a layer of rubble of the ghetto, leveled by the Nazis in the spring of 1943. "The scars of the Holocaust were apparent," Appelbaum said, "and we were struck by how simple things took on another quality. A hook on a wall became something more when you learned that people were hung on it. A field became something more when, after a rain, you saw bits of human bone on the ground." The visceral power of the material remnants of concentration and death camps convinced Smith and Appelbaum that to make the museum's story come alive, visitors would have to be able to be in the presence of the material reality of the Holocaust. Consequently, the museum sent teams throughout Europe to bring back large artifacts designed to further transform exhibition space into a semblance of the world of the Holocaust.

Edward Dziadosz and Edward Balawajder, former director and current director, respectively, of the Majdanek concentration camp's museum, were in favor of lending the museum some of the camp's stark physical evidence. "Most people in the United States," said Balawajder, "will not see Treblinka, Auschwitz, or Majdanek. While nothing can replace the site where an event happened, the museum in Washington will bring the story closer." Perhaps, he went on, "after visiting the museum, some Americans will want to come to Poland and visit the camps." Similar thoughts were

voiced by Krystyna Oleksy, the Deputy Director of the Auschwitz museum. From the perspective of these sites, the museum in Washington,
D.C., was not a center of Holocaust memory, but an extension of the fabric
of the center: the original sites. The museum could connect to the center
through the artifacts. This was the way that Americans could "touch" the
reality of the Holocaust through a museum whose use of artifacts would
shrink the geographical distance between Poland and America and make
permeable the boundaries between Holocaust and American space.[62]

One encounters Holocaust artifacts—like thousands of pairs of victims' shoes—in two quite distinct spaces, in an exhibit in one of the barracks at the Majdanek concentration camp, and once again on display in
the Holocaust Museum. In the camp, the shoes were "at home," framed by
the interpretive lens of the site's exhibit, of course, but more in context,
nonetheless. The smell and the impact of the shoes was overpowering, suf-
focating. —7 KEY .... one of my distinct memories of visiting as a child

One next encounters the shoes in the completed permanent exhibition
in the museum in Washington. Seeing and smelling the shoes, on either
side of the visitor in a tower room on the third floor of the exhibit, brings
one, rather jarringly, to Majdanek. And yet it is easier to view these in
the museum. The shoes are "visitors," and there is the sanctuary of recog-
nizable American space just outside. Even though they—and other artifacts—are skillfully woven into the fabric of an intense Holocaust narrative, their raw power and seemingly unmediated presence in the barrack at
Majdanek is moderated. In both places, of course, the shoes serve as props
in a larger story. In Majdanek however, the story was told within the total environment of the camp, an environment that seemed to collapse
the distance between event and recollection of event, an environment in
which the shoes were actually worn, taken off, left behind, and collected.
They were less a selected artifact—by definition something out of place,
put on display—than a remnant, a material witness to the terrible life
of Majdanek. In Washington, the shoes are elevated to the status of artifact, and their presence as part of a narrative domesticates them, makes
them "safer" to view in the seemingly more controlled environment of the
museum.

"Touching" the Holocaust:
Transforming European Space

While the primary mission of the collection of artifacts for the museum
was to alter the visitors' experience of American exhibition space, the en-

ergetic activities of the museum's collectors led, in one instance, to the symbolic excavation of a forgotten material remnant of the Holocaust—a still-standing section of the Warsaw ghetto wall—and, as a result of the museum's interest in this wall, the creation of a place of memory where none had existed before.

Armed with the museum's "shopping list," for example, Jacek Nowak-owski, the museum's director of collections, searched for evidence of eve-ryday life: a street sign with a bullet hole, for example. Since ghettos made use of Jews as a labor force, he looked for tools, and he obtained a sewer cover symbolizing a means of escape. For the flooring of the museum's display on the ghetto, he was able to negotiate with the City of Warsaw for two thousand square feet of cobblestone, and in 1989 he was taken to one of the only remaining sections of the infamous wall that surrounded the ghetto.

During that trip Nowakowski met with Stanislaw Soszynski, Warsaw's deputy city architect. He had mentioned the museum's interest in find-ing a remnant of the wall to help visitors appreciate ghettos as places of exclusion, confinement, and inevitably, way stations to the death camps. Soszynski said he could help. "I was a witness to the death of this city," he said, and took Nowakowski to a segment of the wall, still standing be-tween two apartment buildings in a nondescript part of the city. "When we got here," Nowakowski recalled, "no one knew about this wall. No one really paid any attention to this piece of history, with the exception of one person who lives here in the neighborhood, who was trying to impress on the city authorities that this is a memorial place and it should be treated this way."[63]

He visited this one-man preservation squad, Mieczysław Jędruszczak, who, after fighting against the Germans with the Polish Home Army, was imprisoned by the Soviets, and returned to Warsaw in 1950, renting the apartment that looks out on the ghetto wall where he still lives. The city, he said, wanted to paint the wall, to "hide" it, but, he added proudly, he was able to muster enough support to preserve it in its original state. Both Nowakowski and Jędruszczak, the collector and the defender, took part in the resurrection of historic space and the creation of memorial space. In August 1989, as part of a major agreement with the Polish government, as well as with the state museums of Auschwitz and Majdanek, a Holocaust Memorial Council delegation—joined by former U.S. ambassador to the United Nations Jeane J. Kirkpatrick, and columnist George Will—arrived in Poland to accept artifacts from various sites. While in Warsaw, they joined in a ceremony at the wall where the Council received two of the

6.9. Visitors see the twisted skylight through the first names of
Holocaust victims. (Photograph © Jeff Goldberg/Esto.

original bricks. A plaque now commemorates the site and the event. In his
spirited defense of the wall, Jędruszczak had kept it "alive," so when
Nowakowski came, he—and the power of the Council—could bring a forgotten place to life. The 1989 ceremony attracted interest, and now this
segment of the wall, and another nearby, have become recognized as places
of memory where the work of commemoration can proceed. Memory cannot be put to work, after all, from a forgotten place. Jędruszczak proudly
showed visitors his scrapbooks with notes and cards from visitors—tourists, official delegations from Israel, the United States, and many European

countries—who now visit this place. For their part, the Holocaust museum, unable to bring the wall to Washington, used dental latex to make an exact casting, which now stands in the permanent exhibition.

Like other memorial space and structures, the Holocaust Memorial Museum is a contested environment, and these examples reveal the powerful interplay between place and memory. The story had to be centered in the appropriate city, then the appropriate site. The potential volatility of the building itself was perceived as a potential agent of defilement so near the mall, hence site line decisions, controversies over windows, and an annex that screened tourists from the museum all became significant issues in symbolic negotiations regarding the terms through which the Holocaust could become an official national memory. Arguments over what the museum is—an urban building on the edge of memorial space, or an addition to the national monuments at the center of this space—give us clues about the intricate ways in which positioning in space governs hierarchy of memory. Where something is remembered determines not only how it is remembered, but the importance of the memory itself.

The location of Holocaust memory was not enough, however. While it succeeded in centering the memory in American memorial space, it did not reduce the distance between European and American space. Consequently, strategies of displacement—in the aesthetics and plan of the building, in the mood of the exhibit, and in the use of artifacts—sought to reduce geographic distance from the sites, and historic distance from the event. Both the act of locating the museum adjacent to the Mall and removing visitors from the Mall were deemed crucial to the mobilization of Holocaust memory in contemporary American life. This was the strategy of memory at work as Holocaust consciousness has broken quite literally into and out of American soil.

Notes

1. *A National Commitment to Remembrance: Official Groundbreaking* (Washington, D.C.: United States Holocaust Memorial Council, 1986), pp. 9, 17.

2. Raul Hilberg, "Developments in the Historiography of the Holocaust," in Asher Cohen, Joav Gelber, Charlotte Wardi, eds., *Comprehending the Holocaust: Historical and Literary Research* (Frankfurt am Main: Verlag Peter Lang, 1988), p. 21.

3. Elie Wiesel, Chairman, *Report to the President*, President's Commission on the Holocaust, Sep. 27, 1979, p. 20 [Appendix A]. A detailed account of the creation of the

President's Commission is found in my book *Preserving Memory: The Struggle to Create America's Holocaust Museum* (New York: Viking Press, 1995).

4. Dawidowicz's statement in President's Commission on the Holocaust miscellaneous files, box 15 [file: "Opening and Closing Remarks, Elie Wiesel"], pp. 5–6, Eliach's statement in box 20 [file: "Subcommittee: Museum & Monument"], p. 5 (Hereafter cited as PCOHMF.)

5. Remarks by Bookbinder and Bernstein found in PCOHMF, box 20 [folder: Subcommittee: Museum & Monument]; Michael Berenbaum to Elie Wiesel, June 5, 1979, Berenbaum files. (Berenbaum was deputy director of the Commission and eventually became project director at the museum. He became director of the museum's research institute in the spring of 1993.)

6. PCOHMF, box 15 [folder: Holocaust Museum—1979, Commission History, file: "Summary of Views Received to Date 3/21/79, Museums and Monuments"].

7. United States Holocaust Memorial Council transcript (hereafter cited as HMCT), Apr. 30, 1981, pp. 20, 17.

8. HMCT, Dec. 2, 1982, pp. 14, 17.

9. Written responses to fund-raising materials found in "DM Sample Letters—incoming," United States Holocaust Memorial Museum files (Hereafter cited as HMMF). Hirsch quoted in the *Atlanta Jewish Times*, May 15, 1992; *Washington Post*, July 10, 1987.

10. Letter to President Ronald Reagan, Mar. 6, 1983, HMMF; *Time*, July 20, 1987. Peter D. Hart, Research Associates, Inc., "Materials from Focus Groups Conducted for the U.S. Holocaust Memorial Museum," HMCF. Avineri's article, originally published in the *Jerusalem Post*, was carried on July 17 in *Jewish Week*. Letters in response are found in *Jewish Week*, Aug. 7.

11. Howard Husock, "Red, White, and Jew: Holocaust Museum on the Mall," *Tikkun*, 5, no. 4 (July/Aug. 1990): 34, 92. Hart, "Materials from Focus Groups."

12. George F. Will, "Holocaust Museum: Antidote for Innocence," *Washington Post*, Mar. 10, 1983.

13. Levine interview, May 3, 1992.

14. Hart, "Materials from Focus Groups."

15. Lance Morrow, "The Morals of Remembering," *Time* (May 23, 1983), p. 88; Bayard Rustin, *New York Times*, May 18, 1984. The Council's fund-raising literature—letters, color brochures—usually included either a map of the Mall and the location of the museum, or a picture of the Mall, usually with the Washington Monument as a point of orientation, and an indicative mark of the museum's location.

16. For a discussion of various American Holocaust memorials and monuments, see James E. Young, *The Texture of Memory: Holocaust Memorials and Meaning* (New Haven: Yale University Press, 1993).

17. L'Enfant's plan for the Mall in a letter to George Washington, June 22, 1791. His comment on the "Grand Avenue" is found in almost any discussion of the L'Enfant plan. See, for example, Paul D. Spreiregen, ed., *On the Art of Designing Cities: Selected Essays of Elbert Peets* (Cambridge, Massachusetts: M. I. T. Press, 1968), p. 88.

18. Pamela Scott, "'This Vast Empire': The Iconography of the Mall, 1791–1848," in Richard Longstreth, ed., *The Mall in Washington, 1791–1991* (Hanover: University Press of New England, 1991), p. 46; George J. Olszewski, *History of the Mall, Washington, D.C.* (Washington, D.C.: Office of History and Historic Architecture, United States Department of the Interior, National Park Service, 1970), p. 25.

19. Quoted in Constance M. Green, *The Secret City: A History of Race Relations in the Nation's Capital* (Princeton: Princeton University Press, 1967), p. 28.

20. The description of Downing's plan is found in Therese O'Malley, " 'A Public Museum of Trees': Mid-Nineteenth Century Plans for the Mall", in Longstreth, ed., *Mall in Washington*, p. 65. Downing quoted in John W. Reps, *Monumental Washington: The Planning and Development of the Capital Center* (Princeton: Princeton University Press, 1967), p. 53.

21. McMillan did not have jurisdiction over Washington's public buildings. His Parks Commission, however, was under the direction of Daniel H. Burnham, who played a key role in the construction of the White City in the Chicago World's Columbian Exposition of 1893. He would be joined by another Exposition veteran, architect Charles F. McKim; by Frederick Law Olmsted Jr., son of the nation's most eminent landscape architect, and a distinguished one in his own right; and by sculptor Augustus Saint-Gaudens.

22. Frederick Gutheim, *Worthy of the Nation: The History of Planning for the National Capital* (Washington, D.C.: Smithsonian Institution Press), p. 135.

23. Charles L. Griswold, "The Vietnam Veterans Memorial and the Washington Mall: Philosophical Thoughts on Political Iconography," *Critical Inquiry*, 12, no. 4 (Summer 1986): 689.

24. Hilberg to Rabbi Bernard Raskas, Feb. 20, 1981, HMMF, Hilberg folder.

25. Cohn worked on this project with Mark Talisman and David E. Altshuler, Professor of Judaic Studies at the George Washington University. Altshuler would join Cohn at the Holocaust museum. He went on to become Director of the Museum of Jewish Heritage, "A Living Memorial to the Holocaust," in New York City. See David Altshuler, ed., *The Precious Legacy: Judaic Treasures from the Czechoslovak State Collections.* (New York: Summit Books, 1983).

26. Cohn interview, Feb. 16, 1994.

27. Cohn memo, June 9,1983, HMMF, "Memos, Micah," and Cohn interview, Feb. 16, 1994. Wiesel had requested that the General Services Administration also transfer annex 3 to the Council, since it was "most suitable for our education and administrative functions and would be an integral part of our unique Memorial/Museum area." Wiesel to Gerald P. Carmen, June 4, 1982. Carmen refused, because the Department of Agriculture thought the annex an "integral part of its overall Master Plan." Carmen to Wiesel, July 16, 1982. Wiesel raised the issue again in 1984, and was again unsuccessful. National Capitol Planning Commission file "Museum-Annex 3." (Hereafter cited as NCPCF.)

28. The Council was able to delist the buildings largely because of the weak case that had been made for their historic value when the General Services Administration nominated them for the National Register of Historic Places in 1978. See Lorenzo W. Jacobs Jr., to Michael F. Mulloy, Historian Preservation Officer, GSA, Feb. 21, 1978. NCPCF 2016-Statues/Memorials-Holocaust Memorial (1981–1987). Naftalin's comment in *Washington Post*, Dec. 27, 1984, p. A11.

29. Benjamin Forgey, *Washington Post*, May 11, 1985, p. G6.

30. Comments by Stone and Chase found in Commission of Fine Arts meeting transcript (hereafter CFAT) May 15, 1985, p. 31, 25.

31. Brown's letter to Hodel, June 5, 1985 also found in transcript. See also Benjamin Forgey, *Washington Post*, May 16, 1985. Letter to editor in *Washington Post*, June 6,

1985. In his letter to Hodel on July 24, 1985, Brown said "there was sufficient improvment . . . to warrant conceptual approval of the present scheme." See CFAT, June 28,1985.

32. PCOHMF box 15, [folder Holocaust Museum—1979, Commission History, file: "February 13, 1979—Summary of Views Received to Date," and "Summary of Views Received to Date, 3/21/79"].

33. The discussion in these paragraphs is found in "Museum Planning Meeting Transcript," July 12, 1985, HMMF box: Museum Concept Materials (various) fy '85. Quoted material on pp. 173, 175, 185–86. A similar discussion took place at a "museum design" meeting on Dec. 13, 1985.

34. Brodecki interview, July 23, 1992, Berenbaum interview, July 20, 1992.

35. CFAT, May 22, 1987, pp. 65–66; CFAT, June 19,1987, p. 26.

36. Finegold interview, Aug. 14, 1991.

37. Freed interview, Mar. 18, 1993; transcript of Freed interview, WETA-TV, "For the Living," roll #93, tape T-6, p. 53. (Hereafter WETA.)

38. Finegold interview, Aug. 14, 1991; I have taken Freed's recollections of the significance of his trip from these sources: Freed interview, Mar. 18, 1993; WETA, p. 65; Jean Lawlor Cohen, "James Ingo Freed," *Museum and Arts Washington* (Mar./April 1988): 41. Final quote from Freed interview, Mar. 18, 1993, WETA, p. 61.

39. Freed also expressed his dislike for a neutral building in Paul Goldberger, "A Memorial Evokes Unspeakable Events with Dignity," *New York Times*, Apr. 20, 1989. On the building as "expressive," see *Washington Post*, Nov. 21, 1986. Freed's comments on different types of buildings in interview, Mar. 18, 1993, WETA, pp. 90–92; on his building, Freed interview, Mar. 18, 1993.

40. Herbert Muschamp, "Shaping a Monument to Memory," *The New York Times*, Apr. 11, 1993, p. 32; "James Ingo Freed: The United States Holocaust Memorial Museum," *Assemblage*, 9 (1989): 70; WETA, p. 69.

41. WETA, pp. 72–73.

42. California congressional representative Thomas Lantos and his wife Annette, both saved as children by Wallenberg, were largely responsible for this act of renaming, and for keeping alive Wallenberg's memory in the United States. Lantos's first piece of legislation, signed by President Reagan on Oct. 5, 1981, made Wallenberg an honorary citizen of the United States, an honor extended to only one other: Winston Churchill. The Lantoses also were responsible for moving the plaque from a largely ignored grassy area across the street from the museum to a prominent place on the wall of annex 3. Annette Lantos interview, June 21, 1993. I also wish to thank Congressman Lantos's legislative assistant, Michelle Rae Marinelli, for her assistance. See also Annette Lantos, "My Fight for Raoul Wallenberg," *Moment* (October 1987): 21–25, 58–59. On the significance of renaming city streets, see Maoz Azaryahu, "Renaming the Past: Changes in 'City Text' in Germany and Austria," *History and Memory* (Winter 1990): 33–53.

43. Benjamin Forgey, "A Miraculous Monument to Catastrophe," *The Washington Post*, Apr. 18, 1993, p. G4; Herbert Muschamp, "Shaping a Monument to Memory," *New York Times*, Apr 11, 1993, sec. 2, p. 1. Freed has stated that he meant the facade on 14th Street to represent the false face that Nazi Germany showed the world, and his intricate entryway introduces "a selection, a segregation of movement, arbitrary if you will, not a life and death situation, but a selection." Freed quoted in *Assemblage*, p. 70.

44. James Ingo Freed, "The United States Holocaust Memorial Museum: What Can

It Be?" Holocaust Memorial Council publicity sheet; Joseph Giovannini, "The Architecture of Death," *Los Angeles Times Magazine*, Apr. 18, 1993, p. 38; Freed interview, Mar. 18, 1993.

45. Freed said of the skylight that it "carries a great deal of information in the way it is built. It is not sleek, it is not pleasant. It is the war structure that we want to see. And when we see it, we will find that it is twisted and deformed as the Holocaust twisted and deformed our perception of justice and our perception of what to expect from a civilized country." HMCT, Nov. 18, 1987, p. 74.

46. WETA, tape 158-159.

47. Freed's comments in CFAT, May 22, 1987, pp. 10, 12. The decision that the Hall of Remembrance would face the Washington Mall was made in 1984. There had been discussion of putting it in the center of the building and the 1985 design suspended it from the museum building. While Freed rejects any necessary religious meaning, there may be an interesting memorial relationship from his own childhood. During *Kristallnacht*, when the streetcar stopped for a moment, his father jumped out and grabbed a hexagonal piece of tile from a synagogue, gave it to Freed, and asked him to keep it. I thank Harry Barone for telling me this story.

For his comments on the "spiritual" nature of the building, see *Jewish Exponent* (Philadelphia), May 29, 1987. In his June 2, 1987 letter to Hodel, J. Carter Brown said that the Commission was "greatly encouraged by what we saw. Many of our previous concerns appear well on the way to being met, and I believe that with some additional study we will have an acceptable design in the near future."

48. *Washington Post*, May 23, 1987; Forgey interview, Aug. 14, 1991; on the annex controversy, see Forgey's article, "Annex 3: Worthy—and Endangered," *Washington Post*, Feb. 20, 1988, pp. B1 & B6. The Council's request to demolish the annex was formally withdrawn in a letter to the executive director of the Advisory Council on Historic Preservation on Apr. 14, 1991.

49. I am indebted to Professor Lawrence Langer for giving me a copy of an unpublished speech in which his comments appear.

50. CFAT, Feb. 18, 1988. Quoted material from pp. 50, 53, 84.

51. See Forgey's comment in *Washington Post*, May 23, 1988. Wolf and Freed's comments in CFAT, Mar. 17, 1988, pp. 15, 16-17, 25-26.

52. WETA, pp. 86, 88. Visitors *can*, through two of the narrow openings in the Hall of Remembrance, see the Washington Monument and the Jefferson Memorial. This was important for Charles Krauthammer, who wrote that the "juxtaposition is not just redemptive. It is reassuring. The angels of democracy stand on watch on this temple of evil. It is as if only in the heart of the world's most tolerant and most powerful democracy can such terrible testimony be safely contained." Charles Krauthammer, "Holocaust Museum," *Washington Post*, Apr. 23, 1993.

53. Quoted material in CFAT, Mar. 17, 1988, pp. 36-38; 40-41; 67; 55. Freed also recalls other attempts to soften his building. Some donors complained about its apparent harshness. One donor asked "Why can't it be more like the National Gallery?" There were constant pressures, he said, to make the building an easier one to look at and move in.

54. Ibid., p. 44. In the first several months after the museum's opening, visitors did not seem to be making use of the Hall of Witness as contemplative space. Roughly sixty percent of the visitors who emerged from the permanent exhibition entered the Hall of Remembrance. Some stood at its entrance, obviously not sure how to inhabit the space.

Others went in and lit candles, or walked around the circular area. Many visitors seemingly wanted to return to "life" immediately. They moved toward the Hall of Witness, always full of people. Of course, part of the problem may be that even tourists coming to the Holocaust museum are not used to being offered the opportunity to inhabit contemplative space in a museum.

55. Fact sheet in author's files. Herbert Muschamp, "How Buildings Remember," *The New Republic* (Aug. 28, 1989): 32.

56. Of use in thinking of the expressive nature of buildings is Nelson Goodman's "How Buildings Mean," in Nelson Goodman and Catherine Elgin, *Reconceptions in Philosophy* (Indianapolis: Hackett Publishing Company, 1988); and Lawrence J. Vale, *Architecture, Power, and National Identity* (New Haven: Yale University Press, 1992). Quoted material from "Report to the President," pp. 11–12.

57. Hilberg interview, Aug. 29, 1992. Freed disagrees strongly with Hilberg's reading of the building. "It is absolutely not about perpetrators," he said, "it says, 'pay attention, something is going on.' " Freed interview, Mar. 18, 1993.

58. These details are in "Exhibition Design Process for the United States Holocaust Memorial Museum," Appelbaum files. Adrian Dannatt, "Bearing Witness," *Building Design* (July 2, 1993): 10–11.

59. Appelbaum interview, Aug. 9, 1993.

60. Ann Farrington interview, July 28, 1993.

61. WETA, roll 128, T-27, pp. 3–4.

62. Interviews with author, Jan. 16, 19, 1993.

63. Interview with author, July 22, 1992. Unless otherwise noted, all quoted materials from Nowakowski from my notes during our trip to Poland in January 1993. I have checked my notes and tape recordings against the WETA transcripts.

7

"A BIG WIND BLEW UP
DURING THE NIGHT"
America as Sacred Space in South Africa
David Chidester

In 1969 ANTHROPOLOGIST James Kiernan was doing fieldwork among small religious communities of Zulu-speaking Christian Zionists in Durban, South Africa. In conversation with a Zionist prophet, Kiernan mentioned that the previous night Americans had landed on the moon. After considering the matter for some time, the prophet responded: "Yes, a big wind blew up during the night." Kiernan was impressed with this answer. He saw the prophet's reply as an illustration of the bounded worldview that had been constructed in the Zionist community, a worldview that was able to dismiss anything outside it, while at the same time accommodating anything within its closed symbolic model. "In terms of his world vision," Kiernan explained, "Americans were rank outsiders, well out on the periphery of his universe. These strangers and outsiders had committed an unnatural act, the effects of which were mystically registered in the here and now, right at the heart of his cosmic model."[1] Here were patterns and processes of a worldview at work, closed and bounded, perhaps, yet resilient in its exegetical elasticity that could assimilate into a natural order an event as unnatural as Americans landing on the moon. That natural order, however, was also a cultural order of worldview construction in which person and place were constantly being negotiated and renegotiated. America was integrated into a classification of persons and an orientation in time and space as rank outsiders, unnatural actors, distant strangers on the periphery of a centered world, as nothing but a big wind that blew up during the night.

Although signifying a distant place, whether across the seas or on the moon, America has nevertheless registered symbolic effects within the space of South Africa. This chapter explores the prismatic effects of America as sacred space in twentieth-century South Africa. I do not merely recall cultural contacts, review foreign relations, or compare aspects of the two societies. There is already a large literature on these topics. Rather, I attempt to advance a spatial analysis of the symbolic productions of "America" in a foreign land. My interests are broadly interpretive, trying to suggest larger patterns of meaning and relations of power. However, although taking in a vast historical sweep, I ask a single question: How has America appeared as a foreign sacred space?

Certain features of American sacred space can only appear outside of the geographical boundaries of America. As a highly charged spatial symbol, America has been appropriated in a vast array of symbolic, religious, and political projects all over the world. As an entry into this dynamic, this chapter examines the various appropriations and interpretations of America as sacred space in South Africa. A historical typology is proposed, following the distinction made by Jonathan Z. Smith between utopian and locative space.[3] First, America has been appropriated as a utopian space of freedom, and even of sudden, apocalyptic liberation. The appearance of America as a utopian space of liberation is dramatically illustrated by the "American" movement of the 1920s, led by Wellington Buthelezi and the Industrial and Commercial Workers Union, that promised an imminent apocalyptic redemption led by the anticipated advent of black Americans, arriving in planes, raining fire from the skies, destroying all unbelievers (especially white South Africans), and restoring the land to the people. Having something in common with "cargo" movements in Melanesia, the "American" movement in South Africa provides a useful illustration of America as a transglobal symbol of a liberating "center out there," extending its liberating power out to the African periphery.

Second, however, more recently, America has registered as the locative "center out there" of a dominant and perhaps oppressive world order. As Nelson Mandela observed in 1958, "It is American imperialism, which must be fought and decisively beaten down if the people of Asia and Africa are to preserve the vital gains they have won in their struggle against subjugation." America, as the symbol of a locative, dominant, and oppressive world order, was most dangerous because "it comes to Africa elaborately disguised."[4] The disguises through which an American center has extended itself have not only been political and military interventions, commercial initiatives, or media penetrations. Religion has also disguised the centrifugal expansion of an American center into Africa. In particular, linkages with South Africa forged by representatives of the New Religious Right in the 1980s helped reinforce the position of America as the locative center of a dominant world order.

During 1990 both Nelson Mandela and F. W. de Klerk had to make a pilgrimage from the periphery to the American center in order to empower their claims on a "New South Africa." In that journey to America, Washington, D.C., continued to operate as the symbolic center of a locative world order. For many Americans, however, South Africa had emerged during the 1980s as a sacred space, even a utopian space that promised sudden, apocalyptic redemption. At a celebration of the 75th anniversary of the African National Congress in Los Angeles in 1987, for example, entertainer and antiapartheid activist Harry Belafonte declared, "When Pretoria falls, South Africa will be liberated. When South Africa is liberated, the entire continent of Africa will be liberated. When Africa is liberated, the whole world will be liberated."[5] In this formula, many Americans during the 1980s appropriated South Africa as a symbol of a utopian space that was prevented from emerging by an oppressive locative order in which America was complicit. Focusing on South Africa, this essay tracks revealing aspects of the history of America as utopian and locative sacred space in order to suggest some of the ways in which American sacred space has been external to America, yet at the same time integral to the meaning and power of America in the world.

1. American Connections

In his *Wealth of Nations*, published in 1776, political economist Adam Smith linked America and South Africa as the twin poles of a new world order. "The discovery of America, and that of a passage to the East Indies by the Cape of Good Hope," Smith declared, "are the two greatest and most important events in the history of mankind." Risking hyperbole, Adam Smith nevertheless identified significant spatial relations of a single world system, an economic order already firmly in place by the end of the eighteenth century. The global economic network marked by the nodal points of America and the Cape had not only expanded the scope of European commerce and industry. These colonial settlements, Smith held, had actually succeeded in "uniting, in some measure, the most distant parts of the world."[6] Although Smith saw that far-flung global order unified under European control, independent American initiatives in trade, diplomacy, and religion by the nineteenth century had established close contacts with South Africa.

[Commerce and religion, sometimes cooperating, sometimes in conflict, were definitely intertwined in the earliest relations between America and South Africa.]The first United States ship anchored at the Cape in 1784.[7] A few years later, U.S. naval captain Stout wrote to President John Adams about the "commercial benefits of establishing a colony from America."[8] Even without actual colonization, however, the United States took an active role in South African trade, so that, by the 1830s, as the British traveler Nathaniel Isaacs observed with some concern, "America is the forerunner of commerce in new countries."[9] In his letter to President Adams, however, Captain Stout had warned against sending missionaries to South Africa who would inevitably interfere with U.S. commercial interests by creating religious confusion and conflict among the settlers and the indigenous people of the region. Nevertheless, in 1834 the first group of six American missionaries, representing the American Board for Foreign Missions, arrived in South Africa and began establishing stations in Natal. British colonial administrators suspected the American missionaries of being agents of the United States. According to Colonial Governor Sir Benjamin D'Urban, "the arrival of American missionaries presaged imminent annexation by the United States."[10] For their part, British missionaries already working in the region feared that American conflicts would be transposed into Africa. For example, the representative of the London Missionary Society, John Philip, worried that Americans would arm the natives, thereby "reenacting on the South African frontier the horrors that had occurred on the frontiers of America." Furthermore, Philip expressed concern that "missionaries from the Southern States should be sent to labor among colored people, in such a country as Africa."[11] In the course of events, however, these fears proved baseless, as American missionaries quickly adapted to conditions of British rule and white supremacy in southern Africa. As one American missionary put it, "God in His providence has sent the Anglo-Saxon race to the southern part of the continent to prepare the way for the dissemination of His truth."[1] Accordingly, American missionaries found it convenient to imagine southern Africa as (1) a spatial nexus for Anglo-American religious, political, and cultural unity.]

For indigenous people, America was a new, unfamiliar place to imagine. Working for the London Missionary Society in the northern Cape during the 1830s, the missionary Robert Moffat recounted an African chief's curiosity about Americans. "He asked from what nation they were," Moffat

(1) Precursor to locate domination power

recalled. "I replied America, but found difficulty in telling him where that country lay."[13] Others in South Africa, however, found different ways to imagine America under the impact of missionary influence. For example, the Voortrekkers in the 1830s, provided with a copy of the U.S. Constitution by one of the American missionaries, Daniel Lindley, imagined America as a symbolic model of political freedom, a portable symbol, because, like the Bible, it could be carried on their journeys of conquest into the interior of Africa. In founding their republic in Africa, these ancestors of modern Afrikaners declared, "We desire to establish our new settlement on the same principles of liberty as those adopted by the United States of America, carrying into effect, as far as possible, our burgher law." One of their settlements, originally named "Pretoria Philadelphia," became the capital of an independent Transvaal Republic in 1860.[14] At the same time, the multi-ethnic Christian community, originally known as Bastaards, subsequently as Griqua, looked to America as a symbol of freedom. In 1838, a Griqua evangelist by the name of Nicholas Kruger argued that his nation ought to be independent and powerful like the United States of America, because the Griqua "began to receive the Gospel at the very same time the colonization of America commenced."[15]

Imagining America, for the Griqua, as well as for the Voortrekkers, meant imagining a space of independence from British domination that could be transplanted from the United States to southern Africa. By the end of the nineteenth century, however, Africans in southern Africa began to discover new ways of reinventing America as a transposable space of freedom. Gradually, America emerged as a sacred space for Africans in South Africa. As we will see in a moment, however, American space was refracted through the specific spatial symbols of Ethiopia, Zion, or Tuskegee. America even appeared in the image of Africa itself, which, in its relational, social production as a symbol, was actually first recognized by Africans in the mirror of America. In a variety of ways, America surfaced as sacred space in South Africa during the early twentieth century.

1.1 Ethiopianism — UNIFIED AFRICAN/AMERICAN IDENTITY

The earliest American connection was established by the "Ethiopian" movement that emerged in the 1890s in the changing urban centers of Pretoria and Johannesburg. As a local initiative in Pretoria, Mangena M. Mokone founded the first independent Ethiopian church, but it was Mokone's niece, Charlotte Manye, who established the American connection by linking the South African church with the African Methodist Episcopal

(2) Roots of utopian thinking

Church (AME) in the United States. On a U.S. tour with the South African Choir, Charlotte Manye was abandoned by white promoters, but was invited to stay and study at the AME's Wilberforce University. Informed by his niece about the religious and educational work of the AME, Mokone and other Ethiopian leaders decided to forge formal links with the American church. As representative of the South Africans, James M. Dwane went to America to arrange for AME Bishop Henry M. Turner to visit South Africa. During his five-week visit in 1898, Bishop Turner consecrated Dwane as assistant bishop, ordained 65 ministers, and bought a site for a school in Queenstown. In 1901, a permanent bishop, the American L. J. Coppin, was established in South Africa. Wilberforce University, based on the American model, was founded in the Transvaal.[16]

In this "Ethiopian" connection, America registered in South Africa, not as the United States, but as Ethiopia, a multidimensional spatial symbol of a unified African and American identity. As a symbol of redemptive space, Ethiopia assumed at least three layers of significance. First, Ethiopia appeared in the biblical psalm, "Ethiopia shall stretch forth her hands unto God" (Ps. 68:31), as a promise of African redemption, a promise frequently announced in African-American sermons.[17] Second, Ethiopia, to a certain extent, was identified with the independent nation of Ethiopia, the ancient Christian kingdom of Abysinnia, that had remained sovereign during the nineteenth-century colonization of Africa. After the Abysinnian victory over European troops at the battle of Adowa in 1896, Ethiopia rose in prominence as a sacred space of African independence from foreign domination. Finally, Ethiopia was employed as a symbol of Pan-African unity, and liberation from white oppression, that was also shared by African Americans. Under the leadership of Bishop Henry M. Turner, the African Methodist Episcopal Church aspired to create a "highway across the Atlantic" that would unify black Christians in America and Africa in human dignity, freedom, and advancement.[10] As a multivalent sacred space, therefore, Ethiopia could stand as a synecdoche for Africa as a whole in the eyes of African Americans. However, from the perspective of Africans in South Africa, Ethiopia also could stand for America, with its redemptive potential and promise of black liberation announced by the African Methodist Episcopal Church.

In the early twentieth century, the "Ethiopian" movement focused black hopes and white fears of an African redemption, a salvation from white oppression formulated in the slogan, "Africa for the Africans." While many Africans saw the black American connection as redemptive, white

③ This type of rhetoric gestures re a little in the fact that a white country is linked to a narrative administrators tended to perceive the Ethiopian movement as dangerous subversion of the political order. Banning AME missionaries in 1902, the Natal governor declared that "American agitators shall not play the deuce with our natives under the guise of religion."[19] Many government officials and representatives of mission churches blamed Americans for fomenting revolt, as the Reverend Scott claimed that "men from America come in and make our natives imagine they have grievances when there are no grievances." Before a government commission in 1905, AME Bishop Charles Spencer Smith, who had replaced Coppin in 1904, tried to reassure the commission by denouncing Bishop Henry M. Turner and his call of "Africa for Africans" by claiming that the bishop was actually regarded in America as "a national character," whose pronouncements about Africa "none of us take seriously."[20] With such assurances, the AME was not banned in South Africa. However, some local leaders of the AME in South Africa grew unhappy with the American connection. Dissatisfied with remaining subservient to African American leadership, James Dwane left the AME to form his Order of Ethiopia, and another local leader, Samuel J. Brander, left to form his own church, complaining that the American church "took, like the old 'Papae Romanorum,' all moneys collected for the interests of the church in Africa to America, and there expended them obviously on purely American interests and not on Ethiopic interests."[21]

1.2 Zionism → ADOPTED AFRICAN PRACTICES, SHARED POWER + REPLACE OPPRESSIVE REGIMES

The American religious connection with independent South African churches was not limited to the influence of the African Methodist Episcopal Church. At the beginning of the twentieth century, a variety of recently formed American baptist, faith-healing, Pentecostal, and millenarian movements entered the South African mission field with dramatic results, but also with unexpected consequences in the proliferation of new independent African churches. One of the most influential of these American churches was the Christian Catholic Church, later known as the Christian Catholic Apostolic Church in Zion (CCACZ), founded in 1896 by the faith healer, John Alexander Dowie. Born in Australia and educated at Edinburgh, Dowie embarked on a faith-healing ministry in America that eventually came to be centered near Chicago, Illinois. As "First Apostle and General Overseer" of the Christian Catholic Church, Dowie attracted a considerable following by proclaiming divine healing, baptism by triple immersion, and the imminent second coming of Christ. In 1899, Dowie acquired land on Lake Michigan, 42 miles north of Chicago, where he began construction of Zion City, Illinois, as a new sacred center of religious purity, healing, and divine law. Residents of Zion City, Illinois observed regular daily prayer, healing services, and prohibitions on alcohol, tobacco, pork, and medicines. Like the biblical mountain of God, or the sacred city of Jerusalem, Zion City, Illinois, was imagined as a pure spiritual center in the midst of a dangerous and defiling world.[22]

In 1897 representatives from Zion City began South African mission work. Certainly, the religion of Zion underwent profound transformations "in the transfer from Lake Michigan to the streams and ponds of Zululand."[23] Eventually, Zionist churches adapted elements of African traditional religion, such as the expression of reverence for ancestors, the practice of detection of witchcraft, and rites of purification, into a Christian framework of spiritual healing. By the end of the 1980s, however, over 5,000 different denominations, accounting for the religious affiliation of roughly 30 percent of the South African population, could be traced back to the sacred center of Zion City, Illinois.[24]

In spatial terms, therefore, America registered for Zionists in South Africa as Zion. Although the United States might be insignificant, even when landing on the moon, the American origin of the Zionist faith, and its founder in America, John Alexander Dowie, remained important for many Zionist churches in South Africa. Like Ethiopia, Zion was also a multivalent spatial symbol. It could represent an alternative enclave of spiritual purity carved out of the oppressive, defiling social space of South Africa. But it could also represent the power to transcend ordinary space. In this respect, the sacred space of Zion had the potential to displace the oppressive domain of the South African political order. Although Zionists tended to be apolitical, the alternative spaces they created, in their purity and power, held the potential for a kind of political liberation in South Africa.

In the 1920s, a related movement, known as the Israelites also with American roots, tried to create an alternative sacred space of political resistance in South Africa. After a series of religious visions, Enoch Mgijima joined the Church of God and Saints of Christ, a black American movement founded by the charismatic prophet William Crowdy, a former cook on the Sante Fe Railroad.[25] Mgijima's increasingly dramatic apocalyptic visions of conflict between whites and blacks, however, caused his excommunication from the American church. Founding his own Israelite movement, Enoch Mgijima adapted some of the ingredients of the American church, particularly its annual observation of Passover as the major religious festival, but developed a unique anticipation of a millenarian end of the world. Refusing to move from their holy place, Mt. Ntabelanga, near Bulhoek in the eastern Cape, the Israelites were attacked on 24 May 1921 by the largest police action during peacetime in South Africa, resulting in at least 183 Israelites killed, 100 wounded, and 150 arrested and sentenced to hard labor. As a local newspaper revealed, just prior to the massacre, the Israelite community had been encouraged by the prospect of "Americans coming to assist them."[26]

1.3 Tuskegeeism

In addition to the religious innovations represented by the Ethiopian, Zionist, and Israelite movements, Africans engaged America as a place representing the promise of education and upliftment. In particular, the American example of Booker T. Washington was embraced by an educated African elite in South Africa as a symbol of redemption. A. B. Xuma, for example, the founder of the African National Congress, embarked in 1914 on a journey to America inspired by the prospect of reaching Booker T. Washington's Tuskegee Institute. According to his wife, Xuma had "heard about a place called Tuskegee Institute, and it was a school that you could get an education." On the way to America, as his wife recounted, A. B. Xuma felt that "it was really just like going to heaven." Xuma lived with Washington's family in Tuskegee while attending the institute. He must have been struck by the symbolic import and redemptive potential of the bronze statue of Booker T. Washington lifting the "veil of ignorance" from the head of an American black man. After completing his education at the University of Minnesota and Northwestern Medical School, A. B. Xuma returned to South Africa, as his wife recalled, convinced that "all things are possible through God." After his educational pilgrimage to America, Xuma, like many other African leaders of his generation, dedicated himself to the spiritual and material regeneration of Africa.[27]

In South Africa, as in America, Tuskegee was an ambivalent symbol of sacred space. Black America might have been divided among adherents of the industrial education for upliftment represented by Booker T. Washington and George Washington Carver, the academic education for liberation advocated by W. E. B. Du Bois, and the preparation for political independence championed by Marcus Garvey. In South Africa, however, although these different strategies were often noted, the conflict among them seemed less relevant, as Africans could sing,

For inspiration we may reach.
Beyond the seas to Negro soil.
In schools our children, let us teach,
Of Carver, Garvey and Du Bois.[28]

[handwritten margin note: wow! Use of music in particular — space for create memory & narrative]

For many Africans, therefore, Tuskegee represented a place of redemption that could be transposed into the South African context. Xuma's American-educated associate, John Dube, first president of the African National Congress, established the Ohlange Institute, based on the Tuskegee model, for African education in Natal. Tuskegee was a sacred place that could be effectively transplanted in African soil.

However, at the same time, Tuskegee was a spatial symbol appropriated by white educators and administrators in South Africa to represent a kind of industrial education that would keep blacks in their subservient social place. For example, Charles T. Loram, the most influential white South African educator in the period, wrote to Booker T. Washington in 1914 to say that his example "proves that with proper training and education the negro can be made a valuable asset to any country."[29] After visiting Tuskegee, Loram became the authority on "The Education of the South African Native." As an ardent segregationist, Charles T. Loram advocated industrial training for Africans, based on the Tuskegee model, at only one institution in South Africa. For the rest, he advised, the mass of Africans only required an elementary education designed to make them efficient and disciplined workers. Not as a symbol of redemption, but of segregation, therefore, Tuskegee was transposed by white administrators into a program for an inferior education that would train Africans for a subservient social position in South Africa.[30]

1.4 Pan-Africanism - *GARVEY*

The first Pan-African congress in 1919, convened by W. E. B. Du Bois, was attended by several South African delegates. But it was Marcus Garvey who came to represent a Pan-Africanism that united South Africa and black America. After the First World War, the message of "Africa for the Africans," proclaimed by the black Jamaican and American activist Marcus Garvey, attracted considerable interest among black South Africans. Garvey's organization, the Universal Negro Improvement Association, with its official organ, *Negro World*, and its plans for a "Black Star Line" of ships that would link America and Africa, gained a large following among black political activists, trade unionists, and independent church leaders in South Africa. Many were inspired by accounts of Marcus Garvey's First International Convention of Negro Peoples of the World, held in New York in August 1920, at which Garvey had predicted, as his message was understood in South Africa, an impending world war that would provide "the Negroes' opportunity to draw the sword for Africa's redemption."[31] In South Africa, Garvey's message was often received in ways that fused political liberation and religious salvation into a single promise of African redemption.

A political activist such as James Thaele, a leader of the African National Congress, drew out the political and religious implications of Marcus Garvey's principle of "Africa for the Africans." In the political sphere, Thaele argued, blacks had to work out their own liberation, just as in the religious sphere they had to seek their own salvation in churches independent of white control. As James Thaele advised, "Keep out of white churches as much as you can."[32] Other political leaders, however, merged religion, politics, and economics. During the 1920s, the Industrial and Commercial Workers Union, under the leadership of Clements Kadalie, drew heavily on the inspiration of Marcus Garvey. Kadalie even declared, at one point, that he wanted to be known as the "great African Marcus Garvey."[33] At a meeting near Cape Town, Kadalie described his union as "a movement which assures every man and woman of his or her salvation. We must therefore unite with racial pride that at least Africans will be redeemed."[34] This fusion of religious, political, and economic salvation was also found in some independent churches. In the northern Cape, for example, a church known as the House of Athlyi, or the Afro-Athlican Constructive Gaathly, which based its teachings on *The Holy Piby*, the "Black Man's Bible," also used literature from Marcus Garvey in its church services.[35] In a variety of ways, therefore, during the 1920s, many black South Africans embraced the promise of redemption associated with Marcus Garvey and black Americans. Increasingly, toward the end of the 1920s, the African nationalism of Marcus Garvey was given a distinctively apocalyptic twist in the popular reception of his promise of liberation from white domination in South Africa.

1.5 The Production of Sacred Space

In the social production of space, as philosopher Henri Lefebvre has argued, spatial practices are oriented by general representations of space and grounded in representational spaces, those specific sites of highly charged symbolic value at which cultural interests, and often countercultural interests, are asserted and contested.[36] The prismatic refractions of America

① new representations of space → freedoms domination
② new representational spaces → churches, white legislation
273

"A Big Wind Blew Up During The Night"

produced in South Africa from the 1890s through the 1930s created both new representations of space and new representational spaces. Whether it registered as Ethiopia, Zion, Tuskegee, or Pan-Africa, America could represent a space of freedom and empowerment that promised to displace the increasingly pervasive regime of white political domination and economic exploitation that engulfed Africans in South Africa. Obviously, African representations of America were counter-productions, alternative representations of America that clashed with the standard, official versions. Nevertheless, imagining America in these alternative ways also provided new ways to represent Africa. Alternative productions of Africa were inspired by America, but they also resulted from local, situational innovations. The slogan, "Africa for Africans," signaling a new representation of South African space, might have originated in America. In South Africa, however, that alternative representation of African space was embedded in local power relations. As the journalist R. V. Selope Thema observed at a conference in 1928, "there are men who preach the doctrine of 'Africa for the Africans' in response to the cry of 'A White South Africa.' "[37] Although drawing on American inspiration, alternative representations of space, and the production of new representational spaces, were forged in local struggles over land, labor, political rights, and human dignity.

As we have seen, Africa itself could be refashioned in the mirror of America as a space of liberating potential. In some instances, Africa could be represented as a generally oppressive space that nevertheless held alternative enclaves of sacred space, whether Zions or Tuskegees, with powerful American roots. In these counter-productions of sacred space, specific sites marked out liberated zones in South Africa. These representational spaces—AME churches, the sacred mountains, rivers, and other centers of Zion, or the African Tuskegees, such as the Ohlange Institute in Natal and the Wilberforce University in the Transvaal—resulted from African initiatives in the production of sacred spaces that transposed American sites into Africa. The geographical transposition of specific sacred sites, often traversing great distances, is an occasional feature of the production of sacred space in the history of religions. For example, Japanese Buddhist sacred mountains are said to have flown by night from their original locations in India.[38] In South Africa, new sacred sites, alternative representational spaces of liberation, symbolically flew from America to Africa. Through local, African initiatives, these specific sacred sites were relocated and grounded in South African space.

At the same time, as we have also seen, Africa as a whole could appear

① Representations of space affecting other representations of space
 - McDonald → home affects church
 - Limehill → Museum affects orientation camps in Europe
 - Chidester → America affects Africa

NO SPACE is INDEPENDENTLY CREATED or GAINS MEANING, THEY ARE DEPENDENT & BASED ON SPACES, RELATES to CHRISTIANS /non-CHRISTIAN ALIGNMENT

(CLASS COMMENT)

as an Ethiopian or Pan-African unity, a sacred space that transcended
spatial limits by also embracing African America. Reflecting on the significance of his 1898 to 1906 American sojourn, ANC leader Pixley
Seme declared, "In Africa, as in America, the Africans shall refuse to
be divided."[39] This new sense of Pan-African unity, forged in America,
promised to transform Africa into a space of regeneration. By the 1930s,
America had become a prominent feature of an African representation of
space in South Africa. For example, in June 1934, during a series of national thanksgiving celebrations to mark the centenary of the British abo-
lition of slavery, the Bantu Dramatic Society in Johannesburg staged a play.
Significantly, this play ignored Britain and focused exclusively on an
American saga of enslavement and emancipation. As historian Tim Couzins has noted, this focus on America suggested a "remarkable bias in consciousness," an orientation of imagination in which African history under
British colonial rule was rewritten as an American drama of slavery and
liberation.[40] By the time black American educator and political activist
Ralph Bunche arrived in South Africa in September 1937, America had
become a common feature of popular African political rhetoric. On his
first day in Cape Town, Bunche listened to the public "soap-boxing" on
the parade grounds by African National Congress representative Arthur
McKinley. As Bunche noted in his journal, the speaker,

> Used American Negro as example constantly. Said they have brains and
> wealth and don't stand for foolishness. Says American Negro says Africa
> belongs to Africans, and are ready to come back home. . . . American Ne-
> gro demanded to be treated as human beings and are equal of any people
> in the world. Praised Joe Louis as a great man—a black man and world
> champion. No white man in all of Africa can challenge him.

Another speaker, as Bunche recalled, held up a copy of the *Philadelphia
Courier*, declaring, "See here how 10,000 American black men march to
show the world that they are equal to any people on earth."[41] These images
of black America—union demonstrators, world champions, powerful human beings—provided alternative resources for imagining the spatial location of Africans in South Africa. Alienated and dispossessed in the land
of their birth, Africans could nevertheless reimagine Africa as home, in
some measure, because they imagined that powerful African Americans
regarded it as home.

In political terms, America represented an ambivalent promise of redemption. On the one hand, African intellectuals admired the American

constitutional system. As R. V. Selope Thema noted in 1928, "The principle which protects the political and legal status of the Negro in the United States is enshrined in the American constitution, and it is the rock upon which all efforts to deny him political, legal and economic rights must in the end break."[42] On the other hand, however, the American example could be held up by white intellectuals as justification for racist disenfranchisement in South Africa. According to the British missionary administrator J. H. Oldham, "American experience proves that the bestowal of political rights cannot confer the power to exercise them to those who do not possess the capacity. The enfranchisement of the Negro population became a dead letter because those enfranchised were not capable of governing."[43] Although the American political system provided ambivalent grounds for hope, America could nevertheless appear, in religious terms, as an unequivocal promise of redemption. The most dramatic instance of that promise in South Africa was the mass religious movement, known as the "American" movement, that swept through the eastern Cape and Natal during the 1920s, promising an imminent, apocalyptic American redemption. "*Ama Melika ayeza*"—the Americans are coming.

2. Utopian America: The Space of Redemption

During the 1920s, the myth of American redemption spread throughout central and southern Africa. The imminent advent of black American liberators was anticipated from the mining centers to the remote rural areas of the region. In the Congo many people expected that American liberators were about to sail up the Congo River at Manyanga in a huge battleship to deliver Africans from bondage and force whites to leave.[44] In Zambia believers in the American redemption anticipated the arrival of a mighty black American army. As one of the Zambian leaders announced in 1924, "America will be the chief of this country with the black people: the whites will go back to England. . . . These white people—the country is not theirs; when America comes you will see that America and we will own the country."[45] In Nyasaland people awaited the arrival of American planes dropping bombs that would only hit white people. This expectation of airborne black American liberators was given voice in a popular song:

> We're pleased that
> We went to America
> To learn the making of aeroplanes
> So as to 'fix up' all foreigners.[46]

Elsewhere in central and southern Africa, the American liberators were expected to arrive on motorcycles, or appear suddenly from under the ground, or drop from the skies in balloons. In all these cases, America represented a utopian space of redemption, a sacred place inhabited by free black people, who could wield the power of the latest military technology, and transcend spatial limits through the most modern modes of transportation, to bring an apocalyptic salvation to Africa.

Several factors contributed to the formation of this redemptive image of America. First, the extensive American missionary activity of the prophetic Watchtower movement, the Watch Tower Bible and Tract Society that came to be known in the United States as the Jehovah's Witnesses, combined an apocalyptic expectation of the end of the world with a tendency to depict America as a land in which either all the people were black or all the people, regardless of race, lived in harmony.[47] In central Africa, the figure of John Chilembwe, who returned from three years of theological training in Virginia in 1900, also stimulated interest in America as a land of opportunity for Africans.[48]

Second, the prominent role of the United States in World War I linked America with images of advanced military technology, the airplanes, battleships, motorcycles, and machine guns that would be used to liberate Africa. Like many other twentieth-century millenarian movements, in Africa and elsewhere, this American movement looked for redemption in a capitalist future, symbolized by westernized black Americans, the latest military technology, and the wealth controlled by whites, rather than looking for salvation in the recovery of a precolonial past. The future was America.

Third, the 1924 tour of the continent by the African-born American educator James K. Aggrey, sponsored by the Phelps-Stokes fund, stimulated widespread expectations of the advent of Americans. In Nyasaland, where, as George Shepperson recounted, "the image of America as a land peopled almost entirely with Negroes was also widespread amongst Africans," the arrival of Aggrey "was seen by many as the prelude to an American Negro invasion, in which all wrongs would be righted and the Europeans driven out of the country."[49] Aggrey was met with a similar reception in South Africa. Although he intended to promote education on the Tuskegee model, Aggrey was received, as Edwin Smith noted, as "the herald of some invading band of Negroes—they (the Africans) thought all Americans were Negroes—who would drive the whites of South Africa into the sea."[50] People came to hear him in Umtata hoping to learn about the coming of the Americans. Some expected that Aggrey, as harbinger of that arrival, would give away trade goods. These listeners were disappointed, according to one account, not only because Aggrey did not distribute wealth but because he failed to mention the "American Government."[51]

Finally, the promise of redemption associated with Marcus Garvey must have featured in the American myth. Reports of Garvey's "Black Star Line" might have inspired rumors of the arrival of Americans in modern forms of transport. In addition, however, stories circulated throughout central and southern Africa about a prophet, named "America," who was distinguished, like Garvey, by a gold tooth. In Zambia, a prolonged criminal investigation even resulted in 1929 in the arrest of a suspect for supposedly being this subversive prophet "America."[52]

In South Africa, popular interest in the redemptive promise of America was widespread. An American redemption was anticipated after the 1906 Bambatha rebellion in Natal and Zululand. Rumors spread that heroes killed in the rebellion would rise from the dead, "assisted by 'black abelungu' (black Americans) with modern weapons."[53] In 1923 in the eastern Cape, a woman by the name of Nonteto preached a message, under the aegis of Ethiopianism, "that American Negroes are coming who will cut the throats of Europeans."[54] Diagnosed as suffering from manic-depressive psychosis, she was confined to a mental hospital. By the end of the 1920s, however, interest in America was so pervasive that it could not be confined. A principal of a Pondoland teacher-training college observed in 1927 that "unsophisticated natives in these parts . . . regard the voice of America as that of a mighty race of black people overseas, dreaded by all European nations. . . . [Americans] manufacture for their own purposes engines, locomotives, ships, motor cars, aeroplanes, and mighty weapons of war . . . today the word America (*iMelika*) is a household world symbolic of nothing else but Bantu National freedom and liberty."[55] This enthusiasm for American redemption was initially mobilized in South Africa by the enigmatic religious leader, Wellington Buthelezi. Eventually picked up by the Industrial and Commercial Workers Union, the American myth inspired the largest mass religious movement in South Africa during the 1920s.

2.1 American Redemption

Although born in Natal, Wellington Buthelezi claimed to have been born in Chicago and trained as a medical doctor in North America. In 1925 he initiated a religious movement based on the promise that black Ameri-

cans were coming to South Africa as powerful liberators. Buthelezi announced "that a new and powerful race of people is to come shortly out of
the sea, and an end will be made of all tyranny and wrong."[56] Buthelezi
announced that imminent redemption was coming from America. "The
American negroes have decided to fight the Europeans and will help the
local natives," Buthelezi taught, according to one account. "There are already three ships with ammunition on this side of the sea" and "balloons
are also coming over."[57] As he traveled around the region, Buthelezi supported his prophetic message with the use of medicinal herbs, a battery to
give patients electric shocks, and a crystal in which followers "would see
numbers of aeroplanes and motor cars filled with negro troops sailing in
the sky, awaiting the call to land."[58] Wellington Buthelezi rapidly gained a
large following that included local chiefs, headmen, ministers, and congre-
gations of both independent and mission churches. In particular, Wellington Buthelezi mobilized the rural poor and migrant laborers who were
most responsive to the prospect of liberation. Followers of this millenarian movement were known as Wellingtonites, or "Americans," but they
were also known by a term that signified their preparation for an imminent apocalyptic war of liberation, *Amafela Ndawonye*, "those who are
prepared to die together."[59] At Wellingtonite meetings, hymns, prayers,
and sermons celebrated the coming salvation, which was expected soon,
when black Americans in airplanes would fly over the country, dropping
fire from the skies that would destroy all whites and all black nonbelievers. "The Americans are coming," became the rallying cry of Wellington Buthelezi's millenarian movement, as his followers looked to the skies
for signs of the American planes. "Now when these things begin to take
place," Wellington declared, "look up and raise your heads, because your
redemption is drawing near."[60]

When local government authorities deported Wellington Buthelezi in
March 1927, the "American" movement continued, with its promise of
redemption taken up by other leaders, especially by representatives of the
Industrial and Commercial Workers Union. One ICU organizer in eastern
Pondoland, the American-educated Baptist minister Filbert Mdodana, who
had formed his own independent Regular Christian Baptist Church, played
a prominent role in preparing people for the arrival of the American planes
that was expected in December 1927. Rev. Mdodana and other leaders of
the movement advocated two ritualized means of preparation.
First, people had to purchase membership tickets in the Industrial and

Commercial Workers Union. When the American liberators came, holders of the red ICU tickets would be spared from destruction. During 1927 the ICU membership ticket was transformed into a religious icon of salvation, as a minister of the independent African Native Church told his followers, "You will die if you do not buy the ticket!" People had to obtain the ICU card to show to the "American angels" when they arrived. "They must have a card to show when an angel came from America," an ICU leader in Natal observed. "If you didn't possess that card to show to that angel you were lost." ICU tickets were purchased from activists on the mines, who "said that the Americans were coming and the people working on the mines were going to be released from labour." Although ticket holders were also instructed to stop paying taxes, adding practical interest to membership, the ownership of a ticket itself became a religious symbol of redemption from the impending destruction of whites and white rule in South Africa.[61]

Second, people had to protect themselves through ritual acts of sacrifice, especially by killing their white animals and fowl. If they wanted to avoid being burned to death by the fires descending from the skies, believers in the American redemption had to eliminate animals associated with whites. In particular, believers had to kill pigs. The widespread, ritualized pig slaughters carried out by believers in the "American" movement during 1927 drew on a complex of religious symbolism that associated pigs with whites, not only because pigs had been introduced by Europeans into southern Africa, but, more importantly, because pig fat was associated with lightning, fire, and witchcraft. Although many people in the eastern Cape believed that lard provided protection from lightning sent by witches, leaders of the "American" movement argued that pig fat would attract the lightning flames that descended from the American planes. If the believers killed their pigs, then whites and nonbelievers would be the only ones left in South Africa still owning the animals that would attract the flames of destruction from the skies.[62] Although the ritual killing of pigs drew on "traditional" religious resources, it was clearly linked with a "modern" means of fighting white political domination and economic exploitation, the purchase of a membership ticket in a labor union. Furthermore, both the "traditional" and the "modern" aspects of this movement were woven together by adapting a Christian expectation of a final cosmic battle, a kind of Armageddon, in which the forces of good would defeat and eliminate evil from the world.

hybridization

2.2 America as Utopian Space

In the history of religions, millenarian movements have often been explained as responses to deprivation, natural disaster, or social disruption. During the 1920s in central and southern Africa, however, religious movements with apocalyptic expectations of sudden redemption responded to the more specific historical conditions of colonialism, capital penetration, labor exploitation, and white political domination. Although they occasionally drew on "traditional" symbolic resources, these millenarian movements were not regressions to the "primitive." Rather, these religious movements in the 1920s, promising an imminent, instant, collective, and this-worldly redemption, were modern innovations. As a sacred, redemptive space, America was at the symbolic center of those modern innovations. America stood as an organizing symbol around which other signs of modernity constellated. Modern transport, weapons, trade goods, wage labor, taxation, and the dispossession of the land were all incorporated in the American myth. Although a foreign sacred space, America nevertheless focused local reflections on power relations and local struggles over power. "Whatever its origin," as historian Karen Fields has observed, "a mythic vision of America's greatness was cultivated in Africa—as on other continents during this century—and it gave blacks and whites a luxuriant symbolic language in which to think about African liberation."[63] The apocalyptic myth of American redemption focused black hopes and white fears of dramatic social change. While magistrates and missionaries complained about "American agitators," many Africans looked to the skies for their liberation, waiting for the apocalyptic advent of the American utopia.

America, as we have seen, was a symbolic device appropriated and mobilized by Africans for achieving an inversion of the prevailing organization of space that had alienated, dehumanized, and displaced them in the South African political economy. Since Africans had been submerged under a reign of oppression that pervaded South African space, many aspired to get out of place. America provided one compelling symbol of that utopian hope. Such a utopian orientation toward space, as Jonathan Z. Smith has suggested, can be contrasted with a locative worldview that emphasizes the maintenance of everyone and everything in their assigned places. A locative order is based on a stable, supposedly permanent center that anchors a fixed order "in which each being has its given place and role to fulfill." It depends upon the ongoing reinforcement of order, hierarchy, and

① Looking to the skies marks, in Christianity, the coming of black Americans as the coming of CHRIST.

boundaries, requiring a high degree of conformity to place. It tends to feature prominently in the official ideology of any normative, imperial order. By contrast, a utopian worldview tests boundaries and transcends limits. It is an orientation in space "in which beings are called upon to challenge their limits, break them, or create new possibilities." Rather than the maintenance of place, the utopian worldview calls for liberation from place, often requiring the transgression or destruction of a prevailing social, symbolic, or spatial order. Accordingly, the utopian worldview entails an orientation in space in which "the categories of rebellion and freedom are to the fore."[64]

Smith has qualified this contrast by observing that the locative and the utopian are "coeval possibilities," simultaneously available options in any social world. However, the appearance of America as sacred space in South Africa suggests that the locative and utopian can be, not merely "coeval," but intimately related maneuvers in contests over local space. America appeared as utopian space precisely for Africans who suffered under the imposed locative order inherited from conquest and colonialism. By producing America as a utopian space, people were responding to the specific ① historical conditions of domination. Displaced under a dominant locative order, Africans forged a new, utopian space that bore the name "America." They anticipated a radical transposition of space that is commonplace in apocalyptic movements—the first would be last, the last would be first, the up would be down, the down would be up, the inside would be out, and the outside would be in. In that expectation, America represented the imminent reversal of the prevailing spatial order of domination and exclusion in South Africa.

The myth of American redemption in Africa bears certain resemblances with the "cargo" movements that swept through the Melanesian Islands after World War II. Like the Wellingtonites, some of these movements represented America as the source of their salvation. Perhaps the most adamantly Americanist of these movements, the John Frum movement, began on the island of Tanna in the early 1940s. After the departure of U.S. troops in 1946, leaders of the movement predicted the imminent return of Americans by ship, submarine, or airplanes to establish a new island utopia. The redemptive power of America was even personified in the mysterious figure of John Frum—John from America, the "King of America"—who embodied the American promise of salvation. "He teaches the good road," proclaimed one John Frum hymn, "he points to the place, to America, to America."[65] Into the 1990s, John Frum movements continued to propagate

① How might this relate to MICHAELSON?

their "American Dreams" of utopian redemption. But the hope of American redemption also featured in other religious movements. On the Admiralty Islands, for example, Paliau Maloat, founder of Melanesia's first independent church, declared in 1946 that America would come soon "to show us the road that would make us all right."[66] In the 1960s, similar movements in Melanesia continued to look to America, most notably the Remnant Church on the Solomon Islands, which held that it shared an ancient, theocratic covenant with America, and a Tungak movement in New Hanover that collected money in order to purchase American President Lyndon B. Johnson.[67]

However, the resemblance between the utopian movements in South Africa and Melanesia is more profound than merely the invocation of America. Most "cargo" movements, like the Wellingtonites, engaged in specific practical strategies that directly addressed the historical situation of colonial domination. These strategies were intentionally disruptive of basic colonial structures, designed "to challenge their limits, break them, or create new possibilities." If the dominant, locative order was based on the extraction of native labor, these movements called upon their followers to refuse to work. If its political administration was based on centralized taxation, their followers were forbidden to pay taxes. If its rationale was capital accumulation, resistance could be exercised through the ritualized destruction of symbols of wealth. In these terms, the locative and utopian orientations towards space were contested within specific historical conditions of oppression and resistance. When African prophets in central and southern Africa during the 1920s predicted liberation from colonial domination in the name of "America," colonial administrators labeled them crazy and tracked them down as criminals. However, in the course of events, these prophetic "Americanists" actually turned out to be right, because forty years later the European colonial administrators were gone, everywhere, that is, except in South Africa. There, oppression was only further entrenched, after 1948, under the racist system of domination and exclusion known as apartheid. If America symbolized a utopian space of liberation, Africans in South Africa remained waiting for America.

3. Locative America: The Space of Oppression

When the American forces did arrive, they came in support of the white minority regime and, implicitly, in support of the apartheid system imposed by the government of H. F. Verwoerd. On 31 May 1961, the day marking the birth of the Republic of South Africa, a U.S. naval task force was visiting Durban. Marines demonstrated flame-throwers and machine guns. Helicopters flew over African locations. According to sociologist Pierre van den Berghe, "almost all Africans interpreted the American visit as a show of force in favor of Verwoerd."[68] Rather than ushering in an apocalyptic redemption, therefore, the advent of armed Americans appeared to reinforce the systematic, institutionalized oppression of the African majority of South Africa.

Out of World War II, America emerged with new global security interests. Initially the United States was committed to keeping the remnants of the British colonial order intact. As William Roger Louis noted, "the general policy of the American government, in pursuit of security, tended to support rather than to break up the British imperial system."[69] Eventually, U.S. foreign policy focused on maintaining a Cold War balance of power. Perceiving South Africa as crucial to that balance, as well as to regional security interests, the United States lent tacit support to the apartheid regime. The U.S. abstained from all United Nation votes on antiapartheid resolutions during the 1950s until 1958, based on the argument that the U.N. was not competent to deal with such an internal matter within a sovereign state.[70] In November 1962 the U.S. voted against a U.N. General Assembly resolution to break diplomatic ties with South Africa, expel South Africa from the U.N., and boycott South African exports. The spatial dynamics of this conflict were significant: the campaign against South Africa sought to isolate its government from the international community. American interests, however, were focused on the expansion of its space program. As Richard Hull has speculated, "President Kennedy wanted to deal cautiously with the country, perhaps because the United States was preparing to undergo a rapid expansion of its space program and would need a network of stations around the world to monitor Soviet satellites as well as its own."[71] In this respect, the U.S. needed South Africa, among other reasons, because it wanted to put an American on the moon.

After the nuclear test ban treaty, the United States finally agreed in August 1963 to support an arms embargo against South Africa. Nevertheless, through several presidential administrations, U.S. policy continued to oppose attempts to isolate the South African government. In National Security Study Memorandum 39, summarizing the Henry Kissinger policy towards South Africa, as well as towards other white minority regimes in southern Africa, the U.S. government affirmed that the "whites are here to stay and the only way that constructive change can come about is through them." Accepting the white regimes, the National Security memorandum concluded that the U.S. should "maintain public opposition to racial repression but relax political isolation and economic restrictions on the white states."[72] For all its concern with human rights, the Carter administration continued relations with the white regime of South Africa. In April 1977, President Jimmy Carter described South Africa as "a stabilizing influence in the Southern part of the continent." The following year he invited State President P. W. Botha to Washington, promising a "more normal relationship" between the two governments.[73] During the 1980s, the policy of "constructive engagement" advanced by the Reagan administration reformulated this resistance to the international isolation of the South African government. From 1981 to 1983 the U.N. General Assembly considered 38 resolutions sanctioning South Africa. The U.S. voted against these resolutions 33 times and abstained from the rest.[74] In addition to this international support, the Reagan administration gave encouragement to the South African government through the ill-considered remarks of Ronald Reagan himself in a 1981 interview with Walter Cronkite. Rhetorically, Reagan asked, "Can we abandon a country that has stood beside us in every war we've ever fought, a country that strategically is essential to the free world? It has production of minerals we all must have and so forth." Reagan concluded that "surely we can keep the door open and continue to negotiate with a friendly nation like South Africa." In response to U.S. "friendship" with South Africa, the Organization of African Unity resolved unanimously in 1981 to condemn the United States for "collusion" with the apartheid regime of South Africa.[75]

3.1 American Imperialism

Obviously, U.S. foreign policy towards South Africa was framed in the spatial terms of the balance of forces, stability, and security in a world order, and even in terms of the strategic requirements of a global space program. In South Africa, however, America increasingly came to be experienced by people resisting apartheid as complicit in the oppressive order that pervaded South African space. By the end of the 1950s, the perception of the United States as central to both global and local oppression had become common within South African liberation movements. Speaking on behalf of the African National Congress in 1959, Joe Matthews asked, "Can any African forget what Western democracy has meant to us? Has it not meant colonial slavery? . . . Has this western democracy not meant racial discrimination in the United States and South Africa?" From this perspective, America was not a space of redemption. "To us," Matthews concluded, "it means national oppression and exploitation." During the 1960 treason trials, representatives of the African National Congress identified America as central to the reign of oppression established in South Africa. As one of the accused informed the court:

> My lords, there is a view which we held, that America being a leading Western power, by allowing itself to support the South African Government, was in fact making it difficult for us to get our liberation. . . . We regarded America as the leader of the Western Powers, and South Africa being part of the Western Powers, America was the leader of the oppressor group in South Africa.[76]

During the 1960s, America continued to be perceived by ANC leadership as playing a crucial role in reinforcing oppression in South Africa. In a 1966 essay on passive resistance in South Africa, ANC president Oliver Tambo focused on the ironic contrast between American ideals and practice. "Oppressed people in South Africa," Tambo observed, "have always associated the history of the United States with the great name of Abraham Lincoln." From Tambo's perspective, Lincoln directly faced the issue of human rights, rose to the challenge represented by the principles enshrined in the Declaration of Independence, and translated those principles into positive action. By contrast, the United States, according to Tambo, might occasionally condemn apartheid, but the U.S. nevertheless blocked any action that would contribute to dismantling it. "What puzzles and worries Africans," Tambo concluded, "is the opposition persistently offered by the White House to any action intended to put an end to this bondage."[77]

In these terms, therefore, America was betraying, not only the black majority in South Africa, but also its own most cherished national ideals. By the 1970s, the perception of American imperialism was firmly established. As black consciousness leader Steve Biko noted in 1976, "America's foreign policy seems to have been guided by a selfish desire to maintain an imperialistic stranglehold on this country irrespective of how blacks were made to suffer."[78] During the Reagan era, a prominent religious leader such as Anglican Archbishop Desmond Tutu might refer to the policy of "constructive engagement" as "immoral and un-Christian," but the leadership of the ANC simply identified American foreign policy as imperialism. From their perspective, American foreign policy had two significant spatial effects. First, it enforced a pattern of racist domination over the entire globe, a spatial order of oppression that engulfed, in particular, the so-called Third World. In response to Reagan's remarks about the close friendship between the United States and South Africa, Oliver Tambo observed:

> It was not a slip of the tongue but a frank admission of the truth when Ronald Reagan characterised the apartheid regime as an ally of long standing. His policy of constructive engagement with apartheid represents an engagement with racism that arises from the nature of imperialism—an engagement which, in the context of his goal to dominate the Third World, is constructive because it helps to strengthen the allied apartheid regime.[79]

Even U.S. professions of "neutrality" appeared to opponents of apartheid and most African governments as a duplicitous support for white supremacy.[80]

Second, by apparently reinforcing the white minority government in South Africa, American imperialism shaped the basic contours and the interplay of power relations within the local spatial order of the region. "Given the offensive posture of U.S. imperialism," Tambo noted in June 1985, "the Botha regime also felt that, for the first time, the balance of forces was shifting in its favour."[81] Indeed, America's global crusade against communism provided considerable support for the development of the South African government's "total strategy," a comprehensive military control of the country and the region that defined the basic spatial orientation of the regime during the P. W. Botha era.[82]

While the ANC and other liberation movements advocated sanctions against South Africa, seeking, in spatial terms, a global isolation of the white minority regime, powerful, heavily funded religious interests in the United States sought to establish new spatial and spiritual links between America and South Africa. American representatives of the New Religious Right visited South Africa frequently during the 1980s. Jerry Falwell praised South Africa as a "Christian country" in which human rights were upheld, that is, the human rights of the unborn, because abortion was illegal. Jimmy Swaggert referred to South Africa as a "godly country" on the frontlines of the battle between the communist Antichrist and the "Christian civilization" represented by the white government. Campus Crusade for Christ was active in South Africa, representing, according to one commentator, "a perfect example of an American evangelical group that has completely adjusted and assimilated to the apartheid system."[83] A proliferation of American religious groups, such as the Full Gospel Businessmen's Fellowship International, Youth With a Mission, and Bible Pathways Ministries, lent moral support to the apartheid government of South Africa.[84]

For the South African government, this ideological support was particularly welcome, since the Dutch Reformed Church, which used to be known as the "National Party at prayer," was no longer providing unquestioned legitimation of apartheid. For many within the New Religious Right, however, South Africa was a model that the United States could emulate. "In the area of traditional family values," as one publication, the *Family Protection Scoreboard*, declared, "South Africa puts America to shame."[85] South Africa had no abortion, no Equal Rights Amendment debates, no pornography, no separation of church and state, and no secular humanism. From the perspective of the New Religious Right, therefore, South Africa sometimes appeared as a conservative Christian utopia, a sacred space of family values and anticommunism that could serve as a model for the United States. (1)

However, many South African evangelicals rejected this link between the American New Religious Right and South Africa. In 1986 a group calling themselves "Concerned Evangelicals," based in Soweto, issued a publication that tried to distance evangelicalism from American imperialism. They noted that their "evangelical family has a track record of supporting and legitimating oppressive regimes here and elsewhere." In South Africa, their case in point was the Rhema Church in Randburg, near Johannesburg, with its roots in the Rhema Bible Church of Tulsa, Oklahoma, which displayed the American and South African flags on its pulpit. "The flag of America symbolizes 'enemy number one' in the minds of most Blacks in the townships," the concerned evangelicals reported, "whilst that of South Africa is an insult to their humanity and dignity." For these evangelicals, therefore, America and its flag symbolized the global center of a dominant, dehumanizing order, an order of religious and political oppression that extended throughout South Africa.[86]

Defenders of the order, however, celebrated an armed religious nationalism, a globalism that was centered in America, but was extended in and through the anticommunist regime of South Africa. One of the most remarkable documents to emerge out of the anti-sanctions campaigns of the 1980s was an appeal for U.S. annexation, *South Africa, the 51st State*. This book, authored by two political consultants, suggested that America still retained features of utopian space. "South Africa needs a saviour," the document declared, "and that saviour is the United States." But "salva-

(1) utopias feeding upon utopias !

tion" meant incorporation into the existing political order of the United
States. "We believe," the authors announced, "that only acceptance by
the world's greatest democracy can solve one of the world's most complicated social problems." Not only would annexation save South Africa, but,
the authors argued, it would also be beneficial to the United States. "The
'American-ness' of America," they observed, "comes from centuries of absorbing other cultures. . . . The waves of cultural immigration are over,
and if new stimuli are to revitalise American-ness, Americans must look
beyond their shores for them . . . *to the 51st State.*" By assuming that
America has constituted itself by "absorbing" other cultures, the authors
present an image of America as a centripetal force drawing the entire world
into its central vortex. South Africa's salvation, they suggested, depended
upon being drawn into that U.S. force field. In addition to this imagination
of American space, the authors advanced two other spatial arguments to
seal their case. First, they argued that South Africa, in the modern "global
village," with rapid transportation and instant communication, is actually
closer to Washington, D.C., than California was when it was admitted into
the Union. Second, appealing to an American transcendence of space, the
authors insisted that the proposal of statehood for South Africa was no
more farfetched than "the idea of putting Neil Armstrong on the moon."
If Americans could plant their flag on the moon, the authors concluded,
they could certainly plant it in South Africa.[87]

3.2 America as Locative Space

Once again, Americans landing on the moon provided an occasion for
imagining America. As we recall, the Zionist prophet in Durban, upon
hearing that Americans had landed on the moon, imagined America as a
distant periphery of his centered world. America's effects might register at
that center. A big wind might blow up during the night. But such effects
were incorporated into what anthropologist James Kiernan described as
the prophet's closed worldview. By contrast, the advocates of U.S. annexation imagined America, not as the periphery, but as the fixed center of
a global order, a center that could extend all the way out to the farthest
reaches of the world to absorb South Africa. This orientation in space,
however, should also be regarded as a closed worldview, based, as it was, on
imagining the world as a permanent locative order centered in America.
While some might celebrate that locative order, others in South Africa,
particularly those religious and political movements struggling for libera-

tion from apartheid, experienced America as the center of a normative, imperial order of oppression. South African liberation movements advanced utopian alternatives, promoting worldviews in which the categories of rebellion and freedom certainly were prominent. But unlike the "American" movement of the 1920s, they no longer looked to America as a redemptive symbol of utopian space. Instead, America was the center of a global order that had to be resisted. Whether celebrating or resisting, however, it is clear that South Africans during the second half of the twentieth century increasingly came to imagine America as the center of a "galactic polity."[88] -) GALATIC POLITY

Of course, Americans also tended to imagine the United States as the center of the world. America's move from the geopolitical periphery to the center was anticipated by nineteenth-century American cartographers who by 1850 had began to design world maps with the United States in the middle.[89] This imaginary centering of America, however, was reinforced by international economic, political, and military relations forged during two world wars. Out of World War I, the United States emerged as the center of a global economy. As President Woodrow Wilson declared, "The United States has become the economic center of the world, the financial center. Our advice is constantly sought. Our economic engagements run everywhere, into every part of the globe."[90] After World War II, this economic centrality merged with the expanded international scope of American political and military power. With the destruction of the former world order centered in Europe, the United States became the single fixed center of the world. In 1977, President Jimmy Carter remarked on this transition from periphery to center:

> By the measure of history our nation's 200 years are brief; and our rise to world eminence is briefer still. It dates from 1945, when Europe and the old international order both lay in ruins. Before then, America was largely on the periphery of world affairs. Since then, we have inescapably been at the center.[91]

The symbolic centrality of America—as "city upon a hill," as promised land hidden by God until discovered by "a people of a special kind"—was a familiar feature of the political rhetoric of Ronald Reagan during the 1980s.[92] This tendency to locate the center of the world in America, and, more precisely, in Washington, D.C., recalls a sociocentrism common in the history of religions. As sociologists Emile Durkheim and Marcel

Mauss long ago observed, "so many people have placed the center of the world, 'the navel of the earth', in their own political or religious capital."[93] What is more remarkable, however, is that so many people in the twentieth century have located the center of the world, not in their own capital, but in the foreign political or religious capital of the United States.

In South Africa during the 1980s, the spatial, symbolic relations between periphery and center were focused in the controversy over sanctions. Resisting the oppressive locative order anchored at the American center, the ANC advocated economic, political, and cultural sanctions that would cut the ties connecting Washington, D.C., with the white minority government on the southern African periphery. Other interests, however, including the New Religious Right in America, sought to reinforce connections between the U.S. center and the South African government. At the very least, these struggles revealed the contested relations between center and periphery within the American world order. In that locative order, America was a sacred space, not only because it was central, but because even on the periphery the meaning and power of America was contested. While the center held, those on the periphery could negotiate local power in relation to it. They could even reinforce their claims to power on the periphery by going directly to the center of the world.

4. Contested America: Pilgrimages to the Center

During 1990, two South African political leaders, ANC President Nelson Mandela and State President F. W. de Klerk, journeyed to America. Both visits addressed the issue of sanctions, that symbolic key to the international spatial dynamics that had come to characterize relations between the U.S. and South Africa during the 1980s. While Mandela pressed for sanctions that would further isolate the South African government, De Klerk sought an easing of sanctions that would lead to his nation's readmission to the international community. More than merely efforts to influence American foreign policy, however, these two visits can be regarded as ritual pilgrimages to the sacred center of the world. By asserting their competing claims on the center of America, Mandela and De Klerk hoped to mobilize power back home in the political struggle over the future of South Africa. In this respect, their visits appeared as a ritual contest over America that was, at the same time, part of an ongoing local contest over power in South Africa.

4.1 Pilgrims in America

When Nelson Mandela was released from prison on 11 February 1990, after serving nearly thirty years on charges of treason, his emergence was interpreted by the Reverend Jesse Jackson, in South Africa for the occasion, in dramatically apocalyptic terms. Nelson Mandela, according to Rev. Jackson, "was a Christ-like figure" who had "suffered his way into power." Upon Nelson Mandela's release, Jackson continued, "now that the stone has been rolled away," the world beheld an apocalyptic "second coming."[94] Rather than sudden redemption, however, South Africa entered into a long, slow, and often violent process of negotiation. In symbolic, spatial terms, going to America was a significant maneuver in the contested negotiations over meaning and power in a "New South Africa."

In June 1990 all of America witnessed the "second coming" of Nelson Mandela during his two-week tour of eleven cities in the United States and Canada. Americans, and particularly African Americans, embraced Mandela's visit in highly charged religious terms. Nelson Mandela was publicly hailed as "the most sainted man of our time." He was addressed by New York Mayor David Dinkins as "a modern-day Moses." He was identified by the Reverend Jim Holley, pastor of the Little Rock Baptist Church, as an African Pope, because, as Rev. Holley explained, "Whatever the Pope means to Catholics, that's what Mandela means to us." His wife, Winnie Mandela, was also sacralized, as she was described in one church service as Eve, Esther, and Ruth, "the perfect person God decided to make when He finished creation." Even *Time* magazine had to resort to religious imagery to make sense of the fervor of Mandela's reception in America. "On a more transcendent plane, where history is made and myths are forged," *Time* declared, "Mandela is a hero, a man, like those described by author Joseph Campbell, who has emerged from a symbolic grave 'reborn, made great and filled with creative power.' " In these potent symbolic terms, therefore, as Messiah, Moses, Pope, and Hero-with-a-Thousand-Faces, Nelson Mandela was welcomed by America.[95]

Beyond the extravagance of the rhetoric, the Mandela tour obviously resonated with deep religious and political interests in America. In particular, many African Americans found the Mandela visit an opportunity to reassess their position in American society. At one ritual tribute to Mandela in New York City, a reading of "praise songs" by thirty political poets, the organizer observed, "We're so troubled by racial conflict in New York that we desperately need some kind of Messiah." In this search for

(2) Another example of utopias replacing utopias

local salvation, South Africa, which had stood for so long as a symbol of racist evil, was ironically transposed into a sacred place, the distant birthplace (and re-birthplace) of an African savior. At the same time, however, Mandela's visit produced several significant spatial effects that promised to alter the location of African Americans in America. First, every place Mandela visited became a temporary sacred place, a shrine for American pilgrims. As one commentator observed, "Like pilgrims contemplating a joyous vision, millions of black Americans are trying to gauge the long-term effects of Mr. Mandela's visit to the United States." Second, among the possible long-term effects, Mandela's visit raised the possibility of reviving the social activism and aspirations of the civil rights movement. Benjamin F. Chavis Jr., executive director of the Commission for Racial Justice of the United Church of Christ, announced this promise specifically in terms of the creation of a new sacred space for African Americans in America: "I think you're going to see a lot of African Americans break out of the cycle of hopelessness we've had. We have a new Jerusalem. We have to keep that flame alive, and thank God Mandela has lit a flame that was extinguished in the 1960s." Third, the visit promised to relocate African Americans, and African-American interests and concerns, from the periphery to the center of American life. "Whatever its international implications," the *New York Times* observed, "the Mandela visit locally has become perhaps the largest and most vivid symbol of the fact that after years on the edges of New York City power and politics, the black community has arrived." For Americans, therefore, the visit of Nelson Mandela held the potential to transform spatial relations. New sacred places, even a "New Jerusalem," along with new representations of the place of African Americans in the United States and the world, suddenly seemed possible, all because of the visit of a man, who, in the words of the Reverend Joseph Lowery, President of the Southern Christian Leadership Conference, "gives flesh to the struggle against apartheid in South Africa—and against the apartheid mentality in South Georgia and America."[96]

For Mandela and the ANC, however, the American tour had specific goals of local, South African significance. Certainly, the forging of ties with America was an important goal, especially in establishing alternative connections that bypassed the official foreign relations between the United States and South Africa. Indeed, Mandela met with "official" America. After conferring with President George Bush and Secretary of State James Baker, Mandela addressed a joint session of the U.S. Congress.

Back in South Africa, that event reinforced Mandela's standing as an international statesman. However, Mandela's connections with the "other" America probably held greater significance during his trip to America. In addition to participating in all the public celebrations, ticker-tape parades, and church services, Mandela went on a special pilgrimage to Atlanta, to the graveside of Martin Luther King Jr., where he placed a wreath decorated in the ANC colors, black, green, and gold. In this ritual act, Mandela reaffirmed connections between the liberation struggle in South Africa and the Civil Rights movement. But the most dramatic, and publicized, attempt to forge connections with America occurred in New York, at Yankee Stadium, when Nelson Mandela, in baseball cap, announced his identification with all the people of America. "You know who I am," he declared. "I am a Yankee!"[97]

While establishing symbolic links with America, Mandela pursued two other goals of local, South African import during his visit, fund-raising and pressing for sanctions against the government of South Africa. These practical, political goals tended to be controversial in America. Contentious questions were raised that frustrated fund-raising attempts, issues that included the ANC's alliance with the South African Communist Party, its socialist economic policies, its armed struggle, and Mandela's defense of Arafat, Gadhafi, and Castro as "brothers in the struggle." But even those who celebrated Mandela as an African messiah could resent his fund-raising by pointing to the commodification of his charisma during the American tour. As Rashida Ismaili complained, "Every little inch of the man's flesh and every second of his time is being equated with a certain amount of money—the tip of his nose is worth $100, one minute is worth $1000. He has been commodified to such an extent that he no longer has meaning." On the issue of sanctions, Mandela appealed to Americans to maintain the spatial and spiritual isolation of the South African regime from the international community. On this issue as well, however, many Americans observed an incongruity between Mandela's charisma and his political agenda. Mandela's call for sanctions, according to one commentator, was "as if the Second Coming were devoted to pressing Rome for the recall of Pontius Pilate." Mandela, however, had come, not to save America, but to sanction the South African government.[98]

Although the sanctions campaign continued to hold local significance in South Africa, Americans by 1990 were starting to lose interest. In part, the easing of sanctions against the government of South Africa was directly related to the public relations efforts of its State President F. W. de

Klerk. In September 1990, De Klerk embarked upon his own pilgrimage to America. De Klerk's visit was not marked by parades, church services, ceremonies at American shrines, or any other form of public celebration. Rather, De Klerk went straight to the "official" America, on pilgrimage exclusively to the symbolic heart of the locative world order centered in the White House. Nevertheless, that visit to the center was sufficient to produce significant local effects on the South African periphery. As one popular South African newspaper reported, De Klerk's visit to the political center of the world signaled the return of South Africa to the international community. More than that, however, De Klerk's visit to the White House symbolized a mythic journey to the sacred center of the world. "If Washington is the world's informal capital and the United States president its most powerful man," this newspaper report observed, "the Oval Office in the White House must surely be a very important place." With meticulous attention to spatial symbolism, this report described the contours of the oval presidential seal, on the oval carpet, in the Oval Office of the White House. Tracing out a series of concentric circles that seemed to radiate power throughout the entire world, the "Oval Office, De Klerk would have noted, was aptly named."

Standing at the sacred center of the world, surrounded by the flags of the fifty states, the United States, and South Africa, De Klerk participated in one ceremonial act, a "photo opportunity" with George Bush posed under the portrait of George Washington. For the South African press, however, that simple ritual held profound significance for South Africa: "That president F. W. de Klerk met his counterpart, George Bush, in that office last September symbolized the promise of South Africa's eventual return to the global community."[99] This conclusion contained two assumptions. First, it asserted that F. W. de Klerk was the "counterpart" of George Bush, implying that De Klerk was the equivalent of the "most powerful man" in the world. In local South African contests over power, De Klerk, rather than Mandela, according to this account, derived greater empowerment from his pilgrimage to America. Second, it revealed that America continued to operate as a sacred space that held the promise of redemption. Obviously, Mandela and De Klerk sought to empower different kinds of redemption, one seeking liberation from local oppression, the other seeking inclusion in the international community. Although they employed many other strategies toward those ends, both advanced their claims on power during 1990 by means of a journey to America, a pilgrimage from the periphery to the locative center of the world order.

4.2 America as Contested Space

Rituals of pilgrimage enact a symbolic transformation of ordinary space. By going to what anthropologist Victor Turner called the "center out there," pilgrims renegotiate ordinary relations between the center and periphery of their worlds. During 1990, Mandela and De Klerk tried to renegotiate international relations between the South African periphery and the American center by ritual means. Characteristically, pilgrims abandon their conventional roles on the journey to adopt, in Victor and Edith Turner's terms, "an alternative mode of social being." They enter a special world of pure potential, unbound by the familiar temporal and spatial limits of their social worlds. In America, as we have seen, Mandela became an African "messiah," De Klerk became the "counterpart" of the most powerful man in the world. They adopted new roles for America, but also for their own society that was undergoing a violent transition towards a "New South Africa." Accordingly, the full significance of their travels was only realized, as in any pilgrimage, when they returned, bearing signs of new power derived from the sacred center, to what the Turners described as the pilgrim's "warm and admiring welcome at home."[100]

Back home in South Africa, the meaning and power of America, as the locative center of a world order, continued to be contested on the periphery. As negotiations over a political settlement dragged on, it was difficult to assess what had been gained by going on pilgrimage to America. Mandela had raised funds; De Klerk had succeeded in gaining support for lifting sanctions. Nevertheless, neither could claim clear victory in the symbolic appropriation of America as sacred space. In part, their failure to register a convincing claim on America resulted from the fact that the United States, although apparently the center of the world, did not itself revolve around a single center. The United States was comprised of multiple centers—from the White House to the grave of Martin Luther King Jr., from Wall Street to Yankee Stadium, from the John F. Kennedy Library in Boston to Harlem's Africa Square—that were each accessed by different pilgrimage routes. Pilgrimage to the American center, therefore, revealed a center that was fragmented and dispersed. → KEY!

Accordingly, as Mandela's visit especially showed, the meaning and power of America was also contested at the center. Mandela's visit refocused, however briefly, the endemic conflicts between an "official" America and an "other" America that imagined American society, in the mirror of South Africa, as a space of oppression. As we have seen, many

African Americans responded to Mandela's visit as an occasion for reminding America of its own "apartheid mentality." Of course, this vision of America in the mirror of South Africa was not new. In 1960 Martin Luther King Jr. revealed that he had "taken a particular interest in the problems in South Africa because of the similarities between the situation there and our own situation in the United States."[101] Increasingly, during the 1960s, King emphasized the inherent connection between racist oppression at home and abroad, identifying the central role in that oppression played by "the greatest purveyor of violence in the world today—my own government."[102] Thirty years later, these similarities and connections between America and South Africa remained salient, as many African Americans continued to experience the United States as a locative order that dominated oppressed people both at its center and its periphery.[103]

As we have seen, many people in South Africa shared that impression. However, because America was a contested space, echoes of an American utopia reverberated. In their analysis of ritual pilgrimage, Victor and Edith Turner suggested that pilgrims acquire a new sense of possibility, gaining new insight into "what may be," by going to a sacred center. Perhaps Nelson Mandela beheld such a vision on his return to America in 1993. On 20 January 1993, while F. W. de Klerk remained in South Africa, Mandela was in Washington, D.C., for the inauguration of U.S. President Bill Clinton. Invited by the Congressional Black Caucus, Mandela sat with his hosts in the stands. As a South African newspaper reported, Mandela's presence, in dramatic contrast to his reception in 1990, "passed almost unnoticed." Nevertheless, Mandela's second visit held a symbolic significance for South Africa that was even greater than the first. At Clinton's inaugural, while "witnessing the ritual," this report speculated, Mandela must have had a new vision of "what may be" for South Africa, for "he surely must have been impressed by the ease by which such enormous power is transferred."[104] Whatever it meant to Americans, therefore, this ritual of power, from the vantage point of the periphery, symbolized the possibility that a similar transfer might one day occur in South Africa. On 10 May 1994 that transfer occurred when Nelson Mandela was inaugurated as the first democratically elected president of a new South Africa.

5. American Space

Mythic visions of America have been generated in South Africa. Appearing as a symbolic totality, whether utopian or locative, America has registered local effects in a foreign land. Incorporated into South African symbolic space, America has signified both boundless possibility and the bounds of possibility. Certainly, these symbolic effects have depended upon several factors, including the social location of the perceiver in South Africa. Wherever located in South African society, however, South Africans have contributed to the production of America as a space of mythic proportions. Not only "insiders," but also "outsiders," have generated American sacred space. -> Key to McDannel

The production of America as symbolic space in South Africa corresponds in important respects to the ways in which Americans have imagined America. In analyzing the role of ideology in American history, Sacvan Bercovitch has identified "the culture's controlling metaphor—'America' as synonym for human possibility." This poetics of human possibility, however, has simultaneously been the site for a politics of social conflict in which, as Giles Gunn has noted, "the term 'America' has always served the political interests of both cultural consensus and cultural dissensus."[105] "America," therefore, has been mobilized as a symbol of human possibility, but also as a symbol for dissent and resistance against forces that limit the realization of human possibility in the United States. Martin Luther King Jr. might have identified America as "the greatest purveyor of violence in the world"; but he had a utopian dream of human realization in community that also bore the name "America." As a multivalent symbol, therefore, the significance of "America" has oscillated between fixed pattern and open promise, between limits and opportunities, between oppression and redemption. Accordingly, like South Africans, Americans have also experienced American space as both a locative and utopian world. -> Key!

5.1 Imagining America

Outside the United States, people all over the world have imagined America. The long history of the European production of images of America reveals certain characteristic strategies of symbolic representation. In the earliest "inventions" of America, dating back to the age of European explorations, the continent and its indigenous population represented the boundary of the world. America was Europe's "other." Reports of America were used to place Europe in silhouette, to circumscribe its familiar features with images from a strange world. Travelers described America's unfamiliar topography, unknown vegetation, wild animals, savage humans, and even bizarre, semihuman monsters as if they represented the ultimate boundary of world. Imagining America as the outer limit of possibility, as the historian Joseph Leerssen has observed, Europe was "defined in its periphery and by its margins, in its contacts with the unknown past and the alien outer world."[106] By representing America as its own boundary, therefore, Europe constituted itself as the center of the world.

In Europe as well, however, "America" could symbolize both consensus and dissent. In consensual terms, America might represent the periphery that defined Europe's central place in the world. But internal critics of European societies could also appropriate America as a symbol of alternative human possibilities. From 1500 to 1800, reports of the "New World" had a profound impact on European social thought. Their occasional descriptions of Native American societies that were in harmony with nature, without oppressive masters, exhaustive labor, private property, or greed for the accumulation of wealth, hinted at a way of life very different from the capitalist order emerging in Europe. These images of human possibility affected European notions of liberty and equality. Visions of America, such as More's "utopia," Montaigne's "noble savage," or Locke's "state of nature," were useful in gaining critical leverage on European society, providing a baseline for imagining both an original human past and a possible human future. Not merely a boundary, therefore, America could be represented as an alternative to European society.[107]

During the nineteenth century, these representations of America as both boundary and alternative proliferated as European visitors recorded their impressions of American space. Certainly, European tourists were impressed by the natural landscape. Many visitors, however, tried to represent the social landscape of America in specifically spatial terms. One of the more perceptive European visitors, the French sociologist Alexis de Tocqueville, touring the United States during the early 1830s, proposed a particular spatial representation of America by suggesting that American society was a dramatic reversal of natural order. "The Americans arrived but yesterday in the land where they live," Tocqueville reported, "and they have already turned the whole order of nature upside down to their profit."[108] By the nineteenth century, therefore, America was not the "state of nature." American space was an inversion of nature, a mirror image of a social order regarded as natural in Europe, not merely reflecting, but actually reversing a familiar European world. This reversal could be celebrated or decried, sometimes simultaneously, as epiphany easily turned to irony in European representations of America. At mid-century, German novelist Ferdinand Kurnberger captured this symbolic tension between

representations of America as a land of opportunity and a land of disillu-
sionment. Kurnberger represented America as a utopian epiphany:

> America! What name is as weighty as this name? Save in the sphere of
> imagination there is nothing loftier in the world. The individual speaks of
> the better self: the globe says "America". The word is the final chord and
> the great cadence in the concert of human perfections.[109]

But the German novelist embedded this celebration of utopian America in
a critical account of the hardships actually suffered by immigrants, under-
scoring the irony of his opening epiphany of America by titling his novel,
Der Amerika-Müde (Tired of America). In contrast to conventional depictions of America as a land of opportunity, therefore, some Europeans resorted to irony to represent the perceived failure of possibility in America.

Recently, Tocqueville's successor as a French intellectual tourist in
America, the postmodernist critic Jean Baudrillard, has pursued this use of
irony by representing the entire space of America as a vast emptiness. In
depicting American space, which he referred to as *l'Amérique sidérale*, or
astral America, Baudrillard focused on "the America of the empty, absolute freedom of the freeways." According to Baudrillard, America appeared
"in the film of days and nights projected across an empty space." Most
importantly, America revealed itself in the emptiness of its deserts. In fact,
Baudrillard asserted, "America is a desert." From the outside looking in,
he claimed to have penetrated the illusion of America, not by discovering
the truth of America, but by exploring the emptiness of the deserts of the
American Southwest. "I know the deserts, their deserts, better than they
do," Baudrillard asserted, "since they turn their backs on their own space
as the Greeks turned their backs on the sea, and I got to know more about
the concrete social life of America from the desert than I ever would from
official and intellectual gatherings." Apparently, the American desert revealed an extermination of meaning, a void that resisted the imposition of
any meaningful social, political, or moral project. As a result, Baudrillard
insisted, "here in the most moral society there is, space is truly immoral."
At the same time, however, the desert was subject to an unrestrained proliferation of meaning. Across the empty space of America, Americans were
entangled in the wild dissemination of signs and images that had turned
America into a "hyperreality," a space of simulation with all the effects
of the real. Because America meant nothing, it could mean anything and
everything. America, the desert, was also astral America, the America of
the stars.[110]

5.2 America as Foreign Sacred Space

Certainly, these strategies for imagining America, as boundary, alternative, reversal, epiphany, irony, or emptiness, have produced an "America" enveloped in mythic space. As humanistic geographer Yi-Fu Tuan has argued, mythic space can have practical effects by framing the "pragmatic space" of localized values in which people act and interact.[111] Mythic images of America have had practical effects. During the nineteenth century, for example, European depictions of America as a land of savagery formed a mythic image beneficial to governments and interest groups trying to discourage emigration. Depictions of America as a land of promise, opportunity, and equality, however, served to encourage emigration.[112] Conflicting myths of America, therefore, were implicated in European social struggles, suggesting that the production of America as mythic space was integral to the production of the social and symbolic space of Europe.

Obviously, foreign perspectives on America, from the outside looking in, have not been confined to Europe. Beyond the European voices that have usually been privileged in accounts of foreign perceptions of America, many others have spoken about American space. Immigrants and refugees from Africa, Asia, South America, and elsewhere, have also perceived America as a space of human possibility. Many, however, have experienced America as an empty space. To cite only one striking example: Chinese sociologist Fei Xiotong, on a tour of the United States in 1943, observed that America lacked enduring traditions that were "part of life, sacred, something to be feared and loved." As a result, American space was empty, a land without the ancestral ghosts that gave meaning to the present by relating it to the past. "In a world without ghosts," Fei Xiotong remarked, "life is free and easy. American eyes can gaze straight ahead. But still I think they lack something and I do not envy their lives."[113] In these terms, therefore, American space was not sacred, because it lacked nurturing temporal connections with the past. Like Baudrillard, perhaps, Fei Xiotong found American space empty of meaning because it could mean anything. America was devoid of sacred reality precisely because everything was humanly possible.

As we have seen, however, America has also been produced and reproduced from foreign perspectives as a space full of sacred meaning and power. Symbolic productions of America as sacred space have significantly affected America's place in the larger world. Inside and outside of the

United States, America has symbolized a utopian transcendence of space. Rising above and going beyond spatial limits, America has been represented all over the world by potent twentieth-century technological symbols of speed, mobility, and flight. While Africans in southern Africa were awaiting the apocalyptic advent of American airplanes, Americans themselves were adopting what Joseph Corn has called the "winged gospel" of aviation. From roughly 1908 through the end of World War II, Corn has argued, Americans perceived air travel as "an instrument of reform, regeneration, and salvation, a substitute for politics, revolution, or even religion."[114] Declining in the 1950s, this "winged gospel," for many Americans, was transferred into the U.S. space program and explorations of outer space, even including those Americans who claim to have actually journeyed to other planets.[115] On the ground, the American "cult of the automobile," which eventually spread throughout the world, promised a transcendence of space by achieving "mass personal automobility."[116] Like airplanes and spaceships, automobiles came to symbolize a transcendence of space that has been, if not uniquely, then at least distinctively, American. —7 American identity

Speed and mobility in transport have been matched by the increasingly rapid transmission of information. American mass media and advertising have also transcended space to encircle the globe. But media have had other spatial effects. Critics have argued that electronic media have changed the "spiritual geography" of social life in America by breaking any necessary link between the social situation of an event and the physical setting in which information about that event is received. As a result, Americans have become dislocated by their media. As Joshua Meyrowitz has suggested, "one of the reasons many Americans may no longer seem to 'know their place' is that they no longer have a place in the traditional sense of a set of behaviors matched to physical locations and audiences found in them."[117]

Presumably, people in foreign countries who are exposed to American media should also be subject to the same dislocating effects. However, as we have seen, the American movement of the 1920s in South Africa used images of American transport and communication, not to "know their place," but to transcend their place, to prefigure an imminent redemption from an oppressive environment. Locked into a dehumanizing social system, they welcomed dislocation. More recently, anthropologist Jean Comaroff has described the use of American symbols of the transcendence of space among Christian Zionists in South Africa. Entering a small, impoverished Zionist church, the Full Witness Church, Comaroff noticed the display of "a large, outdated calendar sporting a photograph of a sleek American car." She noted that "calendars and advertisements, which combine images of manufactured goods with signs of literacy and enumeration, are common in South African Zionist churches." Later, she visited the larger, more prosperous Zion Christian Church, where she observed that its "leaders are equipped with a fleet of sleek American cars." Whether driven or merely depicted, however, the American automobile served as a sign of transcendence over spatial limits. As Jean Comaroff concluded, "Such focal symbols do not seem fortuitous; like the car on the calendar in the Full Witness Church, they connote control not only over white status symbols, but over fluid motion and space."[118] Although the Zionist prophet interviewed by anthropologist James Kiernan in Durban seemed dismissive of Americans on the moon, these Zionists apparently manipulated American spatial symbols to carve a utopian enclave out of South Africa. Although they might agree that the United States was nothing but a big wind, they nevertheless appropriated American symbols of speed and mobility, power and status, to signify the wind of the spirit blowing through and transforming the space of South Africa. Everywhere and nowhere, America continues to be produced as a foreign sacred space through such local symbolic initiatives, even in a place as far away from the United States as South Africa.

At the same time, it should not be forgotten that America still represents for many people the locative center of a fixed world order. At the beginning of the century, Henry Adams lamented the absence of a single, unifying symbol for America, a symbol, like the cross of Constantine, or the Virgin of Chartres, that would capture the core values of a whole cultural complex. Adams proposed the "dynamo" as the central symbol for twentieth-century America. Signifying America's vitality, creativity, and unbounded industry, this symbol also evoked the violent force at the heart of America.[119] Toward the end of the century, in southern Africa and elsewhere, there were those who experienced America as the central dynamo of a violent world order. In 1992, while U.S. President George Bush still celebrated a "New World Order" supposedly emerging from the Gulf War, an obscure publication of a little-known group, the Southern African Non-Governmental Development Organisation Network, decried that same order as "American Hegemony in the Imperial Realm."

The popular image of the new emerging world order is that it is dominated by American Imperialism. This characterisation of the Imperial Realm is a substantially true reflection of reality, but nothing ever is so simple. It is not an American empire, pure and simple. It is, truly speaking, a White-Caucasian, Capitalist, Christian (W-CCC) empire in alliance with Japan and under American hegemony. . . . We are therefore living in a very dangerous period in world history. The problem humanity faces as it enters the twenty-first century is not the threat of small countries endangering world peace, but of US thuggery aimed at holding on to an unjust world order through resort to "precision" bombing and calculated violence.[120]

In spite of the obscurity of this South African organization, and the extravagance of its rhetoric, its basic depiction of an unjust, oppressive world order centered in America has been reproduced at various times and places all over the world. America has been produced as the demonic center of the world, whether the heart of a W-CCC empire or the "Great Satan" of Iran, through local initiatives in the generation and maintenance of sacred space.

As the twenty-first century opens, will the American center hold? Will America maintain its position as the sacred center, whether heavenly or demonic, of a stable, fixed, locative world order? Addressing the question of America's continuing global centrality, geographer Alan Henrikson has suggested that "the American world position, and the international order still dependent upon it, may fragment and blur, like a cubist painting." Out of that process of disruption, however, "new, powerful focal centers may emerge—much as the United States itself emerged from a disintegrating world order."[121] But from the vantage point of southern Africa, the American center fragmented and blurred long ago. From the 1780s, the United States might have had official foreign relations with various governments in southern Africa, but the people of the region found new, creative ways to renegotiate spatial relations with America. In the twentieth century, as we have seen, South Africans reproduced America as sacred space through the refractions of Ethiopia, Zion, Tuskegee, Pan-African unity, apocalyptic redemption, and international oppression. Rather than a single center, America was a sacred space of multiple focal points. In diverse ways, therefore, America's sacred significance in the world has been defined outside of the geographical boundaries of the United States. In the future it is likely that the character of America as sacred space, even if that space extends to the moon, will continue to depend upon such foreign productions.

Notes

1. James Kiernan, "Worldview in Perspective: Towards the Reclamation of a Disused Concept," *African Studies*, 40 (1981): 9.

2. A bibliography of works up to 1980 on relations between America and South Africa has been provided in C. Tshehloane Keto, *American-South African Relations, 1784–1980: Review and Select Bibliography* (Athens, Ohio: Ohio University Center for International Studies, African Studies Program, 1985). Keto has identified five phases in those relations: (1) Trade and Missionary Phase (1784–1869); (2) Transition Phase (1870–1928); (3) The African Colonial Period (1929–1948); (4) Decolonization Era (1949–1960); and (5) African Independence (1961–1980). American presence in Africa through the end of the nineteenth century has been addressed in Clarence Clendenen and Peter Duignan, *Americans in Black Africa up to 1865* (Stanford: Hoover Institution Press, 1964), and Clarence Clendenen, Robert Collins, and Peter Duignan, *Americans in Africa, 1865–1900* (Stanford: Hoover Institution Press, 1966). For a review of recent research on relations between America and Africa, see Andrew Roberts, "Review Article: Americans and Africa," *Journal of African History*, 28 (1987): 295–99. Comparative work has focused upon frontiers and patterns of racial segregation. See Howard Lamar and Leonard Thompson, eds., *The Frontier in History: North America and Southern Africa Compared* (New Haven: Yale University Press, 1981); George M. Frederickson, *White Supremacy: A Comparative Study of Segregation in South Africa and the American South* (Oxford: Oxford University Press, 1981); and John W. Cell, *The Highest Stage of White Supremacy: The Origins of Segregation in South Africa and the American South* (John W. Cell: New York and Cambridge, 1982). As America has served as a foreign frame of reference in South Africa, so has South Africa recently become a reference point for comparative observations about American society. Consider the following example: "The United States imprisons black males at four times the rate of South Africa and now leads the world in overall incarceration rates, surpassing even the Soviet Union over the past decade, a study reported Friday" (*Los Angeles Times*, 5 January 1991).

3. Jonathan Z. Smith, *Map Is Not Territory: Studies in the History of Religions* (Leiden: E. J. Brill, 1978), 100–102; and *Drudgery Divine: On the Comparison of Early Christianities and the Religions of Late Antiquity* (Chicago: University of Chicago Press, 1990), 121.

4. Nelson Mandela, *The Struggle Is My Life* (New York: Pathfinder Press, 1986), 72, 76.

5. Author's notes, 75th Anniversary of the African National Congress, Los Angeles, California, 8 January 1987.

6. Adam Smith, *An Inquiry into the Nature and Causes of the Wealth of Nations*, R. H. Campbell, A. S. Skinner, and W. B. Todd, eds. 2 vols. (1776; Oxford: Clarendon Press, 1976), II: 626.

7. Peter Duignan and L. H. Gann, *The United States and Africa: A History* (New York: Cambridge University Press, 1984), 68.

8. Eric Rosenthal, *Stars and Stripes in Africa* (London: George Routledge and Sons, 1938), 92.

9. Nathaniel Isaacs, *Travels and Adventures in Eastern Africa.* 2 vols. (London: Edward Churton, 1836), II: 322.

10. John S. Galbraith, *Reluctant Empire: British Policy on the South African Frontier, 1834-54* (Berkeley: University of California Press, 1963), 182; Harold Graham Mackeurtan, *The Cradle Days of Natal, 1497-1845* (London: Longmans, Green, 1930), 329.

11. Alan R. Booth, *The United States Experience in South Africa 1784-1870* (Cape Town: Balkema, 1976), 57.

12. Thomas J. Noer, *Briton, Boer, and Yankee: The United States and South Africa, 1870-1914* (Kent, Ohio: Kent State University Press, 1979), 38. On the American adaptation to British political dominance, see Norman Etherington, *Preachers, Peasants, and Politics in Southeast Africa, 1835-1880: African Christian Communities in Natal, Pondoland, and Zululand* (London: Royal Historical Society, 1987). On nineteenth-century American missionaries in southern Africa, see D. J. Kotzé, ed., *Letters of the American Missionaries, 1835-1838* (Cape Town: Van Riebeeck Society, 1950); Eleanor S. Reuling, *First Saint to the Zulus* (Boston: American Board of Commissioners for Foreign Missions, 1960); Edwin W. Smith, *The Life and Times of Daniel Lindley* (London: Epworth, 1949); and Alan R. Booth, ed., *Journal of the Reverend George Champion, American Missionary in Zululand, 1835-1839* (Cape Town: C. Struik, 1967).

13. Robert Moffat, *The Matabele Journals of Robert Moffat, 1829-1860*. 2 vols. (London: Chatto and Windus, 1945), I: 114-15.

14. J. A. I. Agar-Hamilton, *The Native Policy of the Voortrekkers: An Essay in the History of the Interior of South Africa 1836-1858* (Cape Town: Maskew Miller, 1928), 120; Rosenthal, *Stars and Stripes in Africa*, 176-77; Eric Anderson Walker, *The Great Trek* (London: Black, 1948), 216.

15. Martin Legassick, "The Northern Frontier to c. 1840: The Rise and Decline of the Griqua People," in Richard Elphick and Hermann Giliomee (eds.), *The Shaping of South African Society, 1652-1820* (Cape Town: Maskew Miller Longman, 1989), 403.

16. On relations between the American center and the South African periphery of the AME, see Josephus R. Coan, "The Expansion of Missions of the African Methodist Episcopal Church in South Africa, 1896-1908," Ph.D. dissertation, Hartford Seminary, 1961; Beaulah M. Flournoy, "The Relationship of the African Methodist Church to Its South African Members," *Journal of African Studies*, 2 (1975/76): 530-46; J. Mutero Chirenje, "The Afro-American Factor in Southern African Ethiopianism, 1890-1906," in David Chanaiwa, ed., *Profiles of Self-Determination* (Northridge: California State University, 1976), 250-80; Walton R. Johnson, "The AME Church and Ethiopianism in South Africa," *Journal of Southern African Affairs*, 3 (1978): 211-24; and James T. Campbell, "Our Fathers, Our Children": The African Methodist Episcopal Church in the United States and South Africa," Ph.D. dissertation, Stanford University, 1989.

17. Carleton J. Hayden, "Afro-American Linkages, 1701-1900: Ethiopia Shall Soon Stretch Out Her Hands unto God," *Journal of Religious Thought*, 44 (Summer/Fall, 1987): 25-34.

18. Edwin S. Redkey, "Bishop Turner's African Dream," *Journal of American History*, 54 (1967): 271-90.

19. Carol Page, "Colonial Reactions to AME Missionaries in South Africa, 1898-1910," in Sylvia M. Jacobs, ed., *Black Americans and the Missionary Movement in Africa* (Westport, Conn.: Greenwood Press, 1982), 184-91.

20. *South African Native Affairs Commission*. 5 vols. (Cape Town: Government Printers, 1905), III: 375; IV: 962-64.

21. Bengt G. M. Sundkler, *Bantu Prophets in South Africa*, 2nd ed. (Oxford: Oxford

University Press, 1961), 42; J. Mutero Chirenje, *Ethiopianism and Afro-Americans in Southern Africa, 1883-1916* (Baton Rouge: Louisiana State University Press, 1987), 105. See Trevor David Verryn, *A History of the Order of Ethiopia* (Pretoria: Ecumenical Research Unit; Cleveland: Central Mission Press, 1972).

22. Rolvix Harlan, *John Alexander Dowie and the Christian Catholic Apostolic Church in Zion* (Evansville, Wisc.: Press of R. M. Antes, 1906); Grant Wacker, "Marching to Zion," *Church History*, 54 (1985): 496-511; and Donna Quaife Knoth, "John Alexander Dowie: White Lake's Healing Evangelist," *Michigan History*, 74 (May/June, 1990): 36-38.

23. Sundkler, *Bantu Prophets in South Africa*, 49.

24. G. C. Oosthuizen, *The Birth of Christian Zionism in South Africa* (KwaDlangezwa: University of Zululand, 1987).

25. Elmer T. Clark, *The Small Sects of America* (New York: Abingdon Press, 1957), 151-53; Elly M. Wynia, *The Church of God and Saints of Christ* (Hamden, Conn.: Garland, 1993).

26. Robert A. Hill and Gregory A. Pirio, " 'Africa for the Africans': The Garvey Movement in South Africa, 1920-1940," in Shula Marks and Stanley Trapido, eds., *The Politics of Race, Class, and Nationalism in Twentieth-Century South Africa* (London: Longman, 1987), 213-14. See Helen Bradford, *A Taste of Freedom: The ICU in Rural South Africa, 1924-1930* (Johannesburg: Ravan Press, 1987), 215; Robert Edgar, "The Prophet Motive: Enoch Mgijima, the Israelites, and the Background to the Bulhoek Massacre," *International Journal of Historical Studies*, 15 (1982): 401-22; and Edgar, *Because They Chose the Plan of God: The Story of the Bulhoek Massacre* (Johannesburg: Ravan Press, 1988).

27. Richard D. Ralston, "American Episodes in the Making of an African Leader: A Case Study of Alfred B. Xuma (1893-1962)," *International Journal of African Historical Studies*, 6 (1973): 75, 79. See R. Hunt Davis Jr., "John L. Dube: A South African Exponent of Booker T. Washington," *Journal of African Studies*, 2 (1975/76): 497-529; Christopher Saunders, "Pixley Seme: Towards a Biography," *South African Historical Journal*, 25 (1991): 196-217; and the American journal of D. D. T. Jabavu, *E-Amerika* (Fort Hare: Lovedale Press, 1932). For an overview, see R. Hunt Davis Jr., "The Black American Education Component in African Responses to Colonialism in South Africa (ca. 1890-1914)," *Journal of Southern African Affairs*, 3 (1976): 65-83.

28. Tim Couzins, " 'Moralizing Leisure Time': The Transatlantic Connection and Black Johannesburg 1918-1936," in Shula Marks and Richard Rathbone, eds., *Industrialization and Social Change in South Africa* (London: Longman, 1982), 336, n. 68.

29. R. Hunt Davis Jr., "Charles T. Loram and an American Model for African Education in South Africa," *African Studies Review*, 19, 2 (1976): 89. See Charles T. Loram, *The Education of the South African Native* (London: Longmans, Green, 1917).

30. For an advocate in South Africa of segregated education based on the Hampton and Tuskegee model, see Maurice S. Evans, *Black and White in the Southern States: A Study of the Race Problem in the United States from a South African Point of View* (London: Longmans, Green, 1915). The British missionary administrator J. H. Oldham also advocated segregated education on the American model. See Kenneth King, "Africa and the Southern States: Some Notes on J. H. Oldham and American Negro Education for Africans," *Journal of African History*, 10 (1969): 659-77. On Booker T. Washington as "the white hope" in the United States, see Louis Harlan, *Booker T. Washington: The*

Making of a Black Leader, 1856-1901 (New York: Oxford University Press, 1972), 324. See also Manning Marable, "Booker T. Washington and African Nationalism," *Phylon*, 35 (1974): 398-406; and "Black Skins, Bourgeois Masks: John Langalibalele Dube, Booker T. Washington, and the Ideology of Conservative Black Nationalism," in Chanaiwa, ed., *Profiles of Self-Determination*, 320-45.

31. Hill and Pirio, " 'Africa for the Africans,' " 212.

32. Ibid., 232.

33. Clements Kadalie to S. M. Bennett Ncwane, 20 May 1920, Marwick Papers, File 74 (KCM 8315), Killie Campbell Africana Library, Natal.

34. *Negro World* (23 October 1920).

35. Hill and Pirio, " 'Africa for the Africans,' " 221.

36. Henri Lefebvre, *The Production of Space*, trans. Donald Nicholson-Smith (Oxford: Blackwell, 1991), 33, 38-39.

37. R. V. Selope Thema and J. D. Rheinallt Jones, "Our Changing Life and Thought in South Africa," in Milton Stauffer, ed., *Thinking with Africa: Chapters by a Group of Nationals Interpreting the Christian Movement* (London: Student Christian Movement, 1928), 63.

38. Allan G. Grappard, "Flying Mountains and Walkers of Emptiness: Toward a Definition of Sacred Space in Japanese Religions," *History of Religions*, 20 (1982): 218-19.

39. Saunders, "Pixley Seme," 217.

40. Couzins, " 'Moralizing Leisure Time,' " 322-23.

41. Robert Edgar, ed., *An African American in South Africa: The Travel Notes of Ralph J. Bunche* (Athens: Ohio University Press, 1992), 55-56. According to Edward Roux, Arthur McKinley was one of Marcus Garvey's "most vociferous followers in South Africa." *Time Longer than Rope: A History of the Black Man's Struggle for Freedom in South Africa.* 2nd ed. (Madison: University of Wisconsin Press, 1964), 112.

42. Thema and Rheinallt Jones, "Our Changing Life and Thought in South Africa," 57.

43. J. H. Oldham, *White and Black in Africa: A Critical Examination of the Rhodes Lectures of General Smuts* (London: Longmans, Green, 1930), 184. For a similar assertion, see Evans, *Black and White in the Southern States*, 280.

44. Efraim Andersson, *Messianic Popular Movements in the Lower Congo* (Uppsala: Almqvist and Wiksell, 1958), 153-54.

45. Karen E. Fields, *Revival and Rebellion in Colonial Central Africa* (Princeton: Princeton University Press, 1985).

46. George Shepperson, "Nyasaland and the Millennium," in Sylvia L. Thrupp, ed., *Millennial Dreams in Action: Essays in Comparative Study* (The Hague: Mouton, 1962), 145.

47. John Higginson, "Liberating the Captives: Independent Watchtower as an Avatar of Colonial Revolt in Southern Africa and Katanga, 1908-1941," *Journal of Social History*, 26 (1992): 55-80.

48. George Shepperson and Thomas Price, *Independent African: John Chlembwe and the Origins, Setting and Significance of the Nyasaland Rising of 1915* (Edinburgh: Edinburgh University Press, 1958).

49. Shepperson, "Nyasaland and the Millenium," 145.

50. Edwin W. Smith, *Aggrey of Africa: A Study in Black and White* (Garden City, N.Y.: Doubleday, 1929), 181.

51. Bradford, *A Taste of Freedom*, 215. See Kenneth King, "James E. K. Aggrey: Collaborator, Nationalist, Pan-African," *Canadian Journal of African Studies*, 3 (1970): 511-30.

52. Fields, *Revival and Rebellion in Colonial Central Africa*, 11.

53. Shula Marks, *Reluctant Rebellion* (Oxford: Clarendon Press, 1970), 251.

54. Clifton C. Crais, *The Making of the Colonial Order: White Supremacy and Black Resistance in the Eastern Cape, 1770-1865* (Johannesburg: Witwatersrand University Press, 1992), 219.

55. W. D. Cingo, "Native Unrest," *Kokstad Advertiser* (30 September 1927).

56. Bradford, *A Taste of Freedom*, 219.

57. William Beinart and Colin Bundy, *Hidden Struggles in Rural South Africa* (Berkeley: University of California Press, 1987), 252.

58. Bradford, *A Taste of Freedom*, 217.

59. Beinart and Bundy, *Hidden Struggles in Rural South Africa*, 222-69.

60. Robert Edgar, "Garveyism in Africa: Dr. Wellington and the American Movement in the Transkei," *Ufahamu*, 6, 3 (1976): 31-57.

61. Bradford, *A Taste of Freedom*, 229, 127, 218.

62. Edgar, "Garveyism in Africa," 41; Bradford, *A Taste of Freedom*, 224-28; Monica Hunter (Wilson), *Reaction to Conquest*. 2nd ed. (London: Oxford University Press, 1961): 570-71.

63. Fields, *Revival and Rebellion in Colonial Central Africa*, 12.

64. J. Z. Smith, *Map Is Not Territory*, 100-101, 293, 309. This distinction between locative and utopian has been employed to good effect in analyzing the spatial dynamics of the emergence of Rabbinic Judaism. See Baruch Bokser, "Approaching Sacred Space," *Harvard Theological Review*, 78 (1985): 279-99. As Bernard Faure has shown, however, locative worldviews are not always embedded in a normative, imperial order; utopian worldviews are not always implicated in rebellion. In China, a utopian worldview, Ch'an Buddhism, became normative for the empire. As a result, the indigenous folk religions, with locative worldviews, registered as disruptive of the imperial order. Bernard Faure, "Space and Place in Chinese Religious Traditions," *History of Religions*, 26 (1987): 337-55.

65. Lamont Lindstrom, *Knowledge and Power in a South Pacific Society* (Washington, D.C.: Smithsonian Institution Press, 1990): 104. On John Frum, see Jean Guiart, "Forerunners of Melanesian Nationalism," *Oceania*, 22, 2 (1951): 87; "Culture Contact and the 'John Frum' Movement on Tanna, New Hebrides," *Southwestern Journal of Anthropology*, 12 (1956): 105-16; *Un siècle et demi des contacts culturels à Tanna, Nouvelles-Hébrides* (Paris: Musée de l'Homme, 1956), and Lamont Lindstrom, "Cult and Culture: American Dreams in Vanuata," *Pacific Studies*, 4 (1981): 101-23. On Cargo movements more generally, see the classic works of Kenelm Burridge, *Mambu: A Melanesian Millennium* (New York: Humanities Press, 1960; *New Heaven, New Earth* (Oxford: Oxford University Press, 1969); Peter Lawrence, *Road Belong Cargo: A Study of the Cargo Movement in the Southern Madang District, New Guinea* (Manchester: Manchester University Press, 1964); and Peter Worsley, *The Trumpet Shall Sound: A Study of "Cargo" Cults in Melanesia*. 2nd ed. (New York: Schocken Books, 1968); and, on more recent research, see Andrew Lattas, ed., "Special Issue: Alienating Mirrors: Christianity, Cargo Cults, and Colonialism in Melanesia," *Oceania*, 63 (1992): 1-93. For reflections on the significance of cargo movements for the study of religion, see Charles H.

Long, *Significations: Signs, Symbols, and Images in the Interpretation of Religion* (Philadelphia: Fortess Press, 1986).

66. Theodore Schwartz, *The Paliau Movement in the Admiralty Islands, 1946-1954* (New York: American Museum of Natural History, 1962), 256-57.

67. Gary Trompf, "The Cargo and the Millennium on Both Sides of the Pacific," in Trompf (ed.), *Cargo Cults and Millenarian Movements: Transoceanic Comparisons of New Religious Movements* (Berlin and New York: Mouton de Gruyter, 1990): 72.

68. Pierre L. van den Berghe, *South Africa, A Study in Conflict* (Middletown, Conn.: Wesleyan University Press, 1965), 258-59; Anthony Lake, "Caution and Concern: The Making of American Policy Towards South Africa, 1946-1971," Ph.D. dissertation, Princeton University, 1974, 87.

69. William Roger Louis, *Imperialism at Bay: The United States and the Decolonisation of the British Empire, 1941-1945* (New York: Oxford University Press, 1978), 567. See D. C. Watt, *Succeeding John Bull: America in Britain's Place, 1900-1975* (Cambridge: Cambridge University Press, 1984).

70. William Minter, *King Solomon's Mines Revisited: Western Interests and the Burdened History of Southern Africa* (New York: Basic Books, 1986), 134.

71. Richard W. Hull, *American Enterprise in South Africa: Historical Dimensions of Engagement and Disengagement* (New York: New York University Press, 1990), 257.

72. Mohamed A. El-Khawas and Barry Cohen, eds. *The Kissinger Study of Southern Africa* (Westport, Conn.: Lawrence Hill and Co., 1976), 105-106.

73. Thomas Karis, "United States Policy Toward South Africa," in Gwendolen M. Carter and Patrick O'Meara, eds., *Southern Africa: The Continuing Crisis.* 2nd ed. (Bloomington: Indiana University Press, 1982), 344, 356-57.

74. Lee Cokorinos and James H. Mittelman, "Reagan and the Pax Afrikaana," *Journal of Modern African Studies*, 23 (1985), 551-73.

75. U.S. Department of State, "Interview with Walter Cronkite," *Department of State Bulletin*, 81,2049 (1981): 11; Hull, *American Enterprise in South Africa*, 316.

76. Thomas Karis and Gwendolen M. Carter, *From Protest to Challenge: A Documentary History of African Politics in South Africa 1882-1964.* Vol. 3: *Challenge and Violence 1953-1964* (Stanford: Hoover Institution Press, 1977): 539, 615-16.

77. Oliver Tambo, "Passive Resistance in South Africa," in James A. Davis and John K. Baker, eds., *Southern Africa in Transition* (New York: Frederick A. Praeger, 1966), 217.

78. Steve Biko, *I Write What I Like*, Aelred Stubbs, ed. (San Francisco: Harper and Row, 1986), 140.

79. E. S. Reddy, ed., *Oliver Tambo and the Struggle Against Apartheid* (New Delhi: Sterling Publishers, 1987), 110.

80. Robert Fatton, "The Reagan Foreign Policy toward South Africa: The Ideology of a New Cold War," *African Studies Review* 27 (1984): 68; Robert M. Price, "U.S. Policy toward Southern Africa," in Gwendolen M. Carter and Patrick O'Meara, eds., *International Politics in Southern Africa* (Bloomington: Indiana University Press, 1982): 73-78.

81. Adelaide Tambo, ed., *Preparing for Power: Oliver Tambo Speaks* (London: Heinemann, 1987): 155.

82. See David Chidester, *Shots in the Streets: Violence and Religion in South Africa* (Boston: Beacon Press, 1991), 87-111.

83. L. Jones, "Right-wing Evangelicals and South Africa," *Moto*, 64 (April, 1988): 12.

84. See Pippa Green, "Apartheid and the Religious Right," *Christianity and Crisis*, 47, 14 (1987): 326-28; Paul Gifford, *The Religious Right in Southern Africa* (Harare: University of Zimbabwe Publications, 1988); and Gifford, *The New Crusaders: Christianity and the New Right in Southern Africa* (London: Pluto Press, 1991). American evangelical, fundamentalist, or pentecostal ministries, often with right-wing political agendas, have established themselves widely throughout Africa and the so-called Third World. As Edwin S. Gaustad has noted, the ministry of an evangelist such as Oral Roberts "is most likely to endure far from Tulsa in the Third World, where his special brand of healing pentecostalism has demonstrated its sweeping appeal." Gaustad, "Review: David Edwin Harrell Jr., *Oral Roberts: An American Life*," *Journal of American History*, 72 (1986): 952.

85. R. Hunsicker, "South Africa: Nation of Strong Religious Values," *Family Protection Scoreboard* (Costa Mesa, CA: Biblical Scoreboards, 1987), 13.

86. Concerned Evangelicals, *Evangelical Witness in South Africa: A Critique of Evangelical Theology and Practice by Evangelicals Themselves* (Dobsonville: Concerned Evangelicals, 1986), 4, 34.

87. Peter Major and Stephano Ghersi, *South Africa, the 51st State* (Randburg: Fastdraft, 1989), 239, 215, 233, 10.

88. Stanley Tambiah introduced the term "galactic polity" into the analysis of centralized religiopolitical systems in southeast Asia. "The Galactic Polity," in Stanley J. Tambiah, *Culture, Thought, and Social Action* (Cambridge: Harvard University Press, 1985), 252-86.

89. Alan K. Henrikson, "America's Changing Place in the World: From 'Periphery' to 'Centre'?," in Jean Goffmann, ed., *Centre and Periphery: Spatial Variation in Politics* (Beverly Hills and London: Sage, 1980), 79.

90. Hamilton Foley, ed., *Woodrow Wilson's Case for the League of Nations* (Princeton: Princeton University Press, 1923).

91. *New York Times* (23 May 1977).

92. David Chidester, "Saving the Children by Killing Them: Redemptive Sacrifice in the Ideologies of Jim Jones and Ronald Reagan," *Religion in American Culture: A Journal of Interpretation*, 1 (1991): 177-201; Tami R. Davis and Sean M. Lynn-Jones, " 'Citty upon a Hill,' " *Foreign Policy*, 66 (Spring, 1987): 20-38.

93. Emile Durkheim and Marcel Mauss, *Primitive Classification*, trans. Rodney Needham (London: Cohen and West, 1963), 87.

94. *Cape Times* (17 February 1990).

95. *International Herald Tribune* (30 June-1 July 1990); *Daily Mail* (20 June 1990); *New York Times* (17 June 1990); *Vrye Weekblad* (29 June 1990); *Time* (2 July 1990): 12.

96. *Daily Mail* (20 June 1990); *International Herald Tribune* (2 July 1990); *New York Times* (24 June 1990); *The Tennessean* (28 June 1990).

97. *Time* (2 July 1990): 14.

98. *Daily Mail* (20 June 1990); *International Herald Tribune* (30 June-1 July 1990).

99. *Argus* (31 January 1991).

100. Victor Turner and Edith Turner, *Image and Pilgrimage in Christian Culture* (New York: Columbia University Press, 1978), 39, 3. See Victor Turner, "The Center Out There: The Pilgrim's Goal," *History of Religions*, 12 (1973): 191-230; and "Pilgrimages as Social Processes," *Dramas, Fields, and Metaphors: Symbolic Action in Human Society* (Ithaca: Cornell University Press, 1974), 166-230.

101. Lewis V. Baldwin, *To Make the Wounded Whole: The Cultural Legacy of Mar-

tin Luther King, Jr. (Minneapolis: Fortress Press, 1992), 203. See George M. Houser, "Freedom's Struggle Crosses Oceans and Mountains: Martin Luther King, Jr., and the Liberation Struggles in Africa and America," in Peter J. Albert and Ronald Hoffman, eds., *We Shall Overcome: Martin Luther King, Jr., and the Black Freedom Struggle* (New York: Pantheon Books, 1990), 169–96.

102. Minter, *King Solomon's Mines Revisited*, 137.

103. An alternative account of how America became the "center of the world"—through African labor—was advanced by W. E. B. Du Bois: "From being a mere stopping place between Europe and Asia or a chance treasure house of gold, America became through African labor the center of the sugar empire and the cotton kingdom and an integral part of that world industry and trade which caused the Industrial Revolution and the reign of capitalism." *The World and Africa* (New York: International Publishers, 1965), 227–28.

104. *Cape Times* (21 January 1992); Turner and Turner, *Image and Pilgrimage in Christian Culture*, 3.

105. Sacvan Bercovitch, "The Problem of Ideology in American Literary History," in Sacvan Bercovitch and Myra Jehlen, eds., *Ideology and Classic American Literature* (Cambridge: Harvard University Press, 1986), 645; Giles Gunn, *Thinking Across the American Grain: Ideology, Intellect, and the New Pragmatism* (Chicago: University of Chicago Press, 1992), 32.

106. Joseph Th. Leerssen, "On the Edge of Europe: Ireland in Search of Oriental Roots, 1650–1850," *Comparative Criticism*, 8 (1986): 109. See Peter Mason, *Deconstructing America: Representations of the Other* (London: Routledge, 1990). On European first images, discovery, invention, or conquest of the space of America, see Fredi Chiapelli, ed., *First Images of America: The Impact of the New World on the Old*. 2 vols. (Berkeley: University of California Press, 1976); Edmundo O'Gorman, *The Invention of America: An Inquiry into the Historic Nature of the New World and the Meaning of Its History* (Bloomington: Indiana University Press, 1961); Tzvetan Todorov, *The Conquest of America*, trans. R. Howard (New York: Harper and Row, 1984); and C. Vann Woodward, *The Old World's New World* (New York: Oxford University Press, 1991).

107. William Brandon, *New Worlds for Old: Reports from the New World and Their Effect on the Development of Social Thought in Europe, 1500–1800* (Athens: Ohio University Press, 1986); Herman Lebovies, "The Uses of America in Locke's *Second Treatise on Government*," *Journal of the History of Ideas*, 47 (1986): 567–81.

108. Cited in Gunther Barth, *Fleeting Moments: Nature and Culture in American History* (New York: Oxford University Press, 1990), xviii.

109. Ferdinand Kurnberger, *Der Amerika-Müde: Amerikanisches Kulturbild* (Frankfurt a. Main: Meidinger, 1855): 1; cited and trans. in Hugh Ridley, *Images of Imperial Rule* (London: Croom Helm; New York: St. Martins Press, 1983), 30. On British, French, and German images of America, see Hugh Honour, *The New Golden Land: European Images of America from the Discoveries to the Present Time* (London: Allen Lane, 1975); Honour, *The European Vision of America* (Cleveland: Cleveland Museum of Art and the National Gallery, 1976); Allan Nevins, ed., *America through British Eyes* (New York: Oxford University Press, 1948); Richard L. Rapson, *Britons View America* (Seattle: University of Washington Press, 1971); Durand Echeverria, *Mirage in the West: A History of the French Image of American Society to 1865* (Princeton: Princeton University Press, 1968); and Theresa Mayer Hammond, *American Paradise: German Travel Literature from Duden to Kisch* (Heidelberg: Carl Winter Universitätsverlag).

110. Jean Baudrillard, *America*, trans. Chris Turner (London: Verso, 1989), 5, 99, 63, 9.

111. Yi-Fu Tuan, *Space and Place: The Perspective of Experience* (Minneapolis: University of Minnesota Press, 1977), 99.

112. Ray Allen Billington, *Land of Savagery, Land of Promise: The European Image of the American Frontier in the Nineteenth Century* (New York: Norton, 1981).

113. R. David Arkush and Leo O. Lee, eds., *Land Without Ghosts: Chinese Impressions of America from the Mid-Nineteenth Century to the Present* (Berkeley: University of California Press, 1989), 177–80. For a collection of immigrant accounts of America, see Thomas Kessner and Betty Boyd Caroli, *Today's Immigrants, Their Stories: A New Look at the Newest Americans* (New York: Oxford University Press, 1981).

114. Joseph J. Corn, *The Winged Gospel: America's Romance with Aviation, 1900–1950* (New York: Oxford University Press, 1983), 30.

115. Douglas Curran, *In Advance of the Landing: Folk Concepts of Outer Space* (New York: Abbeville Press, 1985). In general, the U.S. space program has had an ambivalent effect on American spatial orientations, symbolizing the potential, as Dale Carter has argued, for both national unity and global totalitarianism. See Dale Carter, *The Final Frontier: The Rise and Fall of the American Rocket State* (New York: Verso, 1988).

116. James J. Flink, *The Automobile Age* (Cambridge: MIT Press, 1988).

117. Joshua Meyrowitz, *No Sense of Place: The Impact of Electronic Media on Social Behavior* (New York: Oxford University Press, 1985), 7.

118. Jean Comaroff, *Body of Power, Spirit of Resistance: The Culture and History of a South African People* (Chicago: University of Chicago Press, 1985), 203, 238. See Sundkler, *Bantu Prophets of South Africa*, 183.

119. Harold Kaplan, *Power and Order: Henry Adams and the Naturalist Tradition in American Fiction* (Chicago: University of Chicago Press, 1981).

120. *Weekly Mail* (23 October 1992).

121. Henrikson, "America's Changing Place in the World," 94.

8

AMERICAN SACRED SPACE AND
THE CONTEST OF HISTORY

Rowland A. Sherrill

The state is nearly 400 miles across, but the twisting road must
have added at least 100 miles to that. In any case, every time I
looked at the map I seemed to have moved a remarkably tiny distance. From time to time I would pass a sign that said HISTORI-
CAL MARKER AHEAD, but I didn't stop. There are thousands
of historical markers all over America and they are always dull. I
know this for a fact because my father stopped at every one of
them. He would pull the car up to them and read them aloud to
us, even when we asked him not to. . . . You knew before you
got there that they would be boring because if they had been even
remotely interesting somebody would have set up a hamburger stand
and sold souvenirs.　　　　　　—Bill Bryson, *The Lost Continent:*
　　　　　　　　　　　　　　　Travels in Small-Town America

THIS CHAPTER EXPLORES the concept and questions of sacred space in
America as they have been rendered problematical by the cultural conditions pressing on them at the close of the so-called "American Century."
Deeply imbedded in the mythography of American civil religion, as it is
both localized and nationalized, special revered or "hallowed" sites have
long been fundamental elements of a powerfully sustaining worldview
in American self-understanding. The designation of a spot in the landscape or culturescape as "sacred" results from human decision-making, a
result flowing from perceptions of the special, spiritual meanings associated with the site. If the designation is collectively compelling, it subsequently entails the imaginative operations of coordinating those religious meanings with others in the community of belief and commitment
and of interpreting and maintaining the place, role, and significance of the
"site" in the continuing traditions of the community. Recently, however,

313

predicaments of social and social-psychological, economic, and political experience in contemporary cultural existence have conspired not only to fracture collective senses of American meaning about these symbolic places and indeed to create conflict over them but also to hamper the perception and imagination of sacrality itself at its very sources and in its integral operations.

In what follows, then, the purpose is to clarify the complexities of "sacred space"—its sources, terms, and dynamics—in such a way that critical inquiry can detect its entanglements with American religious meanings and why and how it might have suffered some losses in the contest with American history. First, the exploration will examine the implications of this sacralization process in some elements of the stuff of American civil religion and pose questions about how the process might be thought compromised in transitions into the current era. Then, in composing a rudimentary anatomy of American sacred space out of three recent, representative works, the inquiry devotes itself to the manner and matter of the sacralization process as it has worked in some crucial cases in American experience. Finally, the essay will turn to those courses and directions, dilemmas and conditions, which, also running deeply in the American grain, might be thought to have *dis*-located the senses and meanings of American "place" and to put extreme pressures on this form of American religious imagination at century's end.

Senses of Sacred Place and American Religious Meanings

In 1982, Dan Wakefield published *Under the Apple Tree*, one of his less-celebrated novels set in the Midwest, which depicts the "home front" during World War II. The narrative arrives through the experiences and reflections of fourteen-year-old Artie, whose older brother Roy has been sent overseas. Artie, at home, struggles not only with his version of small-town adolescence but with his own felt implication in the national war effort—standing home-guard for enemy aircraft, gathering metal, and the like—and the musings at the closure of the novel present a compact crystallization of some issues and ideas of sacred space in America:

> In the crisp clear days of October, America was beautiful, just like in the song. Artie had never been "from sea to shining sea," nor had he seen "the purple mountains' majesty" but he knew they were out there, believed in them, and saw every day with his own eyes the beauty of the

gentle hills, the creeks and cornfields, the solid old white frame houses and the ancient oaks of Town. He believed, in fact, that God had "shed his grace" on this land, that this grace was tangible, visible, in the arch of rainbows over wet fields, the slant of shed sunlight on the sides of old barns. His pride in his country was sustained by the signs of nature and the symbols of men, not only the bright stars and stripes that flew from public buildings and hung from private porches but the comforting, everyday emblems of home: Bob's Eats, Joe's Premium, Mail Pouch Tobacco. This was what Roy and all the other boys were fighting to save, preserve, and protect, along with the people who were lucky enough to live in and of it, and all this was sacred, worthy of any sacrifice, including life itself, for without it, life would be hollow and dumb.

Sometimes home seemed so beautiful and right it was hard to believe the War was really going on out there in the fringes of the world, the bleak foreign battlegrounds and alien oceans.[1]

Compressed within these paragraphs, a little gem of American civil religious "evidence," are perceptions and processes which bear decisively on the question of sacred space in America in the second half of the Twentieth Century: home, place, projection; location, sense, and imagination; center, orientation, and *terra incognita*.

On its face, the quotation might seem easily dismissed as just so much nostalgia on Wakefield's part, as he writes in the more complicated 1980s about a somehow ideally less complicated and more mythically sound time and place or as just so much chimerical conflation on Artie's part of "home" and "homeland" pressed into the service of the author's depiction of a metaphysics of patriotism. But, even as evidence constituted out of imaginative expression, there is that here which "rings true" with respect to a number of discursive interpretations of sacred space stemming from the various intellectual disciplines. Jonathan Z. Smith issues the reminder that, for all its frequent distortions of memory, a sense of meaningful "[p]lace as home-place appears to be pre-eminently a category of nostalgia (a word derived from the Greek *nostos*, 'to return home'), of *Heimweh* ('homesickness')."[2] Even with the possibility that Wakefield wants to create an American primordium as a purely fictive venture, to conjure a time in which an identification of a "sacred America" could be recognized and warranted by a broad civic faith, Artie's particular homologization of national space with locative place evinces some of the rudiments and dynamics of the sacralization process.

The passage certifies, in its way, the insistence of humanistic geography both that "space" must become significant "place" in the sacralization process and that "to interpret the meaning of places . . . is to interpret the subjective meaning of persons."[3] As a locus of meaning, Yi-Fu Tuan argues: *Meaning of places = subjective meaning of persons.*

> "Space" is more abstract than "place" [although their meanings often merge]. What begins as undifferentiated space becomes place as we get to know it better and endow it with value. . . . The ideas "space" and "place" require each other for definition. From the security and stability of place, we are aware of the openness, freedom, and threat of space, and vice versa. Furthermore, if we think of space as that which allows movement, then place is pause; each pause in movement makes it possible for [spatial] location to be transformed into place.[4]

Thus, for Artie, "Town," local artifact, topography, take on the "virtues" of significant place—experienced in the "pause" of childhood, made more intimate still by the "storied" character of the scene (as the novel inscribes this), taken up in feeling and endowed with religious meaning and value (for those lucky enough to be "of it"), demarcated or differentiated from and yet continuous with the larger abstract or as-yet-untravelled space, centered symbolically (the apple-tree) and orienting with respect to general landscape ("purple mountains' majesty"), nation (America as blessed), world (fringed with "bleak battlegrounds" and "alien oceans"), and cosmos (a universe in which God sheds grace on some).

Following from elements of this experiential geography, the understanding of sacred space can be complicated with a lexicon drawn from studies of visual, poetic, and narrative arts, as, for instance, with the definition Alan Gussow provides of "a sense of place"—a set of perceptions issuing from deep experience of "a piece of the whole environment that has been claimed by feelings".[5] Such a place, in turn, establishes "a place of sense," a place in which life achieves fuller coherence and significance, in which place the religious person can identify the sacred and from which sacred place a "sense of the whole" can be developed.[6] If such a sense of the whole environment can be thought grounded in the empirics of an immediate "setting," experienced as sacred in terms of what Tuan elsewhere describes as "topophilia,"[7] then it matters not at all if this piece of sacred "ground," claimed *in situ* "by feelings," is a mythically designated natural location (Mount Fuji), a ritually inscribed "rational landscape" (Mecca) or edifice (the Church of the Holy Sepulchre), a personally discovered patch of "wilderness" acreage (Annie Dillard's Tinker Creek), or a slowly realized small setting coalescent of topography, artifactual life, storied events,

In this sense, could meditation on "groove spaces" become spaces of significance as well?

317
American Sacred Space and the Contest of History

sensations, and beliefs (Artie's "Town"). To the extent, in fact, that one gains "a sense of place" of any of these which renders it also "a place of sacred sense," then it matters not at all if it is "a place of big sense." It can just as easily be "a place of little sense," when that phrase is used, as Gary Comstock invokes it, to indicate not "no sense" but that anchoring, orienting, unifying view composed out of the small incidents, images, visuals, tactiles, and associations, which come to occupy inordinately large, even centralizing "space" in memory and meaning.[8] For Comstock, the sense of the place is grounded in memories of "Grandma's Backbone, Dougie's Ankles"; for Artie, "Joe's Premium," "Bob's Eats," "old white frame houses," just as much as "the signs of nature and the symbols of men". When vested with the sacred, the "place of sense" establishes and orders the whole environment situationally and relationally: as Smith might put it, such a sense, such a place, locates one "in place" and construes a world in which everything has "its place".[9]

Accounts of "sacred space" in sociopolitical theory extend the consideration outward toward the places of "bigger sense". As Carlton Hayes and Wilbur Zelinsky have pointed out in their analyses of religious implications in nationalism, the "sacred nation," which encompasses and is referent for inclusive geographical territory, has become for many in the modern world a potent, if abstract locus of sacred space, even as its symbolic substance might work at some remove from the daily experience of the people.[10] For Artie, of course, America is "out there" symbolically, including home and him in its reservoir of meanings and under its protective canopy; he is lucky enough to be "in it" and "of it". Thus, even with distinctions like those Hayes, Zelinsky, and others want to make among "nationalism" (a *mentalité* respecting the collective identity of a "people" spread over vast territories),[11] "patriotism" (associated with *patrie*, "fatherland," and referent to a smaller, more specific space), and "homeland" (the stuff of *pays*, "topophilia," the more immediate locale),[12] it seems clear with regard to the question of sacred space that these forms of commitment can interpenetrate. The most empirically local "home" can help make the meaning of the symbolic nation; the sacred nation, in turn, can help supply the meaning made of home. If Artie's sacred America seems grounded ineluctably in "patriotism," in what Zelinsky defines as "an emotion experienced as love of, or loyalty toward, one's immediate environs,"[13] as *pays* and *patrie* become coextensive, the religious vocabulary of Artie's "Americanism" suggests, for him, the transcendent character of the nation. In short, he expresses "nationalism . . . [an] intense devotion to

relates to McDannell

the nation, that real or supposed community of individuals who are convinced they share a common set of traditions, beliefs, and cultural characteristics so precious that no sacrifice is too great for its preservation or
advancement."[14] Sacred space, in this formation, is symbolic space, abstraction realized in collective subjectivity, funded by local experience and
vaunting imagination, held intact by social faith.] → Key Definition

For a more explicit grammar of faith respecting sacred space, however, the views of the religionists can be called to contribute. Utilizing
thematics apparently derived from Mircea Eliade's *The Sacred and the Profane*,[15] Joel P. Brereton, for instance, explains the establishment and functions of sacred space for the sensibility of *homo religiosus.* For Brereton,
the sacred place combines one or more of several elements: the place is
differentiated, discrete from ordinary spaces; the place is mythically
inscribed, inherited from a community, a tradition; the place is consecrated through ritual actions performed there; the place is discovered to
be endowed with religious meanings; the place contains the presence of
the gods.[16] While these elements are probably fully sensical only to those,
like Artie, whose perceptions of the landscape are molded by and filtered
through a certain style of religious conviction and interpretation, they can
intersect with the other kinds of descriptions and analyses of sacred space.
They have the explanatory effect of describing how certain rudiments of
"a sense of place" might transform a site into "a place of sacred sense"
under the presiding aegis of a theological imagination, even a vague or un-
tutored one like Artie's, charged only by a broad civic faith. In such interpretations, sacred space is not only, or simply, a matter of an experiential
or perceptual geographics, or a depth or unity of coherence achieved in
aesthetics, or a transcending abstraction of sociopolitics, some "sacred nation" built on and out of homeland patriotics, but, rather, a matter of "the
holy" made manifest, of transcendence and immanence, of the numinous
palpable or "felt" in the landscape. Without connection to some such lexicon of religious sensibility, as Tuan at least recognizes, no space large or
small, regardless of how taken up in loyalty or emotion, gets the adjectival
empowerment of "sacred".[17]

Now, while there are other entrances into the understanding of sacred
space, these four broad viewpoints—from geography, aesthetics, sociopolitics, religion—can be held in tension and yet in balance, and together they
provide a particular vantage point for taking up the question of sacred
space in America toward the end of the twentieth century.[18] It seems to
follow from these four avenues into the question of sacred space that, as

Smith asserts, no space or place is intrinsically sacred,[19] that the sacrality of a place, sensible or symbolic, is a function of human recognition or attribution, that the sense of the sacred is always implicated in local forms of culturally conditioned sense-making, and that, as Belden Lane argues, any space, so transformed into "place" by discovery, experience, communal decision, mythic prescription, royal decree, ritual action, or perceived numinal modifier, can become an "emplacement" of the sacred.[20]

On this line of reasoning, sacred space can be thought to exist largely as potentiality, its realization or recognition or maintenance completely predicated and dependent on responsive religious sensibility. It becomes problematical when the warrants or conditions for such a response are removed or eroded or somehow invalidated. What happens when a so-called secular age, stripped for many of any credible prospect of "the holy," stunted in its senses of any transcendent and yet present spirit, makes the identification of any sacred space—in fact, the whole category of "the sacred"—a difficult, even whimsical matter? What happens when the "symbolic space" of the "sacred nation" is discovered to be just so much finite and exigent business or when the very idea of "the nation" is sundered by pervading rifts in any, now dubious, shared traditions, experiences, and values, much less any "collective identity"? What happens when the current experience and the defining logic of the contemporary sociolcultural imagination undermine the discernment of any orienting "places of sense"? What happens, indeed, when the claim and character of modern social-psychological conditions work to prevent even any "senses of place"? What happens when the people in a place suffer the loss of such primary and symbolic spatial orientation and identity, when such *loci* of meaning and commitment become problematical? What *has* happened, at last, when Artie's equations—of place, sacrality, symbolic space, home, homeland, and sacred America—seem possible, even rightful for nostalgic faith, even as late as the 1940s but somehow "merely" adolescent in the 1990s?

Such questions are not merely rhetorical when some of the most compelling recent critical testimony suggests that these things *have* happened, broadly and decisively, in America in the late twentieth century. Nor are such questions pertinent and significant only to those whose religious and ideological efforts seek to reify the "sacred nation" or to those whose restive spiritual cravings must, even yet, find objective outlet. If in a different way, the questions are also serious ones for those fields of cultural studies that attend to elements of tradition and change, cultural predicament and response, the ways and means of cultural diagnosis and revision. From that standpoint and in terms of that intellectual charter, three recent studies of American sacred space seem broadly representative of work on distinctively American and decidedly modern facets and forms of the sacralization process. John Sears's *Sacred Places*, a study of nineteenth-century tourist sites, provides clues about what might now be altered by detailing what seemed more broadly possible under earlier, far different religious and cultural warrants and conditions.[21] Edward Tabor Linenthal's *Sacred Ground*, elaborating a pattern of American veneration of historic battle-fields, provokes attention to the dynamics of mythohistorical accretion in the work of tradition-maintenance even today.[22] And Belden Lane's *Land-scapes of the Sacred*, which traces the modes and possibilities of some spiritual seeking, suggests how sacred space might yet be located in the responses of American spirituality in quests for even personal "enclaves" of religious location.[23] While each of these, and a number of other works, isolate various responses to the situation, described in Joshua Meyrowitz's title, of *No Sense of Place*,[24] they also help to lift up some crucial terms and conditions of the sacralization process as it flows in historical currents which might be thought to wash it away.

Sacred Space and American "Evidentiary" Places

Among others, Sears, Linenthal, and Lane all concentrate on the matter of American sacred space and do so in ways which, cumulatively, compose at least a general anatomy of the complex of issues surrounding studies in this area. One facet of the subject at hand is pressed forward immediately by all three studies—namely, that, in the world of naming the "sacred," the receptive and attributive imagination is surely the name of the game. By examining the modes in which the three conceive the sacralization process, by assaying their analyses of sources, mechanisms, and channels through which Americans have identified and "constructed" sacred places, and by following out the logic of their interpretations, it becomes more possible to "clear" American "sacred space" as a concept, to begin to determine what makes Artie's sacralizing imagination tick and, indeed, what might have happened to Artie in the meantime.

Sears's *Sacred Places* follows a cultural-historical approach which takes the key terms of its approach with full seriousness. As he surveys the national scenes which allured the nineteenth-century American tourist,[25] he is fully attentive to the cultural situations that condition allure, the historical factors and forms of consciousness at play in specific times and places. He wants to know what in a specific site evokes the recognition of its sacred character—that is, how a place in its own physical make-up might be thought to elicit the adjectival attribution "sacred" and how, then, that attribution ramifies as a broad cultural phenomenon. In this way, he is bent on deciphering the fundaments and dynamics of a process that begins with the allusive nature of a scene as that then is met by the receptive imagination, itself in turn apparently self-commissioned to articulate the sacrality of the place. That articulation subsequently lends itself to a broader cultural *production* of the scene for future pilgrims or tourists, with the process reaching closure in considerations of the *fate* of the sacred site when the cultural modifiers dissipate or are altered. At its best, this inquiry teaches crucial lessons about the ways propelling and defining religious energies are *always* entangled in America with other forms of cultural desire.

Among the clear strengths of Sears's book, therefore, one finds especially valuable the canny ways he is able to specify some of the toe-holds that a form of American imagination, most particularly under the charge of a mounting nativist romanticism, once located in an abundant and variegated physical setting, the stuff of America Wakefield's Artie knows is "out there". Sears is especially astute in showing how the receptions and articulations of these specific sites, these (unique) places, are pinned on and are elaborated in answer to an American craving for a more general sacred and abstract nationalistic "space," articulations to which Artie is also heir. Among other clear virtues, *Sacred Places* provides refined critical angles on how Sears's cases in point index what might be a kind of class-structure in the rudiments of the sacralization process and demonstrates the power of "marketing" principles for selling the efficacy of the "sacred" site in a large, plural, and spread-out society.

For theoretical underpinnings, Sears relies heavily on the thought of Mircea Eliade for a conceptual vocabulary of religion—a tactic which at first blush would seem to implicate his agenda in Eliade's insistence on the "ontic" character of "the sacred". It is finally clear, however, that while Sears views the sacred place as allusive, to be sure, he nonetheless concludes that sacrality is a function of the attributive imagination at its seat and center. And, while Eliade deals in over-arching "genera," the universal phenomenon, Sears clearly deals as historian in the localized specificities of the phenomena. If Sears occasionally seems short on attention to the implications of his own demonstraton that the "sacrality" of the sites he studies is finally inscribed by, with, and in *narrative* formulation, his work even so keeps itself firmly grounded in the particularities of perception brought to and iterated out of these spots in the American terrain.

With Edward Linenthal's *Sacred Ground*, the title itself signals a different approach, aimed at a different objective. As with Sears, "sacred" remains an adjective, but Sears's plural "places" now become singular "ground," a ground on which broad and commanding features of national faith might be disclosed. Thus, while Linenthal remains attentive to the cultural-historical particularities of his various battlefields, he is rather more bent on locating the containing pattern—from Lexington and Concord, to the Alamo, to Gettysburg, to the Little Bighorn, to Pearl Harbor—and on tapping the successive stuff of "veneration, defilement, and redefinition" which represents the common denominator from one field to the next. Out of these discrete "grounds," he digs a structural pattern of complex reciprocities between the stuff of univocal memory and the crucible of contemporary plural and competitive desires, an interflow which belongs to the matter of the *maintenance of sacrality* in a heterodox social world. Each of these places comes to qualify as "sacred ground" as it moves from ordinary and only locally storied "site" through a "hallowing" experience which makes it nationally storied, then ritually inscribed by the constructive imagination, into a situation of "custodianship vs. conflict". By tracking this processive structure from case to case, Linenthal is able to locate decisive clues about some crucial, competing facets in the nature of the American symbolic imagination—at once, ostensibly, somewhat "Protestant" in its seriousness respecting history, somewhat Catholic in its location of the telling icon, but surely also somewhat New World in the chimerical terms of its operative memory.

Among other assets, *Sacred Ground* provides alert exposition of the ways historical experience is gobbled up by nationalistic faith in the dynamics of the American imagination, with both experience and faith captive ultimately to a metaphysics of craving distinctively American. Part of this can be seen in the ways Linenthal centers on the structures of heroism and sacrifice in the American frame: these various grounds are hallowed by historical incident, by the spilled blood of patriots (thus using Lincoln, in effect, as a key religious-studies conceptual resource on sacred space), and, with this, Linenthal teaches something important about the martial dimension of the American mind, a dimension clearly charging young Artie's home-front efforts, not to mention his assertion "that all this was sacred, worthy of any sacrifice." On this same count, the study demonstrates well how certain "sacred" sites arrive not only "topographically" (as the expectant romantic imagination Sears explores finds its sacralizing occasion in an allusive physical scene) but "historically," grounds hallowed by actions on them and thus presented to the operations of receptive patriotic faith not by virtue of what was discovered there but of what "*happened* there" quickly made mythic. In this account, moreover, a unique form of access opens to the ideas and issues of canon-formation as enacted in a democratic and pluralistic framework, to the terms of subsequent custodianship in the theological labors of "patriotic orthodoxy," and to the situation and necessities of a continuing hermeneutics in a culture, a believing community, greatly defined by its malleable memory.

Although Linenthal takes only indirect recourse to theoretical resources in the study of religion, only small extrapolations can work to determine how his work gives approaches to American religion different subjects to look at and different angles of vision for the looking. With his examination of the mobilized "rhetorics" of the relative orthodoxies and heresies at moments of contention, for instance, the consideration can quickly extend to a calculation of how those "rhetorics" borrow from or are grounded in the stuff of a larger commanding and containing mythic framework, in civil-religious terms, which enables the rhetorics of orthodoxy and heterodoxy alike.[26]

Belden Lane's *Landscapes of the Sacred* returns inquiry to the plural places or grounds on which the sacralizing imagination might be thought to work. But "sacred" has now become a noun, an entity, a thing which, if abstract, clearly overrides any particular landscape or indeed all cultural and physical landscapes. The compelling specities of natural scene or historic site dealt with by Sears and Linenthal are replaced for Lane by the power or prospect of numinous presences. The book explores the character of that form of religious imagination which might be restorative for a sustaining spirituality, itself in turn conducive for a revitalized sense of the sacrality of the whole landscape. Lane proposes four axioms for studying the "mythogenesis" of sacred space: (1) the place, vested with numinous power, "chooses" the seeker; (2) the place can be ordinary, only recognized as sacred through ritual actions performed there; (3) the place is existentially discovered by way of a concording state of consciousness; (4) the place is both local and universal as God is there and everywhere.[27] All of this depends on a form of religious disposition and desire as the seeker moves toward that which he or she needs. Lane finds instructive guides to such cultivated spirituality in the narrative voices of the nature-religionists, mystic-saints, poets and artists, whose quickened sense of the "presences" to be felt, thought, intuited, even conjured, in this place or that might lead a renewed spirituality to a perception of "the sacred," as a noun, generated out of something at least akin to a revived sacramentalist vision of experience. Just so, young Artie in the Wakefield novel does not directly encounter "the holy" so much as he has inherited the belief, confirmed by his own perceptions, "that God had 'shed his grace' on this land, that this grace was tangible, visible." The key, Lane argues, is the recognition of numinous inscriptions, the discovery of the independent existence and the portentous work of the Holy in the landscape, and then, somewhat paradoxically, the consumed, consuming, and consummating work of the attributive human imagination. For Lane, then, the sacralization process thus pivots at an existential triangulation of time and space and supernature (human imagination and the Holy having "met" in some locale) in moments made possible by a spirituality itself stemming from a faith in the possibility of just such moments).

Belden Lane's study issues the reminder that, in treating of the matter of sacred space, the originating subject is *homo religiosus.* Concentrating on what religious people have said they religiously experienced, Lane's four axioms for the study of sacred place refuse to reduce that testimony. In this, Lane bedrocks on a fact apparently less attended these days but one which adamantly will not go away—viz., that a condition for the recognition or designation of sacrality is being religious to begin with. With all of the insistence of the book about this, however, Lane also displays some dexterity in appropriating and then building from the best of those so-called "secular" articulations of senses of place—in narratives supplied by, say, Edward Abbey—without baptizing them in the name of the sought spirituality.

Landscapes of the Sacred might vex some students of American sacred space because Lane's own spiritual desires and the forms of his intellectual inquiry sometimes disappear into each other, thus making his work at such junctures a subject, evidence of a case in point, to study more than a theoretical resource with which to study. And, utilizing an approach that finally sails over particular landscapes for the sake of a cultivated soulscape, Lane pursues his topic in a way that equally sails past what might be thought quite distinctively American in it with respect to physical, cultural, and temporal modifiers. In many ways, Edward Abbey's desert of the American Southwest might as well be the Sahara as not. Nonetheless, even if topography and significant occurrence are displaced by a kind of timeless soul-scape in which the situated character of the actors is not sufficiently plumbed, the study recalls to attention the idea that the sacred "geography" referred to in Lane's subtitle is a map, a cartography, of human interiority and that, to deal with sacred space is to struggle, as Yi-Fu Tuan argues, with the subjective meanings of persons.

Accumulated in terms of these characterizations, then, it is possible to see how the three studies in part converge—or at least stand contiguously—to compose at least a broad anatomy of the concept of American sacred space. With Sears, one gets a concentration on the *origins* and *productions* of American sacred places founded on the allusive character of the landscape itself: it is a matter, at least at first, of what the site does to the onlookers. With Linenthal, one gets a different angle, this focused on *arrivals* and *recognitions* of sacred grounds founded on the momentous character of historical actions and commemorative responses: it is a matter, at least at first, of what the onlookers do to the site. With Lane, one gets yet another vista, this time centered on the *senses* and *structures* of immediacy, of "being there" in a sacred spot, taken into interiority by the receptive character of faith: it is a matter, at least at first, of what existentially occurs in the onlooker by virtue of inlook and outlook. Respecting all three studies, there is the reminder that senses of "sacred space" work in abstractions derived from and extended out of senses of sacred "places"—or, as Tuan puts it, "the pause in movement makes it possible for [spatial] location to be transformed into place." Thus, singly and cumulatively, these three authors establish and refine some terms of access and assessment for students of American religion as they approach and enter the complex territory of sacred space.

Furthermore, on the bases of this little anatomy, it seems possible to argue that something like this combination of inquiries might well be just the thing to begin to reinvigorate or rehabilitate the utility of the "civil religion" constellation of ideas in approaches to American religion. Because these ways of encircling and addressing the matter of American sacred space might put one kind of substance into the notion of "civil religions" deeply pluriform—and might as well "translate" into approaches to American sacred time, American sacred "this" or "that"—they insist that there are in fact ways both to acknowledge the power of the socially "organized" formations of religious life in America and at once to cut beneath or above or across all those species of religious association (whether institutional, doctrinal, denominational, traditional) to get to a kind of widely pervading religious *energy* in the general populace which is entangled in

Kay

locale, modified by the specificities of cultural existence, and yet referential to and at once constitutive of a pervading American faith whose essential ingredients and overall character might well always be exemplified most broadly by this "American" sacralizing imagination.[28] But there is much in the current age that conspires against such an imagination, as can be seen when one considers even only a few of the combatant factors against the sacralization of space in its contest with American history.

No Sense of Place, No Place of Sense

It is not difficult to suppose on the bases of most assessments of contemporary American experience that Artie's 1940s participation in the consecration of his hometown and his homologization of "home" with the blessed nation he knew was "out there" might well be compromised by the time of the last decade of the twentieth century. The flow of history itself would seem to veer away from the proper environment for such an imagination. Quite apart from the increasingly conflictual character of its once celebrated social pluralism and quite beyond the heightened mobility of Americans which truncates or diffuses the sense of home-place, the country has also passed through the kind of fracturing of its "national faith" portrayed in Robert Bellah's *The Broken Covenant*.[29] With that, America becomes a theater of pluriform, competing desires—a plethora of discrete and frequently contradictory meanings. Moreover, the loss of the sense of home "place," which in some respects was a loss that fueled additional fervor about nationalist "space," was also met by a hazard to the sensibilities promoting and sustaining the largest civil-religious meanings. The war in Southeast Asia, of course, had the effect, among other obvious consequences of social and generational divisiveness, of calling into radical question a rudiment of the very *mythos* of America, its blessed and exceptional character. The country could be seen, and certainly was felt, no longer to elude the claims of history: America was just one more erstwhile empire caught up in the finite and maculate stuff of geopolitical experience. Then, as the corruptions of leadership became more and more apparent, many had and have had to ponder whether, as Artie asserted, it was "worthy of any sacrifice". This question of "sacrifice" loomed larger still as economic factors began to attenuate any remaining senses that "home seemed so beautiful and right." Vaunted American abundance, the material signal of visibly shed "grace," might well have been—as for Artie—a linchpin of American senses of spiritual plenitude and well-being, or a palpable cornerstone of the *mythos*,[30] but now, trapped in the equations of intricate international economic vectors, American "prosperity" itself could be viewed much less as a result of the blessedness of the nation than as simply a matter of great, good, but altogether temporary luck. The majesty of purple mountains and "amber waves of grain" might yet be present, but the failures of ecological consciousness seemed to doom even these. Moreover, there soon arrived keener public senses of scarcity in the face of all that abundance. Homelessness and poverty clearly did not, do not, end relative general affluence, but they stand increasingly as reminders of something gone dreadfully wrong, just as riots in the street signal not only fractious social realities but the existence of what seems a permanent underclass. In the midst of all of this, as the broadest terms of identity and common meaning in American society seemed less and less possible, there is reason to think that, perhaps as a result, the cravings for community only intensified, though now directed, on the one hand, into the smaller enclaves of interest groups or, on the other, into the drives of new ethnic consciousness at more and more immediate levels—from nation to region, to neighborhood, to tribe. Whether cause or effect, such directions in the "shapes" of community conspire against any broad American community.

If these convolutions of contemporary experience contest the mythic framework of American civil-religious sensibilities in general, there are still other much more direct challenges, pressed forward in recent decades, that confront the particular imagination of "American sacred places" and thus America as abstract "sacred space". For one thing, an indisputable "homogenization" of the American landscape has created a kind of "sameness" about the environment: the superhighway, the proliferation of the strip mall, the growing "constancy" of what Artie referred to as "the symbols of men" from one place to the next (Burger King here is Burger King there), all have reduced the distinctiveness of those various landscapes which, as one moves through abstract space, might give one reason to pause, to gather in the unique sense of a site, to make space into "place," much less to make one or the other a "place of sense," to experience its symbolic potency. For another thing, the tendency pointed out by Sears with respect to the "production of place" has clearly been exacerbated, as if the beauty and even sublimity of certain sites were insufficient without the marketing of them, the re-creation and packaging of them for American appetites whetted to expect "more". Further, the current modes of "tourism" itself militate against being possessed by "the power of place" as the objective of the tour seems, rather, to be to possess the place in ever-increasing acquisitive acts of American consumption.[31]

Each and all of these factors can be seen to erode the landscape in ways which stunt the potential of places to seize upon the receptive imagination. But each is also part and parcel of a deep and growing disposition of the American mind to insert itself in the world technologically, and, quite beyond what the machine has done to the garden, this technology has created conditions as well which conspire profoundly against the very *forms* of imagination decisive for the recognition of sacred space. The flow of history in this direction forces inquiry to grapple with the more or less obvious facts that the imagination of sacred place also has a determining temporal dimension and that, for the receptive and attributive self, some cultural-historical moments afford more effectual prospects, more heightened possibilities, than others. The final throes of the twentieth century, having enshrined the universe of technology, seem to many cultural analysts especially to pose conditions and dilemmas for the American self that, in turn, can be thought deeply to undermine the work of the sacralizing imagination.

Kenneth Gergen's exploration of what he calls "the technologies of social saturation"[32] represents one kind of case in point. While not dealing directly with the ways modern communication modes might blockade the imagination of place, Gergen's study of the effects of "low" and "high" technologies leads to his insistence that these media have had consequences on forms of modern "selfhood" that put "the self under siege". Specifically, he argues, everything from the railroad, radio, postal service, television, to electronic mail and facsimile machines, has so rapidly accelerated the range and numbers of one's social relationships that an individual self finds itself "overpopulated" and indeed overwhelmed by its frequently obligatory or at least unavoidable connectedness to far too many other selves. While in some respects this technological creation of social propinquity might generate a self's surer appreciation of human interdependency, Gergen believes it can also eventuate in a person's becoming saturated to the extent that he or she experiences a "multiphrenic condition," the sensation of a "vertigo of unlimited multiplicity"[33] that costs one any persisting, stable sense of self. Out of balance, the self becomes nothing other than a function of myriad other selves, a residence inhabitated by the ghostly, commanding voices of those "others" from whom, now, the populated self cannot distinguish its separate identity, agency, or authorizing form of outlook and, so, cannot either choose among or coor-

dinate the numerous competitive and often contradictory values and perspectives of the multitudes in it.[34]

In the diagnostic musings about contemporary life in *The Message in
the Bottle*, Walker Percy picks up this matter of the contemporary dismantling of the authority of the self from a different but at least comparable
angle—namely, by considering the increasing hurdles posed by technology
necessarily faced by anyone who would seek "the sovereign discovery of
the thing before him,"[35] whether it be the Grand Canyon, a dogfish, or a
Shakespearean sonnet. The problem, according to Percy, is that modern
technological life has created a situation in which experience has become
so utterly mediated, or packaged for consumption, or overridden by theory,
or surrendered to the cult of experts, that a person stands little chance of
eluding the intermediations between him or her and the thing encountered. One's approach to the Grand Canyon, Percy contends, is by now
preceded by a preformulation of it delivered by postal cards, snapshots,
home movies, and television, which conditions the encounter to the degree
that the fullest "term of the sightseer's satisfaction . . . is the measuring up
of the thing to the criterion of the preformed symbolic complex."[36] Moreover, if one pushes on in the effort to experience what might be the extraordinary character of the place, the tour is prepackaged by the National Parks
Service, which manipulates or dictates just how the experience is to be
entered and, indeed, even understood. Similarly, the confrontation of a student with a dogfish in the biology lab not only extracts the thing out of the
environment in which it can be most fully appreciated and not only pack-
ages it for inspection but preconditions the encounter by regarding the
dogfish as a specimen to be understood under and only under the aegis of
"piscinological" theory and convention and, of course, the presiding peda-
gogue.

Even were one to stumble upon a scene or thing unprecedented by a
"preformed symbolic complex," the inclination of the modern self, having in effect "waived" the capacity for integral encounter, would be to
doubt the authenticity of his or her experience until or unless it could be
"certified" by some expert. Percy depicts the amusing, but also poignant,
plight of the young couple who, off the beaten path, quite inadvertently
witness a native ritual but who, though thrilled to think they just might
have seen "the real thing," need then to seek out and bring back to the
scene an ethnologist friend to accredit the genuineness of the experience.
Relinquishing the right of sovereign response, Percy makes clear, is not so
much a voluntary or even conscious surrender as it is virtually an inevita-

bility in an historical era and cultural circumstance under the sway of that technology, advertising, and consumerism, which create the self's expectations of experience, generate the craving for "products," and package and market them just so.

Such dilemmas of the American self presented by Gergen and Percy are compounded when the very structures of technology, quite apart from questions of saturation or advertising and consumption, change the nature of experience itself. As Joshua Meyrowitz argues, the omnipresence of electronic media especially makes it not only possible but actual that one need not even leave the room to gain access to "experience" once closed out to him or her by being situated in a particular physical place. "More and more," he observes, "people are living in a national (or international) information-system rather than a local town or city."[37] Although his study concentrates mainly, as the subtitle indicates, on "the impact of electronic media on social behavior," Meyrowitz recognizes that one of the significant alterations wrought by the media of simultaneity—particularly television—has been the felt obliteration of the distinction between "here," the place one is in, and "there," that place physically and formerly "other". And, as he recognizes along with Daniel Boorstin, among others, the technical capacity for "simultaneity" can also lead to the creation of "pseudo-events"—that is, *apparently* important "happenings" arranged, framed, edited, and presented by the media as "significant experience," at which and to which the place-bound viewer can be "present" and indeed is told she cannot afford to miss.[38] Thus, not only do technological delivery-systems have the potential effect, on the one hand, of leveling trivial and important matters to a common plane but, inadvertently or not, they can so manipulate matters, on the other hand, that the responding self has difficulty determining even the validity of the occurrence, much less its mundane or commanding character.

Such determinations become more difficult still when the self has been dislocated from any sense of "placement" that might help him or her gain some bearings at least. The communications technology might well mean, of course, that "home"—as the advertisement suggests—is anywhere there is a telephone, but it can also clearly rob "home" of any sense of distinctiveness and orientation, and all the more so, Gergen would add, when the "population" can enter it so freely. The imagination of the other so crucial for the identification and definition of the self can suffer deep atrophy when the other grows so present and so familiar. Additionally, however, the sheer range of exposure to "there" made possible by what Meyrowitz calls "homogenized access to space" has the effects both of

FB as sacred space?

; CRUCIAL - but are we really at this point?

creating a kind of "limitlessness" (really "placelessness") and of promoting "a new sense of access and openness to all places." Despite this counterfeit sensation of freedom from confinement, Meyrowitz contends, all "these exposures further increase the demystification of 'place' "[39]—one's own and the others—and dislocate the self from any center.

Directly or indirectly, each of these dilemmas of and challenges to American selfhood—all of which flow from contemporary historical aspirations themselves deeply embedded in the American grain—stand as obstacles to the imagination of sacred places, radically hamper the work of that receptive and interpretive sensibility involved in the sacralization process. This is not a matter simply of some so-called secular turn of mentality generated by new, massive image and information dispersals: the reasons are plentiful to think that *homo religiosus Americanus* is alive and well and serious about the work of consecration even in the midst of such cultural-historical binds. But it should be clear that these developments in recent history contest that work in significant ways. If Jonathan Z. Smith is accurate in thinking meaningful place is associated with the sense of the home-place, then the compromises of "home" experienced by the "saturated self" begin to debilitate the association. If Yi-Fu Tuan is correct that space must become significant "place" in the sacralization process, then the increasing dislocation, the "placelesness," of the contemporary self makes difficult indeed that pause in which a place is taken up in feelings or endowed with the self's subjective meanings, actions made all the more arduous when the "meanings" of that self are perhaps nothing other than functions of his or her population by myriad, contending others. Achieving a "sense of place," as Gussow contends is necessary, becomes no minor feat when the variety, distinctiveness, or special character of this or that site in the *plenum* might yet exist but when the conditions on perception in the technological universe work to reduce, to preformulate, to package the scene. How, indeed, can a place become a "place of sense" when one stands full of doubt about either the authenticity of the experience or the integral nature of one's own responses to it?

Such questions about the gnawing effects of contemporary history on the experience and imagination of place have an added bite when taken to the anatomy of the concept of sacred space constructed out of the work of Sears, Linenthal, and Lane, and the others their works can be thought in large measure to represent.

For Sears, the attribution of "sacred" to a particular site follows originally from the inhering allusive or symbolic character of the scene itself for those onlookers who possess a feel for the aesthetic or spiritual dimensions of its beautiful or mysterious or extraordinary character. While the late modern constrictions on this romantic imagination of the stuff of "the marvelous" are perfectly evident as a chapter in the shifting interpretive theories of Western cultural history, the fact should not be missed that, at center, the work of the sacralization process in this case is predicated decisively and simply on those alluring, unique "visuals" which still exist or which have their contemporary counterparts. In short, what compelled could yet—at least theoretically—compel the sacralizing sensibility, even if in a different interpretive mode. But the odds against this are grown formidable because the eradication of the senses of "here" and "there" reduce the mysterious difference on which "sacred place" rides, the bombardment of the self with an unlimited multiplicity of images homogenizes the uniqueness of any spot and dilutes senses of its special character, the "preformed symbolic complex" of the scene will never again permit one's seeing the place as if for the first time, the packaging of the scene will stymie one's own sovereign pause to make of it "a place of sense," much less a place of sacred sense. The special landscapes which attracted and fascinated those nineteenth-century tourists Sears studies might yet present their stunning vistas, but the sensibility now brought to such sights suffers such conditions of truncation that the attribution of "sacred" to them seems far less likely. Indeed, according to the current diagnoses, the more probable responses would be either dumb bafflement about what one ought to feel in the first "discovery" of such a place or disappointment about the failure of an already-inscribed scene to render consistently with the preformulated expectation of it.

A comparably attenuating situation might be thought to emerge with respect to those "hallowed" sites explored in Linenthal's study and to such new ones yet to be identified and claimed in memorialization. The sacrality of the battlegrounds—and of parallel cases of powerful historic moment—arrives not from the allusive natural vistas so much as from human recognitions that significant human actions and events, replete with religious meanings, have occurred on them. Present or not at such events, those who take custody of their significance and memory claim the "sites" in feelings and invest them with meanings, thereby constructing these grounds in ritual consecrations founded upon and expressive of frameworks of religious meaning central and authoritative in the attribution of sacrality. As Linenthal describes the matter, sure and certain interpretive faith guides those who "own" the site with the conviction that the "event" there and its meaning occurred within and should endure within the frame of canonical or orthodox memory. The preserved meaning and memory may be contested by "others," as Linenthal makes clear, but never by any lapse of custodial faith. For those who now, more recently, go to visit, to encounter, such reputedly sacred grounds, however, the conspiracy of historical developments against the sacralizing imagination is powerful. Although it could be thought that the temporal distance from the hallowing events might lend additional power and mystery to the grounds, it is also inevitable in the technological world that the approach to the Alamo or Pearl Harbor will be predictably conditioned by an already established symbolic complex. Moreover, upon arriving on the scene, one finds not the scene but a site constructed, packaged, for desired "orthodox" responses. Should these prove insufficient to channel or mediate the experience, or to convince the stranded self of the correct response, the expert stands nearby quite prepared not only to authenticate the proper experience but to certify the genuine meaning of it. ⊐ ᴵⁿᵗᵉˡˡᵉᶜᵗᵘᵃˡ journal re: Penn center & MLK

On the question of whether "new" such grounds—potent for the cravings of the sacralizing imagination—might yet be recognized and valorized for the religiously significant human actions suffered or performed upon them, the answer is obviously "yes": the fact that there exist obstacles to such recognitions does not necessarily diminish the needs and efforts of sensibilities bent on such work of consecration. Such historic "events," perhaps rich for religious interpretation, are indeed perhaps more possible now than the discovery of new natural vistas of spiritual allusiveness. Indeed, there are perhaps even now such events that loom large and portend much in American existence, but that have yet to be fully recognized, and that await the organizations of memory, emotion, and intellect to be inspired toward memorializations in space. But, again, the odds would seem considerable. The technics of simultaneity—making all events immediately near to the "self" which lives in vast information systems—not only rob such events of their mystery and power but have the effect of eroding their potential magnitude by leveling them with all of those other images delivered in proximity. Even were this not the case, the dislocated self, here but at once everywhere, and now having lapsed into dubiety about the authority of personal response, would have to hesitate before the possibility that the electronically witnessed scene lacked authenticity, that he or she was "viewing" only one more pseudo-event staged for media consumption. Even the most receptive sacralizing imagination would be forced to beat against such contemporary currents.[40]

Similar conditions would seem to beset the imagination of those "landscapes of the sacred" which Belden Lane explores. In Lane's view, of course, the location and attribution of sacrality occurs when the faithful self existentially encounters those places whose numinous character looms up for discovery or whose mystical "presence" meets that person prepared for its spiritual potency. The axis of sacrality is the spiritual seeker himself or herself, for the scene need not be religiously allusive or historically storied so much as it is any place wherein a cultivated religiosity runs upon the immediacies of holy power and mystery. Such a vibrant sacramentalist form of imagination, receptive to the presence of deity in "place," in *any* place, no doubt remains a possibility even in the universe of technology. If for no other reason than its functioning in inner life, in passionate subjectivity, it might appear less prey to the corrosive effects of those cultural-historical developments which contest the sacred character of a particular natural vista or a topographical field of human valor or sacrifice. Numinal presence, for those of faith, cannot be compromised by cultural history. But, just because it is so much a matter of the self's interiority, the necessary responsiveness of such a self to possible inscriptions of the holy in the landscape might well be thought to suffer compromise or, at least, to meet obstacles. In Gergen's point of view, positing that secure and stable inner life—out of which flows the work of sacralization—is problematical from the outset: one could never be certain, he would contend, that the cravings of spirituality were decisively one's own; indeed, it is more probable that such felt need was other-directed, a result of the multitude of other voices populating the self. And there are additional difficulties. Beyond the homogenizations of place confounding a self's identification of a locale's distinctiveness and beyond the electronic diffusions tending largely to demystify or to "familiarize" every place and, thus, precluding any sense of the extraordinary character of any place, Lane's sacralizing agent, just by dint of living in the technological world, might be thought victim of some effects of the radical "displacement," identified by Meyrowitz, that shakes the inner orientation, that atrophies the stabilizing faith, anchoring for its spiritualizing certitude or orienting for its craving. Moreover, if the contemporary self has suffered what Percy thinks an endemic "loss of sovereignty," then the vital responsiveness of Lane's spiritual seeker might, with good reason, fail to grasp the immediacies of the existential moment of sacred discovery even were he or she to encounter them. Given such conditions, the sacramentalist sensibility or the sacralizing imagination, if not in decline, faces a terrifically difficult ascent.

None of this, it should go without saying, represents the stuff of a jeremiad. At the last, to recite the ways new massive technological systems conspire against the "traditional" forms of the sacralizing imagination is not at all to call for the appearance of some latter-day American version of Ned Ludd, this time to be bent on the destruction of electronic ways and means. The expansive faith and energy that went into the dream and creation of such systems is as American as the religious valorizations of "purple mountains' majesty" or Gettysburg. The purpose has been only, rather, to carry out an exposition of some of those dilemmas of selfhood that, in this time and place, deeply contest the ways Wakefield's Artie innocently enough situated himself in the world of the 1940s. If the historical course of social, economic, and political events suffered by the country in those decades following on Artie's adolescence did not strip him of his civil-religious cravings, the odds are, according to the cultural analysts, that the transformations of American life subsequently affected not only his sense of the home-place and not only the facility of his symbolic extension of home into homeland but also that personal identity and orientation, those staples of selfhood, which earlier nourished both his conversion of a sense of place into a place of sense and his more expansive patriotic projects in the sacralization of space.

Even without blinking the exigencies of contemporary life which conspire so heavily against the imagination of sacred space, however, one has to suppose that, though these conditions are particular to the era, sacralizing sensibilities have always undergone comparable situations. They have faced them whenever historical changes altered the grounds on which the religious imagination had hitherto stood. Now as then, it would be foolish to predict the demise of religion in general or the death of religious sensibility more particularly or, indeed, the end of the sacralizing imagination of space more specifically still. As conservative as religious life might be in many respects, religious peoples frequently have shown remarkable adaptive capacities, renewal strategies, and interpretive ingenuities, which have been utilized in the work of what Jonathan Z. Smith calls "the persistence of the sacred."[41] And, if Smith is correct in his notion that the location of meaningful, "sacred" place is in some respects reiterative of the sense of the home-place, a function of a kind of homesickness,[42] then it might well be thought that the "homeless" condition of the modern American self would only go to intensify the desires and work of the sacralizing sensibility, even if now it might need to invent new experiential and interpretive tactics to gain sacred grounds.

If the conditions outlined by Gergen, Percy, and Meyrowitz, among others, blockade that work, Percy for one knows full well that there are tactics of irony and indirection available to those who seek the tenable terms for the restoration of the self's sovereign responses to its experience.[43] Some of these tactics in the arena of sacred space will surely seem to have peculiar recourse to old traditions, like the new forms of hygenic "monasticism" designed conscientiously to avert the pollutions of the modern world, as people retreat into spaces of repudiation and austerity for purposes of atonement or self-purification. Others will involve complex self-rediscoveries, as with Gretel Ehrlich's relocation in space and life-way in order to achieve a kind of new naivete respecting embodiment, ritually realized.[44] Still others will seek out the "peak experiences" to be devised, then realized, in an athletics "on the edge," devoutly associated with specific sites, religious visions and patterns, and spiritual possibilities.[45] And, quite beyond the cloisters and rites of passage and old goddesses like Nike, the new universes of virtual reality will no doubt prompt new forms of the consecration of space. In short, however much contested by the historical situation, the self intent on the effort of sacralizing some island of its disovery or desire can still be a bright and nimble blockade-runner.

For their part, students of the matter of American "sacred space" should realize that the contest with history does not itself spell any closure of the religious imagination: threading through all of that conspiring against it, it will reveal more and more of the depth and intricacy of its performance; indeed, potentially, the power of that which contests it will only make the exercise and exertion of that imagination even more profoundly disclosive of its resilience and ingenuity. Those students should be prepared as well, then, to reckon with the high probability that the very nature of the contest in the present age will now and hereafter make the American location and attribution of sacred space operate in some unprecedented and perhaps even startling ways, complicating further still the issue of any American civil religion.

Notes

1. *Under the Apple Tree* (New York: Delacorte Press, 1982), pp. 189–90.

2. *To Take Place* (Chicago: University of Chicago Press, 1987), p. 29.

3. E. Gibson, "Understanding the Subjective Meaning of Places," in David Ley and Marwyn S. Samuels, eds., *Humanistic Geography: Prospects and Problems* (Chicago: Maaroufa Press, 1978), p. 138.

4. Yi-Fu Tuan, *Space and Place: The Perspectives of Experience* (Minneapolis: University of Minnesota Press, 1977), p. 6.

5. Gussow, *A Sense of Place: The Artist and the American Land* (New York: Seabury Press, 1971), p. 27.

6. See Tuan, *Space and Place*, pp. 67–84.

7. Tuan, *Topophilia: A Study of Environmental Perception, Attitudes, and Values* (Englewood Cliffs, N.J.: Prentice Hall, 1974), *passim*.

8. Comstock, "Grandma's Backbone, Dougie's Ankles," in *A Place of Sense: Essays in Search of the Midwest*, ed. Michael Martone (Iowa City: University of Iowa Press, 1988), pp. 111–32. For another example of the work of converting immediate locale to one of these little "places of sense," see Tony Hiss, *The Experience of Place* (New York: Knopf, 1990), and for such conversions frequently implicated with a controlling religious imagination, see Thomas H. Rawls, *Small Places: In Search of a Vanishing America* (Boston: Little, Brown, 1990).

9. J. Z. Smith, *To Take Place*, p. 45.

10. See Carlton J. H. Hayes, *Nationalism: A Religion* (New York: Macmillan, 1960); and Wilbur Zelinsky, *Nation into State: The Shifting Symbolic Foundations of American Nationalism* (Chapel Hill: University of North Carolina Press, 1988), especially pp. 232–46, on "Americanism as a Civil Religion". A somewhat different perspective on how the "spatial" dimension of American life has been determinative of meanings for the national existence can be found in Sara M. Evans and Harry C. Boyte, *Free Spaces: The Sources of Democratic Change in America* (New York: Harper & Row, 1986).

11. Anthony D. Smith, *Nationalist Movements* (New York: St. Martin's Press, 1977), p. 7.

12. Hayes, *Nationalism*, p. 9.

13. Zelinsky, *Nation into State*, p. 4.

14. Ibid., p. 6.

15. Trans. Willard Trask (New York: Harper & Row, 1961).

16. Brereton, "Sacred Space," in *Encyclopedia of Religion*, ed. Mircea Eliade (New York: Collier Macmillan, 1987), XII: 526–35.

17. Yi-Fu Tuan, "Sacred Space: Explorations of an Idea," in *Dimensions of Human Geography*, ed. Karl W. Butzer (Chicago: Department of Geography Research Paper No. 186, 1978), pp. 84–99.

18. For another kind of entrance, see Robert S. Michaelsen, "Sacred Land in America: What Is It, How Can It Be Protected?" *Religion* (1968): 249–68.

19. Jonathan Z. Smith, *Imagining Religion: From Babylon to Jonestown* (Chicago: University of Chicago Press, 1982), p. 55.

20. Belden Lane, *Landscapes of the Sacred: Geography and Narrative in American Spirituality* (New York: Paulist Press, 1988), pp. 11–33.

21. *Sacred Places: American Tourist Attractions in the Nineteenth Century* (New York: Oxford University Press, 1989). Although a number of other studies discuss the compelling power of "place," Sears's inquiry provides combinations of facets of the issue highly salient for deciphering the American sacralizing imagination at work. For other kinds of entrance to the ways natural sites themselves "capture" human emotion, see the pertinent essays in James A. Swan, ed., *The Power of Place: Sacred Ground in Natural and Human Environments* (Wheaton, Ill.: Quest Books, 1991), which treat places of natural power; and Winifred Gallagher, *The Power of Place* (New York: Poseidon Press, 1993), which, proposing a "science" of place, examines not only topography and climate but "subtle geophysical energies" which allure. On another feature of Sears's work, the stuff of pilgrimage, scholarly work is legion, and many accounts of the

fascination with the dynamics of travel to *loca sancta* in general can illumine the question of American sacred place as Sears approaches it. See, for instance, Robert Ousterhout, ed., *The Blessings of Pilgrimage* (Urbana: University of Illinois Press, 1990). Fewer studies exist of pilgrimages to American scenes, but see, for example, the more popular approach in Paul Lambourne Higgins, *Pilgrimages USA: A Guide to the Holy Places of the United States for Today's Traveller* (Englewood Cliffs: Prentice-Hall, 1985).

22. *Sacred Ground: Americans and Their Battlefields* (Urbana: University of Illinois Press, 1991). The individual studies devoted to the various sites of Linenthal's survey are abundant. As his notes make clear, his own interpretive "gathering," designed to decipher the containing pattern, the consecration and subsequent contestation of "sacred ground," is broadly representative of the facets of the matter of sacred space having to do with the recognition and valorization of historic human actions performed on certain fields. Other works of comparable or related theoretical interest in the "rational" designation and construction of sacred space include the pertinent essays in Swan, ed., *The Power of Place*; Butzer, ed., *Dimensions of Human Geography*; D. W. Meinig, ed., *The Interpretation of Ordinary Landscapes: Geographical Essays* (New York: Oxford University Press, 1979); Jamie Scott and Paul Simpson-Housley, eds., *Sacred Places and Profane Spaces: Essays in the Geographics of Judaism, Christianity, and Islam* (Westport, Conn.: Greenwood Press, 1991). The last of these also contains essays on the contestation of sacred space, as, among others, does John Eadie and Michael J. Sallnow, eds., *Contesting the Sacred: The Anthropology of Christian Pilgrimage* (London: Routledge, 1991).

23. Beyond Lane, there are a number of other critical studies on the ways American writers have deeply inscribed "senses of place" and "places of sense," actual or imagined. Even if these do not always treat the matter of senses of *sacred* space, it should be remembered that a place must be taken up in the pause of sensibility as an originating episode in the sacralization of space. See, among others, Frederick Turner, *Spirit of Place: The Making of an American Literary Landscape* (San Francisco: Sierra Club Books, 1989); Alfred Kazin, *A Writer's America: Landscape in Literature* (London: Thames and Hudson, 1988); Patricia Nelson Limerick, *Desert Passages: Encounter with the American Deserts* (Niwot: University Press of Colorado, 1989) for three rather different kinds of approaches. Such literary renditions of "place" are frequently so powerfully articulated that later writers make their own kinds of "pilgrimages" to them in the forms of subsequent narratives. See, for instance, Jonathan Raban, *Old Glory: An American Voyage* (New York: Simon and Schuster, 1981); Michael Pearson, *Imagined Places: Journeys into Literary America* (Jackson: University Press of Mississippi, 1991); and Fred Setterberg, *The Roads Taken: Travels through America's Literary Landscapes* (Athens: University of Georgia Press, 1993).

24. *No Sense of Place* (New York: Oxford University Press, 1985).

25. Sears's field of survey includes Niagara Falls, Mammoth Cave, the Hudson River Valley, the Willey House in the White Mountains, Yosemite forest, Yellowstone, and Mauch Chunk.

26. Linenthal does not deal in the vocabulary of civil religion, but, as with Sears and others, the approaches he utilizes cut across broad patterns of American religious perception, the identification, analysis, and interpretation of which seem quite promising for those who want to pursue civil-religious studies but who realize both that such intellectual work must have recourse to different evidence than simply pulpit and politi-

cal "rhetorics" and that it cannot privilege any particular segment of the American population. But see note 28 below.

27. Lane, p. 15. Of course, by now, students of religion realize full well that even those who do not consider themselves "religious" often go about sacralizing this, that, or the other, a sure sign of vestigial or parallel religious energies at work if camouflaged even from those busiest at such work. Still, as Lane recognizes, this is a matter to be approached with the kind of delicacy required for interpreting others in ways true to their own terms for themselves.

28. There remains much work ahead on this, however, because, among a number of other things, Sears, Linenthal, and Lane have not resolved—as someone now *needs* to resolve—an issue imbedded in the ways and means of each of their studies, as each, in its way, quenches its thirst at the well of narrative. The question, in brief, is this: how does this business of the "sacred place" work for the "inarticulate" members who compose the great aggregate, or better "congregate" of any American "civil religion"? To the extent that these three focal studies all gain their evidentiary ground largely from highly articulate narrators, then to the same extent the interpretive conundrum arises about how the more dumbly faithful might perceive, recognize, conceive, sense, discover, or interpret the same phenomena, perhaps in radically different receptive and attributive terms. Do they do it through the mediumship of the articulate or through a more rudimentary channel which belongs more or less exclusively to them? If the former, then how must scholarship reckon with this fact? If the latter, then how can Religious Studies students conceive, measure, and study the forms of articulation which, however halting or obscure or nonverbal, might belong to this more "silent" group? That that "congregate" is muted at least in this round of consideration, must need be admitted.

To locate and plumb the American senses of the sacred possessed by that recalcitrant group, critical research stands in the situation now of needing to take a next step, a movement forward made possible in part by studies like those of John Sears, Edward Linenthal, and Belden Lane. It might well be that the work of imaginative literature can help to turn up the volume of the voices of quieter, ordinary people in the American "congregate," for the work of the novelist seems in some ways most empowered to explore that world of experience and feeling, as Wakefield imagines "what makes Artie tick". Or it might be that students of American civil-religious life need to intersect more completely with those new ethnographers out there bent on tracking across the field of the American folk.

29. *The Broken Covenant: American Civil Religion in a Time of Trial* (New York; Seabury Press, 1975).

30. Several recent studies have noted or detailed the predication of American religion in *many* of its formations on the perception of "abundance". See Robert L. Ferm, *Piety, Purity, Plenty: Images of Protestantism in America* (Minneapolis: Fortress Press, 1991); Roland A. Delattre, "Supply-Side Spirituality: A Case Study in the Cultural Interpretation of Religious Ethics in America," in Rowland A. Sherrill, ed., *Religion and the Life of the Nation: American Recoveries* (Urbana: University of Illinois Press, 1990), pp. 84-108; Catherine Albanese, *Nature Religion in America: From the Algonkian Indians to the New Age* (Chicago: University of Chicago Press, 1990).

31. See Dean McCannell, *The Tourist: A New Theory of the Leisure Class* (New York: Schocken Books, 1976); and John Jakle, *The Tourist: Travel in Twentieth-Century North America* (Lincoln: University of Nebraska Press, 1985).

32. *The Saturated Self: Dilemmas of Identity in Contemporary Life* (New York: Basic Books, 1991), pp. 49–53.

33. Ibid., p. 49.

34. Ibid., pp. 72–80. Gergen's point would seem to render moot the notion of John P. Hewitt that the fundamental issue facing the self in contemporary American culture is that of "staying" or "leaving," conformity or rebellion *(Dilemmas of the American Self* [Philadelphia: Temple University Press, 1989], pp. 99–107). The options in either set are reduced to the same predicament with Gergen's "cadre of social ghosts" in one regardless of his or her leaving or rebellion. At its center, of course, all of this might simply point to the complete ascendancy of the "other-directed" over the "inner-directed" human being as David Reisman described the matter in *The Lonely Crowd: A Study of the Changing American Character* (New Haven: Yale University Press, 1950). But Gergen's depiction of the "overpopulation" of the self surely puts a new cutting edge on the analyses of Christopher Lasch in *The Culture of Narcissism: American Life in an Age of Diminishing Expectations* (New York: W. W. Norton, 1978) and *The Minimal Self: Psychic Survival in Troubled Times* (New York: W. W. Norton, 1984).

35. *The Message in the Bottle* (New York: Farrar, Straus and Giroux, 1975), p. 47.

36. Ibid.

37. Meyrowitz, *No Sense of Place*, p. 146.

38. Boorstin, *The Image: A Guide to Pseudo-Events in America* (New York: Harper & Row, 1964), pp. 7–44.

39. Meyrowitz, *No Sense of Place*, p. 181.

40. If one could in fact recognize through the media delivery the profundity of an event, Meyrowitz and Boorstin would further point out the very real difficulties of establishing custody, much less custodianship of any such event in view of the technologies of "simultaneity." If everyone "views" an event at virtually the same moment and even if they could wrestle its meaning away from the resident expert, the matter of anyone's owning or controlling those meanings in a pluralistic society, wherein all have equal and immediate access, seems compromised from the outset.

41. See Smith, *Imagining Religion*, the chapter entitled "The Persistence of the Sacred".

42. Smith, *To Take Place*, p. 29.

43. Percy, *Message*, pp. 48–49.

44. *The Solace of Open Spaces* (New York: Penguin Books, 1986).

45. See, for instance, Rob Schultheis, *Bone Games: One Man's Search for the Ultimate Athletic High* (New York: Random House, 1984).

CONTRIBUTORS

David Chidester is Professor of Comparative Religion and Director of the Institute for Comparative Religion in Southern Africa at the University of Cape Town. His recent books include *Salvation and Suicide: An Interpretation of Jim Jones, the Peoples Temple, and Jonestown; Shots in the Streets: Violence and Religion in South Africa; Word and Light: Seeing, Hearing, and Religious Discourse;* and *Religions of South Africa.*

Matthew Glass is Associate Professor of Religion in American Culture at South Dakota State University. He is author of *Citizens Against the MX: Public Languages in the Nuclear Age* and is currently completing a cultural history of Mt. Rushmore.

Edward T. Linenthal is Professor of Religion and American Culture at the University of Wisconsin, Oshkosh. His publications include *Preserving Memory: The Struggle to Create America's Holocaust Museum; Sacred Ground: Americans and Their Battlefields;* and *Symbolic Defense: The Cultural Significance of the Strategic Defense Initiative.* He is also co-editor of *A Shuddering Dawn: Religious Studies and the Nuclear Age.*

Colleen McDannell holds the Sterling McMurrin Chair in Religious Studies and is Associate Professor of History at the University of Utah. Her publications include *Heaven: A History,* and *The Christian Home in Victorian America, 1840–1900,* and numerous articles ranging from examinations of Irish-American masculinity to interpretations of religious material culture.

Robert S. Michaelsen is J. F. Rowney Professor of Religion and Society Emeritus at the University of California, Santa Barbara. He has authored more than fifty publications dealing with various aspects of American religious history, including public or tax-supported education, the religion clauses of the First Amendment, and Native American religious freedom issues.

Rowland A. Sherrill is Professor and Chair of Religious Studies and Adjunct Professor of American Studies at Indiana University/Purdue University, Indianapolis. The author of *The Prophetic Melville,* he is also editor of *Religion and the Life of the Nation,* co-editor of *Religion, the Independent Sector, and American Culture,* and co-editor of the journal *Religion and American Culture.*

Bron Taylor is Associate Professor of Religion and Social Ethics at the University of Wisconsin, Oshkosh. He is author of *Affirmative Action at Work: Law, Politics, and Ethics* and numerous articles on environmental movements. He is also editor of *Grassroots Resistance: The Global Emergence of Popular Environmental Rebellion* and *Once and Future Primitive: The Spiritual Politics of Deep Ecology* (forthcoming).

INDEX

Abbey, Edward, 105–10, 113, 114, 115, 116, 141n9, 143nn56,65, 145n101
Abramson, Albert, 237, 239
Adams, Henry, 302
African Methodist Episcopal Church (AME): in South Africa, 266–68, 273, 305n16
Aggrey, James K., 276–77
Albanese, Catherine, 13, 151n164
Altshuler, David E., 258n25
America: as center of the world, 289–90, 311n103; commerce with South Africa, 164–65; conquest of, 51–58; Europeans' images of, 297–99; religious connection to South Africa, 265–66; response to apartheid, 282–88; as symbol of oppression, 263–64, 284–88, 289; as Turtle Island, 110–11, 144n78. *See also* America as sacred space
America as sacred space: commodification of, 28; as foreign sacred space, 263–64, 300–302; and the frontier experience, 25–26; in the information revolution, 28–29; and the legal system, 26–27; managerial ethos of, 27–28; as symbol of liberation, 263, 266, 273–75; as symbol of redemption, 275–82; symbols of speed and mobility in, 301–302; as synonym for human possibility, 297–300; as utopian space, 263, 280–82; as Zion, 269–70, 273
American Indian Movement (AIM), 27, 137–38, 167; Mount Rushmore protests, 171–78, 181
American Indians, 13, 20–22, 34n26, 39n36; federal powers over, 72–77, 93nn122,129, 94nn138,140; tribal sovereignty of, 72–78, 95n152. *See also* Land claims, Indian; Mount Graham Observatory controversy; Mount Rushmore
Ames, Michael M., 41n39
Ammerman, Nancy T., 193, 216nn10,12

Animals: wild vs. domestic, 117, 142nn28,33
Animism, 99, 100, 102–103, 111–14, 116, 141n8, 142n34, 144n84
Apache Indians: and the Earth First! meeting on Mount Graham, 130–38, 150n150; and the Mount Graham Observatory controversy, 119–26, 145n110, 146n114, 147nn117,119,120,123
Appadurai, Arjun, 41n43
Appelbaum, Ralph, 249–51, 252
Arizona: Indian land restitution in, 93n115. *See also* Mount Graham Observatory controversy
Asylums: as sacred space, 14, 39n37
Attakai v United States, 49, 81, 86n28
Avineri, Shlomo, 227

Bachelard, Gaston, 32n6, 214
Badoni v Higginson, 81
Baker, James, 292
Bal, Mieke, 40n39
Balawajder, Edward, 252
Ball, Milner, 62, 65
Balmer, Randall, 191, 216n10
Banks, Dennis, 172–73, 176, 177
Bari, Judi, 98, 140n3
Barsh, Lawrence Russel, 88n57
Bartlett, Richard A., 35
Battlefields, memorialized, 3–5, 79, 322–23, 338n22
Baudrillard, Jean, 299
Bearss, Edwin C., 4
Beecher, Catharine, 187, 188, 213
Belafonte, Harry, 264
Bell, Catherine, 33n14
Bellah, Robert, 30, 326
Bercovitch, Sacvan, 297
Berenbaum, Michael, 225, 238, 257n5
Berkey, Curtis G., 93n122
Bernstein, Irving, 224
Bhabha, Homi, 19

343